T3-BVW-560

Learning
Microsoft® Word 97

Iris Blanc
Kathy Berkemeyer

To Our Families
Alan, Pamela, Matthew, and Jaime,
for always keeping me focused on the important things in life.–*I.B.*
Jack Berkemeyer,
for his love, patience, support and sense of humor – *K.B.*

Special thanks to Jennifer Frew,
Managing Editor at DDC, for her
multiple contributions to this project
and to Cathy Vesecky,
for going above and beyond the call of duty.

Project Manager	**English Editor**	**Technical Editors**	**Design and Layout**
Jennifer Frew	Cathy Vesecky	Carol Havlicek	Midori Nakamura
New York, NY	Westmont, IL	Long Beach, NY	New York, NY
			Shu Yun Chen
			New York, NY
		Cathy Vesecky	
		Westmont, IL	Maria Kardasheva
			New York, NY
		Candi Dickerson	Paul Wray
		Westmont, IL	New York, NY
			Julie Janssen
			Westmont, IL

©Copyright 1998 by DDC Publishing

Published by DDC Publishing

All rights reserved, including the right to reproduce this book or portions thereof in any form whatsoever. For information, address DDC Publishing, Inc., 275 Madison Avenue, New York, NY 10016; HTTP://WWW.DDCPUB.COM

10

Printed in the United States of America.

Microsoft®, Internet Explorer, MS-DOS®, Word 97®, and Windows 95 are registered trademarks of Microsoft Corporation.
Netscape™ Navigator is the trademark of Netscape™ Communications Corporation.
Yahoo!™ and Yahoo™ logo are trademarks of Yahoo!™
LYCOS™, LYCOS™ logo are trademarks of LYCOS™.
AltaVista™ and the AltaVista™ logo are trademarks of AltaVista Technology, Inc.
Digital™ and the Digital™ logo are trademarks of Digital Equipment Corporation.
Excite is a service mark of Excite Inc
Some illustrations in this book and on the DDC Web site have been acquired from Web sites and are used for demonstration and educational purposes only. Online availability of text and images does not imply that they may be reused without the permission of the copyright holder, although the Copyright Act does permit certain unauthorized reuse as fair use under 17 U.S.C. Section 107 Word 97 Screen Shots reprinted with permission of Microsoft Corporation.

All registered trademarks, trademarks, and service marks mentioned in this book are the property of their respective companies.

CONTENTS

INTRODUCTION

About Microsoft® Word 97 for Windows 95

Microsoft Word 97 is a word processing application. Word 97 is an extremely versatile program that allows you to create both visually exciting documents that can contain drawings, tables, and charts, as well as basic correspondence and reports.

✓ *Be sure to check with the Microsoft Web site from time to time for updates to and information about MS Word 97.*

About this Book

Learning Microsoft Word 97 will teach you how to create, format, and print documents. In addition, an entire lesson is devoted to accessing the Internet through Word 97 and integrating information from the Internet into Word 97 documents.

Each lesson in this book explains concepts, provides numerous exercises to apply those concepts, and illustrates the necessary keystrokes or mouse actions required to complete the exercises. Lesson summary exercises are provided at the end of each lesson to challenge and reinforce the concepts learned.

After completing the exercises in this book, you will be able to use all the basic features and many of the advanced features of Word 97 with ease.

How to Use this Book

Each exercise contains four parts:

- **NOTES** explain the concept and application being introduced.

- **EXERCISE DIRECTIONS** explain how to complete the exercise.

- **EXERCISES** allow you to apply the new concept.

- **KEYSTROKES** outline the keystroke shortcuts and mouse actions required for completing an exercise.

✓ *Keystrokes and mouse actions are only provided when a new concept is being introduced. Therefore, if you forget the keystroke or mouse action required to perform a task, you can use the either the Help feature (explained in the Basics section) or the index of this book to find the procedure.*

Before you begin working on the exercises in this book, you should read the first introductory section entitled Basics. This section will explain the screens, the Help feature, working in Windows, toolbars, menus, and other necessary preliminary information.

Data and Solution Files

The data files are provided on the accompanying CD-ROM. Please read the installation directions on pages vii and viii to learn how to access these files. Solutions disks may be purchased separately from DDC Publishing. You may use the data files to complete an exercise without typing lengthy text or data. However, exercise directions are provided for both data disk and non-data disk users. Exercise directions will include a keyboard icon ⌨ to direct non-data disk users to open documents created in a previous exercise and a diskette icon 💾 to direct data disk users to open the document available on the CD. For example, a typical direction might read: Open ⌨**TRY**, or open 💾**03TRY**.

The Solution disk may be used for you to compare your work with the final version or solution on disk. Each solution filename begins with the letter "S" and is followed by the exercise number and descriptive filename. For example, **S03TRY** would contain the final solution to the exercise directions in exercise three.

A directory of data disk and solutions disk filenames are provided in the Log of Exercises section of this book.

✓ *Saving files to a network will automatically truncate all filenames to a maximum of eight characters. Therefore, though Windows 95 allows for longer filenames, a maximum of only eight characters can be saved to a network drive.*

The Teacher's Manual

While this book can be used as a self-paced learning book, a comprehensive Teacher's Manual is also available. The Teacher's Manual contains the following:

- Lesson objectives
- Exercise objectives
- Related vocabulary

- Points to emphasize
- Exercise settings
- A Log of Exercises, which lists filenames in exercise number order
- A Directory of Documents, which lists filenames alphabetically along with the corresponding exercise numbers.
- Solution illustrations

A Companion Internet Simulation

The CD-ROM that accompanies this book contains a simulation of Internet sites to be used in Lesson 12, Word and the Internet. This means that you can complete the exercises without an Internet connection, avoiding modems, connection time and fees, wandering to unrelated sites, and long waits for Web sites to load. It's like being live on the Internet with none of the inconvenience.

For example, in Exercise 91, you will do a multi-level search on a site that gives information on Brazil. Launch the simulation following the detailed directions and follow the prompts at the bottom of your screen to find the information that you need. Even if you have never been on the Internet before, you will be able to do the exercises. The results are that you learn how to integrate the power of Word 97 with the power of the Internet. (*See installation instructions on the right.*)

Multimedia Internet Browser Tutorial

For the new user of the Internet, the CD-ROM includes basic computer-based training on how to navigate the Internet using a browser. A browser is a program that helps manage the process of locating information on the World Wide Web. The tutorial introduces the concepts and then shows you how to apply them. (*See installation instructions on the right.*)

Demo of DDC's Office 97 Multimedia Tutorial

In this excerpt of DDC's Office 97 CBT (Computer Based Training), you will receive a sample of step-by-step directions, illustrations, simulations of desired keystroke or mouse actions, and application problems. (*See installation procedures below.*)

Installation Instructions

A separate installation is required for each program. At the designated prompt, indicate which program you wish to install. When installation of one program is complete, you may begin again from step one (above, right) to install another.

System Requirements

Software	Windows 95 or Windows NT 3.51 (or higher)
Hardware	80486DX or higher, 16 MB RAM, 256 Color Monitor, and CD-ROM Drive-
Disk Space	40 MB available hard disk space

To install the programs, place the CD in your CD-ROM drive and follow the listed steps below:

> ***IMPORTANT***: *If at any time you see a warning message similar to the one below, click **No To All** to proceed with the installation.*

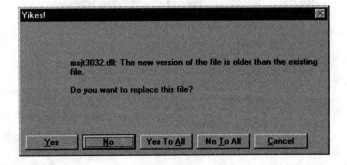

1. **To install from Windows 95:**
   Click Start on the desktop and click Run.
   OR
   To install from Windows NT:
   Go to Program Manager in Main, click File.

2. In the Run window, begin a program installation by typing one of the following:
   - *CD-ROM drive letter:*\WOR97INT\SETUP to install the Internet Simulation.
   - *CD-ROM drive letter:*\OFFICE97\SETUP to install the Office 97 CBT.
   - *CD-ROM drive letter:*\NETCBT\SETUP to install the Browser tutorial.
3. Click NEXT at the Setup Wizard screen.
4. At the following screen, click NEXT to create a DDCPUB directory for storing program files. Then click YES to confirm the directory choice.
5. At the following screen, allow the default folder to be named **DDC Publishing**, and click NEXT.
6. At the next screen, choose one of the following options based on your individual system needs:
   *NOTE: A **Typical** installation is standard for most individual installation.*
   - **TYPICAL:** installs a minimum number of files to the hard drive with the majority of files remaining on the CD-ROM.
     NOTE: With this installation, the CD must remain in the CD-ROM drive when running the program.
   - **CUSTOM:** installs only those files that you choose to the hard drive. This is generally only recommended for advanced users of Innovus Multimedia software.
   - **SERVER:** installs the programs on a network server.
7. Click NEXT to begin copying the necessary files to your system.
8. Click OK at the Set Up status Window and then click YES to restart Windows.

To launch a program, click the Start button on the Windows 95 desktop, select Programs, DDC Publishing, and then select one of the following:
- **WOR97INT (to start the Internet Simulation)**
- **DEMO97 (to start the Office97 CBT)**
- **NETCBT (to start the Browser tutorial)**

Data Files

Since this book is designed to teach you how to use the features of Microsoft Office 97, not how to type, you can use the data files to avoid typing long documents that are used in many of the exercises.

A disk icon 🖫 preceding a filename means that there is a data file for the exercise. Follow the exercise directions to open the data file and complete the exercise as indicated.

   ✓ *Saving files to a network will automatically truncate all filenames to a maximum of eight characters. Therefore, though Windows 95 allows for longer filenames, a maximum of only eight characters can be saved to a network drive.*

To copy data files on to a hard drive:
- Open Windows 95 Explorer (Right-click on **Start** button and click **Explore**).
- Be sure that the CD is in your CD-ROM drive. Select the CD-ROM drive letter from the All Folders pane of the Explorer window.
- Click to Select the **WordData** folder in the Contents of (CD-ROM Drive letter) pane of the Explorer window.
- Drag the folder onto the letter of your hard drive (usually **C:**) in the All Folders pane of the Explorer Window.
- The data files from the CD-ROM are now on your hard drive. To access them, click the Start menu, highlight Programs and Windows Explorer. The folder name for the data files is "WordData."

Log of Exercises

Lesson	Exercise	Filename	Data File	Solution File	Page
6	36	FUND	—	S36FUND	150
	37	MAG	—	S37MAG	153
	38	SELECT	—	S38SELECT	160
	39	RESUME	—	S39RESUME	166
	40	CARS	—	S40CARS	171
		GREEN	—	S40GREEN	173
	41	GREEN	41GREEN	S41GREEN	178
		CARS	41CARS	S41CARS	179
	42	MYRESUME	—	—	182
	43	AUTO	—	S43AUTO	184
7	44	TRAVEL	—	S44TRAVEL	190
	45	PREVIEW	—	S45PREVIEW	196
	46	NET	46NET	S46NET	201
	47	USA	47USA	S47USA	206
	48	BIRDS	48BIRDS	S48BIRDS	212
	49	PREVIEW	49PREVIEW	S49PREVIEW	216
		USA	49USA	S49USA	216
	50	BRAZIL	50BRAZIL	S50BRAZIL	222
	51	INSURANCE	—	S51INSURANCE	224
8	52	TRAVEL	52TRAVEL	—	229
		TOURS	—	S52TOURS	229
	53	BAKERY	53BAKERY	S53BAKERY	234
		BAKERYCAFE	—	—	234
	54	PINEVIEW	54PINEVIEW	S54PINEVIEW	236
		ESTATE	54ESTATE	—	236
	55	WILL	55WILL	S55WILL	240
	56	TRANSFER	—	S56TRANSFER	244
	58	RAVE	—	S58RAVE	248
	59	WORKOUT	—	S59WORKOUT	250
	60	INVEST	—	S60INVEST	252
	61	EMAIL	61EMAIL	S61EMAIL	257
	62	ATSEA	—	S62ATSEA	261
	63	GOODBYE	63GOODBYE	S63GOODBYE	265
	64	PHONE	—	S64PHONE	270
		TC	—	S64TC	270
	65	BOOKMEET	—	S65BOOKMEET	276
		ONTIME	—	S65ONTIME	276
	66	CRUISE	—	S66CRUISE	281
		BOOKMEET	66BOOKMEET	—	281
		BOOKSALE	—	S66BOOKSALE	281
	67	CRUISE	67CRUISE	S67CRUISE	286
		EXPENSES	67EXPENSES	S67EXPENSES	286
	68	INVOICE	—	S68INVOICE	292
9	69	BOOKMEET	69BOOKMEET	S69BOOKMEET	296
		BOOKMEET1	—	S69BOOKMEET1	296
		BOOKSALE	69BOOKSALE	S69BOOKSALE	296
		BOOKSALE1	—	S69BOOKSALE1	296

DIRECTORY OF DOCUMENTS

Filename	Exercise
TICKLE	95
TOURS	52
TOYDATA	95
TRANSFER	56
TRAVEL	44, 52
TRVL	78
TRVLDATA	78
TRVLMAIN	78
TRY	4,10
TRYAGAIN	5,12,14
TRYIT	12, 14
USA	47, 49
VISION	30, 32
VISIONA	32
WALK	31, 33
WILL	55
WORKOUT	59

Word 97

LESSON 1

BASICS

- About Microsoft® Word 97
- Use the Mouse
- Start Word
- The Word Window
- Use the Keyboard
- Close a Document Window/Exit Word
- Toolbars, Menus, and Commands
- Dialog Box Options
- Shortcut Menus
- The Zoom Option
- Window Displays
- Default Settings
- Help Features (Office Assistant, Contents, Index, Find, ScreenTips)
- Exit Help
- Conventions

<table>
<tr><td rowspan="3">**Exercise**
1</td><td>■ **About Microsoft® Word 97** ■ **Use the Mouse** ■ **Start Word**</td></tr>
<tr><td>■ **The Word Window** ■ **Use the Keyboard**</td></tr>
<tr><td>■ **Close a Document Window/Exit Word**</td></tr>
</table>

NOTES

About Word 97

■ Microsoft® Word 97 takes advantage of the capabilities of Microsoft Windows® 95. One advantage of using Word 97 is that you can easily transfer data between other applications running under Windows 95. Word 97 also provides tools and functions that make it easy to access and publish on the Internet.

■ If you are upgrading from Word 7 for Windows 95, you will note a number of differences in toolbars, menus, creating tables and adding borders, spell check features, and getting help.

■ If you worked with Word 6 for Windows 3.1, you will note that the interface, or the look of the window, is somewhat different. The Windows 95 Taskbar appears at the bottom of the screen on all programs running in Windows 95. The Taskbar allows you to start applications and/or to switch between applications. If you are a first-time Word user, this will all be new to you.

■ If you are using Word 97 as part of the Microsoft Office Suite, a Shortcut bar will appear on your screen. The Shortcut bar displays icons (symbols) that represent tasks found in Microsoft Office. This bar is almost always displayed so that you can access Office tasks from within Windows or from any Office application.

Shortcut bar

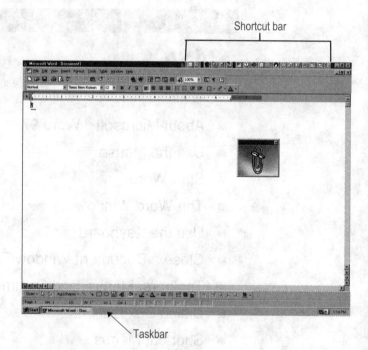

Taskbar

Use the Mouse

■ You must use the mouse to access many features of Word, so if you do not already know how to use the mouse, you need to become familiar with its operation.

■ When the mouse is moved on the tabletop, a corresponding movement of the mouse pointer occurs on the screen. The mouse pointer changes shape depending on the program being used, the object to which the mouse is pointing, and the action it will be performing. The mouse pointer will not move if the mouse is lifted up and placed back on the tabletop.

■ All references to the use of mouse buttons in this book are to the *left* mouse button unless otherwise specified.

■ The mouse terminology and the corresponding actions described below will be used throughout the book:

Point to	Move the mouse (on the tabletop) so the pointer touches a specific item.
Click	Point to an item and quickly press and release the left mouse button.
Right-click	Point to an item and press and release the right mouse button.
Double-click	Point to an item and press the left mouse button twice in rapid succession.
Drag	Point to an item, press and hold down the left mouse button while moving the mouse.
Slide	Move the mouse on the tabletop so that a menu is highlighted.

✓ *Note: You must be using an IntelliMouse™ to use the following mouse actions.*

Scroll	Rotate the center wheel of an IntelliMouse forward or backward to move through a document.
Pan	Press the center wheel of an IntelliMouse and drag the pointer above or below where you first clicked. The farther you drag from the point of the first click, the faster the document will move.
AutoScroll	Click the center wheel of an IntelliMouse to automatically scroll down in a document. Scroll up by moving the pointer above the point of the first click.
Zoom	Hold down the Ctrl key while you rotate the center wheel of an IntelliMouse to zoom in or out by 10% increments.

■ Specific mouse shapes will be discussed within each exercise as they are introduced.

Start Word

■ You may start Word using any one of the following procedures:

- **Using the Windows 95 Taskbar**:
  Click *Start* (a pop-up list appears), slide the mouse to highlight *Programs*, slide the mouse to highlight *Microsoft Word*, then click the left mouse button.

- **Using the Windows 95 Taskbar**:
  Click *Start*, slide the mouse to highlight *New Office Document* and click the left mouse button to select, click to select *Blank Document*, click OK.

- **Using the Shortcut bar**
  (if you are using Word within the Microsoft Office Suite):
  Click the New Office Document button 🗎, click Blank Document, click OK.

The Word Window

■ After you launch the Word program, the following screen appears. Note the description on the next page of each screen part:

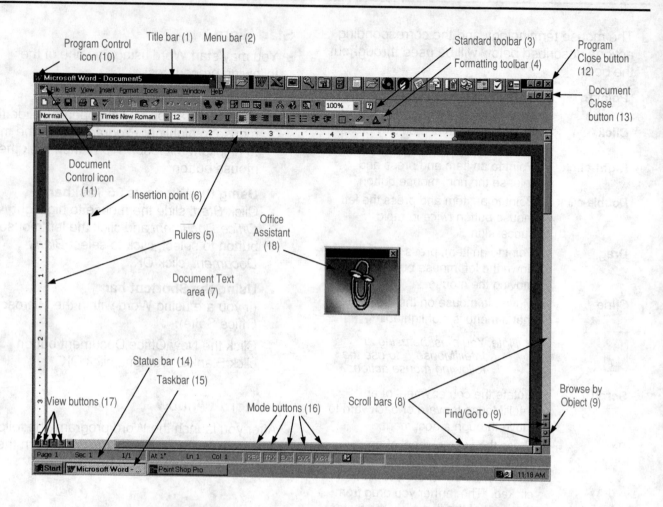

Part	Description
(1) Title bar	Displays the program and document name.
(2) Menu bar	Displays items that you can select when executing commands.
	When an item is selected using either the keyboard or the mouse, a group of subitems appears in a drop-down submenu.
(3) Standard toolbar	A collection of buttons that enable you to accomplish many common word processing tasks easily, like saving and printing a file.
	When you point to a button on the toolbar, a ScreenTip displays below the mouse pointer, and an explanation of that button's function is displayed.
(4) Formatting toolbar	A collection of buttons that lets you easily change the appearance of your document.
(5) Rulers (Horizontal and Vertical)	Measure the horizontal and vertical distance from the margins of the page. You will learn to use these rulers to change tabs, indents, and margins quickly.
(6) Insertion point	The blinking vertical line that appears in the upper left-hand corner when Word 97 is started. It indicates where the next character to be keyed will appear and blinks between characters rather than below them.
	The insertion point does not always appear on the document screen. You may make it visible by clicking the left mouse button at the desired location or by tapping any one of the arrow keys.
(7) Document Text area	The blank space for typing text. You can maximize this area by hiding toolbars.
(8) Scroll bars	Used to move the screen view horizontally or vertically. The scroll box on the vertical scroll bar can be dragged up or down to move the screen view quickly toward the beginning or end of the document. The scroll box on the horizontal scroll bar can be dragged left or right.

(9) Browse by Object Find/Go To	Select an object to search for (field, endnote, footnote, graphic, comment, section, page, bookmark, table, etc.) from the **Browse by Object** menu.

Click the **Find/Go To** button to locate the previous or next item that was selected from the Browse by Object menu.

(10) Program Control icon	Click once to display a menu with commands to control Word program; double-click to close Word program.
(11) Document Control icon	Click once to display a menu with commands to control selected document; double-click to close the document.
(12) Program Close button	Click to exit program.
(13) Document Close button	Click to close current document window.
(14) Status bar	Appears at the bottom of the screen and displays:

Page 1 The page number.

Sec 1 The section number.

1/1 The current page and total number of pages in the document (1/1 meaning page one of a one-page document).

At 1" The measurement in inches from the top edge of the page to the current location of the insertion point.

Ln 1 The line number at which the insertion point is currently located.

Col 1 The distance of the insertion point from the left margin in number of characters.

(15) Taskbar	Used to start applications and switch between applications.
(16) Mode buttons	Mode buttons are located near the center of the Status bar and are activated when double-clicked. They place Word in various **modes**. (Modes will be explained in related exercises.)
(17) View buttons	Let you see your document in different views. Views will be explained in detail in Exercise 4.
(18) Office Assistant	The Assistant (see page 13) can answer questions and offer suggestions about completing a task.

Use the Keyboard

- The best way to access tasks in Word 97 is by using a combination of the mouse and keyboard. Computers contain the following specialized keys:

    - **Function keys** (F1-F12) perform special functions.

    - **Modifier keys** (Shift, Alt, Ctrl—there are two of each on most keyboards) are used in conjunction with other keys to select commands or perform actions. In the keystroke section of this book, you will see combinations of keys indicated with a plus sign (+), such as Alt+V. This means that when you use a modifier key with another key, you must hold down the modifier key while tapping the other key.

    - **Numeric keys**, found on keyboards with a number pad, allow you to enter numbers quickly. When the Num Lock light is ON, the number keys on the pad are operational. When the Num Lock light is OFF, the insertion point control keys (Home, PgUp, End, PgDn) are active. The numbers on the top row of the keyboard are always active.

    - **Escape key** (Esc) is used to cancel some actions, commands, menus or an entry.

    - **Enter key** (there are two on most keyboards) is used to complete an entry.

    - **Directional arrow keys** are used to move the insertion point on the screen.

Close a Document

- When a document has been saved, it remains on your screen. If you wish to clear the screen, you may close the document window by selecting Close from the File menu or double-clicking the Document Control icon. See the illustration on the right.

- If you attempt to close a document before saving it, Word will prompt you to save before exiting. You may respond **Y** for Yes or **N** for No.

- If you make a mistake and would like to begin the document again, close the document window without saving the document.

- To begin a new document after closing the document window, you must select New from the File menu or click the New button 🗋 on the Standard toolbar. This will give you a new document window.

- To quickly exit a program using the mouse, click the Close button (the X in the upper right corner of the screen). In the illustration at right, you will note two Close buttons. The top Close button closes the Word Program; the bottom Close button closes the document window. Other methods of closing documents will be detailed in Exercise 4.

Exit Word

- When you have finished working on your documents (saved and closed them), you will want to exit the Word application. To do so, select Exit from the File menu, or double-click the Program Control icon.

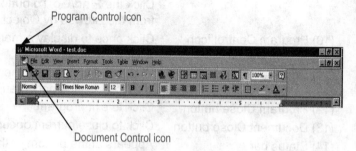

Program Control icon

Document Control icon

In this exercise, you will use the mouse to start and close Word 97.

EXERCISE DIRECTIONS

1. Roll the mouse up, down, left and right on the tabletop or the mousepad.

2. If you are using Word within the Microsoft Office Suite, place the mouse pointer on each button on the Shortcut toolbar and note the ScreenTips notation. Otherwise, skip to step 8.

3. Click the New Office Document icon.

4. Note the New screen (dialog box) with Blank Document highlighted.

5. Click OK to open a new document in Word.

6. Click the bottom Close button (or double-click Document Control icon) to exit the new Word document.

7. Click the top Close button (or double-click Program Control icon) to exit the Word program.

8. Click Start on the Windows Taskbar.

9. Slide the mouse to highlight Programs, then highlight and click Microsoft Word.

10. Place the mouse pointer on each button on the Standard and Formatting toolbars and note the ScreenTips notation for each button.

11. Click the bottom Close button or double-click the Document Control icon to close the Word document.

12. Click the top Close button or double-click the Program Control icon to exit the Word program.

KEYSTROKES

START WORD

USING THE TASKBAR

1. Click **Start** .... Ctrl + Esc
2. Highlight **Programs** .... P
3. Select Microsoft Word.

OR

1. Click **Start** .... Ctrl + Esc
2. Click **New Office Document** .... [icon]
3. Highlight **Blank Document** .... [icon]
4. Click **OK** .... Enter

USING THE SHORTCUT BAR

1. Click **New Office Document** button.. [icon]
2. Double-click **Blank Document** .... [icon]

CLOSE DOCUMENT WINDOW

1. Double-click
   Document Control icon .... [icon]
2. Click **Yes** to save changes............... Y
   OR
   Click **No** to abandon changes .... N

OR

1. Click **File** .... Alt + F
2. Click **Close** C
3. Click **Yes** to save changes................. Y
   OR
   Click **No** to abandon changes .... N

EXIT WORD

1. Double-click **Program Control** icon... [icon]
2. Click **Yes** to save changes .... Y
   OR
   Click **No** to abandon changes. .... N

OR

1. Click **File** .... Alt + F
2. Click **Exit** X
3. Click **Yes** to save changes .... Y
   OR
   Click **No** to abandon changes .... N

Exercise 2

■ **Toolbars, Menus, and Commands**   ■ **Dialog Box Options**
■ **Shortcut Menus**

Standard Toolbar

Formatting Toolbar

NOTES

Toolbars, Menus, and Commands

■ The Menu bar and toolbars may be used to access commands. Word contains two default toolbars that appear when the program is launched. Other toolbars are available and may be displayed when needed. They will be introduced in related exercises.

■ The **Standard toolbar** contains buttons that accomplish many common tasks easily, like saving and printing a file.

■ The **Formatting toolbar** contains buttons that easily change the appearance of text.

■ Toolbars may be moved and displayed anywhere on screen, or you may hide any or all of them to make more room on your screen for text.

■ Toolbars may be customized with the buttons you use most frequently. They may be moved and resized to fit the way you wish to work. (Customizing toolbars will not be covered in this text.)

■ If you are not certain of a toolbar button's function, position your mouse pointer anywhere on the button, and a **ScreenTip** will display with the button's name.

■ You must use the mouse to access toolbar buttons.

To select a command from a toolbar:

• Use the mouse to point to a toolbar button and click once.

To access menu bar items:

• Use the mouse to point to an item on the menu bar and click once.

    OR

Press Alt+*underlined letter* in the menu name.

• When a menu bar item is selected, a drop-down submenu appears with additional options.

• Note the drop-down menus that appear when Edit and View are selected:

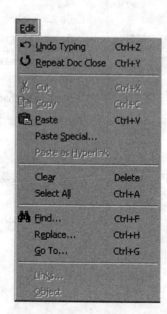

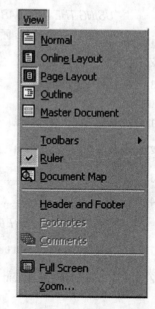

To select a command from a drop-down menu:

- Use the mouse to point to the command on the drop-down menu and click once.

- Press the key for the underlined letter in the command name.

- Use the up or down arrow key to highlight the command, then press Enter.

- Some menu options are dimmed, while others appear black. Dimmed options are not available for selection at this time, while black options are.

- A check mark or bullet next to a drop-down menu item means the option is currently selected.

- Some menu items display shortcut keys that may be used to access the task.

- A menu item followed by ellipsis marks (…) indicates that a dialog box (which requires you to provide additional information to complete a task) will be forthcoming.

Dialog Box Options

- Note the dialog box that appears after Font is selected from the Format menu and the dialog box that appears after Print is selected from the File menu.

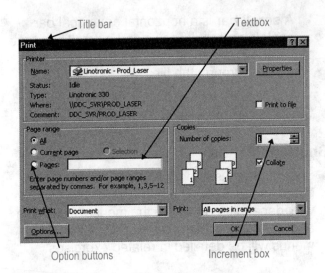

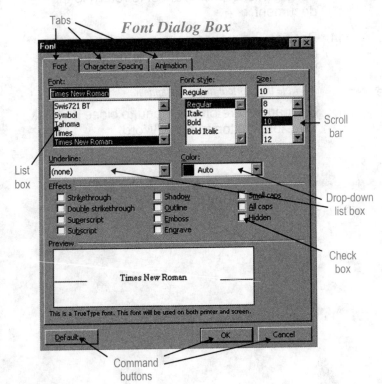

Font Dialog Box

- Dialog boxes let you enter information in a variety of ways. Each dialog box part is described below:

  - The **title bar** identifies the title of the dialog box.

  - A **text box** is a space where you type information.

  - **Command buttons** carry out actions described on the button. When command names have ellipsis marks following them, they will access another dialog box.

  - **Drop-down lists** are marked with a down arrow. Click in the box or on the arrow to access a list of options.

  - An **increment box** provides a space for typing a value. An up or down arrow (usually to the right of the box) gives you a way to select a value with the mouse.

  - A **named tab** displays options related to the tab's name in the same dialog box.

  - **Option buttons** are small circular buttons marking options in a set. You may choose only one option from the set. A selected option button contains a dark circle.

  - A **check box** is a small square box where an option may be selected or deselected. A "✓" in the box indicates the option is selected. If several check boxes are offered, you may select more than one.

  - A **list box** displays a list of items from which selections can be made. A list box may have a scroll bar that can be used to show hidden items in the list.

- A **scroll bar** is a horizontal or vertical bar containing scroll arrows and a scroll box that can be dragged up or down to move more quickly through the file.

  ✓ *Note the labeled parts in the dialog boxes on the previous page.*

Shortcut Menus

- Shortcut menus appear when the *right* mouse button is pressed. The menu items that appear vary depending on where the mouse is pointing and what task is being performed. Shortcut menus will be detailed in related exercises.

✓*Note:*   *Keystroke procedures will be illustrated throughout this book as shown in the example below. Mouse actions are illustrated on the left, while keystroke procedures are illustrated on the right. Keyboard shortcut keys are illustrated below the heading. Use whichever method you find most convenient.*

In this exercise, you will hide and display toolbars, as well as make selections in a dialog box.

EXERCISE DIRECTIONS

1. Start the Word program.

2. Select View from the menu.

3. Deselect Ruler.

   ✔ *Note the change in the screen.*

4. Select View; select Toolbars.

5. Deselect Standard.

   ✔ *Note the change in the screen.*

6. Select View and reselect Ruler to return the ruler to the screen.

7. Select View; select Toolbars. Reselect Standard to return the toolbar to the screen.

8. Place the mouse pointer on each button on the Standard toolbar and note the ScreenTips notation.

9. Select Page Setup from the File menu.

10. Select the Paper Size tab.

11. Click the Paper Size drop-down list arrow and select US Legal 8.5" x 14".

12. Return the paper size to US Letter 8.5" x 11", the default setting.

13. Click on each tab to note the available page setup options; click Cancel to return to the document.

14. Position the mouse pointer anywhere in the document text area and click the right mouse button.

    ✔ *Note the shortcut menu that appears.*

15. Click anywhere off the menu to close it. Click the Close button to close Word.

KEYSTROKES

HIDE/DISPLAY TOOLBARS

1. Click **View** .... Alt + V

2. Click **Toolbars** .... T

3. Select desired toolbar.

4. Repeat steps 1-3 for each additional toolbar you want to appear.

   A ✔ will appear next to toolbars that are currently selected.

   OR

   Click on the ✔ mark next to toolbar(s) to hide.

   The ✔ mark will disappear.

Exercise

3

- **The Zoom Option** ■ **Window Displays** ■ **Default Settings**
- **Help Features (Office Assistant, Contents, Index, Find, ScreenTips)**
- **Exit Help** ■ **Conventions**

Standard Toolbar

Zoom Control   Office Assistant

NOTES

The Zoom Option

- The <u>V</u>iew menu contains a **Zoom** option that allows you to set the magnification of the data on the screen. When <u>Z</u>oom is selected from the <u>V</u>iew menu, the following dialog box appears:

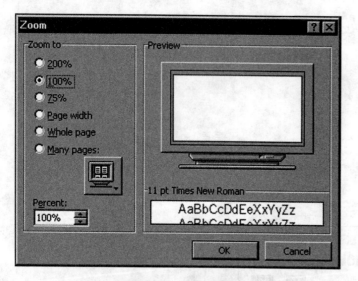

- By clicking the desired option button, you can display text at 200%, 100% or 75% magnification. To set a different magnification, you may enter a magnification amount in the P<u>e</u>rcent increment box. A Preview window shows the effect of your selection.

- If you are using an IntelliMouse, you can hold down the Ctrl key while you rotate the center wheel to zoom in or out by 10% increments.

- You can also change the magnification of a text by entering a magnification amount (or selecting an amount after clicking the arrow) in the Zoom Control box located on the Standard toolbar. This method lets you easily set the magnification of text without opening the menu or dialog box.

Window Displays

Document Control button   Close

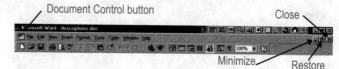

Minimize   Restore

- The **Document Control icon** [icon], located to the left of the menu bar, can be clicked to access a drop-down menu from which you can choose commands to control the *document* window.

- The document window **Minimize, Restore** and **Close buttons** are located on the right of the menu bar. Clicking the Minimize button [icon] shrinks the window to an icon that displays at the bottom of the screen. Clicking the Restore button [icon] creates a document window (below the toolbars), including a Document Title bar.

- The **Document Title bar** contains the Document Control icon and the Minimize, Maximize and Close buttons that also appeared on the menu bar. Clicking the Maximize button on the Document Title bar returns the window to the default opening screen. Clicking the Close button closes the document.

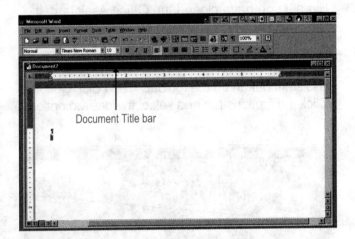

Document Title bar

Default Settings

- Default settings are preset conditions within the program. Settings such as margins, tabs, line spacing, font style, font size and text alignment are automatically set by the Word program. These settings may be changed as desired. Changing margins, tabs, etc., will be covered in later exercises.

  ✔Note: *Word assumes you are working on a standard 8.5" x 11" page. The At indicator in the Status bar shows the insertion point as measured in inches from the top of the page.*

- **Margins** are set at 1.25" on the left and right and 1" on the top and bottom. Margins are measured from the edges of your page.

- **Tab stops** are set every 0.5".

- **Font style** (the design of your characters) is defaulted to either Times Roman or Times New Roman, depending on the printer you are using.

- **Font size** is set to 10 point (font size is measured in points).

- **Line spacing** is set to single.

- **Text alignment** is set to left.

Help Features

- Help is available from a variety of sources in Word. Below is an illustration of the help features available on the Help menu.

  ✔Note: *If you are a WordPerfect user, help is available to assist you in making the transition from that software package to Word 97.*

Office Assistant

- By default, the Office Assistant appears on screen when you open any of the Office applications. The Office Assistant will answer questions, offer suggestions, and provide help unique to the Office program you are using.

- When you click on the Assistant, a help bubble appears, prompting you to type in a help topic. Type your question and click Search. The suggested procedures display. Click on desired procedure to display Help instructions.

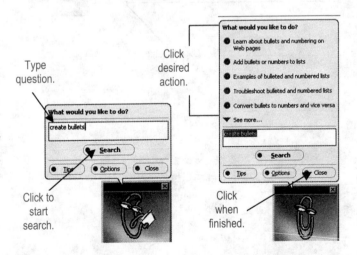

Type question.

Click desired action.

Click to start search.

Click when finished.

■ The Office Assistant can provide help even when you do not ask for it. For example, if you start typing a letter, the Assistant will open and offer help. You can then access a variety of wizards that can walk you through the procedure, or click Cancel and return to your document.

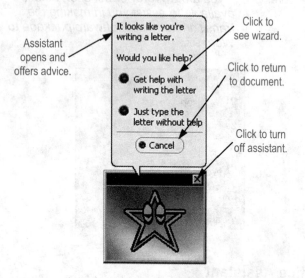

Assistant opens and offers advice.

Click to see wizard.

Click to return to document.

Click to turn off assistant.

■ The Office Assistant also offers tips about features and keyboard shortcuts. A tip is available when a light bulb appears in the Assistant window. Click the Assistant to view the tip.

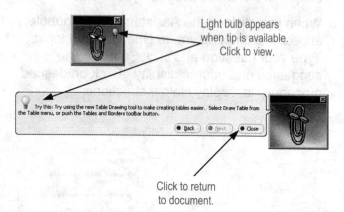

Light bulb appears when tip is available. Click to view.

Click to return to document.

Office Assistant Options

■ You can control the way the Office Assistant appears on screen as well as the kind of information it presents. You can also turn the Assistant off. If you turn the Assistant off, you can easily turn it on again by clicking the Assistant button 🔲 on the Standard toolbar. Even if you have closed the Office Assistant, it may appear when you take certain actions.

■ To change the Assistant options, click the Office Assistant (if it is on screen) or click the Office Assistant button on the toolbar. Then click Options. Click the Options tab and select the desired options.

Options tab

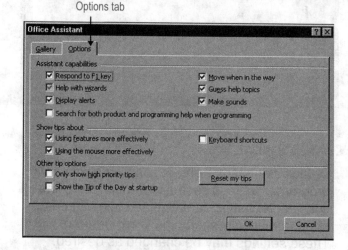

To select a different Office Assistant:

■ The Gallery tab in the Office Assistant dialog box offers several different Assistant characters. Click the Gallery tab on the Office Assistant dialog box and click Next to view the different Assistants. Click OK to select the displayed character.

Gallery tab

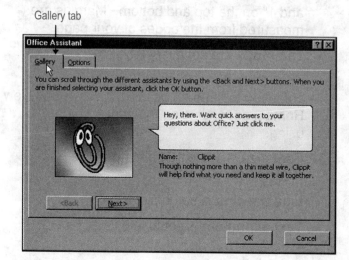

Contents, Index, and Find

■ If you select <u>C</u>ontents and Index from the <u>H</u>elp menu, you will be able to use the Help Contents, Index and/or the Find options to look for help.

Contents

- The **Contents** tab displays a page listing the help contents in the current program by topic. Double-clicking on a topic presents a list of subtopics and/or display screens. Note the Word Help Contents page illustrated below.

Contents tab

Word Help Contents Page

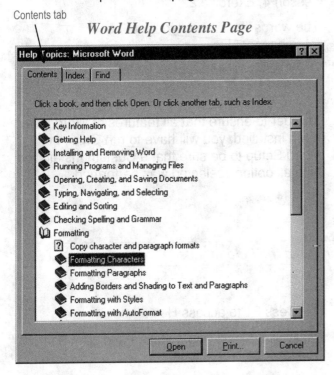

Index

- The **Index** tab allows you to enter the first few letters of your topic; the index feature then brings you to an index entry. Double-click the entry, or select the entry and click <u>D</u>isplay. The help screen related to your topic is then displayed.

Find

- The **Find** tab accesses the Help database feature. It allows you to search the Help database for the occurrence of any word or phrase in a help topic. The Index and Find features are similar; however, Find offers you more options to search for a topic.

ScreenTips

■ You can find information about screen elements by selecting What's <u>T</u>his? from the <u>H</u>elp menu, then pointing to the element you want information about and clicking the mouse.

■ Or you may click the question mark in the dialog box, point to the option, and press Shift + F1.

Microsoft on the World Wide Web

■ If you have access to the Internet, you can connect to Microsoft on the World Wide Web and get up-to-date information and support for Word as well as all the applications in Microsoft Office.

■ Open the <u>H</u>elp menu, select Microsoft on the <u>W</u>eb, and select the site you want to connect to. You can move around from site to site once you are connected to the Internet.

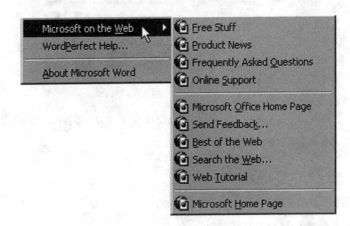

Exit Help

■ Click Cancel or Close, or press Escape to close a dialog box before exiting help.

Conventions

- The default font size is 10 point. The exercises in this book have been created using a larger and more readable 12-point font. If your default font is 10 point, you must change it to 12 point so your work will match the text exercises. Because printers vary, your line endings may not appear exactly like the exercises in this text.

- To change the font size default to 12 point, execute the following procedure:

  1. Click **Format** .... `Alt` + `O`

  2. Click **Style** .... `S`

  3. Click **Modify** .... `Alt` + `M`

  4. Click **Add to Template** .... `Alt` + `A`
     check box if necessary.

  5. Click **Format** .... `Alt` + `O`

  6. Click **Font** .... `F`

  7. Click **Size** .... `Alt` + `S`

  8. Type **12** .... `1` `2`

  9. Press **Enter** .... `Enter`, `Enter`, `Enter`
     three times.

OR

  1. Click **Format** .... `Alt` + `O`

  2. Click **Font** .... `F`

  3. Make the change.

  4. Click **Default** .... `Alt` + `D`

  5. Click **Yes** .... `Y`

- Changing font style and size will be covered in Lesson 4, Exercise 22.

- The words "font" and "type" are used interchangeably.

  ✓ If you do not have the specific font asked for in an exercise, select a similar font from the choices available on your computer.

- In order to ensure that all features of Word have been installed, you will have to run Office or Word Setup to be sure that a Custom Installation with all options selected was performed.

In this exercise, you will change window displays and use the help menus.

EXERCISE DIRECTIONS

1. Start the Word program.

2. Type your name on the screen.

3. Select View from the menu bar.

4. Select Zoom.

5. Select the 200% magnification option.

6. Click OK.
   ✓ Note the change in screen display.

7. Repeat steps 3-6 using the 75% option.

8. Using the Zoom Control box on the Standard Toolbar, set the magnification to 150%.

9. Return to 100% magnification using any desired method.

10. Click the Office Assistant button on the Standard toolbar or click on the Office Assistant image.
    - Type Zoom in the question text box and click Search.
    - Read the Search results.
    - Click Close.

11. Press F1 to access Help.

12. Type the following question and click Search: How do I hide a toolbar?

13. Click one of the topics to display Help screen on selected topic.

14. Press the Esc key to exit Help.

15. Select Contents and Index from the Help menu.

16. Click the Index tab.

17. Type the word Fonts, then click Display. Note the submenu topics.

18. Double-click on a submenu topic and display the help screen.

19. Close the help screen.

20. Click the program close button to exit Word. When prompted to save the file, select No.

KEYSTROKES

ZOOM

To specify a custom zoom:

1. Click **Zoom Control** box .... `100% ▾` on Standard toolbar.

2. Type (10-500) zoom percentage ....*number*

3. Press **Enter** .... `Enter`

To select a zoom:

1. Click drop-down arrow .... `▾` in Zoom Control box.

2. Select zoom percentages.

To change zoom with IntelliMouse:

Hold down the **Ctrl** key and roll the wheel to change zoom option by 10% increments.

START OFFICE ASSISTANT

By default, the Office Assistant will appear when you open any Office application. If the Assistant is not on screen, use these steps to activate the Assistant.

Click **Office Assistant** button .... `🖉` on Standard toolbar.

OR

Press **F1** .... `F1`

✓ *If the Contents, Index, and Find window opens instead of the Office Assistant, the **F1** key option has been disabled in the Office Assistant dialog box. See below for instructions on how to change this option.*

CLOSE OFFICE ASSISTANT

Click **Close** button on Office Assistant balloon.

USE OFFICE ASSISTANT

1. Click **Office Assistant**.......................`F1`

2. Type question in Assistant text box.

3. Click **Search**........................ `Alt` + `S`

4. Select from list of procedures to view more information.

5. Press **Esc** .... `Esc` to close Help window.

CHANGE OFFICE ASSISTANT OPTIONS

1. Click **Office Assistant**...................... `F1`

2. Click **Options**...................... `Alt` + `O`

3. Click **Options** tab................. `Alt` + `O`

4. Select desired options.

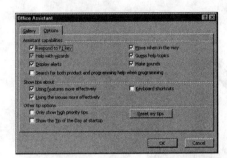

5. Click **OK** .... `Enter`

USE CONTENTS AND INDEX

1. Click **Help**............................. `Alt` + `H`

2. Click **Contents and Index**............... `C`

3. Click desired tab.

Contents

   a. Double-click a book or topic.

   b. Double-click a submenu item or display item.

Index

   a. Type first letters of topic word in Step 1 text box.

   b. Double-click topic that appears in Step 2 box.

   OR

   a. Select topic in Step 2 list box.

   b. Click **Display** .... `Alt` + `D`

Find

   a. Type and enter a search word or phrase in Step 1 text box.

   b. Select matching words in Step 2 list box, if presented.

   c. Double-click topic in Step 3 box.

   OR

   a. Select topic in Step 3 box.

   b. Click **Display** .... `D`

ACCESS SCREEN TIPS

To View Tips in Dialog Boxes:

Click question mark `❓` in dialog box.

OR

Point to option and press........ `Shift` + `F1`

To View Tip for Region of Screen, Menu, or Toolbar Button:

1. Press **Shift+F1**.................... `Shift` + `F1`

2. Click on item to view information about it.

3. Press **Esc** .... `Esc` to exit Help.

EXIT HELP OR HELP SCREENS

Click **Cancel**..................................... `Esc`

OR

Click **Close** button.............................. `✖`

Word 97

LESSON 2

Create, Save, and Print Documents

- If You Make an Error
- Document Views
- Create a New Document
- Save a Document
- Close a Document
- AutoCorrect
- Automatic Spell Checking
- Spelling & Grammar
- Properties
- Insertion Point Movement
- Create a Business Letter
- The Date and Time Feature
- Preview a Document
- Print
- Full Screen View
- Uppercase Mode

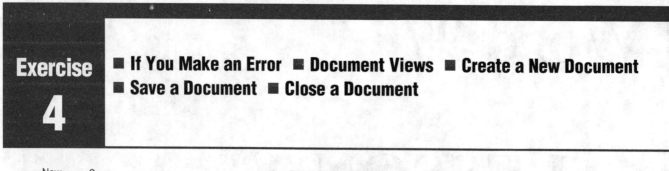

Exercise 4

- ■ **If You Make an Error** ■ **Document Views** ■ **Create a New Document**
- ■ **Save a Document** ■ **Close a Document**

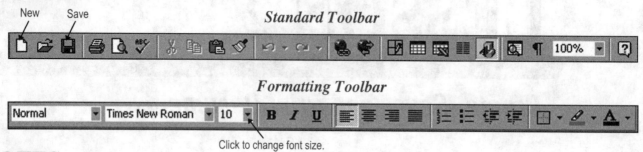

New   Save

Standard Toolbar

Formatting Toolbar

Click to change font size.

NOTES

If You Make an Error

- The following keys will get you out of trouble:

  - **Backspace** will erase characters to the immediate left of the insertion point.

  - **Escape** (or clicking a Cancel button) will back you out of most commands without executing them.

  - **F1** will access Help from the Office Assistant.

Document Views

- Word provides various ways to view documents on screen. The view buttons allow you to quickly switch between views. You may also change document views by selecting the desired view from the Ⅴiew menu.

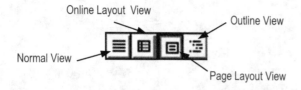

Online Layout View

Outline View

Normal View

Page Layout View

- **Normal view** is the default. It is used for most typing, editing and formatting.

- **Page Layout view** is used to display a document just as it will look when printed. This view allows you to see headers and footers, footnotes and endnotes, columns, etc.

- **Online Layout View** makes it easier to read documents on screen. Text appears larger and is arranged/wrapped to fit the window, rather than appearing as it will print. The Document Map pane *(see page 214)* automatically displays when you switch to Online view.

- **Outline view** is used to see the structure of a document. *(Outline view will be further explained in Exercise 40.)*

Create a New Document

- When you start Word, a blank screen appears, ready for you to begin keyboarding text. Word assigns "Document1" in the Title bar as the document name until you provide a name.

- As you type, the Col (Column) indicator in the Status bar changes. As text advances to another line, the Ln (Line) indicator also changes. If you move the insertion point, the Col and Ln indicators display the new location of the insertion point.

- The At indicator displays the vertical position of the insertion point as measured in inches from the top edge of the page.

- As text is typed, the insertion point automatically advances to the next line. This is called word wrap or wraparound. It is only necessary to use the Enter key at the end of a short line or to begin a new paragraph.

Save a Document

- Documents must be given a name for identification. A filename may contain a maximum of 255 characters, can include spaces, and is automatically assigned the file extension .doc. If you choose not to assign a filename, Word assigns a filename for you. It uses the first phrase of text up to a punctuation mark, new line or character, or paragraph mark, then adds .doc as the filename extension. Filenames and extensions are separated by a period.

  EXAMPLE: travel .doc

  Filename.extension

- Filenames are displayed in the case in which you type them. If you type a filename in uppercase, it will appear in uppercase. You cannot, however, use one filename in uppercase and save another file using the same name in lowercase.

- When saving a file, you must indicate the location where you wish to save it. Documents may be saved on a removable disk or on an internal hard drive. If you save a file to a removable disk, you must indicate that you are saving to the A:\ or B:\ drive. The hard drive is usually designated the C:\ drive.

- If you save to the hard drive, Word provides folders that you may use to save your work. Or you may create your own folders in which to save your work. You will learn to create folders (directories) in a later exercise.

- When saving a file for the first time, select Save from the File menu or click the Save button on the Standard toolbar. The following Save As dialog box appears:

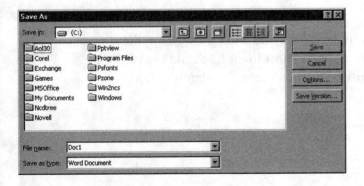

- Note the Save in drop-down list box. Word displays the current default storage location, or folder, to which you can save your file. The large area below the Save in text box displays the contents of the current folder.

- If you wish to save your file to a removable disk, click the drop-down arrow in the Save in drop-down list box and double-click 3½ Floppy (A:).

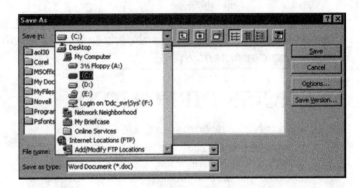

- Once this location is specified, the large area below the Save in box displays the contents of the disk located in the A: drive. Enter a filename or use the one that Word assigns for you in the File name text box, and click Save to save the document.

- You can save your document in a format other than Word by clicking in the Save as type box and selecting the desired format from the drop-down list. Use this option if you intend to use your file with another software program.

- Once your document is named, the filename appears in the Title bar.

- After saving your document for the first time, you can save the document again and continue working (updating it) by selecting Save from the File menu or by clicking the Save button 🖫 on the Standard toolbar. The Save As dialog box does not reappear; Word simply saves any changes you have made to your file. *Save often to prevent losing data.*

- You may also save documents by selecting Save As from the File menu. Use this command when you want to save your document under a different filename or in a different drive/directory (folder).

Close a Document

- When a document has been saved, it remains on your screen. If you wish to clear the screen, you may close the document window by selecting Close from the File menu or by double-clicking the Document Control icon.

- If you attempt to close a document before saving it, Word will prompt you to save before exiting. You may respond Yes or No.

- If you make a mistake and would like to begin the document again, close the document window without saving the document.

- To begin a new document after closing the document window, you must select New from the File menu or click the New button on the Standard toolbar. This will give you a new document window.

In this exercise, you will keyboard two paragraphs using word wrap. You will then save and name the document.

EXERCISE DIRECTIONS

1. Create a NEW document.
   - ✓ *The exercises in this book have been created using a 12-point font size. To have your work appear like the book exercises, you will need to change your font size default. To do so, follow the steps listed in the keystroke section on page 23. (Changing font style and size will be covered in detail in Exercise 22.) However, because printers and available fonts vary, your line endings may not appear exactly like those in the exercises shown in this text.*

2. Hide the Office Assistant.

3. Keyboard the paragraphs below, allowing the text to word wrap to the next line.
   - ✓ *Ignore green wavy lines if they appear.*

4. Begin the exercise at the top of your screen. Press the Enter key twice to start a new paragraph.

5. Correct immediately detected errors using the Backspace key.

6. Save the document; name it **TRY**.

7. Hide and then display the Standard toolbar.

8. Close the document window.

As you type, notice the Col indicator on your status bar changes as the position of your insertion point changes.

The wraparound feature allows the operator to decide on line endings, making the use of Enter unnecessary except at the end of a paragraph or short line. Each file is saved on a disk or hard drive for recall. Documents must be given a name for identification.

KEYSTROKES

CREATE A NEW DOCUMENT

CTRL + N

Click **New Document** button............... 🗋
OR
1. Click **File**.............................. Alt + F
2. Click **New**.................................. N
3. Click **Blank Document** button .... 📄
4. Click **OK**..................................... Enter

SAVE A NEW DOCUMENT

CTRL + S

1. Click **Save** button........................... 💾
   OR
   a. Click **File** .... Alt + F
   b. Click **Save** .... S
2. Click **Save in** box .... Alt + I
   to select drive or folder.
3. Select desired .... ↓, Enter
   drive or folder.
4. To select subfolder,
   if necessary.............. Tab, ↓, Enter
   double-click desired folder.
5. Double-click **File name**........ Alt + N
   text box.
6. Type filename.......................... *filename*
7. Click **Save** .... Alt + S or Enter

CLOSE A DOCUMENT

1. Double-click.................. 📄
   Document Control button.
2. Click **Yes**..................... Y
   to save changes.

   OR

   Click **No** .... N
   to abandon changes.

   OR

   a. Click **File** .... Alt + F
   b. Click **Close** C
   c. Click **Yes** .... Y
      to save changes.

      OR

      Click **No**............................... N
      to abandon changes.

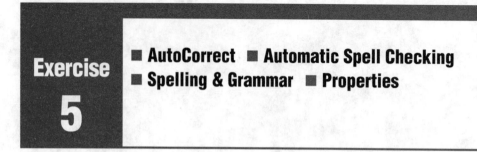

Exercise 5

- ■ **AutoCorrect** ■ **Automatic Spell Checking**
- ■ **Spelling & Grammar** ■ **Properties**

Spell Check

Standard Toolbar

NOTES

AutoCorrect

- The **AutoCorrect** feature automatically replaces common spelling errors and mistyped words with the correct text as soon as you press the spacebar.

- There are numerous words already in the AutoCorrect dictionary. However, you can enter words that you commonly misspell into the AutoCorrect dictionary by selecting AutoCorrect from the Tools menu.

- If you find this feature annoying, you can deselect the Replace text as you type option in the AutoCorrect dialog box.

- You can specify other types of corrections in the AutoCorrect dialog box:

  - **Correct TWo INitial CApitals** automatically converts two initial capital letters of a word to an initial capital letter and a lowercase second letter.

  - **Capitalize first letter of sentences** automatically capitalizes the first letter of a sentence.

  - **Capitalize names of days automatically** capitalizes names of days of the week.

  - **Correct accidental usage of cAPS LOCK Key** automatically assigns the proper case if CAPS LOCK Key was set to ON.

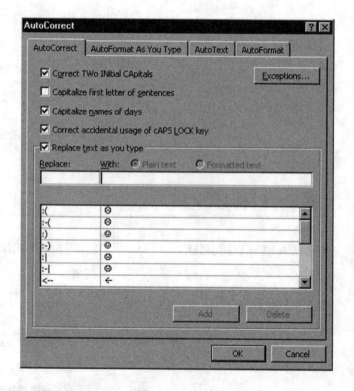

Automatic Spell Checking

- The **Automatic Spell Checking** feature underlines spelling errors with a red wavy line as you type. To correct a misspelled word, point to the underlined error with your mouse and click the *right* mouse button. A shortcut menu displays with suggested corrections. Click the correctly spelled word in the menu, and it will replace the incorrectly spelled word in the document.

- You can also add the word you misspelled (if Word provided a suggestion for the correct spelling) to the AutoCorrect dictionary by selecting AutoCorrect from the shortcut menu, then selecting the correctly spelled word from the submenu that appears.

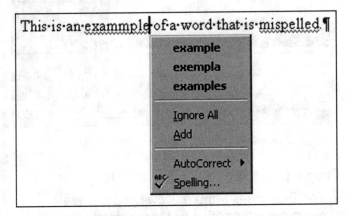

- A book icon appears on the lower right of the Status bar. As you type, a check mark moves from page to page on the book. When you stop typing, a red check mark remains, indicating that no spelling errors were detected by Automatic Spell Checking. If an X appears, it indicates that errors exist in your document. Double-click the book icon and Word will advance you to an error and open a shortcut menu with suggested corrections.

Spelling and Grammar

- Word's Spelling feature checks the spelling of a word, a block of text or an entire document. Occurrences of double words will also be flagged.

- The Speller compares the words in your document with the words in the dictionary. Proper names and words not in the standard dictionary will be identified as errors. When an error is detected, Word will supply a list of suggested spellings. You may accept Word's suggestions or ignore them.

- The Spelling feature may be accessed by selecting Spelling and Grammar from the Tools menu or by clicking the Spelling and Grammar button on the Standard toolbar. The following dialog box appears:

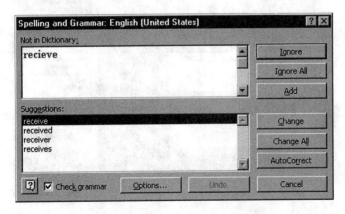

- To avoid having proper names flagged as incorrect spellings during the spell check session, add them to the custom dictionary. To do so, right-click on the word containing a red wavy line that you wish to add, and click Add on the shortcut menu.

- In addition to checking spelling, Word automatically checks for correct word usage and style. Grammatical errors are underlined with a green wavy line. If you right-click anywhere on the underlined sentence, Word will display grammar errors and offer suggestions based on the selected Writing style (Standard, Casual, Formal, Technical, Custom).

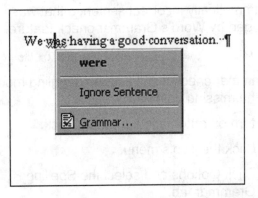

✓ If the grammatical errors in your document are not underlined with green wavy lines, you need to turn on the Grammar Check Option. Click Options on the Tools menu. In the dialog box that follows, make sure Check grammar as you type and Check grammar with spelling are both checked on the Spelling and Grammar tab.

- You can accept the suggestion, ignore it, or select Grammar to go to the Grammar dialog box, where you can see the reason Grammar check has identified this as an error.

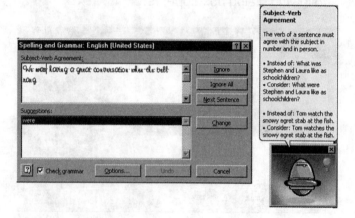

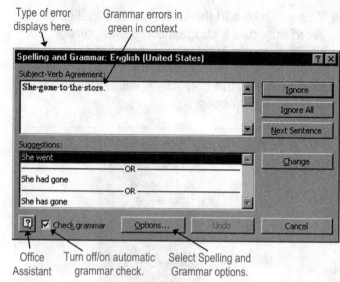

Type of error displays here.

Grammar errors in green in context

Office Assistant

Turn off/on automatic grammar check.

Select Spelling and Grammar options.

- Writing style may be changed by selecting Options in the Spelling and Grammar: English dialog box, then selecting Writing style.

- Remember, neither Grammar nor Spell check eliminates the need for you to carefully check a document.

Grammar Check Limitations

- Grammar check, just like Spell check, is not always correct and can be misleading. Since language is complex, it is difficult for a program to identify everything that is incorrect in a document. In fact, Grammar check can be totally wrong. Note the following example of a grammatically incorrect sentence that was not flagged by Word's Grammar check feature.

    Running down the hall my books fell on the floor.

    Grammar check didn't flag the dangling modifier or the missing comma.

- To turn off automatic grammar check:

    • Click the Tools menu.

    • Click Options and select the Spelling & Grammar tab.

    • Deselect *Check grammar as you type* and *Check grammar with spelling.*

Properties (Summary & Statistics)

- The Properties feature allows you to save summary information with each document. The information includes a document title, subject, author, keywords, and comments.

- You can create, display, and edit summary information at any time by selecting Properties from the File menu. The following dialog box appears for you to enter information about your document:

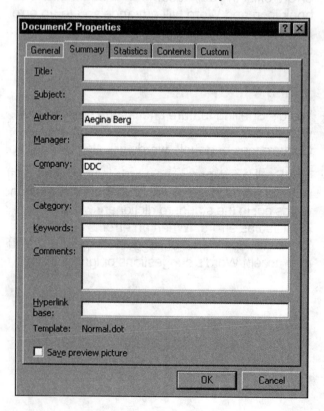

- To see a statistical summary of your document, click the Statistics tab. It lists the number of pages, paragraphs, lines, words, characters and bytes in your document.

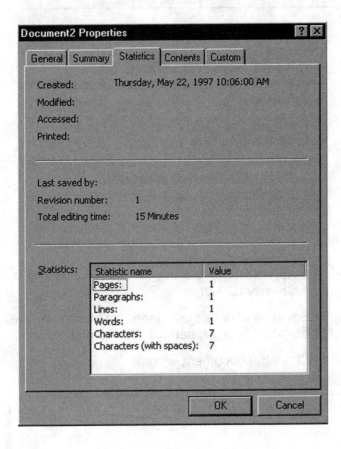

- You may also see a statistical summary of your document by selecting Word Count from the Tools menu. It lists the number of pages, words, characters, paragraphs and lines in your document.

- Statistical summaries are particularly useful if you are required to submit a report with a specified word or page count.

- You may specify that Word display the Properties dialog box each time you save a document. To do so, select Options in the Save As dialog box and select Prompt for document properties.

In this exercise, you will type two short paragraphs using word wrap. The paragraphs contain misspelled words and a grammatically incorrect sentence. After typing the paragraphs, you will note that AutoCorrect corrected some of the words. You will use the Automatic Spelling and the Grammar features to correct the other errors.

EXERCISE DIRECTIONS

1. Create a NEW document.
   - ✔ Be sure to select Check spelling as you type and Always suggest corrections on the Spelling and Grammar tab in the Options dialog box. To do so, select Tools, Options, click the Spelling and Grammar tab and then make your selections.

2. Begin the exercise at the top of your screen.

3. Access the AutoCorrect feature. Be sure Replace text as you type has been selected.

4. Keyboard the paragraphs below exactly as shown, including the circled, misspelled words. Allow the text to word wrap to the next line.

5. Press the Enter key twice to begin a new paragraph.

6. Use the Spelling or Automatic Spelling feature to correct the spelling errors in the document.

7. Use the Grammar feature to correct the grammatically incorrect sentence. Accept Word's suggestion.

8. Using the Properties feature, fill out the following summary information about your document:

Title:	Word 97 Information
Subject:	Ease of use
Author:	Your name
Manager:	Your supervisor or teacher's name
Company:	Your company or school name
Category:	Advertising
Keywords:	simple, margins, tabs
Comments:	first try

9. Save the exercise using the Save button on the Standard toolbar; name it **TRYAGAIN**.

10. Close the document window.

Word 97 is simple to use since you can begin typing as soon as you enter teh program.

THe way text will lay out or "format" on a page is set by the Word 97 program. For example, margins are set for 1.25" on the left and 1.25" on the right; line spaceing is automatic; tabs are set to advance the insersion point ½ inch each time the Tab key is pressed. Formats may be changed at any time and as many times as desired throughtout the document.

KEYSTROKES

AUTOCORRECT

1. Click **Tools** .... `Alt` + `T`
2. Click **AutoCorrect** .... `A`
3. Select **Replace text** .... `Alt` + `T`
   as you type option.

   To add words to AutoCorrect Dictionary:

   a. Click **Replace** text box .... `Alt` + `R`
   b. Type commonly misspelled word to include.
   c. Click **With** text box .... `Alt` + `W`
   d. Type correct version of word.
4. Click **Add** .... `Alt` + `A`
5. Click **OK** .... `Enter`

SPELLING

1. Place insertion point where spell check should begin.
   OR
   Select word or block of text to spell check.
2. Click **Spelling** button .... `ABC✓`
   OR
   a. Click **Tools** .... `Alt` + `T`
   b. Click **Spelling and Grammar** ...... `S`
   ✓ *When the system encounters a word not found in its dictionary, the word is displayed in red in the Not in Dictionary box; the insertion point will appear after the word.*
3. Click **Ignore** .... `Alt` + `I`
   to proceed without changing the word.
   OR
   Click **Change** .... `Alt` + `C`
   to accept word highlighted in Suggestions text box.
   OR
   Edit word in the **Not in Dictionary** box.
   OR
   a. Click **Suggestions** box .... `Alt` + `E`
      and select (highlight) desired suggestion.
   b. Click **Change** .... `Alt` + `C`
   OR

   To add to AutoCorrect:

1. Click **AutoCorrect** .... `Alt` + `R`
2. Click **Close** .... `Esc`
   to discontinue spell check.

AUTOMATIC SPELLING

1. Place mouse on red wavy underlined word.
2. Press right mouse button.
3. Click correctly spelled replacement word on shortcut menu.

PROPERTIES (DOCUMENTSUMMARY)

1. Click **File** .... `Alt` + `F`
2. Click **Properties** .... `I`
3. Click **Summary** tab.
4. Enter relevant information.
5. Click **OK** .... `Enter`

TURN GRAMMAR CHECK ON/OFF

1. Click **Tools** .... `Alt` + `T`
2. Click **Options** .... `O`
3. Select **Spelling &**
   Grammar tab .... `Spelling & Grammar`
4. Select/deselect desired options.

   a. **Check grammar as you type** .... `Alt` + `G`
      Marks errors as you work.

   b. **Hide grammatical errors in this document** .... `Alt` + `E`
      Green wavy lines under possible errors will be hidden when this is selected.

   c. **Check grammar with spelling** .... `Alt` + `H`
      Select this option to check spelling and grammar. Not available if the grammar checker is not installed.

   d. **Show readability statistics** .... `Alt` + `R`
      Shows Readability Statistics dialog box after you run the grammar check.

5. Click **OK** .... `Enter`

GRAMMAR

✓ *By default, spelling will be checked as you check grammar. If you want to check just grammar, deselect* **Check spelling as you type** *in the Spelling & Grammar options dialog box.*

1. Be sure that **Check grammar with spelling** is selected in the Spelling and Grammar Options dialog box (see steps above).
2. Place insertion point where grammar check will begin.
   OR
   Select block of text to check.
3. Click **Spelling** button ....

   ✓ **Check grammar** *should be selected. Word will stop on the first error it finds (spelling or grammar). Grammar errors are underlined with a green wavy line. You can skip or change spelling errors as you go through a document looking for grammar errors.*

4. When you encounter a grammar error, select one of the following options.
5. Click **Ignore** .... `Alt` + `I`
   to reject suggested change and continue grammar check.
   OR
   a. Select desired suggestion if more than one suggestion appears.
   b. Select **Change** .... `Alt` + `C`
      to accept highlighted suggestion and make suggested correction in document.
   ✓ *If no suggestions are made, the Change button will be dimmed. You can edit the text manually in the Spelling and Grammar window.*
6. Continue checking the rest of the document.
   OR
   Click **Cancel** .... `Esc`
   to return to document.

Exercise 6

- ■ **Insertion Point Movement**
- ■ **The Date and Time Feature**
- ■ **Create a Business Letter**

NOTES

Insertion Point Movement

- ■ Use the arrow keys on the numeric keypad or the separate arrow keys located to the left of the keypad to move the insertion point in the direction indicated by the arrow. The insertion point will only move through text, spaces or codes. The insertion point cannot be moved past the beginning or the end of your document.

- ■ To move the insertion point quickly from one point in the document to another, you may use **express insertion point movements**.

    ✔ Note the keystroke procedures on page 33 carefully.

Create a Business Letter

- ■ There are a variety of letter styles for business and personal use.

- ■ The parts of a **business letter** and the vertical spacing of letter parts are the same regardless of the style used.

- ■ A business letter is comprised of eight parts:

    1) **date**

    2) **inside address** (to whom and where the letter is going)

    3) **salutation**

    4) **body**

    5) **closing**

    6) **signature line**

    7) **title line**

    8) **reference initials** (The first set of initials belongs to the person who wrote the letter; the second set belongs to the person who typed the letter.) Whenever you see "yo" as part of the reference initials in an exercise, substitute *your own* initials.

- ■ The letter style illustrated in this exercise is a full-block business letter, because the date, closing, signature, and title lines begin at the left margin.

- ■ A letter generally begins 2.5" from the top of a page. If the letter is long, it may begin 2" from the top of the paper. If the letter is short, it may begin 3" or more from the top.

- ■ Margins and the size of the characters may also be adjusted to make a letter more balanced on the page.

    ✔Note: Changing margins and font size will be covered in a later lesson.

The Date and Time Feature

- ■ The **Date and Time** feature lets you insert the current date and/or time into your document automatically.

- ■ To insert the date or time, select Date and <u>T</u>ime from the <u>I</u>nsert menu. In the Date and Time dialog box that follows, select the desired date format from the list of available formats.

Date and Time Format Dialog Box

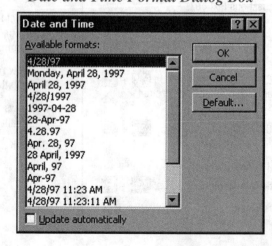

In this exercise, you will create a full-block letter and practice moving the insertion point through the document.

EXERCISE DIRECTIONS

✓ *Directions are given for a 12-point font setting. Be sure your default font is 12 point; otherwise, there will be discrepancies between your document and the one shown in the exercise.*

1. Create a NEW document.

2. With your insertion point at the top of the screen, press the Enter key eight times. Use the date feature to begin the date on Ln 9 (At 2.5").

3. Use the default margins and tabs.

4. Access the AutoCorrect feature. Be sure Replace text as you type has been selected.

5. Keyboard the letter below exactly as shown.

   ✓ *The accent mark is automatically inserted when you type the word Café.*

6. Press the Enter key between parts of the letter as directed in the exercise.

7. Spell and Grammar check using both the Automatic Spell Checking and Spelling features.

8. After completing the exercise, move the insertion point to the top of the screen (Ctrl + Home) and back to the end of the document (Ctrl + End).

9. Save the file; name it **CYBERCAFE**.

10. Close the document window.

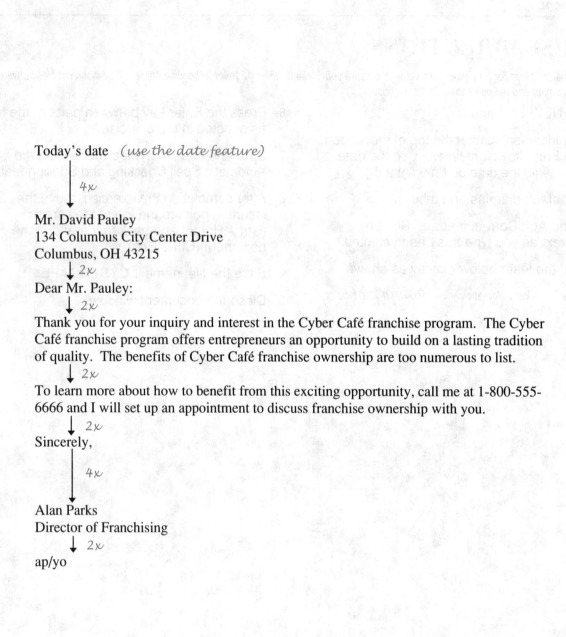

Today's date   *(use the date feature)*

↓ *4x*

Mr. David Pauley
134 Columbus City Center Drive
Columbus, OH 43215

↓ *2x*

Dear Mr. Pauley:

↓ *2x*

Thank you for your inquiry and interest in the Cyber Café franchise program. The Cyber Café franchise program offers entrepreneurs an opportunity to build on a lasting tradition of quality. The benefits of Cyber Café franchise ownership are too numerous to list.

↓ *2x*

To learn more about how to benefit from this exciting opportunity, call me at 1-800-555-6666 and I will set up an appointment to discuss franchise ownership with you.

↓ *2x*

Sincerely,

↓ *4x*

Alan Parks
Director of Franchising

↓ *2x*

ap/yo

KEYSTROKES

INSERT CURRENT DATE AND TIME

1. Click **Insert** .... `Alt` + `I`
2. Click **Date and Time** .... `T`
3. Click desired format .... `↑` `↓`
4. Click **OK** .... `Enter`

EXPRESS INSERTION POINT MOVEMENTS

TO MOVE:	PRESS:
One character left	`←`
One character right	`→`
One line up	`↑`
One line down	`↓`
Previous word	`Ctrl` + `←`
Next word	`Ctrl` + `→`
Beginning of document	`Ctrl` + `Home`
End of document	`Ctrl` + `End`
Top of page	`F5`, *number*, `Enter`, `Esc`

TO MOVE:	PRESS:
Beginning of line	`Home`
End of line	`End`
Top of previous page	`Ctrl` + `Page Up`
Top of window	`Alt` + `Ctrl` + `Page Up`
Bottom of window	`Alt` + `Ctrl` + `Page Down`
To last revision	`Shift` + `F5`

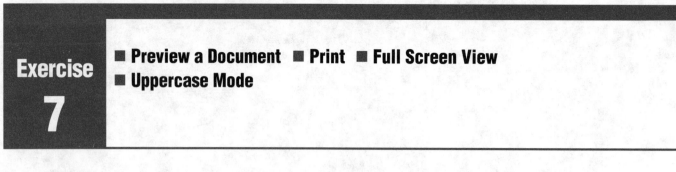

Exercise

7

■ **Preview a Document** ■ **Print** ■ **Full Screen View**
■ **Uppercase Mode**

Print   Preview   *Standard Toolbar*

NOTES

Print Preview

■ The **Print Preview** feature allows you to see how a document will look on paper before you print it.

■ To preview a document, select Print Pre_v_iew from the _F_ile menu, or click the Print Preview button on the Standard toolbar.

■ Clicking the **Multiple Pages** button allows you to view either one page at a time or several pages.

■ Clicking the **View Ruler** button allows you to display or hide the vertical and horizontal rulers. It is suggested that you keep both rulers visible, because they are very useful in viewing and adjusting margin settings. In later lessons, you will learn how to adjust margin settings and page breaks easily in Print Preview mode using the mouse.

■ You may scroll backward or forward through your document in Print Preview mode by pressing the Page Up or the Page Down key on the keyboard or by clicking on the scroll bar using the mouse. Exit Print Preview by pressing the Escape key or by clicking _C_lose.

■ You can also use the wheel on the IntelliMouse to scroll through a multiple-page document in Print Preview. The automatic pan feature, however, will not work in Print Preview.

Print Preview Screen

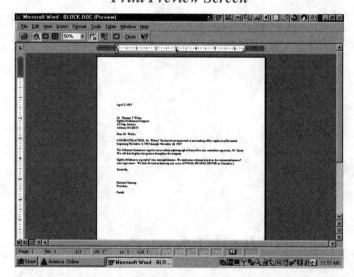

Print Preview Toolbar

Print

■ Word lets you print *part* or *all* of a document that is on your screen. You can print a page of the document, selected pages of the document, one or more blocks of text within the document, or the entire document. You may also print a single document or multiple documents from a disk without retrieving them to the screen. In this exercise, you will print a complete document from a window on your screen.

- Check to see that your printer is turned on and that paper is loaded.

- There are four ways to print an entire document in Word:

  Click the Print button on the Standard toolbar.

  OR

  Select <u>F</u>ile, <u>P</u>rint.

  OR

  Click the Print button on the Print Preview toolbar.

  OR

  Press Ctrl+P, Enter.

Full Screen View

- To see your document without the screen elements (Ruler, toolbars, menu bar, title bar and Taskbar) select F<u>u</u>ll Screen from the <u>V</u>iew menu. Your document will display on the entire screen in either Normal or Page Layout view, depending on what view you were in when you selected Full Screen.

- To return the elements to the screen, click <u>C</u>lose Full Screen or press Escape.

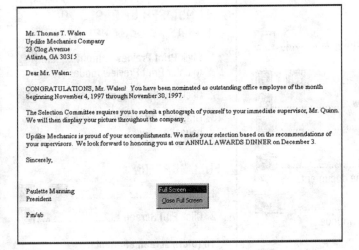

Uppercase Mode

- Pressing the Caps Lock key once allows you to type all capital letters without holding down the Shift key. Only *letters* are changed by Caps Lock. To end uppercase mode, press the Caps Lock key again.

In this exercise, you will create a full-block letter using the Date feature and print one copy of the document.

EXERCISE DIRECTIONS

1. Create a NEW document.

2. Change to Page Layout view.

3. Use the default margins.

4. With the insertion point at the top of the screen, press the Enter key eight times. Use the automatic Date feature to insert the date 2.5" from the top of the page.

5. Access the AutoCorrect feature. Be sure Replace text as you type has been selected.

6. Keyboard the letter on the following page as shown.

7. Press the Enter key between parts of the letter as directed in the illustration.

8. Spell check.

9. Display your document in Full Screen view.

10. Return the elements to the screen.

11. Print one copy either:
    - from the Print Preview screen
    OR
    - using the Print button on the Standard toolbar
    OR
    - by selecting File, Print.

12. Save the file; name it **BLOCK**.

13. Close the document window.

KEYSTROKES

UPPERCASE MODE

1. Press **Caps Lock** .... `Caps`

2. Type text.

3. Press **Caps Lock** .... `Caps`
   to end uppercase mode.

PRINT A DOCUMENT

CTRL + P

Click **Print** button .... 🖨
OR
1. Click **File** .... `Alt` + `F`

2. Click **Print** .... `P`

3. Click **OK** .... `Enter`

PRINT PREVIEW

Click **Print Preview** button .... 🔍
OR
1. Click **File** .... `Alt` + `F`

2. Click **Print Preview** .... `V`

3. Press **Page Up** .... `Page Up`
   OR
   Press **Page Down** .... `Page Down`
   to page through the document.

4. Click **Close** .... `Close`
   to exit Print Preview mode.
   OR
   Press **Escape** .... `Esc`

PRINT A DOCUMENT FROM THE PRINT PREVIEW SCREEN

1. Click **File** .... `Alt` + `F`

2. Click **Print Preview** .... `V`

3. Click **Print** button .... 🖨

SET NUMBER OF PAGES TO DISPLAY IN PRINT PREVIEW

1. Click **Print Preview** button .... 🔍
   to enter Print Preview mode.

2. Click **Multiple Pages** button .... 🔲

3. Drag to indicate desired number of pages to view.

FULL SCREEON

1. Click **View** .... `Alt` + `V`

2. Click **Full Screen** .... `U`

To return screen elements:
   Press **Escape** .... `Esc`
   OR
   Click **Close**
   Full Screen .... `Shift` + `Alt` + `C`

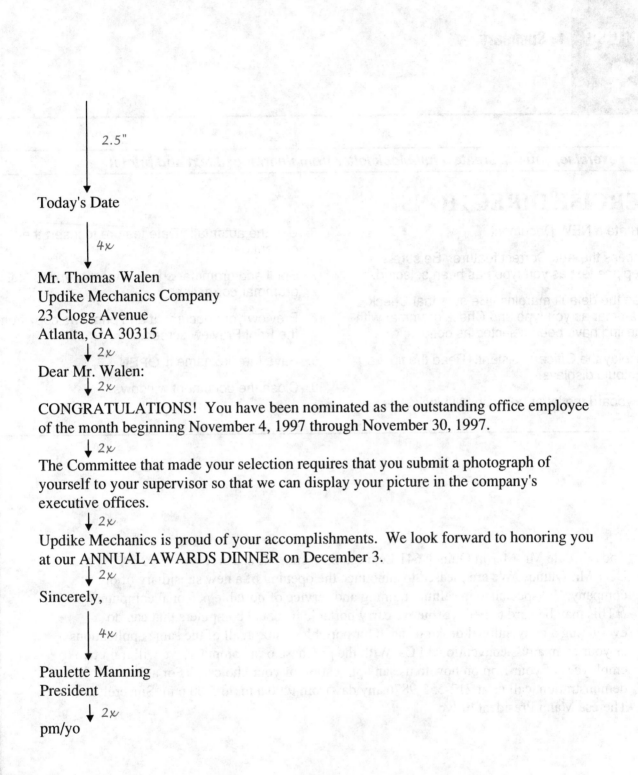

2.5"

Today's Date

4x

Mr. Thomas Walen
Updike Mechanics Company
23 Clogg Avenue
Atlanta, GA 30315

2x

Dear Mr. Walen:

2x

CONGRATULATIONS! You have been nominated as the outstanding office employee
of the month beginning November 4, 1997 through November 30, 1997.

2x

The Committee that made your selection requires that you submit a photograph of
yourself to your supervisor so that we can display your picture in the company's
executive offices.

2x

Updike Mechanics is proud of your accomplishments. We look forward to honoring you
at our ANNUAL AWARDS DINNER on December 3.

2x

Sincerely,

4x

Paulette Manning
President

2x

pm/yo

Exercise

8

■ **Summary**

In this exercise, you will create a full-block letter from unarranged text and print it.

EXERCISE DIRECTIONS

1. Create a NEW Document.

2. Access the AutoCorrect feature. Be sure Replace text as you type has been selected.

3. Use the default margins. Be sure that Check grammar as you type and Check grammar with spelling have been selected as options.

4. Display the Office Assistant. Read the tip if a lightbulb displays.

5. Keyboard the letter below in full-block style.

6. Use the automatic Date feature to insert the current date.

7. Spell and grammar check. Accept Word's first grammar correction.

8. Preview your document and print one copy from the Print Preview screen.

9. Save the file; name it **OPEN.**

10. Close the document window.

Today's date Mr. Martin Quincy 641 Lexington Avenue New York, NY 10022 Dear Mr. Quincy: We are pleased to announce the opening of a new subsidiary of our company. We specialize in selling, training and service of portable personal computers. ⧣This may be hard to believe, but we carry portable personal computers that can do everything a conventional desktop can. Our portables can run all of the same applications as your company's conventional PCs. With the purchase of a computer, we will train two employees of your firm on how to use an application of your choice. ⧣For a free demonstration, call us at 212-555-9876 any day from 9:00 a.m. to 5:00 p.m. Sincerely, Theresa Mann President tm/yo

NEXT EXERCISE

Exercise 9

■ **Summary**

In this exercise, you will create a full-block letter from unarranged text and print it.

EXERCISE DIRECTIONS

1. Create a NEW Document.

2. Access the AutoCorrect feature. Be sure Replace text as you type has been selected.

3. Use the default margins.

4. Display the Office Assistant. Read the tip if a light bulb displays.

5. Keyboard the letter below in full-block style.

6. Use the automatic Date feature to insert the current date.

7. Spell and Grammar check.

8. Preview your document and print one copy from the Print Preview screen.

9. Save the file; name it **CYBERCATERING**.

10. Close the document window.

Today's date Ms. Arlene Fauser 549 Byte Avenue Seattle, WA 98104 Dear Ms. Fauser: We are very pleased you have chosen Cyber Café Catering to fulfill your catering needs. Our goal is to provide you with high quality catering. ¶You can rely on Cyber Café Catering to satisfy all your breakfast, luncheon and office party needs. Our commitment to 100% satisfaction is the basis of our catering service. ¶You may place your order Monday through Friday 8:00 a.m. to 7:00 p.m. by calling 888-8888. ¶On behalf of the staff at Cyber Café Catering, I thank you for choosing us for your catering events. Cordially, Valerie Mana Director of Catering vm/yo

Word 97

LESSON 3

Open and Edit Documents; Manage Files

- Open and Revise a Document
- Insert Text
- Proofreaders' Marks
- Save Changes to a Document
- Overtype Mode
- Comments
- Open a Document As Read-Only
- Save As
- Undo and Redo
- Select Text
- Delete Text
- Show/Hide Codes
- Delete Paragraph Marks
- Change Case
- Nonbreaking Spaces
- Track Changes

- Compare Documents
- Accept/Reject Revisions
- Set Margins
- Set Tabs
- View Margins
- Preview a File
- Print a File without Opening It
- Select Multiple Files to Print
- File Details
- Sort Files
- Find Files

Exercise

10

■ **Open and Revise a Document** ■ **Insert Text** ■ **Proofreaders' Marks**
■ **Save Changes to a Document**

Standard Toolbar

Open

NOTES

Open and Revise a Document

■ A document is revised when corrections or adjustments need to be made.

■ Before a document can be revised or edited, it must be opened from the disk or hard drive to the screen.

Open a Recently Saved Document

■ Word lists the four most recently saved documents at the bottom of the File menu. To open a recently saved document, select the desired filename on the list of recently opened documents.

Open a Previously Saved Document

■ Select Open from the File menu or click the Open button 🖼 on the Standard toolbar. In the Open dialog box that appears, double-click the desired filename from the list of documents displayed. If the desired file is not listed, click the list arrow next to the Look in drop-down list box and select the desired drive and/or folder.

✔ *Note the Open dialog box below.*

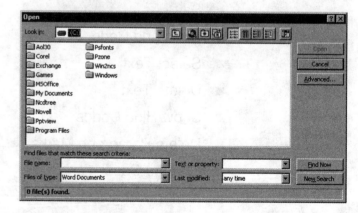

Recently opened files

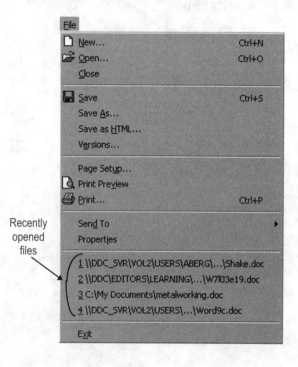

Open a Document from Outside the Word Program

- If you want to open a Word document when you begin working at your computer, you may open a document outside the Word program. Doing so will launch the Word program *and* display the Open dialog box.

- You may open a Word document before launching the program using any one of the following procedures:

Using the Shortcut bar (if you are running Office):

- Click *Open a Document* and select the drive, folder, and document filename from the Open dialog box.

Using the Windows 95 Taskbar:

- Click *Start*, highlight *Documents*, and click one of your last 15 documents.

- Click *Start*, click *Open Office Document* (if you are running Office), and select the drive, folder and document filename from the Open dialog box.

- Click *Start*, highlight *Programs*, select *Windows Explorer*, select the drive and folder, and double-click the document filename.

Insert Text

- To make corrections, you can move through the document to the point of correction using the insertion point movement keys. These keys include End, Home, Page Up, Page Down and the arrow keys. You have already had some practice moving the insertion point through your document in previous exercises.

- To insert text, place the insertion point to the left of the character that will follow the inserted material. When you type inserted text, the existing text moves to the right. When you insert a word, the space following the word must also be inserted.

- To create a new paragraph in existing text, place the insertion point immediately to the left of the first character in the new paragraph and press the Enter key twice.

Proofreaders' Marks

- Proofreaders' marks are symbols on a printed copy of a document that indicate changes to be made. As each proofreaders' mark is introduced in this text, it is explained and illustrated.

- The proofreaders' mark for insertion is: ∧

- The proofreaders' mark for a new paragraph is: ⌗

Save Changes to a Document

- When a document is opened and revisions are made, the revised or updated version must be resaved or replaced. When a document is resaved, the old version is replaced with the new version.

- You may save your changes as you are working or you may save your changes after all corrections have been made. Click the Save button ▣ on the Standard toolbar or select Save from the File menu. Your file will be updated, and the document will remain on the screen for you to continue working.

- It is recommended that you save often to prevent loss of data.

> *In this exercise, you will open a previously saved document and insert new text.*

EXERCISE DIRECTIONS

1. Open ⌨TRY, or open 🖫10TRY.

2. Make the insertions indicated in the illustration below.

3. Save your work.

4. Spell check.

5. Print one copy.

6. Close and save the file; name it **TRY**.

7. Close the document window.

As you type, <ins>you will</ins> notice the Col indicator on your status bar changes as the position of your insertion point changes.

The "wraparound" feature allows the <ins>computer</ins> operator to ~~decide on~~ <ins>determine</ins> line endings, making the use of <ins>the</ins> Enter unnecessary except at the end of a paragraph or short line. Each file is saved on a disk or hard drive for recall. Documents must be given a name for identification <ins>or number</ins>.

(<ins>key</ins>) (<ins>data</ins>)

KEYSTROKES

OPEN A DOCUMENT

CTRL + O

1. Click **Open File** button .... 📂
2. Click **Look in** drop-down list box and select drive and/or folder containing file to open .... Alt + ⬆, ⬇, ↵
3. Double-click desired filename from list under **Look in** box.

OR

1. Click **File** .... Alt + F
2. Click **Open** .... O
3. Click **Look in** box ..... Alt + ⬆, ⬇, ↵ and select drive and/or folder containing file to open.
4. Select or type desired filename.
5. Click **OK** .... Enter

OR

1. Click **File** .... Alt + F
2. Select desired filename .... ⬇, ↵ from list of recently opened files.

OPEN A DOCUMENT OUTSIDE WORD PROGRAM

USING THE SHORTCUT BAR

1. Click **Open Office Document** .... 📄 button.
2. Click **Look in** drop-down list ..... Alt + ⬆, ⬇, ↵ and select desired drive and/or folder.
3. Double-click desired document from those listed.

OR

a. Click **File name** .... Alt + N text box.
b. Enter desired filename. .... *filename*

OR

If document was not saved as a Word file:

a. Click **Files of type** .... Alt + T list arrow.
b. Select desired file type .... ⬇, ↵ (if other than a Word file)
c. Click **Open** .... Enter

USING THE TASKBAR

1. Click **Start** .... Ctrl + Esc
2. Highlight **Documents** .... D
3. Select one of the last 15 displayed documents. .... ⬇, ↵

OR

1. Click **Start** .... Ctrl + Esc
2. Click **Open Office Document**.
3. Select drive and/or folder from **Look in** drop-down list ...... Alt + ⬆, ⬇, ↵
4. Double-click document filename from list beneath **Look in** box.

OR

1. Click **Start** .... Ctrl + Esc
2. Highlight **Programs** .... P
3. Select **Windows Explorer** .... 🔍
4. Select drive and folder.
5. Double-click on desired folder.

RESAVE A DOCUMENT

Click **Save** button .... 💾

OR

1. Click **File** .... Alt + F
2. Click **Save** .... S

OR

1. Click **File** .... Alt + F
2. Click **Close** C
3. Click **Yes** .... Y when prompted to save changes.

INSERT TEXT

1. Place insertion point to left of character that will immediately follow inserted text.
2. Type text .... *text*

Exercise 11

■ **Overtype Mode** ■ **Comments**

NOTES

Overtype Mode

■ Another way to edit text is to put Word into Overtype mode so you can type over the existing text with new text. In Overtype mode, existing text does not move to the right; it is typed over. By default, Word is in Insert mode. You may switch to Overtype mode by double-clicking the OVR indicator on the Status bar. When Word is in Overtype mode, the OVR mode indicator is highlighted in the Status bar.

■ To switch back to Insert mode, double-click the OVR indicator in the Status bar. For most editing, it is recommended that you work in Insert mode.

Comments

■ Comments are hidden notes or annotations that you or a reviewer can add to a document. These comments can be read on screen, hidden when the document is printed, printed with the document, or even incorporated into a document. Each comment is numbered and includes the initials of the person making the comment. By default, Word uses information in the User Information profile to identify the author of the comments inserted into a document.

■ Inserting comments in a document is similar to inserting footnotes and endnotes. Position the cursor where you want to insert a comment or highlight a block of text you want to comment on.

■ Open the Insert menu and select Comment. Enter your comment in the comment pane at the bottom of the screen.

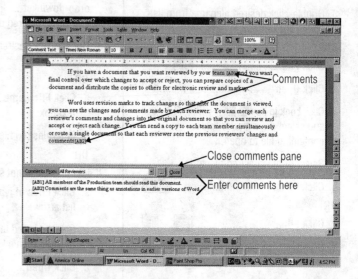

■ Any text that you highlight before you insert a comment will appear in yellow in the document. The initials and the number of the comment will appear in yellow in square brackets.

■ You can continue to add comments with the comment pane open, or you can click the Close button in the Comment pane to return to the document.

■ To view the comment on screen, simply move the mouse pointer over any part of the highlighted text or the initials of the reviewer. The comment will appear under the name of the person making the comment.

✓Note: If comments do not display, you need to select ScreenTips on the View tab under Tools, Options.

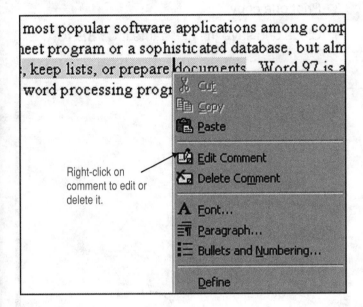

Move mouse pointer over Comments
to view comment on screen.

- You can edit or delete comments easily. Right-click while pointing to the comment and select the desired option.

Right-click on comment to edit or delete it.

- By default, comments will not print.
- To print comments with a document:
  - Select File, Print.
  - Click Options in the lower left corner of the Print dialog box.

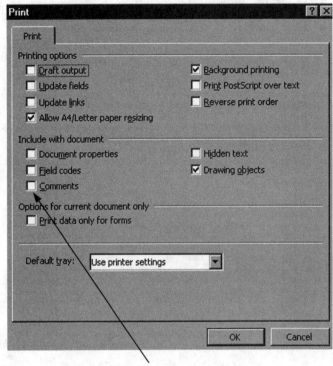

Click here to have Comments print.

  - Click Comments in the Include with document section of the Print options dialog box.
  - Click OK and print the document.

In this exercise, you will open a previously saved document and insert new text.

EXERCISE DIRECTIONS

1. Open 🖳**CYBERCAFE**, or open 🖫**11CYBERCAFE**.

2. Make the indicated insertions.

3. Use the Overtype mode to change the phone number in the second paragraph and to change the closing from Sincerely to Cordially; return to Insert mode immediately following this step.

4. Insert the following comment where illustrated in the letter:

   "Send franchise program information."

5. Spell check.

6. Save your work.

7. Edit your comment to read:

   "Send franchise information next week and follow up with a call."

8. Print one copy.

9. Close and save the file; name it **CYBERCAFE**.

Today's date

Cooper

Mr. David Pauley
134 Columbus City Center Drive
Columbus, OH 43215

Dear Mr. Pauley:

recent   *outstanding*   *long-*

Thank you for your inquiry and interest in the Cyber Café franchise program. The Cyber Café franchise program offers entrepreneurs an opportunity to build on a lasting tradition of quality. The benefits of Cyber Café franchise ownership are too numerous to list.

your potential and   *investment*   *666*

To learn more about how to benefit from this exciting opportunity, call me at 1-800-555-*8888* 6666 and I will set up an appointment to discuss franchise ownership with you.

~~Sincerely,~~
Cordially

Insert comment here.

Alan Parks
Director of Franchising

ap/yo

¶ We urge you to act quickly, because a limited number of franchises will be given in your area.

48

KEYSTROKES

USE OVERTYPE

1. Double-click the **OVR** indicator in the Status bar.
2. Type text .... *text*
3. Double-click the **OVR** indicator in the Status bar to return to insert mode.

INSERT COMMENTS

1. Click anywhere in document where comment will appear.

   OR

   Highlight text about which you want to comment.
2. Click **Insert** .... `Alt` + `I`
3. Click **Co**m**ment** .... `M`
4. Type comment in Comment pane.
5. Click **Close** .... `Alt` + `Shift` + `C`
   in Comments pane.

DELETE COMMENTS

1. Right-click anywhere in comment area.
2. Click **Delete Co**m**ment** .... `M`

EDIT COMMENTS

1. Right-click anywhere in comment area.
2. Click **Edit Comment** .... `E`
3. Make desired edits.
4. Click **Close** .... `Alt` + `Shift` + `C`
   in Comments pane.

Exercise

12

■ **Open a Document As Read-Only** ■ **Save As** ■ **Undo and Redo**

Standard Toolbar

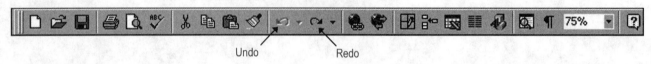

Undo   Redo

NOTES

Open a Document as Read-Only

■ If you wish to open a document but not make changes to it, you may open the document as Read-Only. This option requires you to save your file with a different filename and prevents you from accidentally affecting the original file.

■ To open a file as Read-Only, point to the file you wish to open in the Open dialog box and click the *right* mouse button. Select Open Read-Only from the choices. Or you may select the file you wish to open, then click the Commands and Settings button 🔳, and choose Open Read-Only.

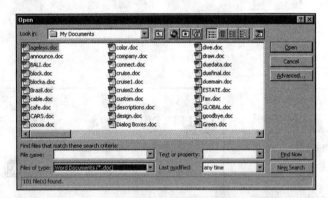

■ If you save, close or exit a document that you opened using the Read-Only option, Word automatically displays the Save As dialog box so you can give the file another name, thus leaving the original document intact.

Save As

■ If you wish to save a copy of any document under a different filename or in a different location, you may select Save As from the File menu. When any document is saved under a new filename, the original document remains intact.

Undo and Redo

■ The **Undo** feature lets you undo the last change you made to the document. Word remembers up to 300 actions in a document and allows you to undo any or all of them. You can undo your most recent actions by repeatedly clicking the Undo button 🔄 on the Standard toolbar, or you can undo a series of actions by clicking the Undo list arrow ▾ next to the Undo button and selecting the consecutive actions to undo, starting with the most recent.

■ The **Redo** feature allows you to reverse the last undo. Like Undo, Redo allows you to reverse up to 300 actions in a document. You can redo your most recent action by clicking the Redo button 🔁 on the Standard toolbar, or you can redo a series of actions by clicking the Redo list arrow ▾ next to the Redo button and selecting the consecutive actions to redo, starting with the most recent.

In this exercise, you will insert text at the top of the page and create a full-block letter. To insert the date, press the Enter key 8 times to bring the At indicator to 2.5", and use the automatic Date feature to insert today's date. Then, press Enter 4 times. After inserting the date, insert the inside address and salutation. Text will adjust as you continue creating the letter.

EXERCISE DIRECTIONS

1. Open ⌨**TRYAGAIN** as a Read-Only file, or open 💾**12TRYAGAIN** from the data disk as a Read-Only file.

2. Make the indicated insertions. Follow the spacing for a full-block letter illustrated in Exercise 6.

3. Use the automatic Date feature to insert today's date.

4. Use Overtype mode to insert the word "start" in the second paragraph; return to Insert mode immediately.

5. Insert the following comment in the document where shown.

   "Check Donna's address. She moved recently."

6. After typing the initials (jo/yo), click Undo to remove your own initials. (Leave as jo/.)

7. Preview your work.

8. Modify the document summary information (Properties) as follows:

Subject:	Inquiry about software programs
Category:	Customer Relations
Manager:	Jerry O'Brien

9. Access the Statistics Tab in the Properties dialog box and note the number of words in this document.

10. Print one copy.

11. Save the file as **TRYIT**.

12. Close the document window.

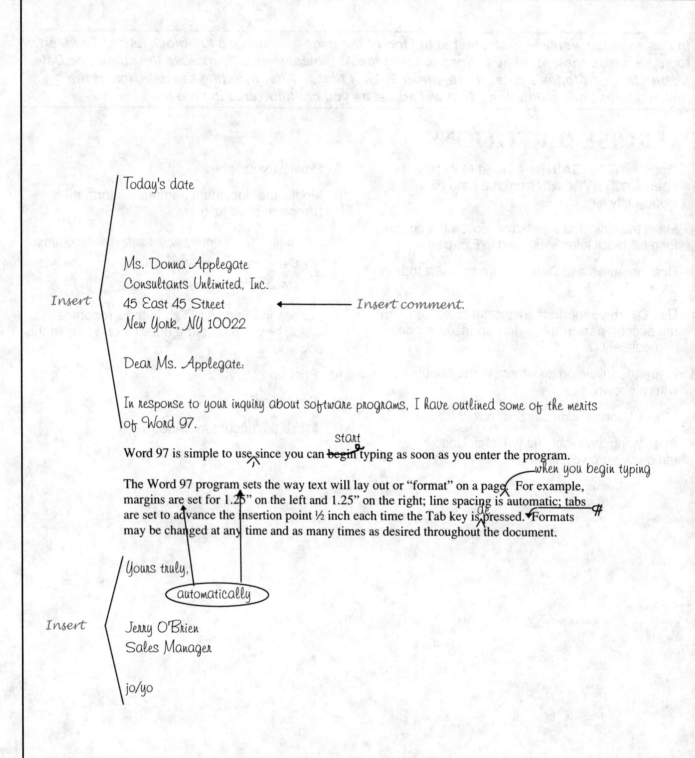

Insert

Today's date

Ms. Donna Applegate
Consultants Unlimited, Inc.
45 East 45 Street   ← Insert comment.
New York, NY 10022

Dear Ms. Applegate:

In response to your inquiry about software programs, I have outlined some of the merits of Word 97.

start
Word 97 is simple to use since you can ~~begin~~ typing as soon as you enter the program.

when you begin typing
The Word 97 program sets the way text will lay out or "format" on a page. For example, margins are set for 1.25" on the left and 1.25" on the right; line spacing is automatic; tabs are set to advance the insertion point ½ inch each time the Tab key is pressed. Formats may be changed at any time and as many times as desired throughout the document.

Yours truly,

automatically

Insert

Jerry O'Brien
Sales Manager

jo/yo

KEYSTROKES

SAVE AS

1. Click **File**.............................. Alt + F
2. Click **Save As** .... A
3. Keyboard new filename in **File name** text box.
4. Click **Save**.............................. Enter

UNDO

CTRL + Z
  ✓ *This procedure is to be used immediately after you execute the command you wish to undo.*

Click **Undo** button.............................. ↺

OR

1. Click **Edit**.............................. Alt + E
2. Click **Undo**.............................. U

OR

Click **Undo** drop-down list arrow and select the series of actions to undo, starting with the most recent.

REDO

  ✓ *This procedure is to be used immediately after you undo a command.*

Click **Redo** button.............................. ↻

OR

1. Click **Edit**.............................. Alt + E
2. Click **Redo**.............................. R

OR

Click **Redo** drop-down list arrow and select the series of actions to redo, starting with the most recent.

Exercise
13

■ **Select Text** ■ **Delete Text** ■ **Show/Hide Codes**

Standard Toolbar

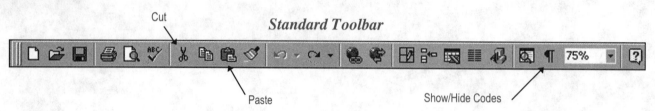

Cut

Paste

Show/Hide Codes

NOTES

Select Text

■ You may highlight or select text in several ways:

- **Using the keyboard** by holding down the Shift key while pressing insertion point movement keys.

- **Using the keyboard in combination with the mouse** by clicking where the selection should begin, holding down the Shift key, and clicking where the selection will end.

- **Using the mouse** by dragging the mouse pointer over desired text.

- **Using the F8 selection extender key** by pressing F8, which places Word in Extend Selection mode (the letters EXT appear in the Status bar).

- **Using the mouse with the selection bar** by clicking in the selection bar. The selection bar is a vertical space alongside the left edge of the Word screen. Note the illustration of the selection bar on the right.

■ Pressing F8 anchors the insertion point and allows you to use the insertion point movement keys to highlight or select text in any direction from the position of the insertion point. When in Extend mode, you can extend the selection to any character or symbol by pressing that character or symbol on the keyboard. Word will instantly highlight from the insertion point to the next occurrence of that character or symbol. Press Esc to cancel the Extend Mode.

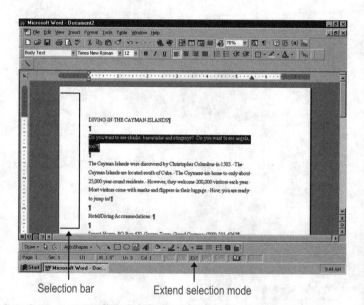

Selection bar   Extend selection mode

■ When you move the mouse pointer into the selection bar, the mouse pointer changes to the shape of an arrow pointing upward toward the top right of the screen.

■ Clicking the left mouse button while the pointer is in the selection bar will highlight the entire line of text opposite the pointer. Holding the left mouse button and dragging the mouse pointer up or down in the selection bar allows you to highlight or select as many lines of text as you wish. To abandon the selection process, release the mouse button and click once anywhere on the Word screen.

Delete Text

- The **Delete** feature allows you to remove text, graphics or codes from a document.

- Procedures for deleting text vary depending upon what is being deleted: a character, previous character, a word, line, paragraph, page, remainder of page or a blank line.

- The Backspace key may be used to delete characters and close up spaces to the left of the insertion point.

- To delete a character or a space, place the insertion point immediately to the left of the character or space to delete, then press the Delete (Del) key located on the right side of your keyboard.

- You may delete blocks of text (words, sentences or paragraphs) by selecting (highlighting) them and either pressing the Delete key

  OR

  selecting either Clear or Cut on the Edit menu

  OR

  clicking the Cut button 🗲 on the Standard toolbar.

- When text is deleted using either the Cut button or Cut on the Edit menu, it disappears from the screen and is placed on the Clipboard. The Clipboard is a temporary storage area in the computer's memory. You can retrieve the text most recently sent to the Clipboard by pressing Shift + Insert or by clicking the Paste button 📋 on the Standard toolbar.

Show/Hide Codes

- As a document is created in Word, codes are inserted that tell the computer how to format the document.

- When you click the Show/Hide button ¶ on the Standard toolbar, codes for paragraph marks (¶), tabs (→), and spaces (•) are visible in your document. These symbols will *not* appear, however, when the document is printed.

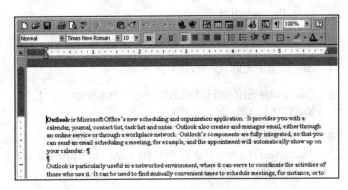

- To combine two paragraphs into one, it is necessary to delete the returns that separate the paragraphs. Returns are represented on the screen by paragraph symbols (¶). Therefore, deleting the symbol will delete the return.

- To delete a tab, place the insertion point to the left of the tab symbol (→) and press the Delete key.

- We recommend that you keep paragraph marks visible when editing a document because:

  - It is easier to combine and separate paragraphs by deleting and inserting the actual paragraph symbols.

  - Each paragraph symbol contains important information about the format of the paragraph preceding it (type size and style, indentation, borders, etc.).

  ✓Note: *You will learn more about this feature in a later lesson.*

- The proofreaders' mark for:

  - deletion is ℰ

  - closing up space is ⌒

  - moving text to the left is [or ⟨{

In this exercise, you will use various deletion methods to edit a document. Use block highlighting procedures to delete sentences, words or blocks of text.

EXERCISE DIRECTIONS

1. Create the exercise as shown in Part I, or open 🖫**13DIVE**.

2. Use the default margins.

3. Disable the Grammar check feature.

4. Begin the exercise At 1".

5. Click the Show/Hide button on the Standard toolbar to display codes.

6. Using the selection and deletion procedures indicated, make the revisions illustrated in Part II.

7. After deleting the last paragraph, undelete (undo) it.

8. Using another deletion method, delete the last paragraph again.

9. Spell check.

10. Print one copy.

11. Save the file as **DIVE**.

12. Close the document window.

PART I

DIVING VACATIONS
DIVING IN THE CAYMAN ISLANDS
¶Do you want to see sharks, barracudas and huge stingrays? Do you want to see gentle angels, too?
¶The Cayman Islands were discovered by Christopher Columbus in late 1503. The Cayman Islands are located just south of Cuba. The Caymans are the home to only about 125,000 year-around residents. However, they welcome approximately 200,000 visitors each year. Each year, more and more visitors arrive. Most visitors come with colorful masks and flippers in their luggage ready to go scuba diving. ¶Because of the magnificence of the coral reef, scuba diving has become to the Cayman Islands what safaris are to Kenya. If you go into a bookstore, you can buy diving gear. ¶Now, you are ready to jump in!

Recommendations for Hotel/Diving Accommodations:

Sunset House, Post Office Box 4791, George Towne, Grand Cayman; (809) 555-4767.

Coconut Harbour, Post Office Box 2086, George Towne, Grand Cayman; (809) 555-7468.

¶Seeing a shark is frightening at first; they seem to come out of nowhere and then return to nowhere. But as soon as the creature disappears, you will swim after it. You will just want to keep this beautiful, graceful fish in view as long as you can.

PART II

Line   ~~DIVING VACATION~~

DIVING IN THE CAYMAN ISLANDS

Word   Do you want to see sharks, barracudas and ~~huge~~ stingrays? Do you want to see ~~gentle~~ angels, too?

Word

Character   The Cayman Islands were discovered by Christopher Columbus in ~~late~~ 1503. The Cayman Islands are located just south of Cuba. The Caymans are ~~the~~ home to only about 25,000

Sentence

Remainder year-around residents. However, they welcome ~~approximately~~ 200,000 visitors each year.

of line   ~~Each year, more and more visitors arrive.~~ Most visitors come with ~~colorful~~ masks and flippers in their luggage, ready to go scuba diving.

Paragraph ~~Because of the magnificence of the coral reef, scuba diving has become to the Cayman Islands what safaris are to Kenya. If you go into a bookstore, you can buy diving gear.~~

Now, you are ready to jump in!

Words   ~~Recommendations for~~ Hotel/Diving Accommodations:

Part of   Sunset House, Post Office Box 4791, George Towne, Grand Cayman; (809) 555-4767.

Word/Character

Coconut Harbour, Post Office Box 2086, George Towne, Grand Cayman; (809) 555-7468.

Remainder ~~Seeing a shark is frightening at first; they seem to come out of nowhere and then return to~~

of page   ~~nowhere. But as soon as the creature disappears, you will swim after it. You will just want to keep this beautiful, graceful fish in view as long as you can.~~

KEYSTROKES

DELETE

Character

1. Place insertion point to the left of character to delete.

2. Press **Delete** .... `Del`

   OR

1. Place insertion point to the right of character to delete.

2. Press **Backspace** .... `Backspace`

Word

1. Double-click desired word.

2. Press **Delete** .... `Del`

   OR

1. Place insertion point to the left of word to delete.

2. Press **Ctrl + Delete** .... `Ctrl` + `Del`

   OR

1. Place insertion point to the right of word to delete.

2. Press
   Ctrl + Backspace .... `Ctrl` + `Backspace`

Block of Text

1. Select (highlight) block to delete using procedures described on the right.

2. Click **Cut** button ....
   to place text on clipboard.

   OR

   Press **Delete** .... `Del`

   OR

   Press **Shift + Delete** .... `Shift` + `Del`
   to move block to clipboard.

   ✓ *The clipboard is a temporary storage area in computer memory. You can retrieve the text most recently sent to the clipboard by pressing Shift + Insert, Ctrl + V, or by clicking the Paste button on the Standard toolbar.*

REPLACE DELETED TEXT WITH TYPED TEXT

1. Select text to replace using procedures described below.

2. Type new text ....*text*

SELECT (HIGHLIGHT) BLOCKS OF TEXT

USING THE KEYBOARD

Place insertion point where highlight is to begin.

TO HIGHLIGHT:	PRESS:
One character to the left	`Shift` + `←`
One character to the right	`Shift` + `→`
One line up	`Shift` + `↑`
One line down	`Shift` + `↓`
To the end of a line	`Shift` + `End`
To the beginning of a line...	`Shift` + `Home`
To the end of a word	`Shift` + `Ctrl` + `→`
To the beginning of a word	`Shift` + `Ctrl` + `←`
To the end of a paragraph	`Shift` + `Ctrl` + `↓`
To the beginning of a paragraph	`Shift` + `Ctrl` + `↑`
To the end of the document..........	`Shift` + `Ctrl` + `End`
To the beginning of the document......	`Shift` + `Ctrl` + `Home`
Entire document......................	`Ctrl` + `A`

USING THE HIGHLIGHT EXTENDER KEY (F8)

1. Place insertion point where block highlighting is to begin.

2. Double-click 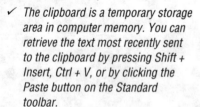 .... `F8`
   on Status bar.

   ✓ *EXT is darkened on the Status bar.*

3. Press any character, punctuation, or symbol to highlight to the next occurrence of that key.

   OR

   Press any of the insertion movement keys to extend the highlighting.

   OR

   Press **F8** repeatedly .... `F8`
   until desired block is selected.

4. Press **Esc** .... `Esc`
   to cancel Extend mode.

USING THE MOUSE

1. Place insertion point where block highlighting is to begin.

2. Hold down the left mouse button and drag the insertion point to desired location.

3. Release the mouse button.

   OR

1. Place insertion point where block highlighting is to begin.

2. Point to where selection should end.

3. Press **Shift** .... `Shift`
   and click left mouse button.

MOUSE SELECTION SHORTCUTS

Select a word

1. Place insertion point anywhere in word.

2. Double-click left mouse button.

Select a sentence

1. Place insertion point anywhere in sentence.

2. Hold down **Ctrl** .... `Ctrl`
   and click left mouse button.

Select a paragraph

1. Place insertion point anywhere in paragraph.

2. Triple-click left mouse button.

Select a line of text

1. Place mouse pointer in selection bar opposite desired line.

   ✓ *Mouse pointer will point upward when you're in the selection bar area.*

2. Click left mouse button once.

Select an entire document

1. Place mouse pointer anywhere in selection bar.

2. Hold down **Ctrl** .... `Ctrl`
   and click with left mouse button.

Cancel a selection

Click anywhere in text.

NEXT EXERCISE

Exercise 14

■ **Delete Paragraph Marks** ■ **Change Case**

NOTES

Delete Paragraph Marks

■ Remember, to combine paragraphs or lines or to eliminate skipped lines, it is necessary to delete the paragraph marks.

    ✓*Note:*   *Paragraph marks will be visible only when you have clicked the Show/Hide button to On.*

■ To delete a paragraph mark, place the insertion point immediately to the left of the paragraph mark and press the Delete key.

■ After you delete paragraph marks between lines, it is sometimes necessary to adjust the text by inserting spaces between the last word of the first line and the first word of the second line.

Change Case

■ The Change Case feature lets you change an existing block of text to sentence case, lowercase, uppercase, title case or toggle case (which changes uppercase to lowercase and lowercase to uppercase in selected text).

■ To change case, select the text, select Change Case from the Format menu, and choose the desired case in the Change Case dialog box. The dialog box selections illustrate the way the text will appear in that case.

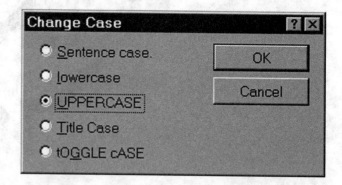

■ The proofreaders' mark for:

• changing uppercase to lowercase is: /

• changing lowercase to uppercase is: ≡

In this exercise, you will edit a previously created letter.

EXERCISE DIRECTIONS

1. Open ⌨**TRYIT**, or open 💾**14TRYIT**.

2. Read the Comment. Change Donna's address to 909 Park Avenue, same city and zip.

3. Using the Change Case feature, change each occurrence of "Word 97" to uppercase.

4. Make the indicated deletions.

5. After completing the letter, restore the last deletion.

6. Print one copy.

7. Close the file; save the file as **TRYAGAIN**.

Today's date

Ms. Donna Applegate
Consultants Unlimited, Inc.
45 East 45 Street ← *Read comment.*
New York, NY 10022 *Change address as*
noted in the directions.

Dear Ms. Applegate:

In response to your inquiry about software programs, I have outlined some of the merits of Word 97.

Word 97 is simple to use, since you can start typing as soon as you enter the program.

The Word 97 program automatically sets the way text will lay out or "format" on a page when you begin typing. For example, margins are automatically set for 1.25" on the left and 1.25" on the right; line spacing is automatic; tabs are set to advance the insertion point ½ inch each time the Tab key is depressed.

Formats may be changed at any time and as many times as desired throughout the document.

Yours truly,

Jerry O'Brien
Sales Manager

jo/yo

Restore the last deletion.

KEYSTROKES

CHANGE CASE

1. Select text to change .... *text*
2. Click **Format** .... `Alt` + `O`
3. Click **Change Case** .... `E`
4. Select a desired case.
5. Click **OK** .... `Enter`

Exercise

15

- ■ **Nonbreaking Spaces** ■ **Track Changes** ■ **Compare Documents**
- ■ **Accept/Reject Revisions**

NOTES

Nonbreaking Spaces

- ■ To prevent two or more words from splitting during word wrap, you can insert a **nonbreaking space** between the words. This is a particularly useful function when you key first and last names, names with titles, dates, equations and times. When inserting a nonbreaking space, you must delete the original space, or the nonbreaking space will have no effect. To insert a nonbreaking space type the first word then press Ctrl + Shift and the spacebar at the same time. Then, type the next word.

- ■ The proofreaders' mark for:

  - nonbreaking space is: △

  - moving text to the right is:] ⟶ or →]

Track Changes

- ■ Making edits and changes to a document is relatively easy. Figuring out what changes were made and by whom can be more difficult. With the Track Changes feature on, you can view all edits (including formatting changes) that are made to a document. Later, you can accept or reject any revisions. You can also see who made the suggested edits.

  ✓Note: *If By Author is selected in the Track Changes options window, Word will assign a unique color to the first eight people who revise a document. (See Customize the Way Revisions Display on the following page for more information.) If more than eight people revise a document, the colors start over with the first color assigned. In addition, when you point to a revision, the name of the person who made the edit will appear if the screen tips option is turned on (see illustration on the following page).*

- ■ You can also determine how the revisions will display on screen and whether or not they will print.

Mark Changes

- ■ Make a copy of the original document before you begin making changes. Having a copy of the original makes it easier to compare documents, which is another way to keep track of revisions. Before you begin to edit an existing document, turn on Track Changes.

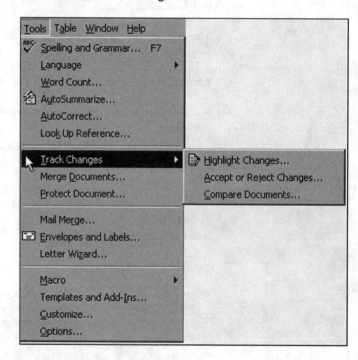

To turn on Track changes:

- Double-click TRK on the Status bar.

OR

- Click Tools menu.

- Select Track Changes.

- Click Highlight Changes.

- Click <u>T</u>rack changes while editing.

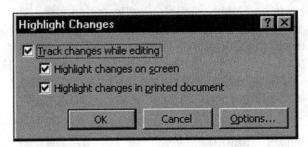

- If you want to view the changes as you make them, be sure that Highlight changes on <u>s</u>creen is selected.

- If you want to have the changes print in a document, be sure that Highlight changes in <u>p</u>rinted document is selected.

- Click OK and make desired edits.

- Below is a sample of how edits will appear in your document.

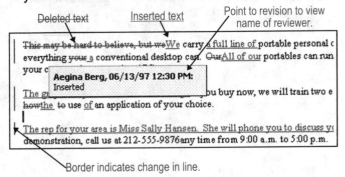

Customize the Way Revisions Display

- You can change the way revisions display or shut off selected marks by selecting various options in the Track Changes options window. Select <u>T</u>ools, <u>T</u>rack Changes, and <u>H</u>ighlight Changes, then click <u>O</u>ptions. The following dialog box appears.

  ✓Note: *You can also access this dialog box by selecting the Track Changes tab in the Tools, Options dialog box.*

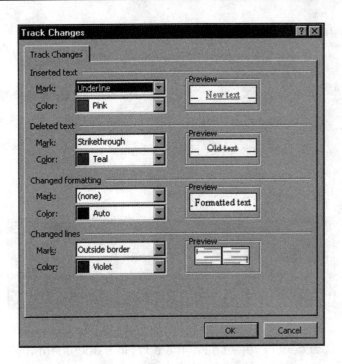

Accept/Reject Revisions

- There are several ways you can accept or reject changes made to the document. You may use the Reviewing toolbar (select <u>V</u>iew, <u>T</u>oolbars, Reviewing), the Accept or Reject Changes dialog box, or the Shortcut menu.

- Open the document containing the revisions that you want to evaluate. If the revision marks do not appear in the document, be sure that Highlight changes on <u>s</u>creen is selected in the Highlight Changes dialog box.

Reviewing Toolbar

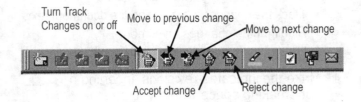

Accept or Reject Changes Dialog Box

■ To use the Accept or Reject Changes dialog box, do the following:

- Click <u>T</u>ools.
- Select <u>T</u>rack Changes.
- Click <u>A</u>ccept or Reject Changes.

■ You can leave the dialog box open while you make various selections.

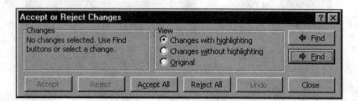

■ You can accept or reject changes individually or accept or reject all of the edits in a document at one time. You can also change the way the changes appear on screen without deleting them from the document. As you click on individual edits, the name of the author will appear on the left in the dialog box.

Compare Documents

■ Edits and revisions to a document can be compared to earlier versions of the document using the Compare Documents feature. Word uses the same revision marks that Track Changes uses to illustrate the changes made to a document.

■ Documents that you are comparing must have different names.

■ To Compare Documents, first open the document where you want to see the revision marks. On the <u>T</u>ools menu, select <u>T</u>rack Changes, then <u>C</u>ompare Documents. In the Select File to Compare With Current Document dialog box, enter the name of the file you want to compare with the open document. Click <u>O</u>pen to view the differences between the documents.

■ Accept or reject changes with the same procedures that are listed under Accept/Reject Revisons.

In this exercise, you will edit a previously created letter.

EXERCISE DIRECTIONS

1. Open ⌨**BLOCK**, or open 💾**15BLOCK**.

2. Print one copy.

3. Access the Track Changes features.
   - Track the changes while editing the document text.
   - Highlight the changes on screen.
   - Highlight the changes in the printed document.

4. Make the indicated revisions, inserting a nonbreaking space where you see the triangular symbol (Δ).

5. After all revisions are made, undo the last deleted sentence.

6. Spell check.

7. Save the edited document as **BLOCKA**.

8. Print one copy.

9. Accept all changes.

10. Turn off the Track Changes feature.

11. Preview your work.

12. Print one copy.

13. Close and save the file.

Today's Date

Mr. Thomas T. Walen
Updike Mechanics Company
23 Clogg Avenue
Atlanta, GA 30315

Dear Mr. Walen:

CONGRATULATIONS, Mr. Walen! You have been nominated as the outstanding office employee
of the month beginning November 4, 1997 through November 30, 1997. ¶ We made
your selection based on the recommendations of your supervisors.
The Committee that made your selection requires that you submit a photograph of
yourself to your immediate supervisor so that we can display your picture in the company's
executive offices. ,Mr. Quinn. will then to throughout

Updike Mechanics is proud of your accomplishments. We look forward to honoring
you at our ANNUAL AWARDS DINNER on December 3.

Sincerely,

Paulette Manning
President

pm/yo

KEYSTROKES

NONBREAKING SPACE

1. Type the first word.
2. Press.................. Ctrl + Shift + Space
   Ctrl + Shift + Spacebar.
3. Type next word............................. *word*

OR

1. Delete the normal space between words.
2. Press.................. Ctrl + Shift + Space
   Ctrl + Shift + Spacebar to insert a nonbreaking space.

TURN TRACK CHANGES ON/OFF

Double-click **TRK** on the status bar.

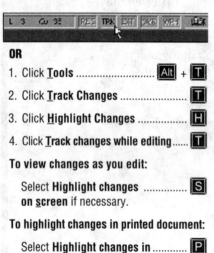

OR

1. Click **Tools** .... Alt + T
2. Click **Track Changes** .... T
3. Click **Highlight Changes** .... H
4. Click **Track changes while editing** ...... T

To view changes as you edit:

Select **Highlight changes on screen** if necessary. .... S

To highlight changes in printed document:

Select **Highlight changes in printed document** if necessary. .... P

CUSTOMIZE THE WAY CHANGES DISPLAY

1. Click **Tools** .... Alt + T
2. Click **Track Changes** .... T
3. Click **Highlight Changes** .... H
4. Click **Options** .... O
5. Select desired **Mark** and **Color** options for the way changes will display:

   • **Inserted text**
   • **Deleted text**
   • **Changed formatting**
   • **Changed lines**

   ✓ *Note that you can turn individual options off/on in this dialog box.*

ACCEPT OR REJECT INDIVIDUAL CHANGES

USING THE TOOLBAR

1. Turn on the **Reviewing** toolbar.
2. Point to change to accept/reject.
3. Click **Accept** button ....
   OR
   Click **Reject** button ....
4. Move to next change.

USING SHORCUT MENU

1. Point to change and right-click.
2. Click **Accept Change** .... E
   OR
   Click **Reject Change** .... R

USING STATUS BAR

1. Click once on a change.
2. Right-click on **TRK**.
3. Click **Accept or Reject Changes** ...... A
4. Click **Accept** .... A
   OR
   Click **Reject** .... R
5. Click **Close** to return to document ...... Esc

ACCEPT OR REJECT ALL CHANGES

USING THE MENU

1. Click **Tools** .... Alt + T
2. Click **Track Changes** .... T
3. Click **Accept or Reject Changes** ..... A
4. Click **Accept All/Reject All** .... C/J

   If message appears asking if you really want to accept/reject all changes without reviewing them:

   Click **Yes/No** .... Y/N
5. Click **Close** to return to document ...... Esc

USING THE STATUS BAR

1. Right-click on **TRK**.
2. Click **Accept or Reject Changes** ...... A
3. Click **Accept All/Reject All** .... C/J

   If message appears asking if you really want to accept/reject all changes without reviewing them:

   Click **Yes/No** .... Y/N
4. Click **Close** to return to document ..... Esc

COMPARE DOCUMENTS

1. Open the document in which you want to display revisions.
2. Click **Tools** .... Alt + T
3. Click **Track Changes** .... T
4. Click **Compare Documents** C
5. Select file to compare with open document.
6. Click **Open**.

NEXT EXERCISE

Exercise 16

■ **Set Margins** ■ **Set Tabs**

NOTES

Set Margins

■ Word measures margins in inches.

■ The default margins are 1.25" on the left and right and 1" margins on the top and bottom of the page.

■ There are three ways to change left and right margins. You can:

• **Drag margin boundaries on the ruler in Page Layout view.** This method is the most convenient way to adjust margins for the entire document, since it allows you to adjust margins as you work and see the immediate effect on text.

Ruler in Page Layout View

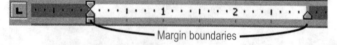
Margin boundaries

• To change margins, position the mouse pointer on the left or right margin boundary. When the pointer changes to a left/right pointing arrow, drag the margin boundary to the desired position. If you hold down the Alt key as you drag, the margin measurements will display on the Ruler.

• The numbers in the white area of the Ruler represent the measurement of the text area in the document; the gray areas represent the margins between the text and the edges of the page.

• **Drag margin boundaries in Print Preview mode.** This method allows you to see the effects of margin changes on the entire document as you make them.

• To change margins, drag the left or right margin boundary on the horizontal Print Preview Ruler. If the Ruler is not displayed, click the View Ruler button.

View Ruler button

Margin boundary

• A vertical ruler also displays in this view, allowing you to change top and bottom margins.

- **Use the <u>F</u>ile, Page Set<u>u</u>p Command** to access the Page Setup dialog box. This method allows greater precision and permits you to limit margin changes to sections of your document.

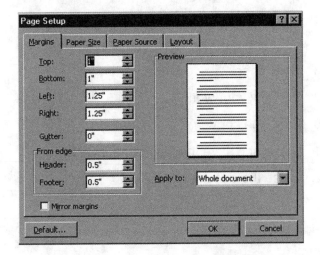

- To set margins in the dialog box, click the Margins tab and enter the margin width in the <u>T</u>op, <u>B</u>ottom, <u>L</u>eft or <u>R</u>ight increment boxes or use the increment arrows to select margin widths. Remember, margins are measured in inches.

- You may apply margin changes to the Whole document (the default) or from This point forward. If you choose This point forward, the margin changes begin at the top of a new page.

- If you wish to apply a margin change to a portion of the document, you must first break the page into sections. To do this, place the insertion point at the point where your margin is to change, select <u>B</u>reak from the <u>I</u>nsert menu, and choose Con<u>t</u>inuous. Then apply the desired margin change. Repeat this procedure each time you wish to apply a new margin change.

  ✓Note: *The same effect of changing left and right margins within a document can also be achieved using left and right paragraph indents.*

Set Tabs

- The Tab key indents a single line of text. Default tabs are set 0.5" apart. When the Tab key is pressed once, text advances 0.5"; when the Tab key is pressed twice, text advances 1", etc.

- It is possible to change the location or the number of tabs. For example, if you desire to advance 0.8" each time the Tab key is pressed, or eliminate all preset tabs except one, you can do so.

- You can change tabs on the Ruler or by selecting <u>T</u>abs from the F<u>o</u>rmat menu. When you change tab settings in a document, changes take effect from that point forward.

Setting Tabs on the Ruler

- Tab settings are displayed on the bottom of the Ruler as gray dots that are set 0.5" apart.

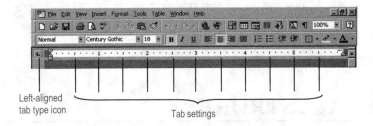

- Default settings are left-aligned. This means that text typed at such a setting will align at the left and move text to the right of the tab as you type.

  > This is an example of left-aligned text. Note that the text on the left edge is aligned, while text at the right edge is jagged.

- The left-aligned tab type icon, located at the left of the ruler, is displayed as an L.

  ✓Note: *Setting custom tabs and tab type icons will be detailed in Exercise 64.*

- To set a new left-aligned tab, click anywhere on the gray area below the Ruler where a new tab is desired; a new tab marker is inserted, and all tabs preceding the inserted tab are deleted.

- To delete a tab setting, drag the tab marker off the Ruler.

- You can also set tabs using the Tabs dialog box (click F<u>o</u>rmat, <u>T</u>abs). This method lets you set and clear tab positions in one operation. You cannot, however, see the result of your changes on text until all settings have been made.

  ✓Note: *This dialog box will be detailed in Exercise 64 when Custom tabs are introduced.*

> *In this exercise, you will set a tab stop at 3.5" and use the Tab key to advance the date and closing to that point, thus creating a modified-block style letter.*

EXERCISE DIRECTIONS

1. Open 🖥OPEN, or open 🖫16OPEN.

2. Select Page Layout view.

3. Set 1.5" left and right margins.

4. Select all text.

5. Set a tab stop at 3.5".

6. Make the indicated revisions.

7. Insert a nonbreaking space between 5:00 and p.m. and 9:00 and a.m.

8. Spell check.

9. Preview your work.

10. Print one copy.

11. Close and save the file; name it **OPEN**.

12. Close the document window.

KEYSTROKES

SET MARGINS IN PAGE LAYOUT VIEW

1. Place mouse pointer over the desired margin boundary on the horizontal or vertical ruler.

2. Hold down **Alt** .... `Alt`
   and drag boundary to desired position.

SET MARGINS IN PRINT PREVIEW MODE

1. Place mouse pointer over the desired margin boundary on the horizontal or vertical ruler.

2. Hold down **Alt** .... `Alt`
   and drag boundary to desired position.

SET MARGINS USING PAGE SETUP DIALOG BOX

1. Click **File** .... `Alt` + `F`

2. Click **Page Setup** .... `U`

3. Click **Margins** .... `Alt` + `M`

4. Click increase or decrease .... `▲▼`
   arrows to set margin.
   OR

Click **Left** .... `Alt` + `F`
AND/OR
Click **Right** .... `Alt` + `G`
AND/OR
Click **Top** .... `Alt` + `T`
AND/OR
Click **Bottom** .... `Alt` + `B`
and type distance from edge of paper.

5. Click **Apply to** .... `Alt` + `A`

6. Click **This point forward** .... `↓` `↑`
   OR
   Click **Whole document** .... `↓` `↑`

7. Click **OK** .... `Enter`

SHOW TEXT BOUNDARIES IN PAGE LAYOUT VIEW

1. Click **View** .... `Alt` + `V`

2. Click **Page Layout** .... `P`

3. Click **Tools** .... `Alt` + `T`

4. Click **Options** .... `O`

5. Click **View**.

6. Click **Text Boundaries** .... `Alt` + `X`
   to select check box.

7. Click **OK** .... `Enter`

CHANGE DEFAULT TAB SETTINGS

1. Click **Format** .... `Alt` + `O`

2. Click **Tabs** .... `T`

3. Click **Default Tab Stops** .... `Alt` + `F`

4. Type distance between tabs ...... *number*

5. Click **OK** .... `Enter`
   OR
   Click below Ruler where new tab is to be set.

To delete a tab:

Drag tab off Ruler.

SET MARGINS FOR A SECTION OF THE DOCUMENT

1. Position insertion point where margin change is to begin.

2. Click **Insert** .... `Alt` + `I`

3. Click **Break** .... `B`

4. Click **Continuous** .... `Alt` + `T`

5. Click **OK** .... `Enter`

6. Set margins as desired
   (follow steps 1-8 in SET MARGINS USING PAGE SETUP DIALOG BOX).

TAB → Today's date ⸻⟶ 3.5"

~~Arnco Industries, Inc.~~

T.   , President
Mr. Martin Quincy
641 Lexington Avenue
New York, NY 10022

Dear Mr. Quincy:

very   *, COMPUSELLTRAIN*
We are pleased to announce the opening of a new subsidiary of our company. We
specialize in ~~selling~~, training and ~~service~~ of portable personal computers.
        service   *sales*   *a full line of*
~~This may be hard to believe, but~~ we carry portable personal computers that can do
            your
everything a conventional desktop can. Our portables can run all of the same applications
as your company's conventional PCs. With the purchase of a computer, we will train *All of*
two employees of your firm on how to use an application of your choice.
                              the   *of*

For a free demonstration, call us at 212-555-9876 any day from 9:00a.m. to 5:00p.m.

TAB → *Very truly yours*
        ~~Sincerely,~~

⟶ 3.5"

*The graphics
capabilities
are outstanding.*

TAB → Theresa Mann
TAB → President

tm/yo

*The rep for your area is Ms.
Sally Hansen.
She will phone you to discuss
your possible needs.*

Exercise 17

■ **View Margins**

NOTES

View Margins

■ Margins display differently in different view modes. In Normal view, margin markers appear on the Ruler, if it is displayed, but margins do not appear in the document itself. In Page Layout view, the margins display, and anything within the margins, such as headers and footers, page numbers and footnotes, also appears. In this view, the page displays as it will print.

Margins in Normal View

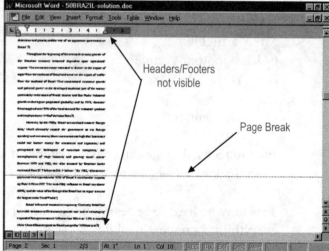

Headers/Footers not visible

Page Break

Margins in Page Layout View

Header visible

Page Margins illustrated

Footnotes visible

Footer visible

■ To change views, select <u>N</u>ormal or <u>P</u>age Layout from the <u>V</u>iew menu, or click the desired view icon on the left of the horizontal scroll bar, just above the Status bar.

In this exercise, you will edit a previously created letter.

EXERCISE DIRECTIONS

1. Open CYBERCATERING, or open 17CYBERCATERING.
2. Select Page Layout view.
3. Set 1.5" left and right margins.
4. Select the whole document and set a tab stop at 3.5".
5. Make the indicated revisions.
6. Insert a nonbreaking space between *8:00* and *a.m.* and *7:00* and *p.m.*
7. Spell check.
8. Preview your work.
9. Print one copy.
10. Close and save the file; name it **CYBERCATERING**.
11. Close the document window.

Today's date)————————————→ 3.5"

Datamation, Inc.

Insert Ms. Arlene Fauser
549 Byte Avenue
Seattle, WA 98104

Dear Ms. Fauser:

              the
We are very pleased you have chosen Cyber Café Catering to fulfill your catering needs.
                              est
Our goal is to provide you with high quality catering. *service possible*

                              for
You can rely on Cyber Café Catering to satisfy all your breakfast, luncheon and office
party needs. Our commitment to 100% satisfaction is the basis of our catering service. ←

                    customer
Join to You may place your order Monday through Friday 8:00 a.m. to 7:00 p.m. by calling 888-
previous ¶. 8888.

                                                        Cyber Café Catering
On behalf of the staff at Cyber Café Catering, I thank you for choosing us for your
catering events.

Cordially,

————————————→ 3.5"   *We deliver high quality*
                                                    food, on time, with the
                                                    same high standards
Valerie Mana   *you'll find in our cafes.*
Director of Catering

vm/yo   *bakery*

Exercise 18

■ **Preview a File** ■ **Print a File without Opening It**
■ **Select Multiple Files to Print** ■ **File Details** ■ **Sort Files** ■ **Find Files**

NOTES

Preview a File

■ The Open dialog box contains options for previewing or printing a file without retrieving it to the screen. These options are important for locating files, particularly when you do not remember the name of a file or the nature of its contents.

■ **To preview a file,** select the drive and folder from the Look in drop-down list in the Open dialog box. Select the file you wish to view and click the Preview button [icon] on the top of the dialog box. The first part of the document displays in the preview window. If this is the document you want to open, click the Open button.

Open Dialog Box

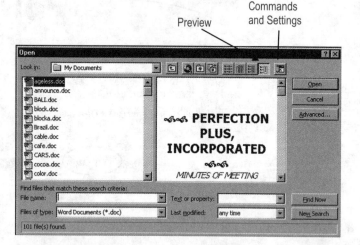

Print a File without Opening It

■ **To print a file without opening it,** point to or select the file you wish to print in the Open dialog box, and click the *right* mouse button. Select Print from the drop-down menu. Or you may click the Commands and Settings button [icon] at the top of the dialog box and select Print.

Open Dialog Box

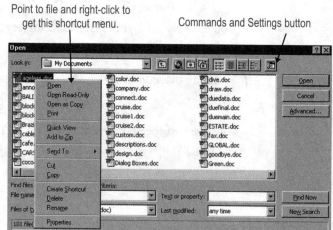

Select Multiple Files to Print

■ **To select multiple non-adjacent files,** click the first file, then hold down the Ctrl key as you click another file.

■ **To select a group of adjacent files,** hold down the Shift key, click the first file, then click the last file.

File Details

- The Open dialog box may also be used to obtain detailed information about a file or group of files. Selecting a file and clicking the Details button 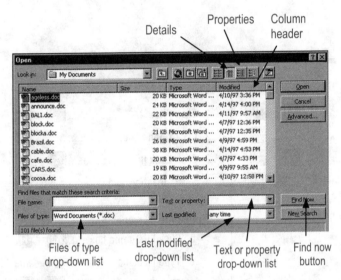 at the top of the dialog box displays the name, size and type of file and the date/time the file was last modified.

Sort Files (in Details View)

- To sort files by Name, Size, Type of file or date/time Last modified in ascending order in Details view, click the column header (Name, Size, Type, Modified). To sort the file in descending order, click the column header again.

Details   Properties   Column header

Files of type drop-down list   Last modified drop-down list   Text or property drop-down list   Find now button

✓Note: Properties, Details and Column header buttons are only visible in details view

- Selecting a file and clicking the Properties button displays summary information such as title, author and keywords that the user added when creating the document.

Find Files

- The Open dialog box also contains options for **finding files**. A file may be searched for by its name, by its type, by its contents or by the date it was created.

  - **To find a file by name**, click File name box, type name of file, and click the Find Now button.

  - **To find a file by date**, click the Last modified box. Select an approximate time you last worked on the file and click the Find Now button.

  - **To find a file by contents,** enter text that might be contained in the document, such as the addressee's name or a subject in the Text or property box, and click the Find Now button.

  - **To find a file by type,** click Files of type box. Select a file type to search and click the Find Now button.

- When you begin a search, remember that Word is searching the current folder. If you wish to expand your search to include subfolders, choose a drive in the Look in drop-down list. Then click the Commands and Settings button and select Search Subfolders.

> *In this exercise, you will edit a previously created letter.*

EXERCISE DIRECTIONS

1. Use the Open dialog box to view ▭CYBERCATERING and ▭OPEN, or view ▭18CYBERCATERING and ▭18OPEN.

2. Open the file that relates to computers (your own or from the data disk).

3. Close the file.

4. Use the Open dialog box to find the last revision of a letter addressed to Mr. Pauley. (Type Pauley in the Text or property box.)

5. Select Page Layout view.

6. Make the indicated revisions.

7. Delete the comment inserted previously.

8. Spell check.

9. Close and save the file; name it **CYBERCAFE**.

10. Use the Open dialog box to print one copy of the last revisions of **CYBERCATERING** and **CYBERCAFE**.

11. Close the document window.

KEYSTROKES

PREVIEW A FILE

1. Click **F**ile .... `Alt` + `F`

2. Click **O**pen .... `O`

3. Click **Look** **in** .... `Alt` + `I`

4. Select the drive and folder .... `↓`, `↵`
   to look in.

5. Select the file to preview.

6. Click **Preview** button .... ▭

PRINT A FILE WITHOUT OPENING

1. Click **F**ile .... `Alt` + `F`

2. Click **O**pen .... `O`

3. Click **Look** **in** .... `Alt` + `I`

4. Select the drive and folder .... `↓`, `↵`
   to look in.

5. Point to or select the file you wish to print.

   OR

To select a group of adjacent files:

   a. Select the first file.

   b. Hold down the **Shift** key.

   c. Select last file in group.

To select multiple nonadjacent files:

   a. Select the first file.

   b. Hold down the **Ctrl** key.

   c. Click additional files.

6. Print the file(s):

   a. Click the right mouse button.

   b. Click **P**rint .... `P`

   OR

   a. Click **Commands and Settings** button. .... ▭

   b. Click **P**rint .... `P`

FIND FILES

1. Click **F**ile .... `Alt` + `F`

2. Click **O**pen .... `O`

3. Click **Look** **in** .... `Alt` + `I`

4. Select the drive and folder .... `↓`, `↵`
   to look in.

To find file by name:

   a. Click **File** **name** box ...... `Alt` + `N`

   b. Type filename .... *name*

   c. Click **F**ind Now .... `Alt` + `F`

To find file by date:

   a. Click **Last** **m**odified box .. `Alt` + `M`

   b. Select an approximate time to search. .... `↑`, `↓`, `↵`

   c. Click **F**ind Now .... `Alt` + `F`

To find file by contents:

   a. Click **Text** or property ..... `Alt` + `X`
      box.

   b. Type any text that might be contained in document .... *text*

   c. Click **F**ind Now .... `Alt` + `F`

To find file by type:

   a. Click **Files** of **t**ype box. ... `Alt` + `T`

   b. Select type of file to search .... `↑`, `↓`, `↵`

   c. Click **F**ind Now .... `Alt` + `F`

Today's date

Pauley Enterprises, Inc.

Mr. David Cooper Pauley
134 Columbus City Street
Columbus, OH 43215

Dear Mr. Pauley:

Thank you for your recent inquiry and interest in the Cyber Café franchise program. The
Cyber Café franchise program offers entrepreneurs an outstanding opportunity to build on
a long lasting tradition of quality. The benefits of Cyber Café franchise ownership are too
numerous to list.

To learn more about your potential and how to benefit from this exciting investment
opportunity, call me at 1-800-555-8888, and ~~I will~~ set up an appointment to discuss
franchise ownership ~~with you.~~ _we can_

~~We urge you to act quickly, because~~ _Since_ a limited number of franchises will be given in your
area. _, we are sending you a brochure under separate cover. It will_

Cordially,   _give you more information about Cyber Café franchises._

Alan Parks
Director of Franchising

ap/yo

What started as a modest coffee house/café in a suburb of Cleveland has emerged to become the country's dominant coffee house/café where computer enthusiasts can surf the Internet.

Exercise
19   ■ Summary

In this exercise, you will create a full-block letter and edit it using the insert and delete procedures learned.

EXERCISE DIRECTIONS

1. Create a NEW document.

2. Set 1.5" left and right margins.

3. Keyboard and format a full-block letter from the text shown in Part I, or open ⊟**19NAVIGATOR** and format a full-block letter.

4. Access the Track Changes feature.
   - Track the changes while editing the document text.
   - Highlight the changes on screen.
   - Highlight the changes in the printed document.

5. Make the revisions shown in Part II.

6. Spell check.

7. Preview your work.

8. Save the edited document as **NAVA**.

9. Print one copy.

10. Accept all changes.

11. Turn off the Track Changes feature.

12. Save the file; name it **NAVIGATOR**.

13. Print one copy.

14. Close the document window.

Today's date Ms. Kristin Anderson 205 Pine Hollow Lane Westport, CT 06880-2498 Dear Ms. Anderson: We are happy to send you the enclosed Internet Navigator program you requested. You may use this product for one month, free of charge. #We know you will be very pleased with this product since it provides high speed access to the Internet and will save you time by multitasking. In addition, its simple point and click navigation will easily help you organize and catalog on-line information. You can send and receive e-mail worldwide while you download. #If you have any questions about connecting, call our toll-free customer support line at 1-800-999-9999. Cordially, Greg Mitchell Customer Service gm/yo enclosure

Today's date Ms. Kristin Anderson 205 Pine Hollow Lane Westport, CT 06880-2498 Dear Ms. Anderson:

→ McAdams International Realty Company

We are happy to send you the enclosed Internet Navigator program you requested. You may use this

unlimited hours and

product for one month, free of charge. #We know you will be very pleased with this product since it

provides high speed access to the Internet and will save you time by multitasking. In addition, its simple

to

point and click navigation will easily help you organize and catalog on-line information. You can send

or problems

and receive e-mail worldwide while you download. #If you have any questions about connecting, call our

toll-free customer support line at 1-800-999-9999. Cordially, Greg Mitchell Customer Service gm/yo

enclosure

After installing the Internet Navigator program, you'll be able to surf the World Wide Web, send and receive e-mail, read news groups and enjoy the rest of the Internet.

Exercise
20

■ **Summary**

In this exercise, you will create a modified-block letter and edit it using the insert and delete procedures learned.

EXERCISE DIRECTIONS

1. Create a NEW document.

2. Set a tab stop at 3.5".

3. Set 1.5" left and right margins.

4. Keyboard and format a modified-block letter from the text shown in Part I, or open 📇**20JOB** and format a modified-block letter.

5. Access the Track Changes feature.
   - Track the changes while editing the document text.
   - Highlight the changes on screen.
   - Highlight the changes in the printed document.

6. Make the revisions shown in Part II.

7. Insert the following comment where shown: "Roberta: Please review all changes."

8. Spell check.

9. Using the Properties feature, note the number of words in this document.

10. Preview your work.

11. Print one copy.

12. Accept all changes.

13. Turn off the Track Changes feature.

14. Save the file; name it **JOBOP**.

15. Print one copy.

16. Close the document window.

Today's date Mr. Bill Demeo ABC Employment Agency 555 Kennedy Avenue Boston, MA 02210-2497 Dear Mr. Demeo: We now have opportunities available in our organization for qualified Partner Managers, Associate Managers and Shift Supervisors who are very interested in a career with a leader in the industry. ⊞We offer an attractive salary, benefits, stock purchase plans and advancement opportunities. ⊞If you have any individuals who you feel are qualified, send their resumes to me. We seek those who demonstrate customer service commitment and strong leadership ability. Some supervisory experience in a restaurant or a retail setting is important. Sincerely, Irene Zofran Director Human Resources iz/yo

Today's date Mr. Bill Demeo ABC Employment Agency 555 Kennedy Avenue Boston, MA 02210-2497

Dear Mr. Demeo: We now have *growth-directed* opportunities available ~~in our organization~~ for qualified Partner

Managers, Associate Managers and Shift Supervisors who are ~~very~~ interested in a *fast-track* career with a leader in *industry* ~~the industry.~~ ¶We offer an attractive salary, *comprehensive* benefits, stock purchase plans and advancement *a comprehensive training program,* *potential* ~~opportunities.~~ ¶If you have ~~any~~ *qualified* individuals ~~who you feel are qualified,~~ send their resumes to me. *or fax* We

seek those who demonstrate *a passion for* customer service ~~commitment~~ *,a genuine "can-do" attitude,* and strong leadership ability. Some

supervisory *or managerial* experience in a restaurant or *a* retail setting is important. Sincerely, Irene Zofran Director *Smith*

Human Resources iz/yo   ⟵———— *Insert comment.*

NEXT LESSON

Word 97

LESSON 4

Text Alignments and Enhancements

- Text Alignments
- Vertical Centering
- Fonts
- Font Faces
- Font Style
- Font Size
- Font Color
- Emphasis Styles: Bold, Underline, Double/Dotted Underline, Italics, Highlight, Strikethrough, Superscript, Subscript and Small Caps
- Remove Emphasis Styles
- Use Symbols
- Format Painter
- Bullets and Numbering
- End Bullets or Numbers

Exercise 21

■ **Text Alignments** ■ **Vertical Centering**

Formatting Toolbar

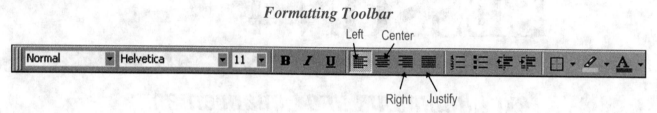

NOTES

Text Alignments

■ Word will align all text following an alignment code until another justification code is entered. Word provides four alignment options:

- **Left** - all lines are even at the left margin but are ragged at the right margin (the default).

- **Center** - all lines are centered between the margins.

- **Right** - all lines are ragged at the left margin and are even at the right margin.

- **Justify** - all lines are even at the left and right margins, except for the last line of the paragraph.

  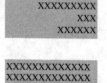

■ Alignments may affect blocks of text as well as individual lines.

■ You may change alignments before or after typing text.

■ Word applies left justification to your text by default.

■ You can align a line of text or a paragraph by positioning the insertion point anywhere within the text and clicking the desired alignment button on the Formatting toolbar.

■ The proofreaders' mark for centering is:] [.

Vertical Centering

■ Text may be centered vertically between the top and bottom edges of the page.

■ To vertically center text, select File, Page Setup from the menu bar. Click the Layout tab. The following dialog box will appear:

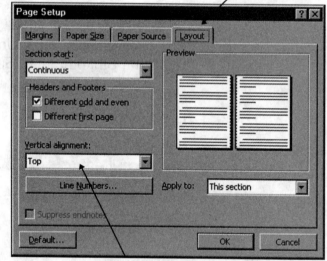

Vertical alignment box

■ Click the Vertical alignment box, choose Center from the choices, and select OK.

  ✓*Note illustration above.*

■ In order to see the position of the vertically centered material on the page, switch to Page Layout view by selecting Page Layout from the View menu.

In this exercise, you will create an advertisement that is vertically centered on the page. You will apply different text alignments and use the Change Case feature.

EXERCISE DIRECTIONS

1. Create a NEW document.

2. Display the Office Assistant.

3. Use the default margins and tabs.

4. Center the page from top to bottom.

5. Type each section of text shown in the exercise, changing the alignment appropriately.

6. Preview your work.

7. Change the case of the last block of text to uppercase.

8. Print one copy.

9. Change the case of the last block of text to sentence.
   - Change the capital H in web site address to lowercase.
   - Change the capital "C" in "Call" to lowercase.
   - Capitalize "C" in "Carat" and "S" in "Shoppe".

10. Print one copy.

11. Save the file; name it **JEWELS**.

12. Close the document window.

THE CARAT SHOPPE

4x

What started as a modest jewelry business in 1962, has emerged to become the country's dominant jewelry manufacturer and distributor--the Carat Shoppe. We are now planning to expand to 1,000 stores and eventually become the dominant jewelry boutique in the world! Our diamond experts can help you select the best quality gem for the lowest price possible.

↓ 2x

What you can expect from us is:

↓ 2x

Expert guidance from our professional diamontologists and gemologists.
Courteous service and a caring attitude.
Full value for your money.
Dependable quality at all times.
Convenient credit plans to suit your needs.

↓ 2x

The 4 "Cs" that determine the quality and value of a diamond:

↓ 2x

CUT—A diamond must be cut to good proportion in order to make the best use of light.
CARAT—The weight of a diamond is measured in carats. The carat is divided into one hundred smaller units of weight called "points."
COLOR—The closer a diamond is to crystal clear and colorless, the more valuable it is.
CLARITY—Refers to a diamond's freedom from tiny bubbles, and carbon spots.

↓ 3x

The Carat Shoppe
Jewelers and Diamond Brokers
234 Mindanao Way
Marina del Rey, CA 90292-9999

↓ 2x

For the nearest Carat Shoppe in your area,
call our toll-free number:
1-800-333-3333.
See our home page on the Web:
http://carat.com

KEYSTROKES

CENTER-ALIGN TEXT

CTRL + E

BEFORE TYPING TEXT

1. Place insertion point where text will be typed.
2. Click **Center** button ....
3. Type text .... *text*
4. Press **Enter** .... Enter

EXISTING TEXT

1. Place insertion point in paragraph to center.

   OR

   Select (highlight) block of text to center.
2. Click **Center** button ....

   ✓ *If you are centering a single line, there must be a paragraph mark (¶) at the end of the line.*

To return to flush left:
Repeat steps above.

JUSTIFY

CTRL + J

BEFORE TYPING TEXT

1. Place insertion point where text will be typed.
2. Click **Justify** button ....
3. Type text .... *text*
4. Press **Enter** .... Enter

EXISTING TEXT

1. Place insertion point in paragraph to justify.

   OR

   Select (highlight) block of text to justify.
2. Click **Justify** button ....

To return to flush left:
Repeat steps above.

FLUSH RIGHT

CTRL + R

BEFORE TYPING TEXT

1. Place insertion point where text will be typed.
2. Click **Align Right** button ....
3. Type text .... *text*
4. Press **Enter** .... Enter

EXISTING TEXT

1. Place insertion point in paragraph to right-align.

   OR

   Select (highlight) block of text to right-align.
2. Click **Align Right** button ....

To return to flush left:
Repeat steps above.

VERTICALLY CENTER TEXT

1. Click **File** .... Alt + F
2. Click **Page Setup** .... U
3. Click **Layout** .... Alt + L
4. Click **Vertical alignment** ..... Alt + V list arrow.
5. Select **Center** .... ↓ , ↵
6. Click **OK** .... Enter

Exercise 22

■ Fonts ■ Font Faces ■ Font Style ■ Font Size ■ Font Color

Formatting Toolbar

Font Face — Font Size

Font Color

| Normal | Helvetica | 11 | **B** *I* U |

Font Face list arrow — Font Size list arrow

NOTES

Fonts

■ A **font** is a complete set of characters in a specific face, style, and size. Each set includes upper- and lowercase letters, numerals, and punctuation. One font that might be available to you in Word is Arial.

■ A **font face** (often called a **typeface** or just a **font**) is the design of a character. Each design has a name and is intended to convey a specific feeling.

■ You should select typefaces that will make your document attractive and communicate its particular message. As a rule, use no more than two or three font faces in any one document.

Font Faces

■ There are basically three types of font faces: serif, sans serif, and script. A **serif** face has lines, curves, or edges extending from the ends of the letter (**T**), while a **sans serif** face is straight-edged (**T**), and **script** looks like handwriting (*T*).

- **Serif Font Face:** Times New Roman
- **Sans Serif Font Face:** Helvetica
- **Script Font Face:** *Freestyle Script*

■ A serif font face is typically used for document text because it is more readable. Sans serif is often used for headlines or technical material. Script typefaces are used for formal invitations and announcements.

■ You can change font faces by selecting Font from the Format menu, then selecting the desired font on the Font tab of the Font dialog box.

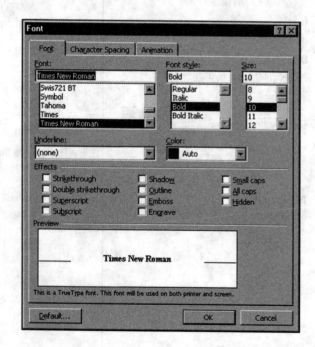

- You can also change font faces by clicking the Font Face list arrow on the Formatting toolbar (which drops down a list of font choices).

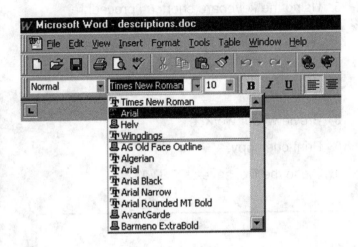

- You can also access the Font dialog box by clicking the right mouse button anywhere in the document window and selecting Font.

- Word supports the use of True Type fonts. When you use True Type fonts, your screen displays text the way it will appear when you print it and can be printed on most printers. True Type fonts are identified by a double **T** in front of the font name.

Font Style

- **Font style** refers to the slant and weight of letters, such as bold and italic.

> Times New Roman Regular
> *Times New Roman Italic*
> **Times New Roman Bold**
> ***Times New Roman Bold Italic***

- Note the Font dialog box illustrated on the previous page. The Font style box lists the styles or weights specially designed and available for the selected font.

Font Size

- **Font size** refers to the height of the font, usually measured in points.

> Bookman 8 point
>
> Bookman 12 point
>
> # Bookman 18 point

- There are 72 points to an inch. Use 10- to 12-point type size for document text and larger sizes for headings and headlines.

- You may change font size in the Font dialog box or by clicking the Font Size list arrow on the Formatting toolbar (which drops down a list of font sizes).

- The currently selected font, style and size are displayed in the Preview window and described at the bottom of the Font dialog box.

- You can change fonts *before* or *after* typing text.

- Font sizes can be changed incrementally using a keyboard shortcut. Select the text you wish to affect and select Ctrl + Shift + > to *increase* to the next largest point size; press Ctrl + Shift + < to *decrease* to the next smaller point size.

Font Color

- You may change the color of text by selecting the text to be affected, then clicking the drop-down list arrow next to the Color option in the Font dialog box and selecting a desired font color. You can also click the drop-down list arrow next to the Font Color button on the Formatting toolbar to select another color to apply to the selected text.

> ✓Note: *You must have a color printer in order to output color.*

In this exercise, you will create an advertisement and apply text alignments and enhancements to the document.

EXERCISE DIRECTIONS

1. Create a NEW document.

2. Using the Properties feature, enter relevant document summary information.

3. Keyboard the exercise exactly as shown in Part I using proper text alignments, or open ⌑**22ESTATE**.

4. Change the font face, font size, font style, and font color as indicated in Part II on page 91.

5. Using the keyboard shortcut procedure, incrementally increase the 6-point text to 8 point.

6. Vertically center the exercise.

7. Spell check.

8. Preview your work.

9. Print one copy.

10. Close the file; save as **ESTATE**.

PART I

PINEVIEW ESTATES.

The country home
that's more like a country club.

Far from the crowds, on the unspoiled North Fork of Long Island, you'll find a unique country home. PineView Estates. A condominium community perfectly situated between Peconic Bay and Long Island Sound on a lovely wooded landscape. And like the finest country club, it offers a community club house, tennis court, pool and a golf course.

Models Open Daily 11 to 4
PineView Estates
Southhold, New York
(516) 555-5555

The complete terms are in an offering plan available from the sponsor.

PINEVIEW ESTATES.

Braggadocio 18 pt. Set font color to green.

The country home that's more like a country club.

Script 22 pt

Far from the crowds, on the unspoiled North Fork of Long Island, you'll find a unique country home. PineView Estates. A condominium community perfectly situated between Peconic Bay and Long Island Sound on a lovely wooded landscape. And like the finest country club, it offers a community club house, tennis court, pool and a golf course.

Arial 10pt

Models Open Daily 11 to 4
Arial 10 pt

PineView Estates
Southhold, New York
(516) 555-5555

Arial 9 pt italics

The complete terms are in an offering plan available from the sponsor.

Arial 6 pt

KEYSTROKES

CHANGE FONT FACE

If all text in a paragraph will be in the same font, we recommend that you include the paragraph mark at the end of the paragraph in your selection (highlighting) before you change the font.

1. Select text for which font is to be changed.

   OR

   Place insertion point where new font is to begin.

2. Click Font Face list arrow on Formatting toolbar and click desired font.

   OR

   a. Click **Format**.................... `Alt` + `O`

   b. Click **Font** .... `F`

   c. Click **Font** tab .... `Alt` + `N`

   d. Select **Font** .... `Alt` + `F`

   e. Click desired font .... `↓` `↑`

   f. Click **OK** .... `Enter`

CHANGE FONT SIZE

1. Select text for which font size is to be changed.

   OR

   Place insertion point where new font size is to begin.

2. Click Font Size list arrow on the Formatting toolbar and click desired point size.

   OR

   a. Click **Format**.................... `Alt` + `O`

   b. Click **Font** .... `F`

   c. Click **Font** tab .... `Alt` + `N`

   d. Select **Size** .... `Alt` + `S`

   e. Click or type......................... `↓` `↑`
      desired point size.

   f. Click **OK** .... `Enter`

CHANGE FONT COLOR

1. Select text for which font color is to be changed.

   OR

   Place insertion point where new font color is to begin.

2. Click Font Color list arrow on Formatting toolbar and click desired color.

   OR

   a. Click **Format**.................... `Alt` + `O`

   b. Click **Font** .... `F`

   c. Click **Font** tab .... `Alt` + `N`

   d. Select **Color** .... `Alt` + `C`

   e. Select desired color............. `↓` `↑`

   f. Click **OK** .... `Enter`

Exercise

23

- ■ Emphasis Styles: Bold, Underline, Double/Dotted Underline, Italics, Highlight, Strikethrough, Superscript, Subscript and Small Caps
- ■ Remove Emphasis Styles

Formatting Toolbar

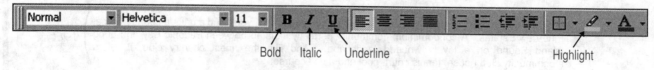

Bold Italic Underline Highlight

NOTES

Emphasis Styles

- ■ **Bold**, <u>underline</u>, <u>double underline</u>, <u>dotted underline</u>, *italic*, and highlight are features used to emphasize or enhance text.

- ■ You may emphasize text before or after you type it.

- ■ To emphasize text *after* typing, select the text to be affected, then click the desired emphasis button on the Formatting toolbar. To emphasize text *before* typing, click the emphasis button to turn on the feature, type the text, then click the emphasis button to turn off the feature.

- ■ Highlighted text will appear yellow on the screen, but will appear gray when printed (unless you have a color printer). To change the highlight color, click the list arrow next to the Highlight button on the Formatting toolbar and choose a different color.

- ■ Numerous underline styles are available in the Format, Font dialog box. Click the Underline drop-down list box and select an underline style.

- ■ As indicated in the previous exercise, font styles include bold and italics, but not all font faces have these styles.

Underline drop-down list box

Font			?
Font	Character Spacing	Animation	

Font:
Times New Roman

Font style:	Size:
Regular	10

Font:
Symbol
Tahoma
Technical
Times
Times New Roman

Font style:
Regular
Italic
Bold
Bold Italic

Size:
8
9
10
11
12

Underline:
(none)

(none)
Single
Words only
Double
Dotted
Thick
Dash
Dot dash
Dot dot dash
Wave

Color:
Auto

adow
utline
mboss
grave

☐ Small caps
☐ All caps
☐ Hidden

Times New Roman

This is a TrueType font. This font will be used on both printer and screen.

Default... OK Cancel

Effects options

92

- In addition to bold, italic, highlight, underline, and double underline, Word provides other effects. These include strikethrough, superscript, subscript, small caps, and all caps. The strikethrough effect is used to indicate that text has been added, deleted, or moved, and is useful when you compare a current document with a different version of the document.

- Superscripts are characters that print slightly higher than the normal typing line; subscripts are characters that print slightly lower than the normal typing line. Note examples below:

SMALL CAPS

ALL CAPS

~~strikethrough~~

~~double strikethrough~~

Shadow

outline

emboss

engrave

subscript

superscript

- Like the other appearance changes, these may be applied before or after you type text. You may access them by selecting one of the Effects in the Font dialog box.

Remove Emphasis Styles

- Bolding, italics, underlines, highlighting and double underlines may be removed using the same procedure as when you applied these special character formats.

- You may remove character formatting individually, or you may remove all character formatting from a selected (highlighted) block of text by pressing the Ctrl key and the Spacebar. This is a useful feature when you wish to remove two or more emphasis styles in one step, such as bolding and underlining and italicizing.

- The proofreaders' mark for each style is:

bold	∼∼∼∼
underline	————
double underline	══════
italic	(ital) *ital*
highlight	(highlight) *hi*

In this exercise, you will create and enhance a letter using bold, double underline, italics, highlight, and small caps.

EXERCISE DIRECTIONS

1. Create a NEW document, or open 🖫**23LONDON**.

2. Begin the letterhead At 1"; begin the date At 2.5". Use the Date feature to insert the date.

3. Use the default margins.

4. Keyboard the exercise as shown, using the alignments and enhancements indicated below.
   - Use a sans serif 14-point bold font for the company name in the letterhead and 10-point sans serif for the remaining letterhead information.
   - Right-align and use a 10-point sans serif italic font for the phone, fax and e-mail information.
   - Use a serif 12-point font for the letter.
   - Center and set the hotel text to small caps.
   - Set the letterhead company name to blue and underline it with a dashed underline.

5. Spell check.

6. Justify paragraph text.

7. Highlight the first two hotels in yellow and the last two in green.

8. Preview your work.

9. Remove all highlighting.

10. Print one copy.

11. Close and save the file; name it **LONDON**.

12. Close the document window.

TRANS-ATLANTIC TRAVEL NETWORK ←——————— *Set to blue*
123-45 Palm Drive
Palm Bay, FL 32905
Phone: 1-800-555-5555
Fax: (407) 777-7777
rep@transtravel.com

Today's date

Mr. Richard Heslin
95 Washington Avenue
Miami Beach, FL 33139

Dear Mr. Heslin:

We are sending you under separate cover your travel itinerary for your upcoming trip to
London. We strongly suggest that you take out the Trip Cancellation Insurance. We are
also sending an insurance brochure for your convenience. Read it carefully.

You had asked us to recommend hotels that serve afternoon tea. The following are some
suggestions:

The Savoy
Dorchester
Connaught
St. James Court

If you have any further questions or needs, call our office. Our experienced staff will
give you prompt and courteous service and will answer all your travel questions. Have a
wonderful trip!

Sincerely,

Lois Marlin
Travel Representative

im/yo

KEYSTROKES

BOLD

CTRL + B

BEFORE TYPING

1. Place insertion point where bold is to begin.

2. Click **Bold** button................................ **B**

   OR

   Press **Ctrl + B** .... Ctrl + B

3. Type text .... *text*

4. Click **Bold** button................................ **B**
   to discontinue bolding.

   OR

   Press **Ctrl + B** .... Ctrl + B
   to discontinue bolding.

EXISTING TEXT

1. Select (highlight) text to bold.

2. Click **Bold** button.......................... **B**

   OR

   Press **Ctrl + B**...................... Ctrl + B

   ✔ *Remove bolding by repeating the steps above.*

UNDERLINE

CTRL + U

BEFORE TYPING

1. Place insertion point where underline is to begin.

2. Click **Underline** button.................. U

   OR

   Press **Ctrl + U** .... Ctrl + U

3. Type text .... *text*

4. Click **Underline** button.................. U
   to discontinue underlining.

   OR

   Press **Ctrl + U** .... Ctrl + U
   to discontinue underlining.

EXISTING TEXT

1. Select (highlight) text to underline.

2. Click **Underline** button.................. U

   OR

   Press **Ctrl + U** .... Ctrl + U

   ✔ *Remove underlining by repeating the steps above.*

ITALICS

CTRL + I

BEFORE TYPING

1. Place insertion point where italics are to begin.

2. Click **Italic** button .... *I*

   OR

   a. Click **Format** .... Alt + O

   b. Click **Font**............................ F

   c. Click **Font tab** .... Alt + N

   d. Click **Font style** .... Alt + Y

   e. Click **Italic**........................ ↓ ↑

   f. Click **OK** .... Enter

3. Type text.................................... *text*

4. Click **Italic** button .... *I*
   to discontinue italicizing.

   OR

   Press **Ctrl + I** .... Ctrl + I
   to discontinue italicizing.

EXISTING TEXT

1. Select (highlight) text to italicize.

2. Click **Italic** button .... *I*

   OR

   Press **Ctrl + I** .... Ctrl + I

   OR

   a. Click **Format** .... Alt + O

   b. Click **Font**............................ F

   c. Click **Font tab** .... Alt + N

   d. Click **Font Style** .... Alt + Y

   e. Click **Italic**........................ ↓ ↑

   f. Click **OK** .... Enter

   ✔ *Remove italics by repeating the steps above.*

HIGHLIGHT

BEFORE TYPING

1. Place insertion point where highlighting is to begin.

2. Click **Highlight** button................

3. Type text..................................... *text*

4. Click **Highlight** button................
   to discontinue highlighting.

EXISTING TEXT

1. Select (highlight) text to highlight.

2. Click **Highlight** button................

   ✔ *Remove highlighting by repeating the steps above.*

DOUBLE UNDERLINE

CTRL + SHIFT + D

1. Place insertion point where double underlining is to begin.

2. Press **Ctrl+Shift+D**... Ctrl + Shift + D

3. Type text..................................... *text*

4. Press **Ctrl+Shift+D**... Ctrl + Shift + D
   to discontinue double underlining.

EXISTING TEXT

1. Select (highlight) text to double underline.

2. Press **Ctrl+Shift+D**... Ctrl + Shift + D

   For double or dotted underline:

   a. Select (highlight) text to underline.

   b. Select **Format** .... Alt + O

   c. Select **Font**........................... F

   d. Click **Font Tab**............... Alt + N

   e. Select **Underline** .... Alt + U

   f. Choose underline style.......... ↓ ↑

   g. Click **OK** .... Enter

   ✔ *Remove underlining by repeating the steps above.*

REMOVE CHARACTER FORMATTING

CTRL+B, CTRL+D, CTRL+I, CTRL+SPACE

Select (highlight) text containing the formatting to remove:

- Click **Bold** button .... `B`
  to remove bold.

  OR

  Press **Ctrl + B** .... `Ctrl` + `B`

- Click **Underline** button .... `U`
  to remove underline.

  OR

  Press **Ctrl + U** .... `Ctrl` + `U`

- Click **Italics** button .... `I`
  to remove italics

  OR

  Press **Ctrl + I** .... `Ctrl` + `I`
  to remove italics.

- Press **Ctrl + Space** .... `Ctrl` + `Space`
  to remove all character formatting.

EFFECTS (STRIKETHROUGH, SMALL CAPS, ALL CAPS, SUPERSCRIPT, SUBSCRIPT)

1. Click **Format** .... `Alt` + `O`
2. Click **Font** .... `F`
3. Click the **Font** tab .... `Alt` + `N`
4. Click desired **Effects**:
   - **Strikethrough** .... `Alt` + `K`
   - **Small Caps** .... `Alt` + `M`
   - **All Caps** .... `Alt` + `A`
   - **Superscript** .... `Alt` + `P`
   - **Subscript** .... `Alt` + `B`
5. Click **OK** .... `Enter`

Exercise 24

■ **Use Symbols** ■ **Format Painter**

NOTES

Use Symbols

■ **Wingdings** is an ornamental symbol font collection that is used to enhance a document. Illustrated below is the Wingdings font collection.

■ A symbol font face must be available with your printer.

Wingdings Font Collection

■ The upper- and lowercase of a letter or character key provide different Wingdings. To create a Wingding, press and then highlight the corresponding keyboard letter or character shown in the chart, then select Wingdings from the Font Face list.

■ You may also add a Wingding to your document by selecting Symbol from the Insert menu and choosing the desired Wingding from the Symbol dialog box. Click the symbol and press Insert, then Close.

Click to select other fonts.

■ There are other ornamental fonts that you may access by clicking the list arrow next to the Font box in the Symbol dialog box.

- Ornamental fonts and special character sets are also treated as fonts. They can be accessed through the Font dialog box.

- You may change the size of a symbol font face as you would that of any other character, by changing the point size.

- Ornamental fonts can be used to:
  - Separate items on a page:

  - Emphasize items on a list:

  - Enhance a page:

Format Painter

- The **Format Painter** feature allows you to copy formatting, such as font face, style and size, from one part of text to another.

- To copy formatting from one location to another, select the text that contains the format you wish to copy. Then click the Format Painter button ⬛ on the Standard toolbar (the I-beam displays a paintbrush). Then select the text to receive the formatting. To copy formatting from one location to several locations, select the text that contains the format you wish to copy, then *double-click* the Format Painter button ⬛. Select the text to receive the formatting, release the mouse button and select additional text anywhere in the document. To turn off this feature and return the mouse pointer to an I-beam, click the Format Painter button.

In this exercise, you will create a menu and add a symbol font face to separate portions of it.

EXERCISE DIRECTIONS

1. Create a NEW document.

2. Keyboard the exercise as shown, using the alignments and enhancements indicated, or open 🖫24BAKERY and format and enhance the text as shown in the exercise.

3. Set 0.5" top and bottom margins.

4. Set the text for the first bakery category (Bagels) to a sans serif 14-point bold blue font.

5. Using Format Painter, copy the character formatting (font face, size, style and color) to the remaining bakery categories.

6. Set the text below each bakery category to a serif 12-point italic font.

7. Using Format Painter, copy the character formatting to the remaining bakery items.

8. Enhance the document with symbols from the Wingdings font collection. **Use any desired symbol.**

9. Spell check.

10. Preview your work.

11. Vertically center the exercise.

12. Print one copy.

13. Close the file; name it **BAKERY**. Save the changes.

14. Close the document window.

KEYSTROKES

INSERT A SYMBOL OR SPECIAL CHARACTER

1. Place insertion point where symbol will be inserted.

2. Click **I**nsert .... `Alt` + `I`

3. Click **S**ymbol .... `S`

4. Click **S**ymbols tab .... `Alt` + `S`

5. Click **F**ont list arrow .... `Alt` + `F`

6. Select desired font .... `↑` `↓`

7. Click desired special character to enlarge it for viewing.

8. Double-click desired special character to insert it into document.

OR

1. Place insertion point where symbol will be inserted.

2. Click **I**nsert .... `Alt` + `I`

3. Click **S**ymbol .... `S`

4. Click **S**pecial .... `Alt` + `P` **Characters** tab.

5. Select desired character .... `↑` `↓`

6. Double-click desired special character to insert it into document.

OR

1. Place insertion point where symbol will be inserted.

2. Type the corresponding letter or symbol shown on the chart.

3. Highlight the symbol.

4. Click **Font** list arrow on toolbar.

5. Select Wingdings.

FORMAT PAINTER

1. Select (highlight) paragraph mark containing the formatting you wish to copy.

2. Click **Format Painter** button .... 🖌

3. When mouse pointer changes to a paint brush, highlight paragraphs to receive the new formatting.

OR

Double-click **Format Painter** .... 🖌 button to copy formatting to multiple locations.

To turn off Format Painter:

Press **Esc** .... `Esc`

Stop Inn Bakery 🔔

Serif 24-pt bold

Sans serif 12 pt

456 Brentwood Lane 🔔
Columbus, OH 43210-1319 🔔
Phone: (614) 292-1882 🔔

Sans serif 14-pt bold blue → **Bagels**

Serif 12-pt italic

Plain
Cinnamon Raisin
Onion
Sesame
❖ ❖ ❖

Classic Muffins

Blueberry
Bran
Corn
Carrot
❖ ❖ ❖

Croissants

Plain
Chocolate
Apple
Almond
❖ ❖ ❖

Loaf Breads and Rolls

Four Grain
Baguette
Country Seed Roll
Cheese
❖ ❖ ❖

Gourmet Cookies

Chocolate Chip
Oatmeal Raisin
Peanut Butter
Shortbread
❖ ❖ ❖

Danish

Raspberry
Sweet Cheese
Pecan Rolls
❖ ❖ ❖ ❖ ❖

Where Freshness and Quality are our Trademark! ← *Narrow sans serif 12-pt italic*

Exercise 25
■ **Bullets and Numbering** ■ **End Bullets or Numbers**

Formatting Toolbar

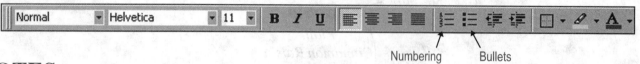

Numbering   Bullets

NOTES:

Bullets and Numbering

■ A **bullet** is a dot or symbol used to highlight points of information or to itemize a list that does not need to be in any particular order.

◆ red	◆ apple
◆ blue	◆ pear
◆ green	◆ orange

■ Using the **Bullets and Numbering** feature, you can insert bullets automatically to create a bulleted list for each paragraph or item you type.

■ The Bullets and Numbering feature also allows you to create numbered paragraphs for items that need to be in a particular order. The numbers you insert increment automatically.

■ The Bullets and Numbering feature allows you to:

- Create numbered paragraphs.
- Create bulleted paragraphs.
- Use symbols instead of the traditional round dot or square bullet.

■ You may access the Bullets and Numbering feature by selecting Bullets & Numbering from the Format menu.

■ In the Bullets and Numbering dialog box that follows, you may click the Bulleted tab and select the bullet style you desire. Or you may click the Numbered tab and select the number style you desire.

Bulleted tab   Numbered tab

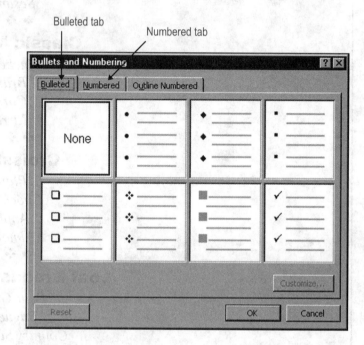

■ Once the bullet or number style is chosen, you may type your text. The bullet or number is entered automatically each time the Enter key is pressed.

■ You can also access Bullets and Numbering by clicking the Bullets ▤ or Numbering ▤ button on the Formatting toolbar.

- You can add bullets and numbers to existing text by selecting/highlighting the text and then choosing Bullets and Numbering from the Format menu and selecting the bullet or number style you desire, or by clicking the appropriate button on the Formatting toolbar.

- Symbols may also be used as bullets.

- When you use the Bullets and Numbering feature for numbered paragraphs, adding or deleting paragraphs will result in all paragraphs being automatically renumbered.

End Bullets or Numbers

- You may remove bullets from a bulleted list by selecting the list and clicking the Bullet button. You may remove numbers from a numbered list by selecting the list and clicking the Numbering button.

- To change the bullet style to a symbol, select the Bulleted item or list and choose Bullets and Numbering from the Format menu. Then click the Bulleted tab in the Bullets and Numbering dialog box and click Customize. Click Bullet. The Symbol dialog box appears, allowing you to select a desired symbol. If you want to see other symbols, click the list arrow to the right of the Font box and select another symbol set.

In this exercise, you will enhance an advertisement created earlier with bullets, symbols and font changes.

EXERCISE DIRECTIONS:

1. Open ▦JEWELS, or open ▤25JEWELS

2. Make the following changes to the advertisement:

   - Set the title to an 18-point bold decorative serif font. Precede and follow the title with symbols from the Windings font collection; set them to 18 point.

   - Center any desired symbol to separate the title and the first paragraph. Set it to a 14-point bold font.

   - Bullet the items listed under "What you can expect from us is." Use any desired bullet except the round dot. Set the items to a sans serif 14-point font.

   - Number the 4 "Cs." Use any desired number style.

   - Set "CUT" to 14-point bold and use the same decorative font used in the title.

   - Using Format Painter, copy the formatting to the remaining "C's".

   - Set the text following "CUT" to a sans serif 12-point font. Using Format Painter, copy the formatting to the text following the other "C's."

   - Bold "Carat Shoppe" in the first paragraph. Use Format Painter to copy the bolding to other bolded text shown in the exercise.

   - Italicize the address below The Carat Shoppe.

   - Insert any desired bullet preceding each line in the phone information.

   - Insert and center any desired symbol in 14-point bold below the phone information.

3. If you have a color printer, change the font color for all bolded text to red.

4. Spell check.

5. Preview your work.

6. Remove the bullets next to the phone information.

7. Print one copy.

8. Close the file; save the changes.

KEYSTROKES

BULLETS

1. Place insertion point where text will be typed.

   OR

   Select text to convert to a bulleted list.

2. Click **Bullets** button........................ ▤

   OR

   a. Click **Format**.................... Alt + O

   b. Click **Bullets and Numbering** ..... N

   c. Click **Bulleted**................. Alt + B

   d. Click desired............ ↑ ↓ → ← bullet style

   e. Click **OK**.................................. Enter

REMOVE BULLETS

1. Select the part of the list from which bullets are to be removed.

2. Click **Bullets** button........................ ▤

   OR

   a. Right-click on selected text.

   b. Select **Bullets and Numbering** ... N

   c. Click **Bulleted** tab .... Alt + B

   d. Click **None**.

   e. Click **OK**............................... Enter

NUMBERING

1. Position insertion point where text will be typed or select (highlight) block of text to convert to a numbered list..

2. Click **Numbering** button ....

   OR

   a. Click **Format** .... Alt + O

   b. Click **Bullets and Numbering**...... N

   c. Click **Numbered** .... Alt + N

   d. Click desired .... ↑ ↓ → ← numbering style.

   e. Click **OK** .... Enter

END NUMBERING

1. Select the list from which numbering is to be removed.

2. Click the **Numbering** button............

   OR

   a. Right-click on selected text.

   b. Select **Bullets and Numbering**.... N

   c. Click **Numbered** tab .... Alt + N

   d. Click **None**.

   e. Click **OK** .... Enter

৯ ∅ THE CARAT SHOPPE ৯ ∅

What started as a modest jewelry business in 1962 has emerged to become the country's dominant jewelry manufacturer and distributor—the **Carat Shoppe**. We are now planning to expand to 1,000 stores and eventually become the dominant jewelry boutique in the world! Our diamond experts can help you select the best quality gem for the lowest price possible.

What you can expect from us is:

◊ Expert guidance from our professional diamontologists and gemologists.
◊ Courteous service and a caring attitude.
◊ Full value for your money.
◊ Dependable quality at all times.
◊ Convenient credit plans to suit your needs.

The 4 "Cs" that determine the quality and value of a diamond:

1. CUT—A diamond must be cut to good proportion in order to make the best use of light.
2. CARAT—The weight of a diamond is measured in carats. The carat is divided into one hundred smaller units of weight called "points."
3. COLOR—The closer a diamond is to crystal clear and colorless, the more valuable it is.
4. CLARITY—Refers to a diamond's freedom from tiny bubbles and carbon spots .

The Carat Shoppe
Jewelers and Diamond Brokers
234 Mindanao Way
Marina del Rey, CA 90292-9999

Copy bold formatting

♦ For the nearest Carat Shoppe in your area,
♦ call our toll-free number:
♦ 1-800-333-3333.
♦ See our home page on the Web:
♦ http://carat.com

Exercise 26 ■ Summary

In this exercise, you will create a flyer and add symbols to separate portions of it.

EXERCISE DIRECTIONS:

1. Create a NEW document.

2. Turn off the Grammar Check feature.

3. Deselect Capitalize first letter of sentences in the AutoCorrect dialog box (Tools, AutoCorrect).

4. Keyboard the exercise as shown, using the appropriate alignments and enhancements and any desired bullet style. Or open 🖫**26DESIGN**, then format and enhance the text as shown in the exercise.

5. Use the default margins.

6. Use Format Painter to copy the formatting from one bulleted item to another.

7. Enhance the document with symbols from the Wingdings font collection. Use any desired symbols.

8. If you have a color printer, highlight each bulleted heading (sans serif text) in a different color. If you do not have a color printer, skip this step.

9. Spell check.

10. Preview your work.

11. Vertically center the exercise.

12. Print one copy.

13. Close the file; save as **DESIGN**.

Script 40 pt bold

Create a

Serif 30 pt bold

Design with Color

48 pt

4 Reasons Why

Sans Serif 24 pt

The world is a colorful place.
So, why not include color in all your
processing?

Serif 14 pt italic

4x

⇒ *Color increases the visual impact of the message and makes it more memorable.*   Don't you want your ads to have impact and be noticed?

Sans Serif 14 pt italic

Serif 12 pt

⇒ *Color creates a feeling and helps explain the subject.* Greens and blues are cool, relaxing tones, while reds and oranges scream with emphasis. Pastels communicate a gentle tone.

Copy formatting

⇒ *Color creates a personality.* You can make your corporate forms and brochures have their own identity and personality with color.

⇒ *Color highlights information.* An advertisement or manual might have warnings in red, explanations in black and instructions in blue.

◆ ◆ ◆

12 point Wingdings

Italic

Our color processing labs will take care of *all* your color processing needs. Just call *1-800-555-6666* for information.   Our courteous staff is ready to assist you with any technical question.

Sans Serif 12 pt

Bold L •A •B •P •R •O
FOR
COLOR PROCESSING

Sans Serif 12 pt

Exercise

27

■ **Summary**

In this exercise, you will create a flyer using text alignments, enhancements, bullets and numbers.

EXERCISE DIRECTIONS:

1. Create a NEW document.

2. Turn off the Grammar check feature.

3. Keyboard the exercise as shown, using the appropriate alignments and enhancements and any desired bullet style for the bulleted items. Or open 🖫**27COLOR**, then format and enhance the text as shown in the exercise.

4. Use the default margins.

5. Enhance the document with any desired symbols from the Wingdings font collection.

6. Set the font color for each occurrence of the word Color in Color Masters to Green.

7. Spell check.

8. Preview your work.

9. Vertically center the exercise.

10. Print one copy.

11. Close the file; save as **COLOR**.

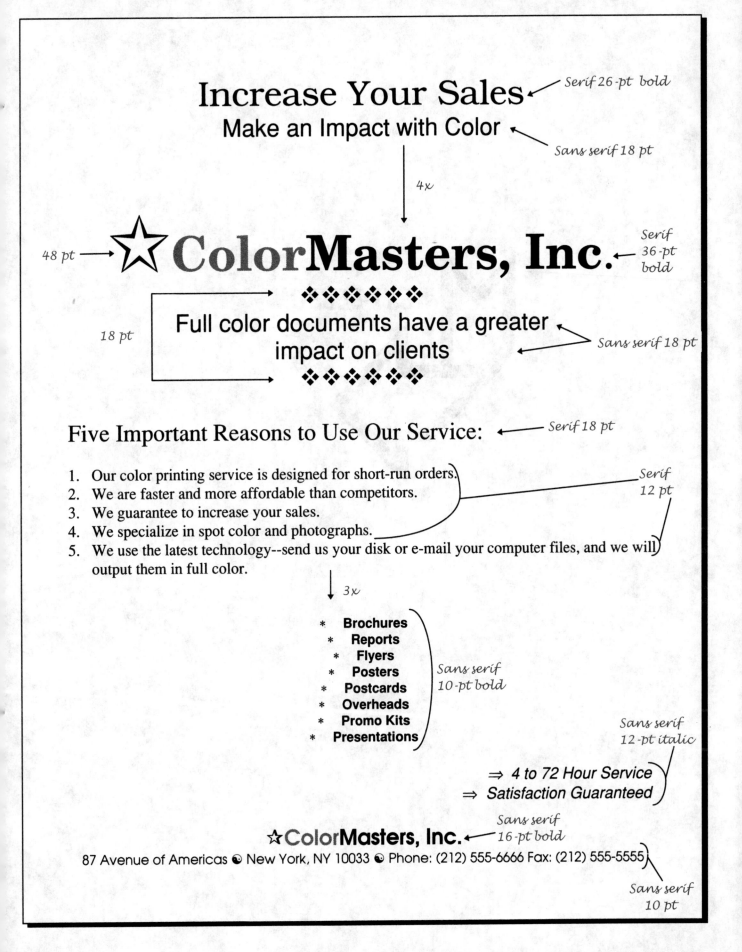

Increase Your Sales

Serif 26-pt bold

Make an Impact with Color

Sans serif 18 pt

4x

★ Color**Masters, Inc.**

48 pt

Serif 36-pt bold

18 pt

Full color documents have a greater impact on clients

Sans serif 18 pt

Five Important Reasons to Use Our Service:

Serif 18 pt

1. Our color printing service is designed for short-run orders.
2. We are faster and more affordable than competitors.
3. We guarantee to increase your sales.
4. We specialize in spot color and photographs.
5. We use the latest technology--send us your disk or e-mail your computer files, and we will output them in full color.

Serif 12 pt

3x

* **Brochures**
* **Reports**
* **Flyers**
* **Posters**
* **Postcards**
* **Overheads**
* **Promo Kits**
* **Presentations**

Sans serif 10-pt bold

⇒ *4 to 72 Hour Service*
⇒ *Satisfaction Guaranteed*

Sans serif 12-pt italic

☆Color**Masters, Inc.**

Sans serif 16-pt bold

87 Avenue of Americas ☻ New York, NY 10033 ☻ Phone: (212) 555-6666 Fax: (212) 555-5555

Sans serif 10 pt

NEXT LESSON

Word 97

LESSON 5

Format and Edit Documents

- Line Spacing
- Paragraph Spacing
- Indent Text
- Hanging Indent
- Format a One-Page Report
- First-Line Indent
- Cut and Paste
- Drag and Drop
- Move Text
- Shrink-to-Fit
- Copy and Paste
- Drag and Drop

Exercise 28

■ **Line Spacing** ■ **Paragraph Spacing**

NOTES

Line Spacing

■ Use **line spacing** to specify the spacing between lines of text. A line spacing change affects text in the paragraph containing the insertion point. Line spacing may also be applied to selected text.

Paragraph Dialog Box

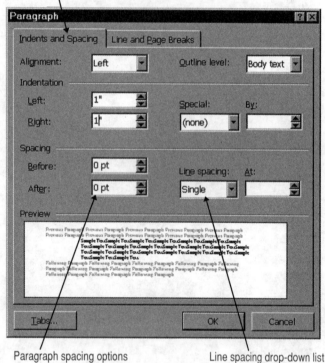

Indents and Spacing tab

Paragraph spacing options

Line spacing drop-down list

■ Line spacing is measured in lines or in points. When line spacing is measured in points, it is referred to as leading (pronounced *ledding*). Reducing leading amounts can reduce the text's readability, while increasing leading can aid its readability.

Leading Examples

> To make text easy to read, fonts that are measured in points usually use leading that is 120% of the font's point size. For example, a 10-point font usually uses 12-point leading.

> The paragraph text in this box has been set to 16-point leading using the specific amount (exactly) setting. Note that the lines appear to be double spaced. They are not.

> The paragraph text in this box has been set to a specific amount (exactly) using 9 point. Note that the lines get less readable as the point size decreases.

■ Line spacing may also be changed to single, double or one-and-a-half lines. The quickest way to change line spacing is to press Ctrl+2 for double, Ctrl+1 for single and Ctrl+5 for 1.5 lines. Other methods for changing line spacing are outlined in the keystrokes section of this exercise.

Paragraph Spacing

■ The paragraph spacing option allows you to add additional space between paragraphs, headings, or subheadings as you type your document. You may choose to add extra space before each paragraph, after each paragraph or before and after each paragraph.

■ To set paragraph spacing, select Paragraph from the Format menu. In the Paragraph dialog box that follows, click the Indents and Spacing tab. Enter a spacing amount in the Before and/or After text box. The amount you enter may be in lines (2 li) or in points (2 pt). If you enter an amount in lines, Word will convert it to points.

In this exercise, you will change line and paragraph spacing in a previously created advertisement.

EXERCISE DIRECTIONS:

1. Open ⌨ **JEWELS**, or open 💾**28JEWELS**.

2. Set 0.5" top and bottom margins.

3. Set line spacing in the first paragraph to 1.5 lines.

4. Set paragraph spacing before and after the "4 C's" paragraphs to 4 point.

5. Change the font size of the Carat Shoppe and phone information paragraphs (at the bottom of the page) to 10 point.

6. Set line spacing for The Carat Shoppe and phone information paragraphs to At Least 12 point.

7. Preview your work.

8. Print one copy.

9. Close the file; save the changes.

10. Close the document window.

ઠ૭ THE CARAT SHOPPE ઠ૭

What started as a modest jewelry business in 1962 has emerged to become the country's dominant jewelry manufacturer and distributor—the **Carat Shoppe**. We are now planning to expand to 1,000 stores and eventually become the dominant jewelry boutique in the world! Our diamond experts can help you select the best quality gem for the lowest price possible.

What you can expect from us is:

◊ Expert guidance from our professional diamontologists and gemologists.
◊ Courteous service and a caring attitude.
◊ Full value for your money.
◊ Dependable quality at all times.
◊ Convenient credit plans to suit your needs.

The 4 "Cs" that determine the quality and value of a diamond:

1. CUT—A diamond must be cut to good proportion in order to make the best use of light.
2. CARAT—The weight of a diamond is measured in carats. The carat is divided into one hundred smaller units of weight called "points."
3. COLOR—The closer a diamond is to crystal clear and colorless, the more valuable it is.
4. CLARITY—Refers to a diamond's freedom from tiny bubbles and carbon spots.

The Carat Shoppe
Jewelers and Diamond Brokers
234 Mindanao Way
Marina del Rey, CA 90292-9999

For the nearest Carat Shoppe in your area,
call our toll-free number:
1-800-333-3333.
See our home page on the Web:
http://carat.com

KEYSTROKES

LINE SPACING

1. Place insertion point where new line spacing is to begin.

   OR

   Select the paragraph in which line spacing is to be changed.

2. Select desired line spacing option:

   a. Press **Ctrl + 2** .... `Ctrl` + `2`
      to change to double-spaced lines.

   b. Press **Ctrl + 1** .... `Ctrl` + `1`
      to change to single-spaced lines.

   c. Press **Ctrl + 5** .... `Ctrl` + `5`
      to change to 1.5-spaced lines.

   OR

   a. Click **Format** .... `Alt` + `O`

   b. Click **Paragraph** .... `P`

   c. Click **Indents and Spacing**. `Alt` + `I`

   d. Click **Line Spacing** .... `Alt` + `N`
      drop-down list.

   e. Click desired
      spacing option .... `↓` `↑`

   To choose a fixed line spacing:

   - Select **Exactly** .... `↓`

   - Click **At** scroll box .... `Alt` + `A`

   - Type desired spacing amount.

   f. Click **OK** .... `Enter`

PARAGRAPH SPACING

1. Position insertion point in the paragraph you want to format or select paragraphs to be formatted.

2. Click **Format** .... `Alt` + `O`

3. Click **Paragraph** .... `P`

4. Click **Indents and Spacing**... `Alt` + `I`

5. Click **Before** and/ .... `Alt` + `B`
   or **After** text box .... `Alt` + `E`

6. Enter a before and/or after spacing amount.

7. Click **OK** .... `Enter`

Exercise 29

■ **Indent Text** ■ **Hanging Indent**

Formatting Toolbar

Decrease Indent   Increase Indent

NOTES

Indent Text

■ The indent feature sets temporary left, right or left and right margins for paragraph text. The indent feature may also be used to set a first-line indent for paragraphs. See the illustration of left and right indents below.

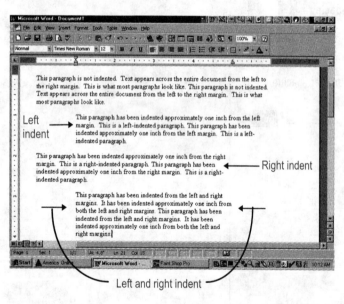

Left indent

Right indent

Left and right indent

■ There are several ways to indent text. You can:

Drag the indent markers on the Ruler.

• This is the most convenient way of setting left *and* right indents. To change indents, drag the left and/or right indent marker to the desired position. Note that the left indent marker consists of three parts. Be sure to drag the correct part to achieve the desired indent.

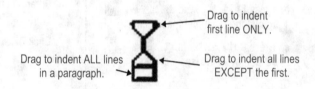

Drag to indent first line ONLY.

Drag to indent ALL lines in a paragraph.

Drag to indent all lines EXCEPT the first.

Page Layout View Ruler

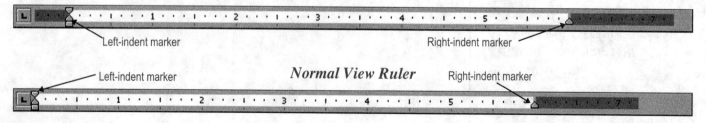

Left-indent marker   Right-indent marker

Normal View Ruler

Left-indent marker   Right-indent marker

Click an Indent button on the Formatting toolbar ▤.

- This is the most convenient way of setting a left indent. Clicking the Increase Indent button indents text to one tab setting. Thus, clicking the Increase Indent button once indents text 0.5"; clicking it twice will indent text 1", etc.

- You can decrease or remove left indents by selecting the indented text and clicking the Decrease Indent button ▤ until the indent reaches the desired location.

Use the Paragraph Dialog Box.

- Access this option by selecting F<u>o</u>rmat, <u>P</u>aragraph, and the <u>I</u>ndents and Spacing tab.

Paragraph Dialog Box

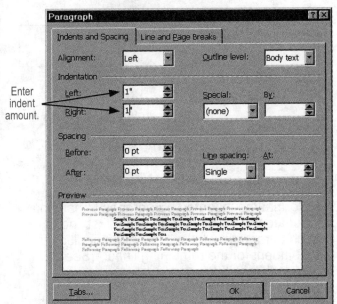

- This option allows greater precision for setting left and right indents. Enter the amount of indentation (or click the increment arrows) in the <u>L</u>eft and/or <u>R</u>ight indent box.

Hanging Indent

- When all lines in a paragraph are indented except the first line, it is called a **hanging indent**. Note the effect of a hanging indent on a paragraph.

Paragraph with a Hanging Indent

> The way text will lay out or format on a page is set by the Word 97 program. For example, margins are set for 1.25" on the left and 1.25" on the right; line spacing is automatic; tabs are set to advance the cursor 0.5" each time the Tab key is pressed. Formats may be changed at any time and as many times as desired throughout the document.

- There are several ways to create a hanging indent. You can:

Drag the hanging-indent and first-line indent markers on the ruler.

- This method allows you to see the changes as you make them. To set a hanging indent, drag the hanging-indent marker anywhere to the right of the first-line indent marker. Note the ruler position of the first-line and hanging-indent markers in the illustration below:

Paragraph with a Hanging Indent

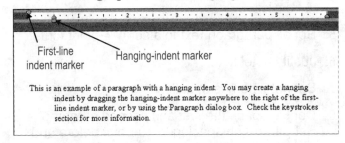

First-line indent marker   Hanging-indent marker

This is an example of a paragraph with a hanging indent. You may create a hanging indent by dragging the hanging-indent marker anywhere to the right of the first-line indent marker, or by using the Paragraph dialog box. Check the keystrokes section for more information.

Press Ctrl+T.

- This method indents all paragraph text, except the first line, to the next tab stop. It is the quickest way to achieve a hanging indent.

- Pressing Ctrl+Shift+T will undo indents created with Ctrl+T.

Use the Paragraph dialog box.

- You may access this dialog box by selecting Format, Paragraph, and the Indents and Spacing Tab.

- This option allows greater precision for setting a hanging indent. Enter the left indent amount in the Left text box. Select Special and choose Hanging. Then select By and enter the desired measurement for the hanging indent.

Paragraph Dialog Box

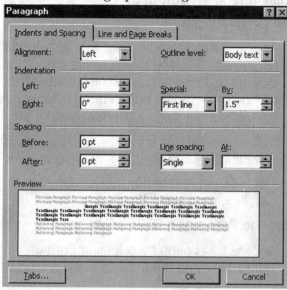

In this exercise, you will change line spacing, indent text and change fonts to create an advertisement.

EXERCISE DIRECTIONS

1. Open ⌨**DIVE**, or open 💾**29DIVE**.

2. Display the Office Assistant and view any suggestions.

3. Make the indicated revisions.

4. Use any desired method to indent hotel paragraphs .5 from left.

5. Set all paragraph text to a serif 14-point font.

6. Justify hotel text.

7. Set hotel names to italic.

8. Double space the first and second paragraphs. Set paragraph spacing to 10-point before and after the first and second paragraphs.

9. Spell check.

10. Preview your work.

11. Print one copy.

12. Reformat the indented paragraphs to hanging indented paragraphs. Leave the first line of each paragraph where it is; set an additional 0.5" indent for the remaining lines. *(See Desired Result II.)*

13. Print one copy.

14. Close the file; save as **DIVE**.

DIVING IN THE CAYMAN ISLANDS] *Center and set to sans serif 18-pt bold*

Press tab →
Do you want to see sharks, barracudas ~~and~~ stingrays? *,and angelfish* ~~Do you want to see angels, too?~~

Press tab →
The Cayman Islands were discovered by Christopher Columbus in 1503 *and* ~~The Cayman Islands~~ are located south of Cuba. The Caymans are home to ~~only~~ about 25,000 year-around residents. However, they welcome 200,000 visitors each year. Most visitors come with masks and flippers in their luggage. ~~Now, you are ready to jump in!~~

Set hotel names to italic {
Hotel/Diving Accommodations:] *Set to sans serif 14-pt bold*

Sunset House, PO Box 479, George Town, Grand Cayman; (800) 555-4767.

Coconut Harbour, PO Box 2086, George Town, Grand Cayman; (809) 555-7468.

Red Sail Sports, PO Box 1588, George Town, Grand Cayman; (809) 555-7965.

Cayman Diving Lodge, PO Box 11, East End, Grand Cayman; (809) 555-7555.

Anchorage View, PO Box 2123, 7 Mile Beach, Grand Cayman; (809) 555-4209.

DESIRED RESULT I

DIVING IN THE CAYMAN ISLANDS

Do you want to see sharks, barracudas, stingrays and angelfish?

The Cayman Islands were discovered by Christopher Columbus in 1503 and are located south of Cuba. The Caymans are home to about 25,000 year-around residents. However, they welcome 200,000 visitors each year. Most visitors come with masks and flippers in their luggage.

Hotel/Diving Accommodations:

Sunset House, PO Box 479, George Town, Grand Cayman; (800) 555-4767.

Coconut Harbour, PO Box 2086, George Town, Grand Cayman; (809) 555-7468.

Red Sail Sports, PO Box 1588, George Town, Grand Cayman; (809) 555-7965.

Cayman Diving Lodge, PO Box 11, East End, Grand Cayman; (809) 555-7555.

Anchorage View, PO Box 2123, Grand Cayman; (809) 555-4209.

DESIRED RESULT II

DIVING IN THE CAYMAN ISLANDS

Do you want to see sharks, barracudas, stingrays and angelfish?

The Cayman Islands were discovered by Christopher Columbus in 1503 and are located south of Cuba. The Caymans are home to about 25,000 year-around residents. However, they welcome 200,000 visitors each year. Most visitors come with masks and flippers in their luggage.

Hotel/Diving Accommodations:

Sunset House, PO Box 479, George Town, Grand Cayman; (800) 555-4767.

Coconut Harbour, PO Box 2086, George Town, Grand Cayman; (809) 555-7468.

Red Sail Sports, PO Box 1588, George Town, Grand Cayman; (809) 555-7965.

Cayman Diving Lodge, PO Box 11, East End, Grand Cayman; (809) 555-7555.

Anchorage View, PO Box 2123, Grand Cayman; (809) 555-4209.

KEYSTROKES

INDENT TEXT FROM THE LEFT MARGIN

1. Place insertion point in paragraph to block indent.

   OR

   Place insertion point where block indenting will begin.

   OR

   Select paragraphs to block indent.

2. Click **Increase Indent** button.......... 〔🔲〕
   on Formatting toolbar to indent text to desired tab stop.

   OR

   Click **Decrease Indent** button.......... 〔🔲〕
   on Formatting toolbar to move text back to left.

   OR

   Drag left-indent marker box .... 〔🔲〕
   to desired position on ruler.

   ✓ *Dragging the left-indent marker box will change both the first line indent and the left indent simultaneously.*

INDENT PARAGRAPHS FROM LEFT AND RIGHT MARGINS

1. Place insertion point in paragraph to block indent.

   OR

   Place insertion point where block indent will begin.

   OR

   Select paragraphs to block indent.

2. Drag left-indent marker box .... 〔🔲〕
   to desired position on ruler.

   ✓ *Dragging the left-indent marker box will change both the first line indent and the left indent simultaneously.*

3. Drag right indent marker .... △
   to desired position on ruler.

   OR

1. Click **F**ormat........................ Alt + O
2. Click **P**aragraph .... P
3. Click **I**ndents and
   Spacing tab...................... Alt + I
4. Click **L**eft text box............... Alt + L
5. Key distance from
   Left margin. .... *number*
6. Click **R**ight text box .... Alt + R
7. Key distance from
   Right margin. .... *number*
8. Click **OK** .... Enter

HANGING INDENT

Place the insertion point in paragraph to be affected.

OR

Select (highlight) the desired paragraphs.

USING INDENT MARKERS ON RULER

1. Drag **hanging-indent marker** .... △
   to desired position.
2. Drag **first-line indent marker**........ ▽
   to desired position.

USING KEYBOARD SHORTCUTS

1. Press **Ctrl+T** .... Ctrl + T
   as necessary to left-indent all paragraph text except first line to the desired tab stop.
2. Press **Ctrl+Shift+T**.... Ctrl + Shift + T
   as necessary to *undo* any left indents created with **Ctrl+T.**

USING THE FORMAT PARAGRAPH COMMAND ON THE MENU BAR

1. Click **F**ormat........................ Alt + O
2. Click **P**aragraph .... P
3. Click **I**ndents and Spacing tab .. Alt + I
4. Click **L**eft text box............... Alt + L
5. Type desired left paragraph
   indent .... *number*
6. Click **S**pecial .... Alt + S
7. Click **Hanging**................................. ↓
8. Click **B**y .... Alt + Y
9. Type distance that all lines, except the first, will be indented .... *number*
10. Click **OK** .... Enter

NEXT EXERCISE

Exercise 30

■ **Format a One-Page Report** ■ **First-Line Indent**

NOTES

Format a One-Page Report

■ A **report** or manuscript generally begins 2" from the top of the page and is prepared in double space. The first line of each new paragraph begins 0.5" or 1" from the left margin. The title of a report is centered and keyed in all caps. A quadruple space follows the title.

■ Margins vary depending on how the report is bound. For an unbound report, use margins of 1" on the left and right.

First-Line Indent

■ A first-line indent lets you set the amount of space that the first line of each new paragraph indents. Each time you press Enter, the insertion point automatically moves to the indented setting. This eliminates the need to use the Tab key to indent the first line of each new paragraph.

■ To set a first-line indent, you may use either the Ruler or the Paragraph dialog box.

■ Using the Ruler, drag the first-line indent marker to the desired position. Using the Paragraph Dialog box, select Special, choose First Line, and enter the amount you wish the paragraph to indent in the By text box.

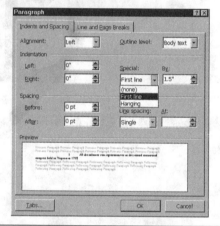

In this exercise, you will create a one-page report and review indent and line spacing procedures.

EXERCISE DIRECTIONS

1. Create a NEW document.

2. Keyboard the report shown, or open 🖫**30VISION**.

3. Set 1" left and right margins and a 0.5" bottom margin.

4. Begin the title At approximately 2". Use any desired Wingdings before and after the title as shown.

5. Center and set the title to a sans serif 14-point bold font.

6. Set a first-line indent at 1" for the first four paragraphs.

7. Set the first four paragraphs to a serif 12-point font.

8. Set the line spacing for the first four paragraphs to At least 16 point.

9. Justify the first four paragraphs.

10. Center and set COMMON VISION PROBLEMS to a sans serif 12-point bold font. Use a dotted underline below the heading.

    • Set vision problem heading text to a sans serif 10-point bold font. (Use Format Painter to copy the bold and sans serif formatting from the first heading to the other headings.)

    • Single-space and indent the vision problem paragraphs (including headings) 0.5" from the left and right margins. Press the Enter key two times before each new paragraph mark.

11. Spell check and preview your work.

12. Print one copy.

13. Save the file; name it **VISION**.

14. Close the document window.

❋ GOOD VISION ❋

Clear vision helps children adapt to the world around them. A large percentage of what a child learns comes through vision. If a vision problem exists, it can affect a child's learning ability. Two common symptoms of a vision problem are when a chalkboard appears blurred and a child has reading difficulties. Vision problems can cause the most intelligent child to become frustrated and lose interest in school. Children's eyes should be examined at the beginning of each school year. By doing so, vision problems can be detected before they affect a child's learning ability.

Safety eye equipment is a must for people working in an industrial environment, working with chemicals, or participating in sports where eye injuries can occur.

For adults, vision problems can affect work performance. Problems such as blurred reading or a reduced desire to do close work, burning eyes, frequent headaches, or difficulty driving can indicate a need for a visual examination.

In senior adults, eye changes do occur. Regular eye examinations can diagnose and treat these problems in the early stages to help preserve one's vision.

COMMON VISION PROBLEMS

NEARSIGHTEDNESS – You can see objects that are close more clearly than objects that are far away.

FARSIGHTEDNESS – You can see objects that are far away more clearly than objects that are close.

ASTIGMATISM – Objects appear blurred or distorted to you at all distances because the cornea (the front of the eye) has an irregular shape.

PRESBYOPIA – An age-related change in the focusing mechanism of your eyes, usually beginning around the age of 40 to 45 years, which causes reading and near vision to be blurred.

GLAUCOMA – An increase in the internal pressure of the eye caused by a buildup of excessive fluid inside the eye.

CATARACTS – A progressive clouding of the lens of the eye which absorbs much of the light entering the eye.

KEYSTROKES

FIRST-LINE INDENT

1. Position insertion point where first-line indent is to begin.

   OR

   Select paragraphs to receive first-line indent.

2. Drag **first-line indent marker**............ ▽
   to desired position on Ruler.

   OR

   a. Click **F**o**rmat**..................... `Alt` + `O`

   b. Click **P**a**ragraph**....................... `P`

   c. Click .... `Alt` + `I`
      Indents and Spacing tab.

   d. Click **S**pecial box............. `Alt` + `S`

   e. Select **First Line**.

   f. Click **B**y box.................. `Alt` + `Y`

   g. Enter an indent amount.

   h. Click **OK**............................. `Enter`

NEXT EXERCISE

Exercise 31

■ Cut and Paste ■ Drag and Drop

Standard Toolbar

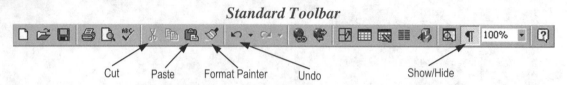

Cut   Paste   Format Painter   Undo   Show/Hide

NOTES

■ **Cut and paste** and **drag and drop** are features that let you move a block of text, a sentence, paragraph, page or column to another location in the same document or to another document.

Cut and Paste

■ The **cut** procedure allows you to cut or delete selected text from the screen and temporarily place it on the Clipboard (temporary storage buffer). The **paste** procedure allows you to retrieve text from the Clipboard and place it in a desired location in the document.

■ There are several procedures for cutting and pasting text. *(See keystrokes on page 129.)*

■ Information remains on the Clipboard until you cut or copy another selection (or until you exit Windows). Therefore, you can paste the same selection into many different locations, if desired.

Drag and Drop

■ The **drag and drop** method of moving text allows you to move selected text using your mouse. This method is convenient for moving a word or a block of text from one location to another.

■ Once text to be moved is selected, place the mouse pointer anywhere on the selected text and click and hold the *left* mouse button as you **drag** the highlighted text to the new location. The mouse pointer changes to a box with a dotted shadow to indicate that you are dragging text.

Hint: If you hold down the Ctrl key as you drag a selection, you can copy a selection to a new location.

■ When you reach the new location, release the mouse button to **drop** the text into place. Be sure to remove the selection highlight before pressing any key, so that you do not delete your newly moved text.

■ When moving a word or sentence, be sure to move the space following the word or sentence. Before you paste the moved text, always place the insertion point immediately to the left of where you want the text reinserted.

■ If text was not reinserted at the correct point, you can undo the move (Edit, Undo). It is sometimes necessary to insert or delete spaces, returns or tabs after completing a move.

■ If you wish to move an indented or tabbed paragraph, be sure the indent or tab code to the left of the text is moved along with the paragraph. To insure this, click the Show/Hide button to reveal formatting codes and check that the insertion point is to the left of the code to be moved before selecting text.

■ In Word, a paragraph is the amount of text followed by a **paragraph mark** (¶). Since all paragraph formatting instructions, such as indents and tabs, are stored in the paragraph mark, it is essential that you move the paragraph mark along with the paragraph; otherwise, you will lose the formatting.

■ The proofreaders' mark for moving text is:

EXERCISE DIRECTIONS:

1. Create a NEW document, or open ⬛31WALK.

2. Set 1.5" left and right margins.

3. Begin the exercise At 1".

4. Keyboard the exercise as shown in Illustration A.

5. Save the file as **WALK**.

   To create Illustration B:

6. Insert an arrow symbol before the 5. Set the symbol and the number 5 to a 72-point bold font. Set the remaining title to a script 28-point font. (Use ShelleyVolante BT font face, if available.)

7. Move the paragraphs in alphabetical order (according to the first word in each). Use any desired move procedure.

8. Press the Enter key once after each paragraph heading. Set a 1" indent from the left and right margins for text below each heading.

9. Set the text for the heading BURN EXTRA CALORIES to a sans serif 14-point bold font. Set the font color to green.

10. Using Format Painter, copy the character formatting (font face size, color, and bolding) to the remaining headings.

11. Set the text below the first heading to sans serif 10-point italics.

12. Using Format Painter, copy the character formatting to the remaining text below each heading.

13. Justify pointer paragraphs.

14. Spell check.

15. Center the page vertically.

16. Preview your work.

17. Print one copy.

18. Close the file; save the changes.

ILLUSTRATION A

5 Ways to Walk Off Weight

TAKE WALKS EVERY DAY. Everyday walking keeps you active and burns calories. Walk at least 20 minutes.

WALK AS FAST AS YOU CAN. Be comfortable in your walking speed. You want to feel energized as you walk and you want to have the motivation to walk again tomorrow.

SET GOALS. Set goals that are challenging and realistic – to walk every day for a week or to take a 4-mile weekend hike.

REMEMBER THE THREE Fs OF WALKING: FASTER, FARTHER, FREQUENTLY. If you can do all three, go for it, but if you can do only one, that's fine.

BURN EXTRA CALORIES. Seize every opportunity to move around. Stand and walk instead of sitting while talking on the phone; walk around the airport instead of sitting at the gate; whatever the occasion (except eating), avoid sitting down.

ILLUSTRATION B

5 *Ways to Walk Off Weight*

TAKE WALKS EVERY DAY.

Everyday walking keeps you active and burns calories. Walk at least 20 minutes.

WALK AS FAST AS YOU CAN.

Be comfortable in your walking speed. You want to feel energized as you walk and you want to have the motivation to walk again tomorrow.

SET GOALS.

Set goals that are challenging and realistic – to walk every day for a week or to take a 4-mile weekend hike.

REMEMBER THE THREE Fs OF WALKING: FASTER, FARTHER, FREQUENTLY.

If you can do all three, go for it, but if you can do only one, that's fine.

BURN EXTRA CALORIES.

Seize every opportunity to move around. Stand and walk instead of sitting while talking on the phone; walk around the airport instead of sitting at the gate; whatever the occasion (except eating), avoid sitting down.

Move into alphabetical order.

KEYSTROKES

MOVE

Cut and Paste:

1. Select text to move.
2. Click **Cut** button .... ✂
   OR
   Press **Shift + Delete** .... Shift + Del
   OR
   Ctrl + X .... Ctrl + X
3. Place insertion point where text will be inserted.
4. Click **Paste** button........................ 📋
   OR
   Press **Shift + Insert**............ Shift + Ins
   OR
   Ctrl + V .... Ctrl + V

Using the Keyboard:

1. Select text to move.
2. Press **F2**.. F2
3. Click to position insertion point where text will be inserted.
4. Press **Enter** .... Enter

Drag and Drop:

1. Select text to move.
2. Point to selected text.
3. Hold down left mouse button and drag text to new location.
4. Release mouse button.
   ✓ *Clicking the Undo button immediately after a move operation will restore moved text to its original location.*

Exercise

32

■ **Move Text** ■ **Shrink to Fit**

NOTES

Move Text

- You can use a shortcut key combination to move an entire paragraph up or down. To move a paragraph up, press and hold the Alt+Shift keys and tap the Up Arrow key. To move an entire paragraph down, press and hold the Alt+Shift keys and tap the Down Arrow key. Repeat the keystrokes as necessary to move the paragraph to the desired location.

Shrink to Fit

- The **Shrink to Fit** feature lets you shrink a document to fill a desired number of pages.

- If, for example, your document fills 1-¼ pages, but you would like it to fit on one page, Shrink to Fit automatically adjusts margins, font size, and/or line spacing so that the text will shrink to one page.

- You may return your document to the original number of pages by selecting Undo from the Edit menu.

- You may access Shrink to Fit by selecting Print Preview from the File menu and clicking the Shrink-to-Fit button 🖼 on the Print Preview toolbar.

Print Preview Toolbar

- The proofreaders' mark for inserting a space is: ⌗.

In this exercise, you will gain more practice moving text. When you select the paragraph to move, be sure you include the paragraph mark.

EXERCISE DIRECTIONS:

1. Open ⌨VISION, or open 💾32VISION.

2. Access the Track Changes feature.
   - Track the changes while editing the document text.
   - Highlight the changes on screen.
   - Highlight the changes in the printed document.

3. Move the paragraphs as indicated. Use any procedure you desire to move the paragraphs.

4. Change COMMON VISION PROBLEMS to italic and change it from center to left-alignment.

5. Change the first vision problem heading to italic.

6. Using Format Painter, change the remaining vision problem headings to italic.

7. Move the vision problem paragraphs into alphabetical order.

8. Create hanging indented paragraphs for the vision problems.

9. Make the remaining revisions.

10. Save the edited document as VISIONA.

11. Accept all changes.

12. Preview your work.

13. Use Shrink to Fit to keep all text on one page, if necessary.

14. Print one copy.

15. Turn off the Track Changes feature.

16. Close the file; save the changes.

❋ GOOD VISION ❋

Clear vision helps children adapt to the world around them. ~~A large percentage of what a child learns comes through vision.~~ If a vision problem exists, it can affect a child's learning ability. ~~Two common~~ symptoms of a vision problem are when a chalkboard appears blurred and a child has reading difficulties. Vision problems can cause the most intelligent child to become frustrated and lose interest in school. Children's eyes should be examined at the beginning of each school year. By doing so, vision problems can be detected before they affect a child's learning ability.

Safety eye equipment is a must for people working in an industrial environment, working with chemicals, or participating in sports where eye injuries can occur. *— and do*

For adults, vision problems can affect work performance. Problems such as blurred reading or a reduced desire to do close work, burning eyes, frequent headaches, or difficulty driving can indicate a need for a visual examination.

In senior adults, eye changes do occur. Regular eye examinations can diagnose and treat these problems in the early stages to help preserve one's vision.

COMMON VISION PROBLEMS *← set to italic*

Move problems into alphabetical order. Create hanging indents.

NEARSIGHTEDNESS – You can see objects that are close more clearly than objects that are far away.

FARSIGHTEDNESS – You can see objects that are far away more clearly than objects that are close.

ASTIGMATISM – Objects appear blurred or distorted to you at all distances because the cornea (the front of the eye) has an irregular shape.

PRESBYOPIA – An age-related change in the focusing mechanism of your eyes, usually beginning around the age of 40 to 45 years, which causes reading and near vision to be blurred.

GLAUCOMA – An increase in the internal pressure of the eye caused by a buildup of excessive fluid inside the eye.

CATARACTS – A progressive clouding of the lens of the eye which absorbs much of the light entering the eye.

KEYSTROKES

MOVE AN ENTIRE PARAGRAPH UP OR DOWN

1. Place insertion point in desired paragraph.

2. Press
   Alt + Shift + Up .... `Alt` + `Shift` + `↑`

   OR

   Press
   Alt + Shift + Dn .... `Alt` + `Shift` + `↓`

3. Repeat steps above as necessary to move paragraph to desired location.

SHRINK-TO-FIT

1. Click **File** .... `Alt` + `F`

2. Click **Print Preview** .... `V`

3. Click **Shrink to Fit** button .... [icon]
   on the Print Preview toolbar.

Exercise

33

■ **Copy and Paste** ■ **Drag and Drop**

Standard Toolbar

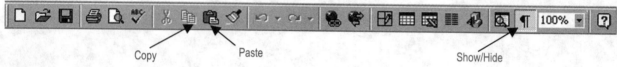

Copy   Paste   Show/Hide

NOTES

Copy and Paste

- **Copy and paste** and **drag and drop** are features that let you copy text from one location to another.

- Copying leaves text in its original location while placing a duplicate in a different location in the same document or another document. (Copying text to another document will be covered in a later lesson.) In contrast, moving removes text from its original location and places it elsewhere.

- The procedure for copying text is similar to the procedure for moving text. *(See keystrokes on page 138.)*

- You may copy text by either:

  - Highlighting it, clicking the **Copy** button 🖹 on the Standard toolbar (which temporarily copies the highlighted text to the clipboard), placing the insertion point in the desired location, and clicking the **Paste** button 🖹 on the toolbar.
    OR
  - Highlighting the text, pressing Ctrl + C to copy the text, then pressing Ctrl + V to paste the text.

- When text is copied, it remains on the screen while a copy of it is placed on the Clipboard. Text remains on the Clipboard until you copy another selection (or until you exit Windows). Therefore, you can paste the same selection into many different locations, if desired.

- Text is reinserted or retrieved from the Clipboard at the insertion point. Therefore, place the insertion point to the immediate left of where the text is to be reinserted before following the paste procedures outlined in the keystrokes.

Drag and Drop

- Use the drag and drop method to copy selected text using your mouse.

- Once text to be copied is selected, place the mouse pointer anywhere on the selected text and press the Ctrl key while **dragging** text to the new location (a box with a plus sign appears). Then **drop** a copy of the text into its new location by releasing the mouse button. Be sure to release the mouse button before releasing the Ctrl key.

- As with the Move feature, if text was not copied properly, you can undo the action.

- As with the Move feature, include the spacing following the word when copying it.

- When moving or copying paragraphs with indent formatting, be sure to include the paragraph mark along with the moved or copied text. To ensure that you do, click the Show/Hide button ¶ so the paragraph marks are visible in your document.

In Part I of this exercise, you will enhance a flyer created earlier using the copy procedure. In Part II of this exercise, you will use move and copy features to edit a previously created document.

EXERCISE DIRECTIONS

PART I

1. Open 🖮WALK, or open 💾33WALK.

2. Insert an arrow symbol to the right of the last word in the first paragraph. Copy and paste the symbol so that there are three arrows at the end of each paragraph as shown.

3. Click the Show/Hide button to display your codes.

4. Type and center **To Summarize:** in a sans serif 12-point italic font followed by three arrow symbols as shown.

5. Copy each bolded sentence as shown.

6. Center-align all summary items and unbold them. Set text to a sans serif 12-point font.

7. Add bullets preceding each summary item (use any desired bullet symbol).

8. Spell check.

9. Preview your work.

10. Print one copy.

11. Close and save the file; name it **WALK**.

PART II

1. Open 🖮DIVE, or open 💾33DIVE.

2. Insert the paragraphs indicated.

3. Single-space paragraph text.

4. Set paragraph spacing before and after the paragraphs to 0 and change the Special option from Hanging to None.

5. Copy and move hotel information as indicated.

6. Set all paragraph text to a serif 12-point font.

7. Using Format Painter, bold each hotel name.

8. Using Format Painter, apply the same font and size format to the second side heading (Hotels Offering Free Diving Instruction) as used in the first side heading.

9. Spell check.

10. Preview your work.

11. Print one copy.

12. Close and save the file; name it **DIVE**.

PART I

5 *Ways to Walk Off Weight*

copy

BURN EXTRA CALORIES.

Seize every opportunity to move around. Stand and walk instead of sitting while talking on the phone; walk around the airport instead of sitting at the gate; whatever the occasion (except eating), avoid sitting down. ☞ ☞ ☞

REMEMBER THE THREE Fs OF WALKING: FASTER, FARTHER, FREQUENTLY.

If you can do all three, go for it, but if you can do only one, that's fine. ☞ ☞ ☞

SET GOALS.

Set goals that are challenging and realistic – to walk every day for a week or to take a 4-mile-weekend hike. ☞ ☞ ☞

TAKE WALKS EVERY DAY.

Everyday walking keeps you active, and burns calories. Walk at least 20 minutes. ☞ ☞ ☞

WALK AS FAST AS YOU CAN.

Be comfortable in your walking speed. You want to feel energized as you walk and you want to have the motivation to walk again tomorrow. ☞ ☞ ☞

To Summarize: ☞ ☞ ☞

⇒ BURN EXTRA CALORIES.

⇒ REMEMBER THE THREE Fs OF WALKING: FASTER, FARTHER, FREQUENTLY.

⇒ SET GOALS.

⇒ TAKE WALKS EVERY DAY.

⇒ WALK AS FAST AS YOU CAN.

DIVING IN THE CAYMAN ISLANDS

Do you want to see sharks, barracudas, stingrays and angelfish?

The Cayman Islands were discovered by Christopher Columbus in 1503 and are located south of Cuba. The Caymans are home to about 25,000 year-around residents. However, they welcome 200,000 visitors each year. Most visitors come with masks and flippers in their luggage.

Single space; set paragraph spacing before and after to 0.

Hotel/Diving Accommodations:

Sunset House, PO Box 479, George Town, Grand Cayman; (809) 555-4767.

Coconut Harbour, PO Box 2086, George Town, Grand Cayman; (809) 555-7468.

Red Sail Sports, PO Box 1588, George Town, Grand Cayman; (809) 555-7965.

Cayman Diving Lodge, PO Box 11, East End, Grand Cayman; (809) 555-7555.

Anchorage View, PO Box 2123, 7 Mile Beach, Grand Cayman; (809) 555-4209.

Move hotels into alphabetical order.

Copy

Copy

Before you descend the depths of the ocean, it is important that you have a few lessons on the don'ts of diving. Don't touch the coral. Don't come up to the surface too fast holding your breath. If you do, your lungs will explode. Now, you are ready to jump in!

Here are some hotel suggestions:

Hotels Offering Free Diving Instruction:

Single-Space

KEYSTROKES

COPY TEXT USING TOOLBAR

1. Select text to copy.
2. Click **Copy** button .... 🔲
3. Place insertion point where text will be inserted.
4. Click **Paste** button .... 🔲

   OR

   Press **Shift** + **Insert** .... Shift + Insert

COPY TEXT USING THE KEYBOARD

1. Select text to copy.
2. Press **Shift** + **F2** .... Shift + F2

   OR

   Ctrl + **C** .... Ctrl + C
3. Position insertion point where text will be inserted.
4. Press **Enter** .... Enter

   OR

   Ctrl + **V** .... Ctrl + V

DRAG AND DROP

1. Select text to copy.
2. Hold down **Ctrl** .... Ctrl
   and point to selected text.
3. Hold down mouse button and drag text to new location.
4. Release mouse button.

NEXT EXERCISE

Exercise

34

■ **Summary**

In this exercise, you will use various formatting techniques to create a full-block letter.

EXERCISE DIRECTIONS

1. Create a NEW document.

2. Set 1" left and right margins and a 0.5" top margin.

3. Keyboard the exercise shown in Illustration A or open 🖫 **34EXPO**.

4. Format a full-block letter as shown in Illustration B on page 142:

   • Begin the letterhead At 0.5". Set the first line of the letterhead to sans serif 14 point, set font color to red, and use left alignment. (Use Swis721BlkEx BT font face, if available.) Set the first letter of each word of the company name to a 20-point font and underline. Set the remaining letterhead information to the same font in 12-point and use right alignment. Use any desired symbol to separate city, state and zip code.

   • Begin the dateline At 2".

   • Set document text to a serif 11-point font.

5. Add the following comment where indicated. "Check New York, New York hotel to see if they are offering a discount."

6. Make the revisions as shown in Illustration B on page 142.

   ✓ *When moving and copying centered text, be sure to copy the paragraph mark and the space following the text, so that the text will be centered in its new location. Click the Show/Hide button on the toolbar to display codes.*

7. Insert a bullet before each hotel. Center all hotel text.

8. Spell check.

9. Preview your work and print one copy from the print preview screen.

10. Delete comment.

11. Save the file; name it **EXPO**.

12. Close the document window.

COMPUTERLEARNINGCENTERS
987 Beverly Boulevard
Los Angeles California 90219
213-888-8888

Today's date Ms. Monique Petersen 765 Birch Lane Los Angeles, CA 90210
Dear Ms. Petersen:
We were happy to arrange your attendance at three workshops at the Las Vegas
Computer Expo next month.   Since you have not made your hotel arrangements as
yet, you might be interested to know that the following hotels have agreed to offer
discounted rates to all attendees of *Computer Expo:*
MGM Grand
Harrahs
Bally's
Caesar's Palace
Mirage
Luxor
Circus Circus
When you make your reservation, mention that you are attending the Computer
Expo at the Convention Center. A limited number of rooms are available at
preferred rates, so plan early. All hotels listed in bold above are within 15 minutes
of the Convention Center. ⌗If we can assist you with anything during your stay in
Las Vegas, please do not hesitate to call us. Sincerely,
Carole Quan Computer Expo Liaison cq/yo

ILLUSTRATION B

COMPUTERLEARNINGCENTERS

987 Beverly Boulevard
Los Angeles▯California▯90219
213-888-8888

Today's date

Ms. Monique Petersen
765 Birch Lane
Los Angeles, CA 90210

Dear Ms. Petersen:

Set to italics

We were happy to arrange your attendance at three workshops at the ⟨Las Vegas⟩ *Computer Expo*
next month.   Since you have not made your hotel arrangements as yet, you might be interested to know that the
following hotels have agreed to offer discounted rates to all attendees of *Computer Expo*.

add comment

move

copy   *move*

* ***MGM Grand***
* *Harrahs*
* *Bally's*
* ***Caesar's Palace***
* *Mirage*
* ***Luxor***
* *Circus Circus*

Set to italics

call to   *explain*
When you make your reservation, ~~mention~~ that you are attending the ⟨*Computer Expo*⟩ at the Convention Center.
A limited number of rooms are available at preferred rates, so plan early. All hotels listed in bold ~~above~~ are
below
within 15 minutes of the Convention Center.

If we can assist you with anything during your ~~stay in Las Vegas~~, please do not hesitate to call us.

Sincerely,

visit to the Computer Expo

Carole Quan
Computer Expo Liaison

cq/yo

 Hotels listed below will offer free overnight parking.

↓2x
≡
↓2x

Exercise 35

■ Summary

In this exercise, you will use various formatting techniques to create a full-block letter.

EXERCISE DIRECTIONS

1. Create a NEW document.

2. Display the Office Assistant and access any suggestions.

3. Set 1" left and right margins and 0.5" top and bottom margins.

4. Keyboard the exercise shown in Illustration A, or open 🖫**35COMPEXPO**.

5. Format a full-block letter as shown in Illustration B:
   - Begin the letterhead At 1". Center the letterhead and set 1997 to a script 48-point font. Set the remaining letterhead to the same font in 18-point. (Use the ShelleyVolante BT font face, if available.)
   - Begin the dateline At 1.5".
   - Insert today's date.
   - Use the inside address, salutation and closing shown.
   - Set document text to a serif 11-point font.

6. Print one copy.

7. Access the Track Changes feature and do the following:
   - Track the changes while editing the document text.
   - Highlight the changes on screen.
   - Highlight the changes in the printed document.

8. Make the revisions shown in illustration B.

9. Indent the event descriptions 1" from the left and right margins to create indented paragraphs.

10. Change the first event title to a sans serif 12-point bold font. Using Format Painter, copy the font face, size and bolding to the other headings.

11. Set the text below the first event description to italic. Using Format Painter, copy the italics to the other descriptions.

12. Set 4-point paragraph spacing after each event description except the last one.

13. Spell check.

14. Save the edited document as **EXPOA**.

15. Print one copy.

16. Accept all changes.

17. Turn off the Track Changes feature.

18. Preview your work and print one copy from the print preview screen.

19. Save the file; name it **COMPEXPO**.

20. Close the document window.

1997 Computer Expo, Las Vegas, Nevada

I strongly urge you to attend this year's <u>Computer Expo</u>. In four days, you will pick up the latest computer news and discover new ways to put your computer to work—in the office, in the lab, in the studio, in the classroom, or in your home.

If you are interested in attending, call Harvey West at 1-800-555-5555. He will pre-register anyone who wishes to attend. This will save you long lines at the show. The pre-registration fee is $150.00. Onsight registration will be an additional $25.00.

Here are some of the events you can look forward to:

Keynote Sessions.

These sessions will feature luminaries from the computer world who will offer you insights from industry.
Application Workshops.
These sessions will provide hands-on experience on the latest software. Tips, new features, and "how-to's" will be presented.
Programmer/Developer Forums.
Veteran and novice computer users will brainstorm so you can learn about innovative advances and techniques.

ShelleyVolante BT
48 pt

ShelleyVolante BT
18 pt

Remove underline;
set to italics

1997 Computer Expo, Las Vegas, Nevada *center*

I strongly urge you to attend this year's <u>Computer Expo</u>. In four days, you will pick up the latest computer news and discover new ways to put your computer to work—in the office, in the lab, in the studio, in the classroom, or in your home.

If you are interested in attending, call Harvey West at 1-800-555-5555. He will pre-register anyone who wishes to attend. This will save you long lines at the show. The pre-registration fee is $150.00. Onsight registration will be an additional $25.00.

Site

move

Here are some of the events you can look forward to:

<u>Keynote Sessions.</u>
These sessions will feature luminaries from the computer world who will offer you insights from industry.
<u>Application Workshops.</u>
These sessions will provide hands-on experience on the latest software. Tips, new features, and "how-to's" will be presented.
<u>Programmer/Developer Forums.</u>
Veteran and novice computer users will brainstorm so you can learn about innovative advances and techniques.

<u>Internet Information Sessions.</u>
These sessions will explore the world of the Internet. Web browsers, terminology, mail boxes, and other vital information needed to connect to the information superhighway will be discussed.

Sincerely,

4x

Gail Saco
Expo Coordinator

gs/yo

Today's date

Mr. Scott Morgan
Corporate Training Director
McKinsey and Stone, Inc.
55 Ridge Way
Portland, OR 97208-9807

Dear Mr. Morgan:

DESIRED RESULT

1997 Computer Expo, Las Vegas, Nevada

Today's date

Mr. Scott Morgan
Corporate Training Director
McKinsey and Stone, Inc.
55 Ridge Way
Portland, OR 97208-9807

Dear Mr. Morgan:

I strongly urge you to attend this year's *Computer Expo*. In four days, you will pick up the latest computer news and discover new ways to put your computer to work—in the office, in the lab, in the studio in the classroom, or in your home.

Here are some of the events you can look forward to:

Application Workshops.
These sessions will provide hands-on experience on the latest software.
Tips, new features, and "how-to's" will be presented.

Internet Information Sessions.
These sessions will explore the world of the Internet. Web browsers,
terminology, mailboxes, and other vital information needed to connect to
the information superhighway will be discussed.

Keynote Sessions.
These sessions will feature luminaries from the computer world who will
offer you insights from industry.

Programmer/Developer Forums.
Veteran and novice computer users will brainstorm so you can learn
about innovative advances and techniques.

If you are interested in attending, call Harvey West at 1-800-555-5555. He will pre-register anyone who wishes to attend. This will save you long lines at the show. The pre-registration fee is $150.00. Onsite registration will be an additional $25.00.

Sincerely,

Gail Saco
Expo Coordinator

gs/yo

Word 97

LESSON 6

Additional Formatting and Editing

- Create a Memo Using a Template
- Thesaurus
- Use a Template Wizard
- Letter Wizard
- Find Text
- Replace Text
- Hyphenate Text
- Create a Résumé
- Styles
- The Outline Feature
- Create an Outline
- Enter Outline Text
- Edit an Outline
- Create/Edit a Word Style

Exercise 36

■ **Create a Memo Using a Template** ■ **Thesaurus**

NOTES

Create a Memo Using a Template

■ A **memo** is a written communication within a company. Word contains predesigned memos called templates. A **template** is a skeleton document that may contain formatting, pictures, and/or text. It may be used over and over again to create new documents.

■ In addition to creating memos using Word's predesigned templates, you can create faxes, letters, and resumes (as well as other documents).

■ To use a template, select <u>N</u>ew from the <u>F</u>ile menu. In the New dialog box that follows, select the desired tab and template style.

New Dialog Box

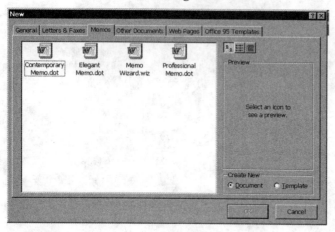

■ For each template group, there are usually several styles from which to choose. The memos group provides three styles: Contemporary, Elegant and Professional. To view a style, select the template; a sample appears in the Preview window.

■ Many template groups also offer a Wizard option. *(Wizards will be covered in Exercise 37.)*

■ If you select Professional Memo as your desired template, a predesigned memo form appears. The date is pulled from the computer's memory and automatically inserted in the proper location. Highlight the bracketed information (including the company name) and enter the relevant information for your memo.

■ Pressing Enter will automatically double return at the end of a paragraph.

Thesaurus

- The **Thesaurus** feature lists the meanings, synonyms and antonyms (if any) of a desired word and also indicates the part of speech of each meaning.

Thesaurus Dialog Box

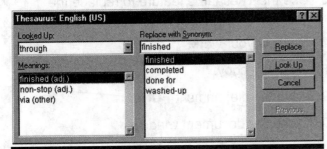

- Note the Thesaurus dialog box in which the word "try" was looked up. You may replace a word in your document with a word listed in the thesaurus by clicking the desired meaning, then selecting the desired synonym (or antonym) and clicking the Replace button. It is sometimes necessary to edit the new word so it fits properly in the sentence *(for example, singular/plural endings)*.

- If you are using the Thesaurus to look up a plural word and it does not produce sufficient synonyms, try looking up the singular form of the word.

- Select the word you want to look up and press Shift+F7 to open the Thesaurus dialog box.

- You can also select the Tools menu, select Language, then Thesaurus to open the dialog box.

    ✓Note: *If Thesaurus does not appear on the Language submenu, you will have to install the Thesaurus.*

In this exercise, you will use a template to create a memorandum and use the Thesaurus feature to replace the highlighted words shown in the exercise.

EXERCISE DIRECTIONS

1. Select New from the File menu; select the Memos Tab.

2. Preview each memo template.

3. Use the Professional Memo template to create the memo illustrated on the following page.

4. Highlight the bracketed prompts and enter the following relevant information:

   Company Name:........ Mark Mutual Funds
   To: .... Mutual Fund Salespeople
   From: ....Pamela Davis
   CC: ....Ira Altchek
   Re:............................. Transaction Fees

5. Type the memo text as shown.

6. Use the Thesaurus feature to replace the highlighted words.

7. Preview your work.

8. Print one copy.

9. Save the file; name it **FUND**.

10. Close the document window.

KEYSTROKES

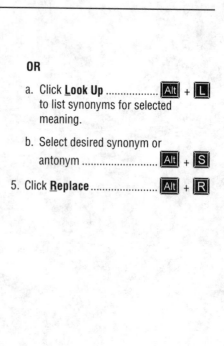

ACCESS TEMPLATES

1. Click **F**ile .... Alt + F

2. Click **N**ew .... N

3. Click **Tab** for desired template group:

   • **Publications**

   • **General**

   • **Memos**

   • **Letters and Faxes**

   • **Reports**

   • **Web Pages**

   • **Legal Pleadings**

   • **Other Documents**

4. Click desired template style.

5. Click **OK**................................... Enter

6. Click prompts and enter appropriate information.

THESAURUS

1. Place insertion point in word to look up.

   OR

   Select word to look up.

2. Press **Shift + F7** .... Shift + F7

   OR

   a. Click **T**ools...................... Alt + T

   b. Click **L**anguage L

   c. Click **T**hesaurus........................ T

3. Select desired meaning...................... Alt + M , ↓

4. Select .... Alt + S , ↓ desired replacement.

   OR

   a. Click **L**ook Up .... Alt + L to list synonyms for selected meaning.

   b. Select desired synonym or antonym .... Alt + S

5. Click **R**eplace .... Alt + R

Memo

To: Mutual Fund Salespeople

From: Pamela Davis

CC: Ira Altchek

Date: Today's date

Re: Transaction Fees

When you communicate with your clients, be sure to emphasize our **Mutual Fund MasterSource Service**. Clients can buy and sell Mutual MasterSource funds at net asset value, without commissions or transaction fees. To offset the costs of short-term trading, our standard transaction fee is charged on each redemption of MasterSource fund shares purchased with no transaction fee and held for 90 days or less.

We retain the right to assess the standard transaction fee in the future, should short-term trading become excessive.

PD/

● Page 1

Exercise 37

■ **Use a Template Wizard** ■ **Letter Wizard**

NOTES

Use a Template Wizard

■ Some template groups contain a Wizard option (such as Memo Wizard, Letter Wizard, Fax Wizard, etc.) as one of the template styles listed in the New dialog box.

New Dialog Box

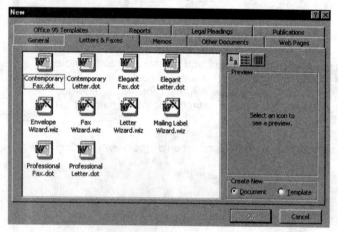

■ **Wizards** walk you through the steps for creating and sending a document.

The Letter Wizard

■ When you access Letter Wizard, for example, the following dialog box appears. The Office Assistant will automatically appear to guide you through the stages of creating a letter. You will be prompted to indicate whether you want to Send one letter or Send letters to a mailing list (multiple recipients).

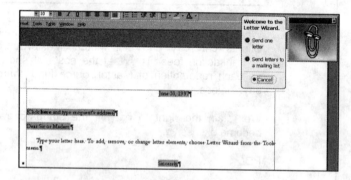

■ If you select the Send one letter option, the following Letter Wizard dialog box displays.

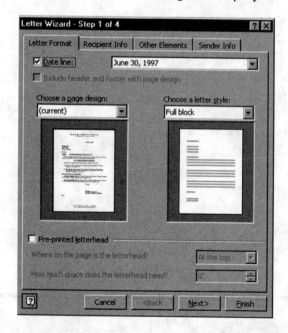

- Click the Choose a page design list arrow and select an option. Click the Choose a letter style list arrow and select an option. The preview window displays your selection. Click the Next button, which will bring you to the Recipient Info tab. Fill out the information in that tab and click the Next button again.

- Continue this procedure until all the information in all the tabs has been filled out. Then click Finish. You will be prompted to indicate whether you wish to Make an envelope, Make a mailing label, Rerun the Letter Wizard, or click Cancel to begin working on the letter.

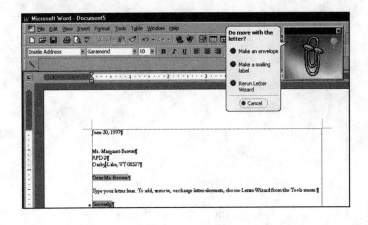

In this exercise, you will use the Letter Wizard to create a letter. You will then use the Thesaurus and Grammar Check features to edit it.

EXERCISE DIRECTIONS

1. Create a NEW document.

2. Select the Letters & Faxes tab.

3. Use the Letter Wizard to create one letter illustrated on the following page.

4. Complete the Letter Format tab information as follows:
   - Use a contemporary letter page design.
   - Use a full-block letter style.

5. Complete the Recipient Info as follows:
   - Send this letter to:
     Ms. Iris Torres
     45 Tryon Park Lane
     New York, NY 10027
   - Select Formal as the Salutation type; change the punctuation after the salutation to a colon.

6. Complete the Other Elements information as follows:
   - Include a subject that reads:
     Our Magazine Program

7. Complete the Sender information as follows:
   - Use your name as the sender.
   - Use Sincerely as the closing.
   - Use Subscription Manager as the Job Title.
   - Include your initials only.
   - Include an enclosure notation.

8. Do not prepare an envelope at this time.

9. Type the letter shown in the illustration on the next page, including the circled grammatical error.

10. Use the Thesaurus feature to substitute the highlighted words.

11. Use the Grammar feature to grammar check the document. Accept Word's suggestions for correcting errors.

12. Preview your work.

13. Center the page vertically.

14. Print one copy.

15. Save the file; name it **MAG**.

16. Close the document window.

June 28, 1997

Ms. Iris Torres
45 Tryon Park Lane
New York, NY 10027

Dear Ms. Torres:

Subject: Our Magazine Program

As you know, the magazine program offers our members a very extensive list of titles at discounted rates. In addition to the popular titles that appears on our printed lists, we have several hundred others available. Call us if you wish to order a magazine not on our regular list or ask for our "extended" list to be sent to you.

Although we offer hundreds of titles, members frequently ask us to obtain discounts on additional titles. I am pleased to report that we have recently obtained significant discounts on a selection of some special titles. Look over our updated list, select a magazine for yourself as a gift, and enjoy the savings, convenience and service.

A magazine subscription is a nice gift for the graduate, particularly someone who will be away at college next year. Review the large selection on the attached list, and place your order today!

Sincerely,

Your Name
Subscription Manager

yo
enclosure

June 28, 1997

Ms. Iris Torres
45 Tryon Park Lane
New York, NY 10027

Dear Ms. Torres:

Subject: Our Magazine Program

As you know, our magazine program offers members a very extensive list of titles at discounted rates.
In addition to the popular titles that appear on our printed lists, we have several hundred others
available. Call us if you wish to order a magazine not on our regular list or ask for our "extended" list
to be sent to you.

Although we offer hundreds of titles, members frequently ask us to obtain discounts on additional
titles. I am pleased to report that we have recently obtained significant discounts on a selection of
some special titles. Look over our updated list, select a magazine for yourself as a gift, and enjoy the
savings, convenience and service.

A magazine subscription is a nice gift for the graduate, particularly someone who will be away at
college next year. Review the large selection on the attached list, and place your order today!

Sincerely,

Your Name
Subscription Manager

Enclosure (1)

yo

KEYSTROKES

CREATE A LETTER USING LETTER WIZARD

1. Click **File** .... `Alt` + `F`
2. Click **New** .... `N`
3. Click **Letters and Memos** tab.
4. Double-click **Letter Wizard**.
   - ✓ *The Office Assistant appears on top of the letter template.*
5. Click **send one letter** in Office Assistant bubble.

IN LETTER FORMAT DIALOG BOX

6. Select desired options:
   - Check **Date line** .... `Alt` + `D` to include date.
   - Click **Date line** drop-down list box ..... `Tab` `↓`, `Enter` and select date format.
   - Click **Choose a page design** .... `Alt` + `P`, `↓`, `Enter` list box and select design.
   - Click **Choose a letter style** .... `Alt` + `S`, `↓`, `Enter` list box and select style.
   - Click **pre-printed letterhead** .... `Alt` + `L` if you plan to print letter on letterhead stationery.

   To allow sufficient space for letterhead:
   - Click **Where on the page** ..... `Alt` +, `W`, `↓`, `Enter` **is the letterhead** and select location.
   - Click **How much space** .... `Alt` + `O`, *number* **does the letterhead need?** and enter amount.

7. Click **Next** .... `Alt` + `N`

IN RECIPIENT INFO DIALOG BOX

8. Select desired options:
   - Click **Recipient's name** .... `Alt` + `R`, *name* and enter name.
   - Click **Delivery address** .... `Tab` `↓`, *address* and enter information.
   - Click **Example drop-down** list .... `Alt` + `E`, `↓`, `Enter` and select desired Salutation (or enter your own text).
   - Select desired salutation style:
   - " **Informal** .... `Alt` + `I`
   - " **Formal** .... `Alt` + `M`
   - " **Business** .... `Alt` + `U`
   - " **Other** .... `Alt` + `O`
9. Click **Next** .... `Alt` + `N`

IN OTHER ELEMENTS DIALOG BOX

10. Select additional options, if desired.
    - Click **Reference line** .... `Alt` + `R` and select from list, or enter text.
    - Click Mailing **instructions** .... `Alt` + `M` and select from list or enter text.
    - Click **Attention** .... `Alt` + `T` and select from list or enter text.
    - Click **Subject** .... `Alt` + `S` and select from list or enter text.
    - Click **Courtesy copies (cc)** .... `Alt` + `O`, *names* and enter names of people to receive copies.
11. Click **Next** .... `Alt` + `N`

IN SENDER INFO DIALOG BOX

12. Select desired options.
    - Click **Sender's name** .... `Alt` + `S` and select from list or enter name.
    - Click **Return address** .... `Alt` + `R` and enter address.

    OR
    - Click **Omit** .... `Alt` + `M` to leave return address out of letter.l
    - Click **Complimentary closing** .... `Alt` + `Y` and select from list or enter text.
    - Click **Job title** .... `Alt` + `J`, *title* and enter title.
    - Click **Company** .... `Alt` + `O`, *name* and enter company name.
    - Click **Writer/typist initials** .... `Alt` + `W`, *initials* and enter initials.

    If you want to include an enclosure:
    - Click **Enclosures** . `Alt` + `E`, *number* and enter number.
13. Click **Finish** .... `F`
14. Select desired option from the Office Assistant bubble:
    - **Make an envelope**
    - **Make a mailing label**
    - **Rerun Letter Wizard**

    OR
    - **Cancel** .... `Esc` to go directly to the document.
15. Compose, edit and save the letter as usual.

NEXT EXERCISE

Exercise 38

■ **Find Text** ■ **Replace Text** ■ **Hyphenate Text**

NOTES

Find Text

■ The **Find** feature will scan your document and search for occurrences of specified text, symbols or formatting. Once the desired text or formatting is found, it can be edited or replaced.

■ You can access Find by selecting <u>F</u>ind from the <u>E</u>dit menu. In the Find and Replace dialog box that follows, type the text to search for in the Fi<u>n</u>d what box.

■ To narrow your search, click the <u>M</u>ore button to display more options.

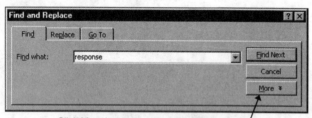

Click <u>M</u>ore button to reveal all search options.

■ You may instruct Word to find only those occurrences of the specified search text that match the capitalization pattern of the search text. In the Find and Replace dialog box illustrated below, all occurrences of the word "response" will be found, regardless of the capitalization, since Matc<u>h</u> Case was not selected.

Click <u>L</u>ess button to hide additional options.

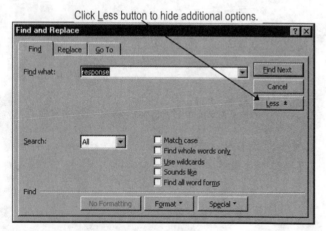

■ You can also access Find by clicking the Select Browse Object button on the vertical scroll bar and clicking the Find icon.

Find icon

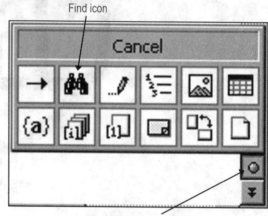

Select Browse Object button

■ You can instruct Word to find separate, whole words rather than characters embedded in other words by selecting the Find whole words onl<u>y</u> option. For example, if this option is *not* selected, a search for the word "and" would find not only "and" but also *sand, candy, Sandusky, android*, etc. It can be helpful to select the Find whole words onl<u>y</u> option, particularly when you are searching for short words.

■ The Sounds li<u>k</u>e check box looks up homonyms (words that sound alike, but are spelled differently) of a word. If you search for the word *sight*, you will also find *cite* and *site*.

■ The Find all word for<u>m</u>s check box looks for all the grammatical forms of a word.

■ The <u>S</u>earch text box contains options for the direction of the search. Word can search a document from the insertion point Down or Up, or it can search the entire document if All is selected.

Replace Text

- The **Replace** feature allows you to locate all occurrences of certain text and *replace* it with different text. In addition to text, you may also search for and replace occurrences of special characters such as tab symbols or paragraph marks, or formatting, such as italic, subscript or indented text.

- You can access Replace by selecting Replace from the Edit menu or by clicking the Replace tab in the Find dialog box. In the Replace dialog box that follows, indicate what you wish to find and what wish to replace it with.

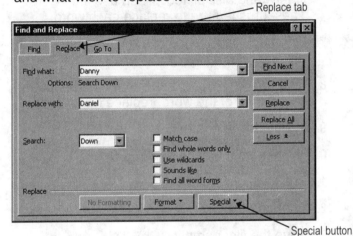

Replace tab

Special button

- To replace all occurrences of text or special characters without confirmation, click Replace All. To find the next occurrence, click Find Next or Cancel.

- To search for and replace special characters, click the Special button in the Replace dialog box and select the desired character from the pop-up list (*see below*).

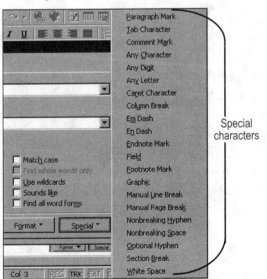

Special characters

- Turn on the Show/Hide codes feature to assist you when searching for and replacing special characters.

Hyphenate Text

- Hyphenating text produces a tighter right margin. If text is justified and hyphenated, the sentences will have smaller gaps between words. Turn on the hyphenation feature when you justify text.

- To automatically hyphenate your document, select Language from the Tools menu, then select Hyphenation. In the Hyphenation dialog box that follows, click the Automatically hyphenate document check box.

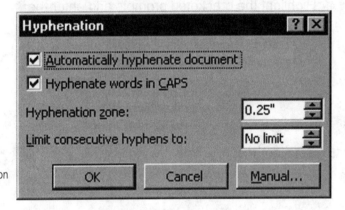

- You may change the distance from the right margin in which to allow hyphenation by changing the Hyphenation zone. *Increase* the width of the zone to hyphenate *fewer* words; *decrease* to hyphenate *more* words.

- If you wish to limit the number of consecutive hyphens, indicate the desired number in the Limit consecutive hyphens to text box.

- Word adds hyphens according to its rules without asking for confirmation from the user.

- To insert manual hyphens, click the Manual button. Word will stop and prompt you for confirmation at each word it suggests should be hyphenated.

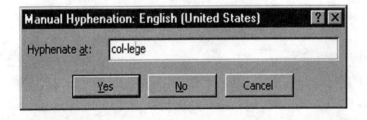

> *In this exercise, you will create a letter using the Contemporary Letter template. You will then use the Find and Replace feature to find and replace words in the document and hyphenate to produce a tighter right margin.*
>
> ✓*Note:* *The template style used in this exercise is the same as the template in the previous exercise. A company may use the same template style to prepare different documents to maintain uniformity of headings and document formatting.*

EXERCISE DIRECTIONS

1. Create a NEW document.

2. Use the Contemporary Letter template to create the letter illustrated on the following page.

3. Use the default margins and font sizes.

4. Highlight the bracketed prompts and enter the following information:

Company Name:	Select Investments, Inc.
Return Address:	60 Wall Street
	New York, NY 10001
	1-555-7SELECT
	http://www.selectvest.com
Slogan:	We SELECT the Best!

5. Set side headings to bold and italic.

6. Use the Find feature to place your insertion point on each of the following words: predicted, timely, and disciplined. Then use the Thesaurus feature to replace each word.

7. Find each occurrence of the word *market* and replace with *markets*.

8. Find the word *Fund*, and except for the last occurrence of the word, replace it with *fund*.

9. Justify document text.

10. Hyphenate the document.

11. Preview your work.

12. Print one copy.

13. Save the file; name it **SELECT**.

14. Close the document window.

60 Wall Street
New York, NY 10001
1-800-7SELECT
http://www.selectvest.com

Select Investments, Inc.

April 24, 1997

Ms. Anne Beyer
65 Pineapple Street
Brooklyn, NY 11201

Dear Shareholder:

We are pleased to present this Annual Report for the U.S. Government Fund, Balanced Fund, and Equity Fund for the fiscal year ended October 31, 1997.

U.S. Markets Soar in 1997

The U.S. financial markets soared in 1997 as investors correctly predicted. It was an outstanding year for U.S. Equity Fund investors. Bond investors also did well, with the yield on 30-year Treasury bonds dropping from 7.96% to 6.32% over the 12-month period, boosting the value of bonds to new highs.

Strong Stock and Bond Sales Raise Investor's Returns

The Select Fund performed well during the period under review. This was largely a result of both the positive economic environment for the U.S. financial market and timely stock and bond selection decisions by fund managers.

As always, we recommend that investors take a long-term disciplined approach to the market. By leaving your money invested for the long term, you will be better able to ride out the down periods.

We appreciate your confidence in SELECT.

Sincerely,

Jillian Mehotra
Chairperson

jm/yo

We SELECT the Best!

KEYSTROKES

FIND TEXT

CTRL + F

1. Click **Select Browse Object**............ 🔘
2. Click **Find**............................... 🔍
   OR
1. Click **Edit**........................... Alt + E
2. Click **Find**............................... F
3. Click **Fi̱nd What**................... Alt + N
4. Type desired search text .... *text*
5. Click **More**........................... Alt + M
   if necessary, to display
   the options listed below.
6. Select desired search options:
   - **Match case**.................... Alt + H
   - **Find whole words only**.... Alt + Y
   - **Use wildcards**................. Alt + U
   - **Sounds like**.................... Alt + K
   - **Find all word forms**........ Alt + M
7. Click **Search**........................ Alt + S
8. Select a search direction:
   - Click **All**.. A
     to search entire document.
   - Click **Up**....................................... U
     to search from insertion point
     to beginning of document.
   - Click **Down**.................................. D
     to search from insertion point
     to end of document.
9. Click **Find Next**.................... Alt + F
   OR
   Press **Enter**........................... Enter
   to find next occurrence
   of search text.
10. Click **Find** next.................... Alt + F
    to skip current occurrence and find
    next one.
    OR
    Click **Cancel**........................... Enter
    to return to document at point
    where most recently located
    search text appears.

REPLACE TEXT OR SPECIAL CHARACTERS

1. Click **Edit**........................... Alt + E
2. Click **Replace**............................ E
3. Click **More**........................... Alt + M
   if necessary, to display
   all the Replace options.
4. Click **Fi̱nd What**................... Alt + N
5. Type desired search text................ *text*
   OR
   a. Click **Special**.................. Alt + E
   b. Select special
      character.............. ↓, ↑, Enter
6. Select **No Formatting**.......... Alt + T
   if necessary, so Word does
   not search for formatting.
   OR
   a. Click **Format**................. Alt + O
   b. Select type of formatting
      to replace.............. ↓, ↑, Enter
   c. Select formatting options to replace
      from dialog box that follows.
7. Click **Replace with**............. Alt + I
8. Type replacement text .... *text*
   OR
   a. Click **Special**.................. Alt + E
   b. Select special
      character................ ↓, ↑ Enter
9. Click **No Formatting**........... Alt + T
   if necessary, to replace found text with
   unformatted text.
   OR
   a. Click **Format**.................. Alt + O
   b. Select format type from
      pop-up list .... ↓, ↑ Enter
   c. Select replacement formatting
      from dialog box.
10. Select a search option:
    - **Match case**.................... Alt + H
    - **Find whole words only** .... Alt + Y
    - **Use wildcards**................. Alt + U
    - **Sounds like**.................... Alt + K
    - **Find all word forms** .... Alt + M

11. Click **Find Next**.................... Alt + F
    to find next occurrence.
12. Click **Replace**..................... Alt + R
    to replace this occurrence.
    OR
    Click **Replace All**.............. Alt + A
    to replace all occurrences of
    search text.
13. Click **Find Next**.................... Alt + F
    as necessary to search
    through entire document.
14. Click **Cancel**..................... Enter
    to return to document at point
    where most recently located
    search text appears.

HYPHENATE (AUTOMATIC OR MANUAL)

1. Select text to hyphenate.
   OR
   Place insertion point where
   hyphenation will begin.
2. Click **Tools**........................... Alt + T
3. Click **Language**......................... L
4. Click **Hyphenation** .... H
5. Click **Automatically**............... Alt + A
   hyphenate document check box.
6. Click **OK**................................. Enter
   OR
   a. Click **Manual**................. Alt + M
      to have Word prompt
      each hyphen.
   b. Click **Yes**........................ Alt + Y
      to accept suggested hyphen.
      OR
      Click **No**.......................... Alt + N
      to reject suggested hyphen.
      OR
      Click to place the insertion point
      where you want hyphen inserted.
   c. Click **Yes**........................ Alt + Y
   d. Press **Cancel**......................... Esc
      to end hyphenation process.
      OR
      Click **OK**............................ Enter
      when hyphenation is complete.

NEXT EXERCISE

Exercise 39

■ **Create a Résumé** ■ **Styles**

NOTES

Create a Résumé

- A résumé is a document that lists your experience, skills and abilities. It is used to gain employment.

- Résumé formats vary depending on the extent of your education and work experience. Unless education and work experience are extensive, résumés should not exceed one page.

- You may access Résumé templates by selecting New from the File menu. In the New dialog box that follows, select the Other Documents tab. Word provides three résumé template styles: Contemporary, Elegant and Professional, as well as a Résumé wizard.

  ✓*Note:* *If you do not see the Other Documents tab, all templates may not have been installed during the typical installation procedure. See software documentation for full installation directions. If a Shortcuts tab is visible, you may access Résumé templates from there. The Résumé templates in the Shortcuts tab have different formats than those under the Other Documents tab.*

- If the résumé template you select does not contain the subheadings you desire, you can edit the subheadings or create new subheading information. Using the Résumé wizard (see right) allows you to easily customize your résumé with the subheadings you desire.

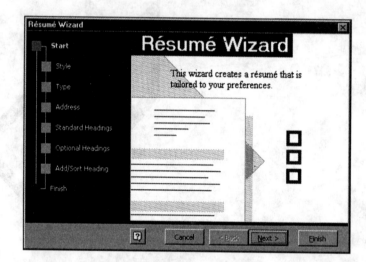

- When you create additional subheading information, you will want to apply the same *style* to the text so that the font face, size and alignments are consistent throughout the document.

Styles

- A style is a collection of formats you can assign to selected text. Templates contain various formatting styles that have been assigned by Word. After you select the template you desire, click on a word in the template and note the style that was applied in the Style drop-down list box on the Formatting toolbar.

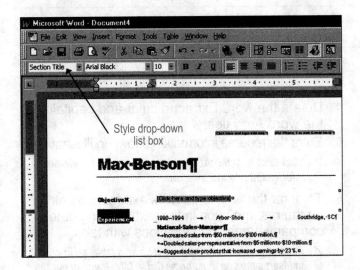

Style drop-down list box

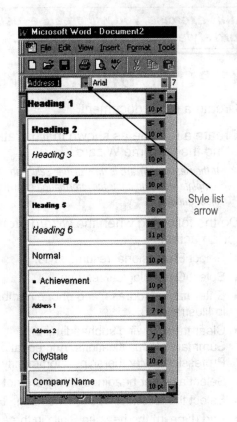

Style list arrow

- For example, the Section Title style applies left-aligned, 10-point Arial Black formatting to text. The Section Title style is used for all the side headings shown in the Professional Résumé template.

- To use a Word style, select the text to which you wish to apply a style. Click the Style list arrow on the Formatting toolbar. Then select a desired style from the style list.

> *In this exercise, you will create a résumé using the Résumé wizard and apply the appropriate Word style to new subheading text.*

EXERCISE DIRECTIONS

1. Create a NEW document.

2. Create a résumé as shown in Illustration A using the Résumé Wizard.

   ✓ *If the Résumé Wizard is unavailable, select any Résumé template style and enter the information shown in Illustration B.*

3. Do the following when the wizard prompts you for an action:
   - Select Professional résumé style.
   - Select Chronological résumé.
   - Enter name, address, and phone number shown in Illustration B.
   - Clear the following subheadings: Summary of Qualifications, Accreditations, Professional Memberships, Community Activities.
   - Select all other headings if they are not checked.
   - Select the following optional heading: Hobbies.
   - Add (type in) the heading Skills in the Add/Sort Heading screen.
   - Change the order of the subheadings to match those in Illustration B.
   - Click Finish to display résumé document.

4. Delete the word Extracurricular and capitalize the word Activities.

5. Enter the résumé information shown in Illustration B.

   ✓ *Click once to highlight bracketed text, then type relevant information into that location.*

6. To enter the additional work experience entries on the resume, type in the text, dividing dates, company names and locations with tabs.

   ✓ *Important: This document is set up as a table, so in order to insert a tab you must press Ctrl + Tab. If you press Tab, you will move to another area in the resume. You will learn about tables in Lesson 9.*

7. Apply the appropriate styles used in the first entry. (For example, click on Company/Institution Name and note that the style used in the first entry was Company Name. Highlight the second Company Name, click on Style list and select Company Name.)

8. Spell check.

9. Preview your work.

10. Print one copy.

11. Save the file; name it **RESUME**.

12. Close the document window.

Address
City, State Zip
Home xxx-xxx-xxxx

Sample

Objective	[Type Objective Here]
Work experience	19xx - 19xx [Company/Institution Name] [City, State]
	[Job Title]
	■ [Details of position, award, or achievement.]
Education	19xx - 19xx [Company/Institution Name] [City, State]
	[Degree/Major]
	■ [Details of position, award, or achievement.]
Extracurricular activities	[Click here and enter information.]
Hobbies	[Click here and enter information.]
References	[Click here and enter information.]

ILLUSTRATION B

201 East 79 Street
New York, NY 10021
Phone 212-555-5555

Pamela Tricia Blane

Objective	To secure a position as a bond trader

Work experience

July 1995-Present   J.P. Gordan   New York, NY
Sales and Trading Trainee
- Rotating on various trading desks to learn transactions and activities.

June-August 1992   J.P. Gordan   New York, NY
Intern in Corporate Finance Department
- Responsible for department correspondence, files and records.

February-June 1991   Rose and Hutton   New York, NY
Administrative Assistant
- Performed administrative tasks.

Summer 1990   Camp Chen-A-Way   Thompson, PA
Administrative Assistant
- Performed administrative tasks.

Education

1991-1995   Yale University   New Haven, CT
Bachelor of Arts/History
- GPA: 3.88

Activities   Yale Freshman Chorus; Assistant Editor and Staff Writer, *The Yale Political Monthly*; Aerobics; Tutor of English as a Second Language.

Hobbies   Reading, cooking, aerobics

Skills   Fluent in Spanish; Keyboarding: 50 wpm; IBM PC: WordPerfect for Windows, Microsoft Office for Windows 95.

References   Will be furnished upon request.

KEYSTROKES

RÉSUMÉ WIZARD

✓ *The following directions cover how to use the Résumé Wizard to set up the style of resume used in this exercise. They can be adapted to create the other resumes available when you select Résumé Wizard.*

1. Click **File**............................ `Alt` + `F`

2. Click **New**................................ `N`

3. Click **Other Documents** tab

4. Click **Résumé Wizard**.

5. Click **OK** .... `Enter`

6. Click **Next**......................... `Alt` + `N`
   in **Résumé Wizard** Start window.

IN STYLE SELECTION

1. Select desired résumé style:

   • **Professional** .... `Alt` + `P`

   • **Contemporary**............ `Alt` + `C`

   • **Elegant** .... `Alt` + `E`

2. Click **Next**......................... `Alt` + `N`

IN TYPE OF RESUME

1. Select type of résumé:

   • **Entry-level résumé** ...... `Alt` + `E`

   • **Chronological**............. `Alt` + `C`

   • **Functional résumé** ..... `Alt` + `U`

   • **Professional résumé**... `Alt` + `P`

2. Click **Next**......................... `Alt` + `N`

IN ADDRESS ENTRY WINDOW

1. Enter desired information in appropriate text boxes:

   • **Name** .... `Alt` + `M`

   • **Address**.................. `Alt` + `A`

   • **Phone** .... `Alt` + `P`

   • **Fax** .... `Alt` + `X`

   • **Email** .... `Alt` + `E`

2. Click **Next**...................... `Alt` + `N`

IN STANDARD HEADINGS

1. Select desired headings for résumé:

   • **Objective** .... `Alt` + `O`

   • **Summary of qualifications**.............. `Alt` + `Q`

   • **Work experience** .... `Alt` + `W`

   • **Education**................. `Alt` + `D`

   • **Extracurricular activities** .... `Alt` + `X`

   • **Accreditations** .... `Alt` + `A`

   • **Professional memberships** .... `Alt` + `M`

   • **Community activities** .. `Alt` + `C`

   • **References** .... `Alt` + `R`

2. Click **Next**........................... `Alt` + `N`

IN OPTIONAL HEADINGS

1. Select desired optional headings for resumé:

   • **Interests and activities** .... `Alt` + `I`

   • **Volunteer experience** .. `Alt` + `V`

   • **Patents and publications** .... `Alt` + `P`

   • **Languages** .... `Alt` + `L`

   • **Security clearance**....... `Alt` + `S`

   • **Civil service grades**.... `Alt` + `G`

   • **Awards received** .... `Alt` + `A`

   • **Hobbies**...................... `Alt` + `H`

2. Click **Next** .... `Alt` + `N`

IN ADD/SORT HEADING

1. Enter additional headings, if desired .... `Alt` + `A`

To rearrange headings:

   a. Click heading to move.

   b. Click **Move Up** .... `Alt` + `U`

   OR

   Click **Move Down** .... `Alt` + `D`

   OR

   Click **Remove**.................... `Alt` + `R`
   to delete a heading.

2. Click **Next**...................... `Alt` + `N`

3. Click **Finish** .... `Enter`

USE A WORD STYLE

1. Select the text to receive the Word style.

2. Click the Style list arrow on the Formatting toolbar.

3. Click the desired style.

Exercise

40

■ **The Outline Feature** ■ **Create an Outline** ■ **Enter Outline Text**

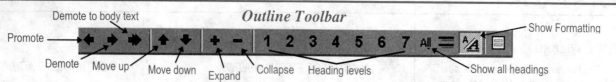

Outline Toolbar

Demote to body text — Promote — Demote — Move up — Move down — Expand — Collapse — Heading levels — Show all headings — Show Formatting

NOTES

The Outline Feature

- A **traditional outline** is used to organize information about a subject before you begin writing a report or delivering a speech.

- An outline contains many topics and subtopics, or levels. The **Outline Feature** automatically formats each level of topics and subtopics differently. Some levels are bolded, some are italicized, and some appear in different font sizes. Word allows up to nine different levels.

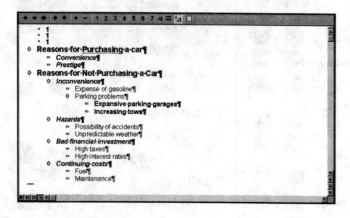

Create an Outline

- To create an outline, Select Outline from the View menu or click the Outline View button. Outline view allows you to see your document in outline format and provides an Outline toolbar to make outlining tasks easier.

Enter Outline Text

- It is easier to type your outline in Outline view, since the level formatting styles are applied as you type. When typing an outline in Outline view, type as you would normally. Use the Tab or click the Demote button on the Outline toolbar to move a heading down a level (to the right). Press Shift + Tab or Click the Promote button to move a heading up a level (to the left).

- Each level is preceded by a heading symbol: or . The plus sign indicates that subheadings associated with the heading are present. A minus sign indicates that no subheadings are below the heading.

- To number and letter the topics and subtopics as you would in a traditional outline, you must use a separate procedure. Select Bullets and Numbering from the Format menu, then click the Outline Numbered tab. Select the desired numbering style and click OK.

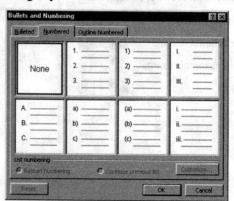

- If you prepare an outline on a single page, the outline generally begins 2" from the top of the page and has a centered heading. A triple space follows the title.

In Part I of this exercise, you will create a topic outline. The outline you create will contain five levels. The keystroke procedures are provided in the exercise directions for Part I. In Part II of this exercise, you will gain more practice creating a topic outline.

EXERCISE DIRECTIONS

PART I

1. Create a NEW document and type the outline shown in Illustration A.

2. Begin the exercise at the top of the page.

3. Set the left margin to 1.75".

4. Click the Outline View button 📄, or select View, Outline to change to Outline view.

5. Key first level heading, *Reasons for Purchasing a Car*.

6. Press the Enter key.

7. Press the Tab key.

8. Key the second level heading, *Convenience*.

9. Press the Enter key.

10. Key the next second level heading, *Prestige*.
    - ✓ There is no need to promote or demote since this heading has the same rank as the preceding heading.

11. Press the Enter key.

12. Click the Promote button ⬅.

13. Key the next level heading, *Reasons for Not Purchasing a Car,* and press the Enter key.

14. Key the remaining headings, promoting or demoting as necessary. *Do not* press the Enter key after the last heading, *Timing*.

15. Insert numbers and letters in the outline using the format shown in Illustration A.
    - Highlight the text to receive the numbers and letters.
    - Select Format, Bullets and Numbering.
    - Click Outline Numbered Tab.
    - Select Numbering style.
    - Click OK.

16. Click the Heading Level button ⬛2 that will display only two levels of headings. Click each Heading Level button from 3 through 5 to see the effect on your outline. Click the Show All Headings button ⬛All to reset the default to display all headings.

17. Spell check.

18. Using the Properties feature, fill out the following summary information about your document:

Title:	Purchasing vs. Not Purchasing a Car
Subject:	Comparison of each
Author:	Your name
Manager:	Your supervisor or teacher's name
Company:	Your company or school name
Category	Economics
Keyboards:	Brakes, Oil, Inconvenience
Comments:	Headings were numbered and lettered.

19. Preview your work. (The document will display as 2 or 3 pages.)

20. Print one copy from Outline view.

21. Save the file; name it **CARS**.

22. Close the document window.

ILLUSTRATION A

I. **Reasons for Purchasing a Car**
    A. *Convenience*
    B. *Prestige*

II. **Reasons for Not Purchasing a Car**
    A. *Inconvenience*
       1. Expense of gasoline
       2. Parking problems
          a) **Expensive parking garages**
          b) **Increasing tows**
    B. *Hazards*
       1. Possibility of accidents
       2. Unpredictable weather
    C. *Bad Financial Investment*
       1. High taxes
       2. High interest rates
    D. *Continuing Costs*
       1. Fuel
       2. Maintenance
          a) **Brakes**
          b) **Oil**
          c) **Filter**
          d) **Tune-up**
             (1) Points
             (2) Plugs
             (3) Timing

PART II

1. Create a NEW document.

2. Set the left margin to 1.5".

3. Switch to Outline view.

4. Create the topic outline shown in Illustration B.

   ✓ *Do not type the numbers or letters that precede the headings; you will use the automatic Numbering feature to add them after completing the outline.*

5. Complete the remainder of the outline *promoting and demoting.*

6. Use the Heading Numbering feature to insert numbers and letters in the outline. Use the default numbering style.

7. Spell check.

8. Preview your work.

9. Print one copy.

10. Save the file; name it **GREEN**.

11. Close the document window.

ILLUSTRATION B

1) **Welcome**
2) **Overview**
   a) *Company history*
   b) *Organizational structure*
   c) *Company mission*
   d) *Sales trends*
   e) *Employee benefits*
   f) *Questions and answers*
3) **Company History**
   a) *Started by Peter Moss in 1965*
   b) *Began as a snow removal company*
   c) *Diversifying into a full landscaping service with a year-round advertising program*
4) **Greenthumb Landscaping Service**
   a) *John Moss, President*
   b) *Wendy Hines, Vice President*
   c) *Pamela Leigh, Finance*
   d) *Matt Chasin, Customer Service*
5) **Company Mission**
   a) *To design quality landscapes in the city*
   b) *To maintain quality landscapes of all customers*
6) **Sales Trends**
7) **Employee Benefits**
   a) *Health Benefits*
      i) Life Insurance
      ii) Medical dental, optical
         (1) **GHI**
         (2) **Major Medical**
      iii) Commissions and Bonus
      iv) Vacation and Sick Leave
         (1) **Vacation: 2 weeks after 12 months**
         (2) **Sick leave: 2.5 days earned each month**
         (3) **Extra provisions for employees who work winters**
8) **Questions and Answers**

KEYSTROKES

CREATE AN OUTLINE

Switch to Outline view:

1. Click **Outline view** button..............
   OR
   a. Click **View** .... `Alt` + `V`
   b. Click **Outline**........................... `O`

2. Type topic or sentence heading.

3. Press **Enter** .... `Enter`

4. Type next heading to keep text at same level as previous heading.
   OR
   Press the **Tab** key or
   click **Demote** button.....................
   to create a lower level heading.
   OR
   Press **Shift** + **Tab** key or
   click **Promote** button....................
   to create a higher level heading.

NUMBER AN OUTLINE

IN OUTLINE VIEW

1. Highlight text to be numbered.

2. Click **Format**........................ `Alt` + `O`

3. Click **Bullets and Numbering** .... `N`

4. Click **Outlined Numbered**..... `Alt` + `U`

5. Click desired format.

6. Click **OK** .... `Enter`

REMOVE NUMBERS FROM ALL HEADINGS

IN OUTLINE VIEW

1. Switch to **Outline view** ... `Alt` + `V`, `O` if necessary.

2. Place insertion point in section from which numbering will be removed.

3. Click **Format**........................ `Alt` + `O`

4. Click **Bullets and Numbering** .... `N`

5. Click **Outlined Numbered**..... `Alt` + `U`

6. Click **None**.

7. Click **OK**.................................... `Enter`

REMOVE NUMBERS FROM A SINGLE HEADING

1. Select the heading.

2. Click **Demote to Body Text** button ...
   on Outlining toolbar.

HIDE OR DISPLAY HEADING LEVELS

IN OUTLINE VIEW

Click appropriate **Heading Level** button to display desired number of levels.

OR

Click **Show All Headings** button ....
to display all heading levels.

MOVE HEADINGS AND TEXT

IN OUTLINE VIEW

Drag heading symbol .... or
to desired location.

OR

1. Select heading, subheadings and text to move.

2. Click **Move Up** button ....
   OR
   Click **Move Down** button ....
   as often as necessary to move heading to desired location.

NEXT EXERCISE

Exercise

41

■ **Edit an Outline** ■ **Create/Edit a Word Style**

NOTES

Edit an Outline

■ To select a topic and its associated paragraph, position your insertion point on the **heading symbol** until it changes to a four-headed arrow and click the left mouse button.

■ To move a heading in an outline without affecting the level or rank, place insertion point in the heading to move and click the Move Up ⬆ or Move Down ⬇ button on the Outlining toolbar. When you use this procedure, only the heading itself moves up or down; any subheadings or subtext under the heading will remain in their original positions.

■ To move all information under a heading (subheadings and subtext), select the heading symbol, then click the Move Up or Move Down button. Or you may select the heading symbol and drag the text to its new location. When you drag text, the mouse pointer changes to a double-headed arrow, and a guideline moves with the mouse to assist you in positioning the heading.

■ You may change the level of text by **promoting** or **demoting** it. First, place the insertion point in the heading to change. To create a lower level subheading (for example, to change text from level II to level B), click the **Demote** button ➡ on the Outlining toolbar. To return the heading to a higher level (for example, to change text from level B to level II), click the **Promote** button ⬅ on the Outlining toolbar.

■ You may collapse (hide) or expand (display) as many levels of headings as desired by clicking the appropriate heading button on the Outlining toolbar. Clicking the Show All Headings button ▣ displays all heading levels, the default in Word.

Create/Edit a Word Style

■ In Exercise 39, you learned that a style is a collection of formats you can assign to selected text. You also learned that templates contain styles applied by Word. Outlines also contain styles applied by Word. You saw in the last exercise that each outline level displays in a different font face, style and size. Word allows you to create your own style or edit one that is contained within Word.

■ For example, to **create a style** that contains a 16-point script font, select the text on which you wish to base your style, click the Style list box on the Formatting toolbar, and replace the current style name with one you type in. Pressing Enter will add that name to the Style list. Whenever you want to apply this new style to text, select the text, click the Styles list and select the new name.

■ However, if you want to keep the same indents for your headings, then you must **edit a Word style**; that is, change the characteristics of a style (Heading 1, Heading 2 or Heading 3), but not its name.

- To edit a style, select text that has the style you wish to change applied to it. Edit the selection, applying the formatting you want to include in the new style and removing any formatting you don't want in the new style. When you are done, select the edited text, click the Styles list box, and select the original style. You will be prompted with the dialog box to the right.

- Select <u>U</u>pdate the style to reflect recent changes and click OK. All headings based on the original style will change to reflect the new style.

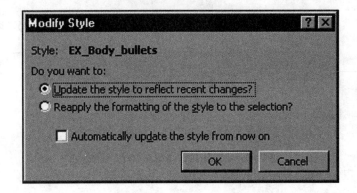

> *In this exercise, you will edit the two outlines you created in the last exercise and apply a new heading style.*

EXERCISE DIRECTIONS

PART I

1. Open ⌨**GREEN**, or open 💾**41GREEN**.

2. Change the Heading 1 style to a 16-point bold font (Use Century Gothic, if available).

3. After you change the characteristics of the Heading 1 style, all Heading 1 text will automatically change to reflect the modification.

4. Move V. information (Company Mission) to become IV. Move IV. information (Greenthumb Landscaping Service) to become V.

5. Print one copy.

6. Close and save the file; name it **GREEN**.

PART I

1) **Welcome**
2) **Overview**
   a) *Company history*
   b) *Organizational structure*
   c) *Company mission*
   d) *Sales trends*
   e) *Employee benefits*
   f) *Questions and answers*
3) **Company History**
   a) *Started by Peter Moss in 1965*
   b) *Began as a snow removal company*
   c) *Diversifying into a full landscaping service with a year-round advertising program*
4) **Greenthumb Landscaping Service**
   a) *John Moss, President*
   b) *Wendy Hines, Vice President*
   c) *Pamela Leigh, Finance*
   d) *Matt Chasin, Customer Service*
5) **Company Mission**
   a) *To design quality landscapes in the city*
   b) *To maintain quality landscapes of all customers*
6) **Sales Trends**
7) **Employee Benefits**
   a) *Health Benefits*
      i) Life Insurance
      ii) Medical dental, optical
         (1) **GHI**
         (2) **Major Medical**
      iii) Commissions and Bonus
      iv) Vacation and Sick Leave
         (1) **Vacation: 2 weeks after 12 months**
         (2) **Sick leave: 2.5 days earned each month**
         (3) **Extra provisions for employees who work winters**
8) **Questions and Answers**

PART II

1. Open ⊟CARS, or open ⊟41CARS.

2. Change the Heading 1 style to a 20-point bold font. (Use BernhardMod BT, if available).

3. Move B. Hazards and the numbered items below it after the items in D. Continuing Costs.

4. Print one copy.

5. Close and save the file; name it **CARS**.

6. Close the document window.

PART II

I. **Reasons for Purchasing a Car**
   A. *Convenience*
   B. *Prestige*

II. **Reasons for Not Purchasing a Car**
   A. *Inconvenience*
      1. Expense of gasoline
      2. Parking problems
         a) **Expensive parking garages**
         b) **Increasing tows**
   B. *Hazards*
      1. Possibility of accidents
      2. Unpredictable weather
   C. *Bad Financial Investment*
      1. High taxes
      2. High interest rates
   D. *Continuing Costs*
      1. Fuel
      2. Maintenance
         a) **Brakes**
         b) **Oil**
         c) **Filter**
         d) **Tune-up**
            (1) Points
            (2) Plugs
            (3) Timing

KEYSTROKES

CREATE NEW STYLE

USING MENU

1. Click **F**o**rmat**, **Style**....... `Alt` + `O`, `S`

   The **Style** dialog box displays.

2. Click **N**ew .... `Alt` + `N`

   The **New Style** dialog box displays.

3. Click **N**ame box............ `Alt` + `N`, text
   and type new style name.

4. Click **Style type** box.... `Alt` + `T`, `↑` `↓`
   and select a style type.

5. Click **Based On** box ... `Alt` + `B`, `↑` `↓`
   and select style to base the new style on.

   ✓ By default, new paragraph styles are based on the style applied to the active paragraph.

6. Click **Style for following paragraph** box ...... `Alt` + `S`, `↑` `↓`
   and select style to apply
   to following paragraphs.

   ✓ This option is not available if **Character** was selected for **Style Type** in Step 4.

7. Click **F**o**rmat**.......... `Alt` + `O`, `↑` `↓`
   and select style element to format.

   Dialog box for selected style element displays.

8. Select formatting options for selected style element.

9. Click **OK**............................. `Enter`

10. Repeat steps 7–9 to format additional style elements.

To assign style to a shortcut key:

a. Click **Shortcut Key** .... `Alt` + `K`

   The **Customize Keyboard** dialog box displays.

b. Click **Commands** list box............. `Alt` + `O`, `↑` `↓`
   and select style to assign
   key sequence to.

c. Click **Press new shortcut key** box..... `Alt` + `N`, keys
   and type new key sequence.

   ✓ If the selected keyboard sequence is already assigned to another command, that command will be displayed in the Press new shortcut key box.

d. Click **Assign**..................... `Tab`, `A`
   to assign new key sequence
   to selected style.

   ✓ Clicking **Assign** overwrites any pre-existing command assignment for the selected shortcut keys with the current selection.

e. Click **Close**................................. `Enter`
   to close **Customize keyboard** dialog box.

11. Select **Add to Template** .... `Alt` + `A`
    check box if desired,
    to add style to current template.

12. Select **Automatically update**..... `Alt` + `U`
    check box to modify style each time you
    apply manual formatting to a paragraph
    formatted in the selected style. Also
    automatically changes all text formatted
    with affected style in active document.

13. Click **OK**................................. `Enter`
    to create new style and
    close **New Style** dialog box.

14. Click **Close** .... `Esc`
    to close **Style** dialog box.

USING TOOLBAR

1. Select text with formatting to include in style.

2. Click **Style** `Normal ▼`
   box .... `Shift` + `Ctrl` + `S`
   in **Formatting** toolbar
   and type new style name. .... text

3. Press **Enter** .... `Enter`

MODIFY STYLE

USING MENU

1. Click **F**o**rmat**, **Style** ...... `Alt` + `O`, `S`

   The **Style** dialog box displays.

2. Click in **Styles** .... `Alt` + `S`, `↑` `↓`
   list box and select style to modify.

3. Click **Modify**........................ `Alt` + `M`

   The **Modify Style** dialog box displays.

4. Follow steps 7–14 in Create New Style Using Menu.

USING TOOLBAR

1. Make desired formatting changes to existing text containing style.

2. Click **Style** `Normal ▼`
   box .... `Shift` + `Ctrl` + `S`
   in **Formatting** toolbar.

3. Select style to modify .... `↑` `↓`

4. Press **Enter** .... `Enter`

   The **Reapply Style** dialog box displays.

5. Select **Redefine the style using the selected as an example?** .... `R`

   OR

   To reapply original style formatting:
   Select **Return the formatting of the selection to the style?** .... `S`

6. Click **OK** .... `Enter`

DELETE STYLE

✓ *Built–in styles, such as heading level styles, cannot be deleted.*

1. Click **F<u>o</u>rmat**, **<u>S</u>tyle** ...... `Alt` + `O`, `S`

    *The **Style** dialog box displays.*

2. Click **<u>L</u>ist** box .... `Alt` + `L`, `↑` `↓`
   and select style options to display.

3. Click **<u>S</u>tyles** list ...... `Alt` + `S`, `↑` `↓`
   box and select style you want to delete.

    Paragraph style names are bold; character styles are not bold.

4. Click **<u>D</u>elete** .... `Alt` + `D`

5. Click **<u>Y</u>es** .... `Enter`
   when **Delete Confirmation**
   dialog box appears.

6. Click **Close** .... `Esc`

    ✓ *The Close button displays after deletion is confirmed.*

EDIT A WORD STYLE

1. Select the text you wish to edit.

2. Click the **Font**

    list box .... `Times New Roman` `▼`
    and select a new font.

3. Click the **Font Size** list .... `9` `▼`
   box and select a new size.

4. Click the **Styles**

    list box .... `Normal` `▼`
    and select the style you wish to change.

5. Click **<u>U</u>pdate the style** .... `Alt` + `U`
   to reflect recent changes
   in the **Modify Style** dialog box.

6. Click **OK** .... `Enter`

Exercise
42

■ Summary

In this exercise, you will use the Résumé wizard to create your own résumé.

EXERCISE DIRECTIONS

1. Create a NEW document.

2. Using the Résumé wizard and a Contemporary Résumé template, create your own résumé.

   ✓ *If the Résumé wizard is unavailable, use any résumé template.*

3. Include or exclude subheadings as they apply to your own experience.

4. If necessary, use the Shrink-to-Fit feature to keep the document on one page.

5. Spell check.

6. Preview your work.

7. Print one copy.

8. Save the file; name it **MYRESUME**.

9. Close the document window.

Your Own

Objective	[Type Objective Here]

Summary of qualifications	19xx - 19xx [Company/Institution Name] [City, State] **[Job Title]** • [Details of position, award, or achievement.]

Work experience	19xx - 19xx [Company/Institution Name] [City, State] **[Job Title]** • [Details of position, award, or achievement.]

Education	19xx - 19xx [Company/Institution Name] [City, State] **[Degree/Major]** • [Details of position, award, or achievement.]

Extracurricular activities	[Click here and enter information.]

Professional memberships	[Click here and enter information.]

Community activities	[Click here and enter information.]

Hobbies	[Click here and enter information.]

References	[Click here and enter information.]

Exercise
43

■ **Summary**

In this exercise, you will create and edit an outline.

EXERCISE DIRECTIONS

1. Create a NEW document.

2. Use the default margins.

3. Switch to Outline view.

4. Create the outline shown in Illustration A.

   ✓ *To insert British pound symbol, press the NUM Lock Key, hold down the Alt key and type 0163 on the numeric keypad. When Alt is released, the British pound symbol will appear.*

5. Spell check.

6. Use the Find feature to locate the word "aging." Use the Thesaurus feature to substitute another word.

7. Change the Heading 1 style to Desdemona 14-point bold.

8. Move the information as shown in Illustration B.

9. Preview your work.

10. Print one copy.

11. Save the file; name it **AUTO**.

12. Close the document window.

I. **Performance of Auto Retailing Stocks in the U.K.**
   A. *Only major market of auto retailing stocks in world*
   B. *Size and length of existence*
      1. range from £8 million to £3 million
      2. privately held for over 20 years
      3. went public in 1980s

II. **Characteristics of U.S. Automotive Retailers**
   A. *Increased efficiency*
   B. *Improved profitability*
   C. *Higher used car sales*
   D. *Lower new car sales*

III. **Recent Trends and Automotive Industry Outlook**
   A. *Increased industry sales*
      1. light vehicle unit sales
      2. dealership service and parts sales
      3. total dealership sales
         a) **Ford - $3 million**
         b) **GM - $8 million**
   B. *Automotive sales mirror the performance of the economy*

IV. **Consolidation of U.S. Automotive Retailing Industry**
   A. *Dealerships decreased in number between 1950 and 1993*
      1. recession of 1990s
      2. aging dealer principal population
   B. *Lower new car sales/Higher used car sales*

ILLUSTRATION B

I.   **Performance of Auto Retailing Stocks in the U.K.**
- A.   *Only major market of auto retailing stocks in world*
- B.   *Size and length of existence*
   1.   range from £8 million to £3 million
   2.   privately held for over 20 years
   3.   went public in 1980s

II.   **Characteristics of U.S. Automotive Retailers**
- A.   *Increased efficiency*
- B.   *Improved profitability*
- C.   *Higher used car sales*
- D.   *Lower new car sales*

III.   **Recent Trends and Automotive Industry Outlook**
- A.   *Increased industry sales*
   1.   light vehicle unit sales
   2.   dealership service and parts sales
   3.   total dealership sales
      a)   **Ford - $3 million**
      b)   **GM - $8 million**
- B.   *Automotive sales mirror the performance of the economy*

IV.   **Consolidation of U.S. Automotive Retailing Industry**
- A.   *Dealerships decreased in number between 1950 and 1993*
   1.   recession of 1990s
   2.   aging dealer principal population
- B.   *Lower new car sales/Higher used car sales*

move

Word 97

LESSON 7

Multiple-Page Documents

- Hard vs. Soft Page Breaks
- Section Breaks
- Headers and Footers
- Letters with Special Notations
- Print Specific Pages
- Bookmarks
- Page Numbers
- Page Number Placement
- Number Formats
- Footnotes
- Widow/Orphan Lines
- Endnotes
- Edit a Footnote or Endnote
- Move Text From One Page to Another
- Document Map

Exercise 44

- **Hard vs. Soft Page Breaks**
- **Headers and Footers**
- **Section Breaks**

NOTES

Hard vs. Soft Page Breaks

- Word assumes you are working on a standard sheet of paper measuring 8.5" wide x 11" long. Remember, Word is defaulted to leave a 1" top and 1" bottom margin. Therefore, there are 9" of vertical space on a standard sheet of paper for entering text.

- The At indicator shows how far you are from the top of the page. When you are working At 9.8", you are working on the last line of the page (one-inch top margin plus 9 inches of text). Therefore, when you enter text beyond 9.8", Word automatically ends one page and starts another.

- When Word ends the page automatically, it is referred to as a **soft page break**. To end the page before 9.8", you can enter a **hard page break** by pressing Ctrl+Enter. In Normal view, a hard page break is indicated by a dotted horizontal line across the screen with the words *Page Break* indicated in the center. In Page Layout view, the hard page break appears as a solid line. When you insert a hard page break, Word automatically adjusts the soft page breaks that follow.

- Once the insertion point is below the Page Break line, the Page indicator on the Status bar displays *Page 2* and the At indicator displays *At 1"*.

- A hard page break may be deleted, which allows text below the break to flow onto the previous page, as room allows. You may also select a hard page break and drag it to a new position (in Normal view).

Section Breaks

- By default, a document contains one section. However, Word allows you to break your document into multiple sections so you can format each section of the document differently. For example, if you wish to apply different margin settings to different parts of your document, you can create a section break, change the margins for that section, then create another section break and return your margins to another setting after the break. Creating section breaks is like creating a document within a document.

- To create a section break, position the insertion point where the break is desired and select Break from the Insert menu. In the Break dialog box that follows, select the desired section break option.

Break Dialog Box

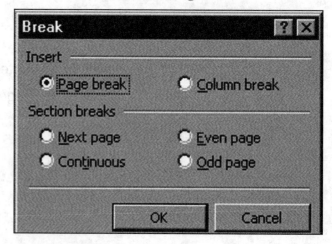

- Next Page creates a new section on the next page.

- Continuous creates a new section at the insertion point.

- Even Page creates a new section on the next even-numbered page (usually a left-facing page).

- Odd Page creates a new section on the next odd-numbered page (usually a right-facing page).

■ Since section break marks store section formatting (the same way paragraph marks store paragraph formatting), removing a section break may also remove all section formatting for the section that precedes the break. To remove a section break, position the insertion point on the section break and press the Delete key.

Headers and Footers

■ A multiple-page letter requires a heading on the second and succeeding pages. The heading should include the name of the addressee (to whom the letter is going), the page number and the date. To include the heading on the second and succeeding pages, you can create a header.

■ A **header** is the same text appearing at the top of every page or every other page, while a **footer** is the same text appearing at the bottom of every page or every other page.

■ After you type the desired header or footer once, the Header/Footer feature will automatically insert it on every page or on specified pages of your document.

■ To see headers, footers, or page numbers on your screen, you must be in either Page Layout view or Print Preview. Although headers, footers, and page numbers do not appear on screen in Normal view, they will print.

■ The header is defaulted to print 0.5" from the top of the page; the footer is defaulted to print 0.5" from the bottom of the page. The header/footer printing position may be changed, if desired.

✓ Note: Headers, footers, and page numbers usually appear on the second and succeeding pages of a letter or report; they generally do not appear on the first page.

■ To add headers or footers, you must display the Header and Footer toolbar by selecting Header and Footer from the View menu.

Header and Footer Toolbar

■ If you wish to include a date or the time as header/footer text, use the **Date** button and/or the **Time** button on the Header and Footer toolbar to insert these items. The Time button causes the time of printing to appear in the header or footer.

■ You may add page numbers to headers or footers by clicking the **Page Number** button on the Header and Footer toolbar. You can position page numbers in the header or footer by pressing Tab to get to the Center tab and pressing Tab again to get to the right-alignment tab.

■ To suppress the header, footer, or page number on the first page, select the Page Setup button on the Header and Footer toolbar, select the Layout tab, and click the Different first page check box.

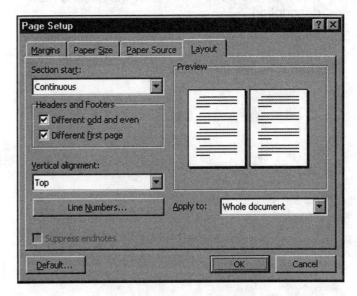

■ Headers, footers, and page numbers may be inserted *before* or *after* the document is typed.

> *In this exercise, you will create a two-page letter and insert a header as the second-page heading. You will also create section breaks and change margins throughout the document.*

EXERCISE DIRECTIONS

1. Create a NEW document.

2. Keyboard the exercise on the next page using the Contemporary Letter template.

3. Use the default margins and tabs.

4. Begin the exercise At 2.6"

5. Insert the company name and address as shown. Add the slogan in the placeholder as shown.

6. Insert a continuous section break after the second paragraph. Set 2" left and right margins.

7. Apply Word's Heading 1 style to the title of each workshop. Apply Word's Heading 4 style to the paragraph covering costs below each workshop description.

8. Insert a hard page break after the second tour description.

9. Insert a continuous section break before the paragraph on the top of the second page. Return margins to the default.

10. Insert a continuous section break after the first paragraph on page 2. Set 2" left and right margins for the two remaining workshop descriptions. Apply the same styles as you did on page 1.

11. Insert a continuous section break after the tour descriptions and return margins to the default.

12. Hyphenate the document. Limit the consecutive hyphens to 2.

13. Modify the header to include the name of the addressee (Ms. Susan Hamilton), the page number and today's date.

14. Spell check.

15. Preview your work using the multiple pages option of Print Preview.

16. Save the file; name it **TRAVEL**.

17. Close the document window.

Time To Travel Tours

Today's date

Ms. Susan Hamilton
110 Sullivan Street
New York, NY 10012

Dear Ms. Hamilton:

Thank you for your inquiry about our summer and fall 1997 travel workshops. These programs tend to fill to capacity, so it is best to enroll as soon as possible. Some of the dates have not yet been finalized, so we will be sending you an update by the end of next week to keep you informed.

This year's week-long workshops will be held in Peru and Egypt.

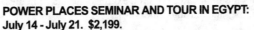

POWER PLACES SEMINAR AND TOUR IN EGYPT:
July 14 - July 21. $2,199.

Journey with others to one of the world's most sacred sites—the Great Pyramid. You will have special access into the Great Pyramid not available to other tourists. Experience a three-hour private tour (closed to the general public) of all three chambers. Learn about the teachings and technologies of ancient Egypt, taught by modern practitioners of these ancient sacred arts. You may choose the optional three-day Nile cruise following the conference.

Price includes airfare from New York, hotel accommodations, 30 meals, entrance into the Great Pyramid, most transportation within Egypt, luggage handling, conference fees and events.

POWER PLACES SEMINAR AND TOUR IN PERU:
June 14 - June 22. $2,299.

This conference has been specifically planned to culminate in Machu Picchu during the summer solstice, the holiest time of the year for the Incas. You will travel through the sacred valley of the Incas, nestled in the serene Urubamba Valley. You will meet native shamans, who will lead a special ceremony on the solstice, and provide insights on Peru's present-day culture, places and people.

Price includes airfare from Miami, hotel accommodations (double occupancy), 30 meals, train and bus transportation within Peru, extensive sightseeing, entrance into Machu Picchu, conference fees and events.

The Perfect Travel Experience Awaits You...

Ms. Susan Hamilton
Page 2
Today's date

This year's weekend panels, lectures and workshops will be held in Sonoma and Napa Valley, California. Unless otherwise announced, the price will include three days and two nights of hotel accommodations, six meals, conference fees and special events.

WOMEN'S RETREAT AT THE SONOMA MISSION INN. (Date to be announced.) $425.
This workshop will focus on women examining their individual power, spirituality, and self-image. In addition to panel discussions and intensive group workshops, there will be plenty of relaxation and therapies at the natural hot springs.

HOLISTIC HEALTH SEMINAR AT THE ST. HELENA HOSPITAL AND HEALTH CENTER. September 20 - September 22. $325.
Open to health professionals and all those interested in health-related issues. The weekend includes seminars and lectures on holistic approaches to western medicine in the areas of diet, exercise, herbal remedies, preventative medicine, and chronic illness.

Some of the lectures will be available to the general public. If you are unable to attend for the entire weekend, please call us to inquire about the dates and times of free lectures.

You may also sign up by phone. Please have a credit card available when you call.

Sincerely,

Angela Bacci
Tour Coordinator

ab/yo

KEYSTROKES

CREATE A HARD PAGE BREAK

1. Position insertion point at desired break point.
2. Press **Ctrl + Enter**.

   OR

   a. Click **Insert**...................... `Alt` + `I`
   b. Click **Break**............................... `B`
   c. Click **Page Break**...................... `P`
   d. Click **OK** .... `Enter`

DELETE A HARD PAGE BREAK

IN NORMAL VIEW

1. Position insertion point on hard page break.
2. Press **Delete** .... `Del`

INSERT SECTION BREAK

1. Position insertion point where desired break is to begin.
2. Click **Insert**...................... `Alt` + `I`
3. Click **Break**................................... `B`
4. Select desired section break:
   - **Next page** .... `Alt` + `N`
   - **Continuous** .... `Alt` + `T`
   - **Even page** .... `Alt` + `E`
   - **Odd page** .... `Alt` + `O`
5. Click **OK** .... `Enter`

CREATE HEADERS/FOOTERS

1. Click **View** .... `Alt` + `V`
2. Click **Header/Footer**................. `H`
   to display the Header and Footer toolbar.
3. Click **Switch between Header/Footer** button .... 🖹
   to switch to header or footer.
4. Type and format header or footer.
   ✓ *Header/footer text may be bolded, italicized, centered, right aligned, etc., just like normal text.*
5. Click **Close** .... `Close`

VIEW HEADERS/FOOTERS

1. Click **View** .... `Alt` + `V`
2. Click **Page Layout**........................... `P`
3. Scroll to header/footer location.

Exercise 45

■ **Letters with Special Notations** ■ **Print Specific Pages** ■ **Bookmarks**

NOTES

Letters with Special Notations

■ Letters may include special parts in addition to those learned thus far. The letter in this exercise contains a mailing notation, a subject line, an enclosure and copy notations.

■ When a letter is sent by a special mail service such as Express mail, Registered mail, Federal Express, Certified mail or By Hand (via a messenger service), it is customary to include an appropriate notation on the letter. This notation is placed two lines below the date and typed in all caps.

■ The subject identifies or summarizes the body of the letter. It is typed two lines below the salutation. One blank line follows it. (Press the Enter key twice.) It may be typed at the left margin or centered in modified-block style. *Subject* may be typed in all caps or in upper- and lowercase. *Re* (in reference to) is often used instead of *Subject*.

> ✓*Note:* *All letter templates contain formatting for a subject line, reference initials, enclosure and copy notations. For example, after you type the inside address and press the Enter key once, Word automatically inserts an appropriate amount of space after the salutation and applies a Subject Line style to the next typed sentence. After you press the Enter key once again, Word automatically inserts the appropriate amount of space after the subject line and sets the font style, size, spacing and indents for the body text.*

■ An enclosure (or attachment) notation is used to indicate that something else besides the letter is included in the envelope. The enclosure or attachment notation is typed one or two lines below the reference initials and may be typed in several ways (the number indicates how many items are enclosed in the envelope):

ENC.	Enclosure	Enclosures (2)
Enc.	Encls.	Attachment
Encl.	Encls (2)	Attachments (2)

■ If copies of the document are sent to others, a copy notation is typed two lines below the enclosure/attachment notation (or the reference initials if there is no enclosure/attachment). A copy notation may be typed in several ways:

Copy to:	c:
CC:	pc: (photocopy)

■ The Letter template also contains formatting for enclosure and copy notations and applies the Enclosure and/or CC style.

Print Specific Pages

■ You may choose to print the entire document, a specific page, several pages, selected (highlighted) text or the current page. You may also specify the number of copies you wish to print.

> ✓*Note:* *When you work with multiple-page documents, use Print Preview to edit text and insert page breaks, because you can see the effect on several pages at once.*

Bookmarks

- The **Bookmark** feature allows you to return quickly to a desired location in a document. This is a convenient feature if, for example, you are editing a large document and have to leave your work for a time. You can set a bookmark to keep your place. When you return to work, you can open your file, find the bookmark in your document and quickly return to the place you marked. Or you may not have all the information needed to complete your document when you begin. Setting bookmarks will enable you to return to those sections of the document that need development or information inserted.

- You can have several bookmarks in a document; however, each bookmark must be named for easy identification. The bookmark name can be the first line of the paragraph or a one-word character name.

- To create a bookmark, position your insertion point where you wish to insert the bookmark. Then select Boo**k**mark from the **I**nsert menu, enter the bookmark name in the Bookmark dialog box as illustrated below, and click **A**dd.

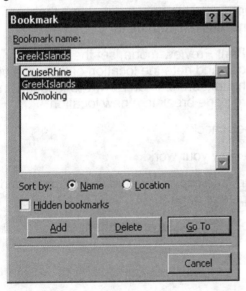

- To return to your bookmark, press F5 to display the **G**o To dialog box and then type the name of your bookmark, or select Bookmark from the G**o** to What list and select desired bookmark from the **E**nter bookmark name drop-down list.

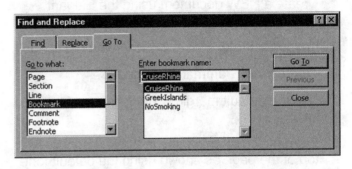

- Your insertion point may be anywhere in the document when you search for the bookmark.

In this exercise, you will create a two-page letter using the Elegant Letter template. The Elegant Letter template will create a modified-block letter with indented paragraphs. You will insert a hard page break to create a second page and insert bookmarks where indicated.

EXERCISE DIRECTIONS

1. Create a NEW document using the Elegant Letter template.

2. Keyboard the exercise shown on the next page.

3. Turn off the Grammar check feature.

4. Use the default margins, font face, and font size.

5. Enter the company name in the text box at the top of the page as shown using the default font face.

   - Size the font to 16 point; set the style to bold.
   - Use the book symbol found in the Wingdings font collection.

6. Enter the address and phone number in the text box at the bottom of the page as shown using the default font face and size.

7. Begin the dateline At approximately 2.5".

8. Press the Enter key once after the date (this will result in a double return) and type REGISTERED MAIL.

9. Type the remainder of the letter as shown. Substitute the template salutation shown with that shown in the exercise.

   ✓ To insert the recipient's name in the salutation line, highlight the words "Sir or Madam" (do <u>not</u> highlight the colon) and replace them with recipient's name. Then place the insertion point at the end of the salutation line and press Enter.

10. Replace "Sincerely" with "Cordially" in the closing.

11. Create a header on the second page that includes the name of the addressee.

    ✓ The Elegant Letter template includes a header with only the page number and today's date. It is only necessary for you to include the addressee's name. It is not necessary for you to suppress the header on the first page; this has been done for you as part of the template design.

12. Set 1" left and right indents for the quoted text as shown.

13. Set bookmarks where indicated; name the first one INDENT1 and the second INDENT2.

14. Save the file; name it **PREVIEW**. **Do not close the document.**

15. Go To the first bookmark, INDENT1. Insert the following sentence at the bookmark location:
    "Furthermore, they have captured the objects on film so true to life that anyone watching them is captivated."

16. Go To the second bookmark, INDENT2. Insert the following sentence as the third indented paragraph:
    "I will institute a program which will make schools throughout the country aware of their vocational potential."

17. Hyphenate the document. Limit the consecutive hyphens to 1.

18. In Print Preview mode, set the display for two pages and note the location of the page break. If the text broke in an awkward location, insert a hard page break in a new location.

19. Spell check.

20. Preview your work.

21. Print one copy of the entire document and two copies of page 2.

22. Close the file; save the changes.

📖 EDUCATIONAL FILM LIBRARY

Today's date

REGISTERED MAIL

Ms. Michelle Mancuso
Aventura College
77 Palm Way
Aventura, FL 33180

Dear Ms. Mancuso:

SUBJECT: EDUCATIONAL FILMS FOR HIGH SCHOOLS AND COLLEGES

Thank you for your interest in the films that we have available for high school and college students. We are pleased to send you the enclosed flyer, which describes the films in detail. Also enclosed is a summary of those films that have recently been added to our collection since the publication of the flyer.

There have been many positive reactions to our films. Just three weeks ago, a group of educators, editors and vocational experts were invited to view the films at the annual EDUCATORS' CONFERENCE. Here are some of their comments:

We will be sure to send the films in time for you to preview them. Please be sure to list the date on which you wish to preview the film.

Mr. William R. Bondlow, Jr., president of the National Vocational Center in Washington, D.C. and editor-in-chief of *Science Careers,* said,

> I like the films very much. They are innovative and a great benefit to all those interested in the earth sciences as a professional career. ⟵⎯⎯⎯⎯⎯⎯⎯⎯ *Create Bookmark.*

Ms. Andra Burke, a leading expert presently assigned to the United States Interior Department, praised the films by saying that,

> They are a major educational advance in career placement, which will serve as a source of motivation for all future geologists.

444 SAMARITAN AVENUE • WASHINGTON, DC • 40124
PHONE: 301-444-4444 • FAX: 301-777-7777

Ms. Michelle Mancuso   – 2 –   Today's date

A member of the National Education Center, Dr. Lawrence Pilgrim also liked the films and said,   ⟵ ———— *Create a Bookmark*

These are some of the reactions we have had to our films. We know you will have a similar reaction.

We would very much like to send you the films that you would like during the summer session. You can use the summer to review them. It is important that your request be received quickly, since the demand for the films is great, particularly during the summer sessions at the colleges and universities throughout the country.

Cordially,

David Chen
Vice President, Marketing

dc/yo

Enclosures (2)

Copy to: Robert Williams, Nancy Polansky

KEYSTROKES

PRINT SPECIFIC PAGES OF A DOCUMENT

CTRL+ P

Print Entire Document:

Click **Print** button .... 🖶

Print Multiple Copies:

1. Click **File** .... `Alt` + `F`

2. Click **Print** .... `P`

3. Type desired **Number of copies**. ...*number*

4. Click **OK** .... `Enter`

Print Specific Pages:

1. Click **File** .... `Alt` + `F`

2. Click **Print** .... `P`

3. Click **Pages** .... `Alt` + `G`

4. Type nonsequential page numbers separated by commas.

   Example: 3,7,9

   OR

   Type range of pages separated by a hyphen

   Example: 3-9

   OR

   Type a combination of nonsequential pages and a range of pages.

   Example: 2,5,7-10

5. Click **OK** .... `Enter`

Print Selected Text:

1. Select (highlight) text to print.

2. Click **File** .... `Alt` + `F`

3. Click **Print** .... `P`

4. Click **Selection** .... `Alt` + `S`

5. Click **OK** .... `Enter`

Print Current Page:

1. Click **File** .... `Alt` + `F`

2. Click **Print** .... `P`

3. Click **Current Page** .... `Alt` + `E`

4. Click **OK** .... `Enter`

INSERT A HARD PAGE BREAK

1. Place insertion point where you would like to place page break.

2. Press **Ctrl + Enter** .... `Ctrl` + `Enter`

   OR

   a. Click **Insert** .... `Alt` + `I`

   b. Click **Break** .... `B`

   c. Click **Page Break** .... `P`

   d. Click **OK** .... `Enter`

EDIT TEXT IN PRINT PREVIEW MODE

1. Click **Print Preview** button .... 🔍 on the Standard toolbar.

   OR

   a. Click **File** .... `Alt` + `F`

   b. Click **Print Preview** .... `V`

2. Click the **Multiple Pages** button....... ▦ and drag down and to the right to display the number of pages desired.

3. Click **Magnifier** button .... 🔍 to enter Edit mode.

4. Edit text and page breaks as usual.

5. Click **Magnifier** button to exit Edit mode or press **Esc** to return to document.

CREATE A BOOKMARK

1. Position insertion point where bookmark is to be inserted.

2. Click **Insert** .... `Alt` + `I`

3. Click **Bookmark** .... `K`

4. Type **Bookmark** name .... `Alt` + `B`

5. Click **Add** .... `Alt` + `A`

GO TO BOOKMARK

1. Press **F5** .... `F5`

   OR

   a. Click **Edit** .... `Alt` + `E`

   b. Click **Go To** .... `G`

2. Click **Bookmark** .... `Alt` + `O`, `↓` in **Go to what** list box.

3. Type Bookmark name.. `Alt` + `E`, *name* in **Enter Bookmark name** box.

   OR

   Select bookmark from drop-down list.

4. Click **Go To** .... `Alt` + `T`

Exercise 46

■ **Page Numbers** ■ **Page Number Placement** ■ **Number Formats**

NOTES

Page Numbers

■ The **Page Numbering** feature lets you insert page numbers independently of headers and footers. It also lets you indicate where the page number should appear on the printed page.

■ If you plan to use only page numbers or you plan to insert the page number in a different location than the header/footer, use the Page Numbering feature. If you plan to insert a header or a footer and page number, it is easier to use the Header and Footer feature to enter the header/footer along with the page number.

■ Page numbers may be inserted before or after the document is typed.

■ To insert page numbers independently of the header/footer text, select Page Numbers from the Insert menu.

Page Number Placement

■ Word provides numerous page numbering position options. Numbers may be positioned at the top or bottom of the page and aligned left, center, right, inside or outside. Select the page numbering position in the Page Numbers dialog box (which appears after Insert, Page Numbers is selected). The position you select displays in the Preview window.

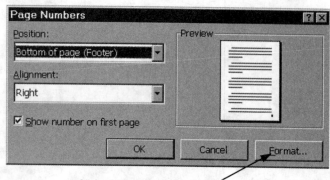

Click to change number format.

Number Formats

■ Word provides five different number formats:

• Numbers	1, 2, 3, 4, 5, etc.
• Lowercase Letters	a, b, c, d, e, f, etc.
• Uppercase Letters	A, B, C, D, E, F, etc.
• Lowercase Roman	i, ii, iii, iv, v, etc.
• Uppercase Roman	I, II, III, IV, V, etc.

■ To change Number formats, click the Format button in the Page Numbers dialog box (shown at left).

■ In the Page Number Format dialog box that follows, click the Number format list arrow and select a desired format.

Click to select number format.

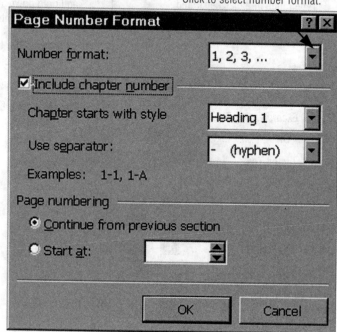

In this exercise, you will create a multiple-page report and include a header and separate page numbers. You will also gain more practice using bookmarks.

✓Note: While the exercise is shown in single space, you are to use double space. Your printed document will result in two or three pages, depending on the selected font.

EXERCISE DIRECTIONS

1. Create a NEW document and keyboard the report shown on the next page, or open 💾46NET.

2. Set 1.5" left and right margins.

3. Begin the exercise At approximately 2".

4. Center and set the title to a serif 14-point bold font.

5. Set line spacing to double.

6. Set a .5" first-line indent.

7. Use a serif 13-point font for the body text.

8. Set bookmarks where indicated; name the first one PAR1; name the second WWW.

9. Use Word's Heading 1 style for each side heading.

10. Right-align and set the following header on the second and succeeding pages to a sans serif 10-point italic font:

    THE BIRTH OF THE "NET"

11. Include an Uppercase Roman page number on the bottom center of the second and succeeding pages.

12. Edit Word's Heading 1 style. Change the font to italic.

13. Reapply the Heading 1 style to the first side heading (the remaining side headings should automatically change to the edited version).

14. Spell check.

15. Edit the header to read:

    THE BIRTH OF THE INTERNET

16. Preview your work.

17. Print one copy.

18. Save the file; name it NET. Do not close the document.

19. Go to the first bookmark, PAR1. Insert the following sentences at the bookmark location:

    In the 1970's, nonmilitary computer users began to borrow this networking idea from the Defense Department. This was the beginning of the Internet.

20. Go to the second bookmark, WWW. Insert the following sentences at the bookmark location:

    While it is possible to search for information on the Internet (surf the Internet) by using hypertext, it is easier to search the Internet using a Web browser. A Web browser allows the user to click on a key word, which causes a more specific list of words to appear, and so on.

21. Justify and hyphenate the document. Limit consecutive hyphens to 2.

22. Spell check.

23. Print one copy of pages one and two and two copies of page three.

24. Close the file; save the changes.

25. Close the document window.

THE BIRTH OF THE INTERNET

HOW IT BEGAN

In 1966, a U.S. Defense Department agency decided to try linking computers around the country through regular telephone hookups. By connecting computers around the country, the Defense Department intended to create a computer network that could survive an atomic strike—or any natural or unnatural disaster. This computer network allowed military researches across the country to share data easily and quickly.

WHAT IT HAS BECOME

Insert Bookmark.

Today, the Internet has become an information superhighway connecting over 5,000 computers and approximately 20 million users throughout the world! It has become the information base for colleges and universities, governmental agencies, research firms and television networks. In addition, many businesses including catalog companies, mail services and magazine publishers have made themselves accessible through the Internet. News services on the Internet also allow users to receive information on the most current events anywhere in the world.

FUNCTIONS OF THE INTERNET

E-mail, one of the most common functions of the Internet, allows users to send letters, documents or pictures over computer wires to other Internet users. E-mail is a fast, cheap and effective way to communicate with people all over the world. It may take only several minutes to send a letter or document from New York to Japan.

THE WORLD WIDE WEB

The World Wide Web is another function of the Internet. It has become the newest, most fascinating and most talked about aspect of the Internet.

The World Wide Web is a service that organizes and searches information on the Internet. Without it, the Internet would be a vast pile of information that would be so enormous, it would be virtually unusable. The World Wide Web links the information on the Internet by key words or hypertext, making the vast amount of information on the Internet manageable.

Insert Bookmark.

Just a few years ago, only people who worked or studied at colleges, universities and research facilities had access to the Internet. Today, an increasing number of Internet access services are available to the average computer user.

KEYSTROKES

INSERT PAGE NUMBERS

1. Click **Insert**.......................... `Alt` + `I`

2. Click **Page Numbers** .... `U`

3. Click **Position**...................... `Alt` + `P`

4. Click **Bottom of Page(Footer)** ..... `↓`,`↑`

   OR

   Click **Top of Page (Header)** ..... `↓`,`↑`

5. Click **Alignment**.................... `Alt` + `A`

6. Select desired alignment:

   - **Right** .... `↑`,`↓`,`↵`

   - **Left**........................ `↑`,`↓`,`↵`

   - **Center** .... `↑`,`↓`,`↵`

   - **Inside** .... `↑`,`↓`,`↵`

   - **Outside** .... `↑`,`↓`,`↵`

   To change format:

   a. Click **Format** button........ `Alt` + `F`

   b. Click **Number format** .... `Alt` + `F`
      list box.

   c. Select desired format.......... `↓`,`↑`

   d. Click **OK**.................... `Enter`

7. Click **OK** .... `Enter`

Exercise 47
■ **Footnotes** ■ **Widow/Orphan Lines**

NOTES

Footnotes

■ A **footnote** is used to give information about the source of quoted material in a document. The information includes the author's name, the publication, the publication date and the page number from which the quote was taken.

■ There are several footnoting styles. Traditional footnotes are printed at the bottom of a page. A **separator line** separates footnote text from the text on the page.

■ A **reference number** appears immediately after the quote in the text, and a corresponding footnote number or symbol appears at the bottom of the page.

■ An **endnote** contains the same information as a footnote but is typed on the last page of a report. (Endnotes will be covered in the next exercise.)

■ The Footnote feature automatically inserts the reference number after the quote, inserts the separator line, numbers the footnote and formats your page so that the footnote appears on the same page as the reference number. If you desire endnotes instead of footnotes, Word will compile the endnote information on the last page of your document.

■ Each footnote number is indicated by a superscripted Arabic numeral (1, 2, 3, etc.). You can change the note number style by clicking the Options button in the Footnote and Endnote dialog box.

IMMIGRATION'S IMPACT IN THE UNITED STATES

The opportunity to directly transfer a skill into the American economy was great for newcomers prior to the 1880s. "Coal-mining and steel-producing companies in the East, railroads, gold- and silver-mining interests in the West, and textile mills in New England all sought a variety of ethnic groups as potential sources of inexpensive labor."[1] Because immigrants were eager to work, they contributed to the wealth of the growing nation. During the 1830s, American textile mills welcomed hand-loom weavers from England and North Ireland whose jobs had been displaced by power looms. Ip was this migration that established the fine-cotton-goods trade of Philadelphia. "Nearly the entire English silk industry migrated to America after the Civil War, when high American tariffs allowed the industry to prosper on this side of the Atlantic."[2]

Whether immigrants were recruited directly for their abilities or followed existing networks into unskilled jobs, they inevitably moved within groups of friends and relatives and worked and lived in clusters.

Reference number →

Separator line

[1] E. Allen Richardson, *Strangers in This Land* (New York: The Pilgrim Press, 1988), 67.

[2] John Bodnar, *The Transplanted* (Bloomington: Indiana University Press, 1985), 54.

Footnote number

Footnote and Endnote Dialog Box

Footnote →

Footnote and Endnote   ? ☒

Insert
◉ Footnote   Bottom of page
○ Endnote   End of document

Numbering
◉ AutoNumber   1, 2, 3, ...
○ Custom mark: [   ]

                  Symbol...

   OK   Cancel   Options...

- You can view the actual note in Page Layout view if you scroll to the bottom of the page. In Normal view, you must double-click the footnote number or reference mark to view the footnote in a pane at the bottom of the screen.

- You can insert footnotes by selecting Foot<u>n</u>ote from the <u>I</u>nsert menu. Press the Enter key once after keying each footnote to create a blank line between each note.

- After you select <u>F</u>ootnote or <u>E</u>ndnote in the Footnote and Endnote dialog box that follows, a footnote screen appears, ready for you to type the text of the first footnote.

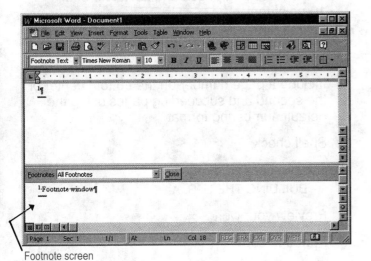

Footnote screen

- It is possible to have both footnotes and endnotes in the same document. In this exercise, however, you will create only footnotes.

- When a footnote or endnote is inserted or deleted, Word automatically renumbers all existing footnotes or endnotes as necessary.

Widow/Orphan Lines

- A widow line occurs when the last line of a paragraph is printed by itself at the top of a page. An orphan line occurs when the first line of a paragraph appears by itself on the last line of the page. Widow and orphan lines should be avoided.

- The Widow/Orphan Control feature eliminates widows and orphans in a document and may be accessed by selecting <u>P</u>aragraph, Line and Page Breaks, <u>W</u>idow/Orphan Control from the F<u>o</u>rmat menu.

In this exercise, you will create a report with footnotes, a header, and bottom-centered page numbers. Remember to suppress headers and page numbers on the first page.

✓*Note:* *When a quotation is longer than two sentences, it is single spaced and indented. In this exercise, you will indent the quoted material, as directed.*

✓*Note:* *While the exercise is shown in single space, you are to use double line spacing. Your printed document will result in two or three pages, depending on the selected font, and footnotes will appear on the same page as reference numbers.*

EXERCISE DIRECTIONS

1. Create a NEW document and keyboard the report shown on the following page, or open 🖫**47USA**.

2. Set 1.5" left and right margins.

3. Begin the exercise At approximately 2".

4. Set line spacing to double.

5. Use a serif 13-point font for the document.
   - ✓ *When creating the footnote text, check to see that the footnote font style and size is the same as the document text. Also, be sure to press Enter after each footnote text entry.*

6. Center and set the title to a serif 14-point bold font.

7. Set a .5" first-line indent for body text.

8. Use widow and orphan control.

9. Indent and single space the quoted text, as indicated. Return to the default format when resuming body text.

10. Left-align the following header on the second and succeeding pages and set it to a serif 10-point font:
    BUILDING THE UNITED STATES OF AMERICA

11. Insert the comments where shown.

12. Include a page number on the bottom center of the second and succeeding pages using the default numbering format.

13. Spell check.

14. Edit the header to read:
    BUILDING THE U. S. A.

15. Preview your work.

16. Print one copy.

17. Delete both comments.

18. Save the file; name it **USA**.

19. Close the document window.

IMMIGRATION'S IMPACT IN THE UNITED STATES

The opportunity to directly transfer a skill into the American economy was great for newcomers prior to the 1880s. "Coal-mining and steel-producing companies in the East, railroads, gold- and silver-mining interests in the West, and textile mills in New England all sought a variety of ethnic groups as potential sources of inexpensive labor."[1] Because immigrants were eager to work, they contributed to the wealth of the growing nation. During the 1830s, American textile mills welcomed hand-loom weavers from England and North Ireland whose jobs had been displaced by power looms. It was this migration that established the fine-cotton-goods trade of Philadelphia. "Nearly the entire English silk industry migrated to America after the Civil War, when high American tariffs allowed the industry to prosper on this side of the Atlantic."[2]

Add comment: Check approximate number of factories operating at this time.

Whether immigrants were recruited directly for their abilities or followed existing networks into unskilled jobs, they inevitably moved within groups of friends and relatives and worked and lived in clusters.

As the Industrial Revolution progressed, immigrants were enticed to come to the United States through the mills and factories who sent representatives overseas to secure cheap labor. An example was the Amoskeag Manufacturing Company, located along the banks of the Merrimack River in Manchester, New Hampshire. In the 1870s, the Amoskeag Company recruited women from Scotland who were expert gingham weavers. Agreements were set specifying a fixed period of time during which employees would guarantee to work for the company.[3]

Single space and indent .5" from left and right margins.

In the 1820s, Irish immigrants did most of the hard work in building the canals in the United States. In fact, Irish immigrants played a large role in building the Erie Canal. American contractors encouraged Irish immigrants to come to the United States to work on the roads, canals, and railroads, and manufacturers lured them into the new mills and factories.

Add comment: Check contribution of Italian immigrants.

"Most German immigrants settled in the middle western states of Ohio, Indiana, Illinois, Wisconsin and Missouri."[4] With encouragement to move west from the Homestead Act of 1862, which offered public land free to immigrants who intended to become citizens, German immigrants comprised a large portion of the pioneers moving west. "They were masterful farmers and they built prosperous farms."[5]

---

[1] E. Allen Richardson, *Strangers in This Land* (New York: The Pilgrim Press, 1988), 67.

[2] John Bodnar, *The Transplanted* (Bloomington: Indiana University Press, 1985), 54.

[3] Bodnar, 72.

[4] David A. Gerber, *The Making of An American Pluralism* (Chicago: University of Illinois, 1989), 124.

[5] Bodnar, 86.

KEYSTROKES

FOOTNOTES

1. Place insertion point where footnote reference number will appear.

2. Click **Insert** .... `Alt` + `I`

3. Click **Footnote** .... `N`

4. Click **Footnote** .... `Alt` + `F`
   OR
   Click **Endnote** .... `Alt` + `E`

5. Click **OK**........................... `Enter`

6. Type footnote/endnote information.

IN NORMAL VIEW

7. Press **Shift + F6** .... `Shift` + `F6`
   to leave footnote pane open
   and return to where you were working
   in the document.

   OR

   Click **Close** to close footnote pane and
   return to where you were working in
   the document.

IN PAGE LAYOUT VIEW

Press **Shift + F5** .... `Shift` + `F5`
to return to where you were
working in the document.

VIEW FOOTNOTES

IN NORMAL VIEW

Double-click the footnote reference mark.

OR

1. Click **View** .... `Alt` + `V`

2. Click **Footnotes** .... `F`

IN PAGE LAYOUT VIEW

Double-click the footnote reference mark.

OR

Scroll to footnote location.

OR

1. Click **View** .... `Alt` + `V`

2. Click **Footnotes** .... `F`

WIDOW AND ORPHAN CONTROL

1. Click **Format**....................... `Alt` + `O`

2. Click **Paragraph** .... `P`

3. Click **Line and Page Breaks** ... `Alt` + `P`

4. Click **Widow/Orphan Control** .... `Alt` + `W`
   check box to turn Widow/Orphan
   Control off or on.

NEXT EXERCISE

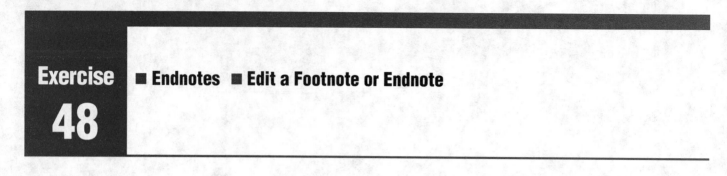

Exercise

48

■ **Endnotes** ■ **Edit a Footnote or Endnote**

NOTES

Endnotes

■ As indicated in Exercise 47, an **endnote** contains the same information as a footnote but appears at the end of document text.

■ Each endnote number is indicated by a superscripted Roman numeral (i, ii, iii, etc.). You can change the note number style by clicking the Options button in the Footnote and Endnote dialog box (see below).

Footnote and Endnote Dialog Box

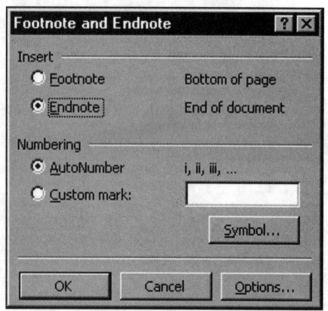

■ Like footnotes, endnotes may be viewed in Page Layout view if you scroll to the bottom of the page. In Normal view, you must double-click the endnote number or reference mark to view the footnote in a pane at the bottom of the screen.

■ Access the Endnote feature by selecting Foot<u>n</u>ote from the <u>I</u>nsert menu. In the Footnote and Endnote dialog box that follows, select <u>E</u>ndnote, OK. The bottom of the document displays, ready for you to type the text of the first endnote.

Document Window

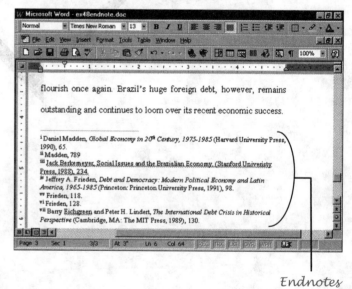

Endnotes

Edit a Footnote or Endnote

■ If you need to make a correction to the footnote/endnote, you may return to the footnote/endnote pane and edit the note. In Normal view, double-clicking the reference number will bring you to the footnote/endnote pane.

■ To delete, copy or move a footnote or endnote, edit the reference mark, not the footnote/endnote text. If you delete, copy or move the footnote/endnote text, the reference number will remain where it was inserted. When you delete, copy or move reference numbers, Word renumbers and reformats all footnote/endnote references and text.

■ You may also view your footnotes/endnotes by selecting Footnotes from the View menu. In Page Layout view, choosing this command will scroll the cursor down to the footnote/endnote text at the end of the page/document. In Normal view, choosing this command will open the note pane.

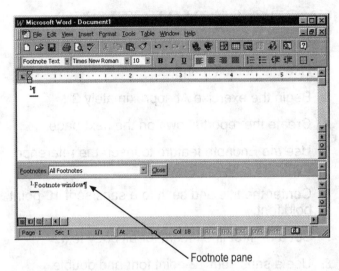

Footnote pane

■ Remember to set the font style and size of footnote/endnote text to match the document text. By default, footnote/endnote text is set to a 10-point font for the note text and a 10-point font for the reference mark. Reference marks automatically match the font size of the text they're noting.

In this exercise, you will create a report with endnotes, a header, and bottom page numbers. Remember to suppress headers and page numbers on the first page.

✓Note: When a quotation is longer than two sentences, it is single-spaced and indented. In this exercise, you will indent the quoted material, as directed.

✓Note: While the exercise is shown in single space, you are to use double line spacing. Your printed document will result in two or three pages, depending on the selected font, and endnotes will appear on the last page of the document.

EXERCISE DIRECTIONS

1. Create a NEW document, or open 🖫**48BIRDS**.

2. Use the default margins.

3. Begin the exercise At approximately 2".

4. Create the report shown on the next page.

5. Use the Endnote feature to insert the reference numbers and endnote text.

6. Center the title and set it to a sans serif 16-point bold font.

7. Set a .5" first-line indent for all body text.

8. Use a sans serif 12-point font and double spacing for the document.

9. Single-space and indent quoted text 1" from the left and right margins.

10. Use Word's Heading 2 style for each side heading.

11. Create the following header on the second and succeeding pages:
The Sport of Bird Watching

12. Right-align and set it to a script 16-point font.

13. Include a page number on the bottom right of the second and succeeding pages using the default numbering format.

14. Spell check.

15. Hyphenate the document. Limit the consecutive hyphens to 3.

16. Use Widow/Orphan control.

17. Preview your work.

18. Print one copy.

19. Save the file; name it **BIRDS**.

20. Close the document window.

KEYSTROKES

ENDNOTES

1. Place insertion point where endnote reference number will appear.

2. Click **Insert** .... `Alt` + `I`

3. Click **Footnote** .... `N`

4. Click **Endnote** .... `Alt` + `E`

5. Click **OK** .... `Enter`

6. Type endnote information.

IN NORMAL VIEW

7. Press **Shift** + **F6** .... `Shift` + `F6`
to leave endnote pane open and return to where you were working in the document.

OR

Click **Close** to close endnote pane and return to where you were working in the document.

IN PAGE LAYOUT VIEW

Press **Shift** + **F5** .... `Shift` + `F5`
to return to where you were working in the document.

VIEW ENDNOTES

IN NORMAL VIEW

Double-click the endnote reference number.

OR

1. Click **View** .... `Alt` + `V`

2. Click **Footnotes** .... `F`

IN PAGE LAYOUT VIEW

Double-click the endnote reference mark.

OR

Scroll to endnote location.

OR

1. Click **View** .... `Alt` + `V`

2. Click **Footnotes** .... `F`

DELETE ENDNOTES

1. Select the endnote reference mark.

2. Press **Delete** .... `Del`

OR

a. Click **Edit** .... `Alt` + `E`

b. Click **Cut** .... `T`

BIRD WATCHING

Single space and indent 1" from left and right.

> Birds symbolize the power that helps people to speak reflectively and leads them to think out many things in advance before they take action. Just as birds are lifted up into the air by their feathers and can remain wherever they wish, the soul in the body is elevated by thought and spreads its wings everywhere.[i]
> --St. Hildegard of Bingen, 1098-1179

Each year millions of people enjoy the sport of bird-watching, nowadays more commonly known as "birding."[ii] Some birders enjoy trying to spot as many different species as possible; others simply try to become better acquainted with local and regional birds. No matter what the level or degree of interest you might have in birding, it takes very little to get started and begin having success in identifying birds.

HOW TO GET STARTED

The first thing to do is purchase a field guide to birds native to your geographical region. These guides can be very helpful in teaching you how to identify species, but they can also be frustrating to the beginner. Most standard field guides are arranged according to bird families, such as warbler, vireo, or finch, and you need to know these families in order to locate any bird in the book. Depending on your knowledge of bird families, you will want to keep this in mind when you purchase a field guide.

WHAT TO TAKE WITH YOU

Although you need no equipment to watch birds, it can be very helpful to have a notebook, camera (preferably with a telescopic lens), and binoculars. Since you may only catch a brief glimpse of a bird, it is important to try and note as many essential details as possible, which can help you identify the bird later. These details include **field marks**, **relative size**, **voice**, and **behavior**. It may also be helpful to note the time of year, as many birds undergo plumage changes and color phases throughout the seasons.

WHAT TO LOOK FOR

Field marks include any distinctive features of the bird, such as length of the bill, size and shape of the tail and wings, color patterns, eye rings, size, shape, and color of the head.

Relative size is also important, as some birds are easily identified by size alone. It is best to become familiar with the relative sizes of some common species, such as the House Sparrow, the Blue Jay, the Common Crow, and the American Robin, so that you can more easily estimate the size of an unfamiliar species.

Voice can be one of the most distinguishing features of a bird. Of course, there are several types of bird calls, including mating calls, alarm cries, territorial claims, and simple calls used to maintain contact. You may try to transcribe these sounds into words, such as *chip, peek, cheerio, cheerie-up,* and *cheerily* to help you remember the call.

Behavior is also important in helping identify a particular species. Pay close attention to what the bird is doing. Does it walk or hop? Does it forage on the ground or hitch up a tree? Does it seem shy or bold? Is it alone or in a flock? How quickly or slowly does it flap its wings? Does its flight seem to be smooth or undulating? If it is a water bird, does it feed at the surface or dive under water?

BIRDING

The more time you spend at home studying your field guide, the more easily you will be able to identify birds in the wild. For the most part, however, experience will be your teacher. You will likely have better luck watching birds if you move quietly and stand very still. There are exceptions to that rule: If you learn to imitate a bird's call, curious species might come closer to investigate. Under no circumstances should you ever disturb birds or their habitats. Bird life in general has declined significantly with the advancement of technology and human population. "Many local and national organizations work tirelessly toward the preservation of bird habitats and species, and welcome your support and participation."[iii]

---

[i] Biederman, Hans, *Dictionary of Symbolism: Cultural Icons and the Meanings Behind Them,* (New York: Meridian, 1989), 41.

[ii] Bull, John and John Farrand, Jr., *The Audubon Society Field Guide to North American Birds,* (New York: Alfred A. Knopf, 1977), 13.

[iii] Scott, Shirley L., ed., *National Geographic Society Field Guide to the Birds of North America*, Second Edition (Washington, D. C.: The National Geographic Society, 1987), 14, 16.

Exercise 49

■ **Move Text From One Page to Another** ■ **Document Map**

Standard Toolbar

Document Map

NOTES

Move Text From One Page to Another

- The procedure for moving blocks of text from one page to another is the same as that for moving blocks of text on the same page. However, if you are moving text from one page to another, you can use the **Go To** key (F5) or the Select Browse Object button [O] on the vertical scroll bar to quickly advance to the page where you want to insert the text.

- When you move text from one page to another within two or three pages of each other, it is helpful to work in Print Preview mode using the drag-and-drop technique.

- If a hard page break was inserted, delete the break, then move the text. Word will then insert a soft page break. If the soft page break is not in a satisfactory location, insert a hard page break in the desired location.

Document Map

- Word provides several ways for you to view your documents on screen. You may be used to viewing a document in Normal, Page Layout, and Outline views. You can also view documents using the Document Map.

- The Document Map is especially useful when you want to navigate quickly to specific locations in long documents or online documents. Document Map also keeps track of your current location in the document.

- Document Map appears as a separate pane on the left of the document. To quickly jump to a new location in the document, click on its heading in the Document Map pane. You can access Document Map by clicking on the Document Map button [🔍] on the Standard toolbar, or by selecting Document Map from the <u>V</u>iew menu.

Document Map View

Click to move to another location.

Click to expand or collapse.

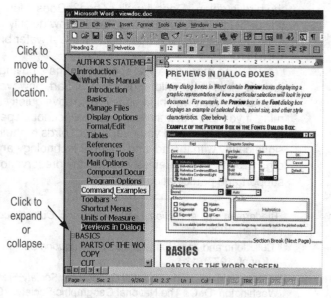

- You can change the level of the displayed headings in the same way you change how Outline levels display. Right-click in the Document Map pane and select the level of heading that you want to display.

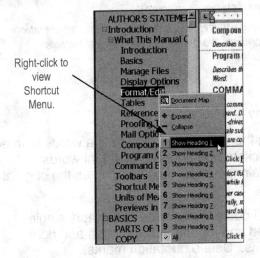

Right-click to view Shortcut Menu.

- You can also click on the expand and collapse buttons in the Display Map window.

- If you do not see many heading levels when you activate Document Map, it is probably because you have not used the heading styles that Word looks for to create the map. If Word does not find Heading levels, it will look for paragraphs that resemble headings and use those to create a map. The Document Map will be empty if Word cannot find Headings or paragraphs that seem to function as headings.

- Close Document Map by clicking the Document Map button on the Standard toolbar or by clicking Document Map on the View menu.

In this exercise, you will edit two different documents and gain practice moving text from one page to another. In addition, you will use the Thesaurus and other editing features.

EXERCISE DIRECTIONS

PART I

1. Open ⌨PREVIEW, or open 💾49PREVIEW.

2. Set Widow/Orphan Control to off.

3. Display the Document Map.

4. Access Print Preview mode and set the display for two pages; make the indicated revisions in Print Preview or Page Layout views.

5. Return to Page Layout view.

6. Change EDUCATORS' CONFERENCE to Title Case.

7. Preview your document.

8. Close the Document Map.

9. Print one copy.

10. Save the file; name it **PREVIEW**.

11. Close the document window.

PART II (PAGES 219 AND 220)

✓ *Moving paragraphs in this exercise will not affect footnote placement. Word automatically readjusts footnote placement.*

1. Open ⌨USA, or open 💾49USA.

2. Display the Document Map.

3. Using the Thesaurus, replace the words marked in brackets. Be sure replacement words maintain the same tense/ending as the original words.

4. Set off quote in separate paragraph, single-spaced and indented .5" from left and right margins. Delete quotation marks.

5. Access Print Preview mode and set the display for two (or three) pages; make the indicated revisions in this mode.

6. Return to Page Layout view.

7. Justify the body text and hyphenate the document.

8. Preview your document.

9. Print one copy.

10. Save the file; name it **USA**.

11. Close the document window.

📖 EDUCATIONAL FILM LIBRARY

Today's date

REGISTERED MAIL

Ms. Michelle Mancuso
Aventura College
77 Palm Way
Aventura, FL 33180

Dear Ms. Mancuso:

SUBJECT: EDUCATIONAL FILMS FOR HIGH SCHOOLS AND COLLEGES

Thank you for your interest in the films that we have available for high school and college students. We are pleased to send you the enclosed flyer which describes the films in detail. Also enclosed is a summary of those films that have recently been added to our collection since the publication of the flyer.

There have been many positive reactions to our films. Just three weeks ago, a group of educators, editors and vocational experts were invited to view the films at the annual EDUCATORS' CONFERENCE. Here are some of their comments:

A

We will be sure to send the films in time for you to preview them. Please be sure to list the date on which you wish to preview the film.

Move to next page.

Insert B.

Mr. William R. Bondlow, Jr., president of the National Vocational Center in Washington, D.C. and editor-in chief of Science Careers said,

I like the films very much. They are innovative and a great benefit to all those interested in the earth sciences as a professional career. Furthermore, they have captured the objects on film so true to life that anyone watching them is captivated.

Indent 1" from left and right margins.

Ms. Andra Burke, a leading expert presently assigned to the United States Interior Department, praised the films by saying that,

444 SAMARITAN AVENUE • WASHINGTON, DC • 40124
PHONE: 301-444-4444 • FAX: 301-777-7777

They are a major educational advance in career placement, which will serve as a source of motivation for all future geologists.

B

Move to page 1.

A member of the National Education Center, Dr. Lawrence Pilgrim, also liked the films and said,

I will institute a program which will make schools throughout the country aware of their vocational potential.

Insert A.

These are some of the reactions we have had to our films. We know you will have a similar reaction.

We would very much like to send you the films that you would like during the summer session. You can use the summer to review them. It is important that your request be received quickly since the demand for the films is great, particularly during the summer sessions at the colleges and universities throughout the country.

Cordially,

David Chen
Vice President, Marketing

dc/yo

Enclosures (2)

Copy to: Robert Williams, Nancy Polansky

IMMIGRATION'S IMPACT IN THE UNITED STATES

The opportunity to directly transfer a skill into the American economy was great for newcomers prior to the 1880s. "Coal-mining and

Single space and indent quote .5" from left and right margins. →

steel-producing companies in the East, railroads, gold- and silver-mining interests in the West, and textile mills in New England all sought a variety of ethnic groups as potential sources of inexpensive labor."[1] Because

immigrants were eager to work, they contributed to the wealth of the growing nation. During the 1830s, American textile mills welcomed hand-loom weavers from England and North Ireland whose jobs had been displaced by power looms. It was this migration that established the fine-cotton-goods trade of Philadelphia. "Nearly the entire English silk industry migrated to America after the Civil War, when high American tariffs allowed the industry to prosper on this side of the Atlantic."[2]

Insert A. →

Whether immigrants were recruited directly for their abilities or followed existing networks into unskilled jobs, they inevitably moved within groups of friends and relatives and worked and lived in clusters.

[1] E. Allen Richardson, *Strangers in This Land* (New York: The Pilgrim Press, 1988), 67.

[2] John Bodnar, *The Transplanted* (Bloomington: Indiana University Press, 1985), 54.

BUILDING THE U. S. A.

As the Industrial Revolution progressed, immigrants were enticed to come to the United States through the mills and factories who sent representatives overseas to secure cheap labor. An example was the Amoskeag Manufacturing Company, located along the banks of the Merrimack River in Manchester, New Hampshire. In the 1870s, the Amoskeag Company recruited women from Scotland who were expert gingham weavers. Agreements were set specifying a fixed period of time during which employees would guarantee to work for the company.[3]

A Move to Page 1.

In the 1820s, Irish immigrants did most of the hard work in building the canals in the United States. In fact, Irish immigrants played a large role in building the Erie Canal. American contractors encouraged Irish immigrants to come to the United States to work on the roads, canals, and railroads, and manufacturers lured them into the new mills and factories.

"Most German immigrants settled in the middle western states of Ohio, Indiana, Illinois, Wisconsin and Missouri."[4] With encouragement to move west from the Homestead Act of 1862, which offered public land free to immigrants who intended to become citizens, German immigrants comprised a large portion of the pioneers moving west. "They were masterful farmers and they built prosperous farms."[5]

---

[3]Bodnar, 72.

[4]David A. Gerber, *The Making of An American Pluralism* (Chicago: University of Illinois, 1989), 124.

[5]Bodnar, 86.

KEYSTROKES

GO TO

1. Click **Select Browse Object** button .
   on vertical scroll bar.

2. Click **Go to** button .... →
   on palette.

   OR

   a. Press **F5**.................................... `F5`

   b. Click **Enter page number**... `Alt` + `E`

   c. Type page number to go to ...*number*

   d. Click **Go To**...................... `Alt` + `T`

SWITCH TO DOCUMENT MAP

1. Click **Document Map** button ....
   on Standard toolbar.

   OR

   a. Click **View** .... `Alt` + `V`

   b. Click **Document Map**................. `D`

   ✓ *Document Map pane will appear on the left of the document.*

2. Click heading you want to go to.

   To turn off Document Map:

   Right-click in Document Map pane and click Document Map icon.

   OR

   a. Click **View** .... `Alt` + `V`

   b. Click **Document Map**................. `D`

CHANGE LEVEL OF HEADING IN DOCUMENT VIEW

1. Right-click in Document Map pane.

2. Select desired heading level to view.

   OR

   Click **Expand** or **Collapse** buttons next to heading levels in Document Map pane.

Exercise

50

■ **Summary**

In this exercise, you will create a report with footnotes. This report will be bound on the left. Therefore, you will need to place the footer and page number accordingly.

EXERCISE DIRECTIONS

1. Create a report using the text on the following page, or open 🖫**50BRAZIL**.

2. Set a 2" left margin and a 1.5" right margin.

3. Begin the exercise At approximately 2.5".

4. Create a right-aligned footer in a sans serif 12-point bold font on the second and succeeding pages that reads:
   BRAZIL: Investment Opportunities.

5. Include a page number at the top right corner of the second and succeeding pages.

6. Set line spacing for document text to double.

7. Set a .5" first-line indent for all body text.

8. Use a serif 13-point font for the document; center and set the title to a serif 16-point bold font.

9. Use the Footnote feature to insert the reference numbers and footnote text.

10. Use widow and orphan control.

11. Edit the footer to read BRAZIL.

12. Justify and hyphenate the document. Limit the consecutive hyphens to two.

13. Spell check.

14. Preview your work.

15. Print one copy of page one and an extra copy of pages 2 and 3.

16. Save the file; name it **BRAZIL**.

17. Close the document window.

BRAZIL

Brazil is often viewed as the economic giant of the Third World. Its economy and territory are larger than the rest of South America's and its industry is the most advanced in the developing world. Brazilian foreign debt is also the Third World's largest. The problem of foreign debt has plagued the Latin American economies since the 1960s when foreign borrowing was the only way for Latin American nations to sustain economic growth. However, when international interest rates began to rise in the 1980s, the debt these nations accumulated became unmanageable. In Brazil, the debt crisis of the 1980s marked the decline of an economy that had flourished since 1967 when foreign borrowing enabled the nation to develop its own productive industries and lessen its dependence on foreign manufactured goods. "Similar to other Latin American nations, Brazilian overseas borrowing between 1967 and 1981 became a drain on the economy when international interest rates rose; by 1985, its excessive borrowing resulted in economic disaster, political dissension and protest, and the rise of an opposition government in Brazil."[1]

Throughout the beginning of the twentieth century, growth of the Brazilian economy remained dependent upon agricultural exports. The twentieth century witnessed a decline in the export of sugar from the northeast of Brazil and a rise in the export of coffee from the southeast of Brazil. This concentrated economic growth and political power in the developed southeast part of the nation, particularly in the states of Rio de Janeiro and Sao Paulo. Industrial growth in this region progressed gradually and by 1919, domestic firms supplied over 70% of the local demand for industrial products and employed over 14% of the labor force.[2]

However, by the 1980s, Brazil accumulated massive foreign debt which ultimately caused the government to cut foreign spending and investment, drove interest rates so high that businesses could not borrow money for investment and expansion, and precipitated the bankruptcy of numerous companies, the unemployment of wage laborers, and growing social unrest. Between 1979 and 1982, the debt amassed by Brazilian banks increased from $7.7 billion to $16.1 billion. "By 1982, debt-service payments were equivalent to 91% of Brazil's merchandise exports, up from 51% in 1977."[3] In mid-1988, inflation in Brazil ran above 500% and the value of the foreign debt Brazil has to repay remains the largest in the Third World.

Brazil's financial situation is improving. Currently, Brazil has been able to sustain a 5% economic growth rate and is encouraging expanded foreign investment. Inflation in Brazil has fallen to 1.5% a month while United States exports to Brazil jumped by 35% last year.[4]

Rising international trade which may culminate in a South American free trade zone has enabled the Brazilian economy to flourish once again. Brazil's huge foreign debt, however, remains outstanding and continues to loom over its recent economic success.

---

[1] Jeffrey A. Frieden, *Debt, Development and Democracy: Modern Political Economy and Latin America, 1965-1985* (Princeton: Princeton University Press, 1991), 98.

[2] Frieden, 118.

[3] Frieden, 128.

[4] Barry Eichgreen and Peter H. Lindert, *The International Debt Crisis in Historical Perspective* (Cambridge, MA: The MIT Press, 1989), 130.

Exercise

51

■ **Summary**

In this exercise, you will create a multiple-page letter.

EXERCISE DIRECTIONS

1. Create the letter shown on the following pages using the Contemporary Letter template.

   ✓ *To insert the recipient's name in the salutation line, highlight the words "Sir or Madam" (do <u>not</u> highlight the colon) and replace them with recipient's name. Then place the insertion point at the end of the salutation line and press Enter.*

2. Use the default margins and start line.

3. Insert the company name, address and logo as shown.

4. Modify the header to include the name of the addressee, in addition to the page number and today's date.

5. Insert a continuous section break before the first numbered item.

6. Set 2" left and right margins.

7. Use the Bullets and Numbering feature to number the four indented paragraphs.

8. Set line spacing to 1.5 for numbered paragraphs.

9. Set the first sentence in each numbered paragraph to bold italics.

10. Insert a continuous section break after the last numbered paragraph and return the margins to default (1.25" left and right). Return line spacing to single space.

11. Highlight all body text (do not include the company name or address) and change font size to 11 point.

12. Insert hard page breaks where desired so that the text does not break awkwardly.

13. Spell check.

14. After completing the exercise, move the sentence as shown.

15. Preview your work using the Multiple Pages option of Print Preview.

16. Print one copy.

17. Save the file; name it **INSURANCE**.

18. Close the document window.

5550 West Cypress
Tampa, FL 33607-1707
Phone: 1-800-888-8888
Fax: 1-800-333-3333

Equinox Life Insurance Company

Today's date

Ms. Jackie Ng
87 Miami Gardens Drive
Miami, FL 30122

Dear Ms. Ng:

SUBJECT: NEW LIFE INSURANCE PROGRAM AT EQUINOX

Congratulations on your retirement! Ms. Janet Leigh, your friend and a client of ours, indicated that you were interested in purchasing life insurance. Equinox has just developed a new life insurance program that makes good sense for newly retired individuals.

For example, our Premium Term Life coverage is ideal for short term needs, such as paying off mortgages or other obligations that may decrease over time. This policy is available to members who are 50-64 years of age. Premiums are expected to remain constant. Our Permanent Life coverage can help build a nest egg for your survivors.

Move to page 2.

Ms. Leigh did tell us that you were considering other insurance carriers for your life insurance needs. Let me assure you that Equinox has an insurance program for you. Here are four reasons why you should choose Equinox:

1. *We provide affordable, quality life insurance designed for people over the age of 50.* There's no physical exam, just three health questions to answer. And members' spouses age 45 and older are also eligible.

2. *We provide the coverage you want at a price you can afford.* Coverage of up to $25,000 is available. And you can choose from several term or permanent products. Whether you are seeking to maximize family protection or minimize premium costs, this Program has a product for you.

EQUINOX for all your insurance needs.

Ms. Jackie Ng
Today's date
Page 2

3. ***We offer you more value for your dollar.*** Among the Program's special features are a waiver of premium for nursing home care, plus a living benefit. Further details on these features, plus facts on costs, eligibility, limitations and exclusions—are detailed in the enclosed information kit.

4. ***Equinox Life Insurance has been in business for over 40 years.*** Equinox has earned the highest possible ratings from financial institutions for its financial stability and claims paying ability.

Please read the enclosed information kit, which will describe in detail how Equinox can protect your family better. I will phone you early next week to answer any questions you might have about our life insurance programs. We know you will be pleased with our numerous life insurance products and our very personalized service.

Sincerely,

Insert A.

John Roth
Manager

jm/yo

enclosure (1)

Word 97

LESSON 8

Multiple Documents; Macros

- ■ Switch Among Open Documents
- ■ Display Multiple Documents
- ■ Copy/Move Text from One Document to Another
- ■ Close/Maximize a Document Window
- ■ Save All
- ■ Close All
- ■ Insert a File
- ■ Create AutoText Entries
- ■ Insert AutoText
- ■ Record a Macro
- ■ Run a Macro

Exercise 52

- ■ **Switch Among Open Documents** ■ **Display Multiple Documents**
- ■ **Copy/Move Text from One Document to Another**
- ■ **Close/Maximize a Document Window**

NOTES

Switch Among Open Documents

- ■ It is often convenient to work with more than one document at a time. To switch (cycle) between open documents and view one document at a time, press Ctrl + F6.

Display Multiple Documents

- ■ If you wish to copy or move information from one document to another, it is convenient to display more than one document on your screen. You can display multiple documents by opening the documents you wish to view, then selecting Arrange All from the Window menu.

- ■ The document that contains the insertion point is known as the active document. To make a document active, press Ctrl + F6 and click in the desired document, or select the document name from the Window menu.

Copy/Move Text from One Document to Another

- ■ The procedure for copying or moving text from one document to another is the same as that for copying/moving text within the same document. With your insertion point in the active document, select the text you wish to move or copy. Use whatever copy/move procedure you desire (cut/copy and paste or drag and drop). Click the document to receive the copied/moved text to make it active, and complete the copy/move procedure.

Close/Maximize a Document Window

- ■ As you close each document window, you can save its contents. To close a window, double-click the Document Control button 📄 to the left of the title bar. Or click the document you wish to close and select Close from the File menu. Or click the document you wish to close and click the Close button ❌ on the title bar.

- ■ To return a document to the full screen size, click the maximize button 🔲 to the right of the document title bar.

- ■ After closing one of your open documents, you may rearrange the remaining documents on the screen by selecting Arrange All from the Window menu.

Window Displaying Multiple Documents

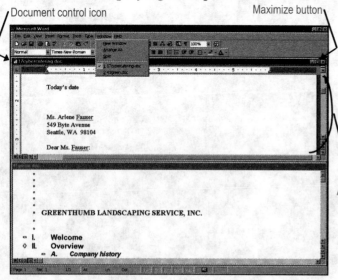

Document control icon

Maximize button

Active window

In this exercise, you will display two documents and copy text from one document to another. This procedure may also be used for moving text from one document to another.

Reminder: Copying text leaves text in its original location and pastes a copy of it in a new location.

EXERCISE DIRECTIONS

1. Create a NEW document using the Contemporary Memo Template.

2. Display the Office Assistant.

3. Create the memo as shown in Illustration A on page 230.

4. Open ⌨TRAVEL, or open 💾52TRAVEL.

5. Display both documents by selecting Arrange All from the Window menu.

6. Click the Show/Hide button to display screen codes.

7. Copy the first two workshop descriptions from TRAVEL and insert them below the first paragraph in the NEW document.

   ✓ *To copy the formatting, be sure to highlight the paragraph symbol at the end of the last paragraph to be copied.*

   ✓ *When copying, the document to be copied from must be the active document. When you are ready to place the text, the new document must become the active document. Follow keystrokes carefully.*

8. Adjust line spacing as necessary to match illustration.

9. Close TRAVEL.

10. Maximize the NEW document window.

11. Spell check the NEW document.

12. Print one copy of the NEW document.

13. Save the new document; name it TOURS.

14. Close the document window.

Memorandum

To: Kristy Langham, Manager

CC: All Travel Agents

From: Angela Bacci, Tour Coordinator

Date: Today's date

Re: Summer 1998 Travel Workshops

The following summer 1998 travel workshops have been arranged. You can now promote these programs to your travel clients. Since these programs tend to fill to capacity, please keep track of how many workshops you sell.

CONFIDENTIAL

1

Memorandum

To: Kristy Langham, Manager

CC: All Travel Agents

From: Angela Bacci, Tour Coordinator

Date: Today's date

Re: Summer 1998 Travel Workshops

The following summer 1998 travel workshops have been arranged. You can now promote these programs to your travel clients. Since these programs tend to fill to capacity, please keep track of how many workshops you sell.

POWER PLACES SEMINAR AND TOUR IN EGYPT:
July 14–July 21. $2,199.
Journey with others to one of the world's most sacred sites—the Great Pyramid. You will have special access into the Great Pyramid not available to other tourists. Experience a three-hour private tour (closed to the general public) of all three chambers. Learn about the teachings and technologies of ancient Egypt, taught by modern practitioners of these ancient sacred arts. You may choose the optional three-day Nile cruise following the conference.

Price includes airfare from New York, hotel accommodations, 30 meals, entrance into the Great Pyramid, most transportation within Egypt, luggage handling, conference fees and events.

POWER PLACES SEMINAR AND TOUR IN PERU:
June 14–June 22. $2,299.
This conference has been specifically planned to culminate in Machu Picchu during the summer solstice, the holiest time of the year for the Incas. You will travel through the sacred valley of the Incas, nestled in the serene Urubamba Valley. You will meet native shamans, who will lead a special ceremony on the solstice, and provide insights on Peru's present-day culture, places and people.

Price includes airfare from Miami, hotel accommodations (double occupancy), 30 meals, train and bus transportation within Peru, extensive sightseeing, entrance into Machu Picchu, conference fees and events.

CONFIDENTIAL

1

KEYSTROKES

OPEN MULTIPLE DOCUMENTS

1. Click **File** .... `Alt` + `F`
2. Click **Open** .... `O`
3. Hold down **Ctrl** .... `Ctrl`
   and click each file to open.

   OR

   ✓ *You must be selecting adjacent files to use the following procedure.*

   a. Click first file to open.
   b. Hold down **Shift** .... `Shift`
   c. Click last file to open.
4. Click **Open** .... `Enter`

MAKE A DOCUMENT ACTIVE

Press **Ctrl + F6** .... `Ctrl` + `F6`
until desired document is active.

OR

1. Click **Window** .... `Alt` + `W`
2. Click .... `↓` `↑`, `Enter`
   document name or number
   to switch to desired document.

DISPLAY MULTIPLE DOCUMENTS

1. Open desired documents.
2. Click **Window** .... `Alt` + `W`
3. Click **Arrange All** .... `A`

RETURN TO SINGLE DOCUMENT DISPLAY

1. Make desired document active.
2. Click **Maximize** button......... `Ctrl` + `F10`

COPY TEXT FROM ONE DOCUMENT TO ANOTHER

1. Open both documents.
2. Make source document the active file.
3. Select (highlight) text to copy.

   USING TOOLBAR

   a. Click **Copy** button....................... 🗐
   b. Make the destination document active.
   c. Place insertion point where text will be inserted.
   d. Click **Paste** button .... 📋

   OR

   Press **Shift + Insert** .... `Shift` + `Ins`

   OR

   Press **Ctrl + V** .... `Ctrl` + `V`

   USING MOUSE

1. Display both documents.
2. Hold down **Ctrl** .... `Ctrl`
   and point to selected text.
3. Hold down left mouse button and drag text to new location.
4. Release left mouse button.

MOVE TEXT FROM ONE DOCUMENT TO ANOTHER

1. Open both documents.
2. Make the source document the active file.
3. Select (highlight) text to be moved.
4. Click **Cut** button .... ✂
5. Do one of the following:

   Click destination document.

   OR

   Press **Ctrl + F6**.................... `Ctrl` + `F6`

   OR

   a. Click **Window** .... `Alt` + `W`
   b. Select name of destination document to make it active.
5. Place insertion point where copied text will be inserted.
6. Click **Paste** button .... 📋

   OR

   Press **Shift + Insert**........... `Shift` + `Ins`

   OR

   Press **Ctrl + V** .... `Ctrl` + `V`

NEXT EXERCISE

Exercise 53

■ **Save All** ■ **Close All**

NOTES

Save All/Close All

■ When several documents are open at once, you can save all or close all of them simultaneously by holding down the Shift key and then selecting Save All or Close All from the File menu. Word will display a Save As dialog box for any document that was not previously saved.

In this exercise, you will open more than one document and gain more practice copying text from one document to another.

EXERCISE DIRECTIONS

1. Create a NEW document.

2. Open ⌨ **BAKERY**, or open 💾 **53BAKERY**.

3. Display both documents by selecting Arrange All from the Window menu.

4. Click the Show/Hide button to display screen codes.

5. Copy the text shown in Part I to the NEW document. Insert the highlighted text shown in Part II to complete the exercise.

6. Use Format Painter to copy the font formatting (face, style and size) to each section.

7. Spell check the NEW document. Make any necessary adjustments to the text and/or formatting.

8. Save all open documents; name the NEW document **BAKERYCAFE**.

9. Maximize the NEW document window.

10. Print one copy of the NEW document.

11. Close each document.

KEYSTROKES

SAVE ALL OPEN DOCUMENTS

1. Hold Down the **Shift** key............... `Shift`

2. Click **File**.

3. Click **Save All**.............................. `L`

CLOSE ALL OPEN DOCUMENTS

1. Hold Down the **Shift** key............... `Shift`

2. Click **File**.

3. Click **Close All**............................. `C`

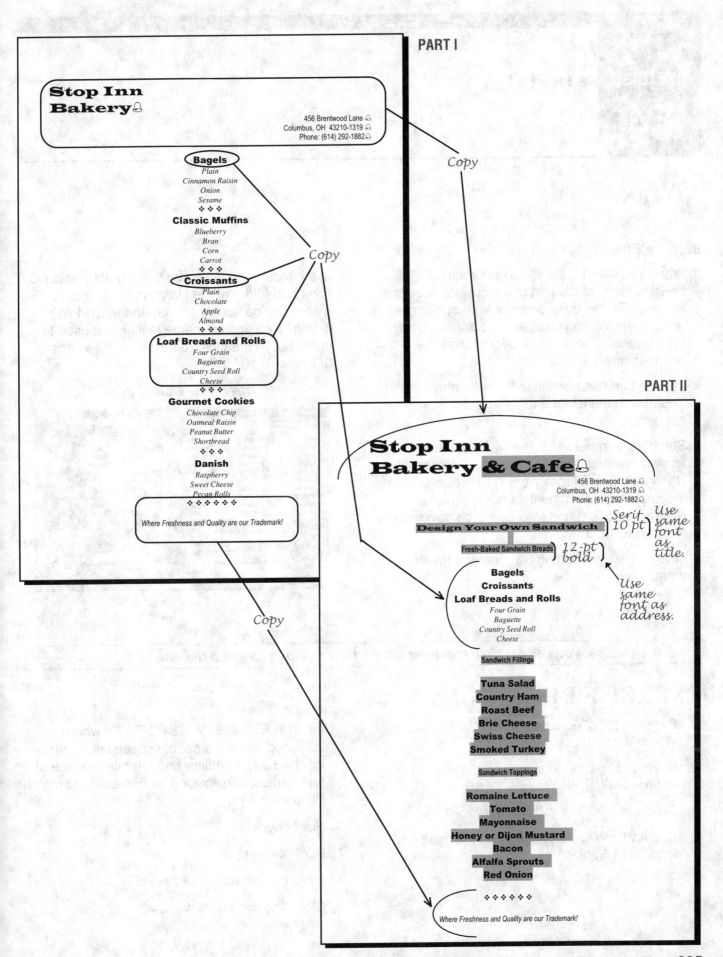

Exercise
54

■ **Insert a File**

NOTES

Insert a File

■ When you insert a file into a document, the inserted file is made part of the current document window. This is quite different from opening a document. When you open a document, each new, opened document is layered over the previous one.

■ The file that has been inserted will remain intact. You may insert it into another document when needed.

■ Standard or repetitive text may be saved under its own filename and inserted into a document when needed. (Repetitive text may also be inserted into a document as AutoText or as a Macro. AutoText and Macros will be covered in later exercises.)

■ Insert a file by selecting File from the Insert menu.

■ In the Insert File dialog box, you must select the drive and folder of the file you wish to insert. (Files may be accessed from the Insert File dialog box using the same techniques used to open files in the Open dialog box. See Lesson 3, Exercise 10.)

Insert File Dialog Box

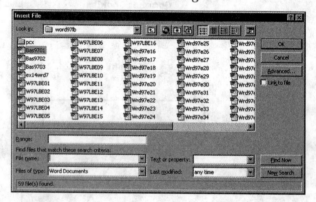

In this exercise, you will create a memo and insert a previously created file into it.

EXERCISE DIRECTIONS

1. Create a NEW document using the Professional Memo template.

2. Keyboard the memo shown on the right, or open 🖫**54PINEVIEW**.

3. Delete the CC line in the memo heading.

4. Use a Wingdings flag symbol in the company logo in a 16-point font.

5. Insert ⌨**ESTATE** or 🖫**54ESTATE** where indicated. Leave a double space before the inserted ad's headline and after its final line of text. Adjust line spacing as necessary to match illustration.

6. Spell check.

7. Print one copy.

8. Save the file; name it **PINEVIEW**.

9. Close the document window.

FLAGSHIP REALTY

Memo

To: Floyd West, Branch Manager

From: Jasmine Baker, Vice President

Date: 09/02/97

Re: Exclusive Listing for Pineview Estates

We just received notice that we have been given the exclusive listing for Pineview Estates, the country condominium residence on the North Fork. The builder placed an advertisement for this new development in several local newspapers. The ad ran last Sunday and will run again next Sunday; a copy appears below.

As a result of this local exposure, you should have considerable activity on these properties. Keep me apprised of all inquiries.

jb

Insert the ESTATE file.

● Page 1

KEYSTROKES

INSERT A FILE

1. Place insertion point where you want file inserted.

2. Click **Insert**......................... Alt + I

3. Click **File**.................................. L

4. Select document to insert.

5. Click **OK**................................... Enter

Exercise 55

■ **Create AutoText Entries** ■ **Insert AutoText**

NOTES

Create AutoText Entries

- The **AutoText** feature allows you to save standard or repetitive text and insert it into a document when needed. For example, creating an AutoText entry for a letter closing eliminates the need to retype a closing each time a letter is generated. In a Last Will and Testament, many of the paragraphs are standard and are used for all clients. Only those paragraphs that relate to specific items or names are changed. An AutoText entry may be created to save the repetitive paragraphs.

    ✓ *Repetitive text may also be inserted into a document as a macro. Macros will be covered in Exercise 57.*

- An unlimited amount of text or graphics may be stored in an AutoText entry. You may use up to 31 characters in naming AutoText entries, and you may include spaces, but it is recommended that you use short names that are easy to remember.

- To create an AutoText entry, keyboard and highlight the text (or graphics) that you want to become an AutoText entry. Open the Insert menu, select AutoText, and then select New from the submenu.

- In the Create AutoText dialog box that follows, type the name of your AutoText entry in the Name text box, and click OK to create the entry. Use a one-letter abbreviation as your AutoText name if you use the entry frequently.

Create AutoText Dialog Box

Insert AutoText

- To insert an AutoText entry into a document, type the name (or abbreviation) of the AutoText entry and press F3. As you begin to type the name of your entry, a pop-up box will display, suggesting the entry name. Press Enter to accept Word's suggestion. This feature is active only when the Show AutoComplete tip for AutoText and dates check box on the AutoText tab in the AutoCorrect dialog box is selected. You can access the AutoText dialog box by selecting AutoText, AutoText from the Insert menu .

AutoCorrect Dialog Box

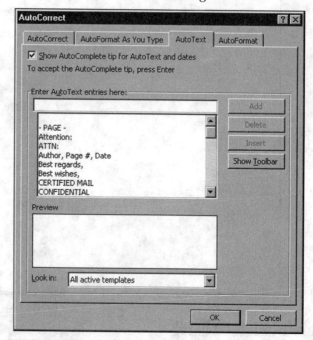

- You can edit an AutoText entry by inserting it into a document, making the desired changes, and resaving it as a new AutoText with the same name as the original entry. Click Yes when asked if you would like to redefine the AutoText entry.

- If you are not certain of the name or content of the AutoText entry, open the Insert menu, select AutoText, then select Normal from the submenu. By default, all your most recently created AutoText entries are stored in the Normal option. View the entries, then select the desired entry. You can also select AutoText from the submenu, select the desired entry from the list in the AutoText dialog box, and then click OK.

- If you use the AutoText feature frequently, you may want to display the AutoText toolbar. Click the Show Toolbar button in the AutoText dialog box, or right-click on the Standard toolbar and select AutoText.

AutoText toolbar

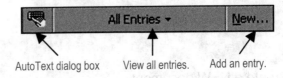

AutoText dialog box   View all entries.   Add an entry.

AutoText Submenu

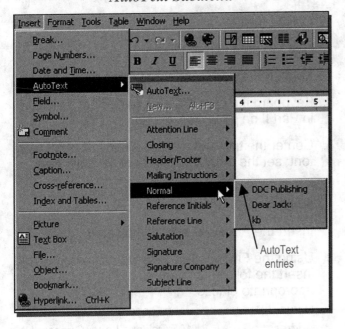

> *In Part I of this exercise, you will create several AutoText entries and save each entry under a different AutoText name. In Part II of the exercise, you will assemble a Last Will and Testament, inserting the appropriate standard paragraph files. Other AutoText entries will be used in subsequent exercises.*

EXERCISE DIRECTIONS

PART I

1. Create a NEW document.

2. Display Office Assistant.

3. Use the default margins.

4. Keyboard the first standardized paragraph for a Last Will and Testament as shown in Part I on the next page, including the asterisks (*). (Do not include the AutoText name in the paragraph.)

5. Spell check.

6. Create an AutoText entry using the AutoText name indicated above the paragraph (Will1).

7. Keyboard the second standardized paragraph for a Last Will and Testament, including the asterisks. Create an AutoText entry using the AutoText name indicated above the paragraph (Will2).

   ✓ *Create the first signature line (residing at) and copy it twice.*

8. Spell check.

9. Create an AutoText entry for each item shown in the table and use the AutoText name indicated. Do not include paragraph mark at end when saving AutoText entry.

10. Close the document window without saving.

PART II

1. Create a NEW document.

2. Use the default margins.

3. Begin the exercise At approximately 2".

4. Keyboard the Last Will and Testament as shown in Part II on page 241, or open ⌨55WILL.

5. Center the title and set it to a serif 14-point bold font; set the body text to a serif 12-point font.

6. Set a first-line indent at 1" for the three numbered paragraphs.

7. Insert the AutoText entries indicated.

8. Using the Find feature, locate each asterisk and insert the following information in the appropriate places:

Name (I,):	John Richard Adams.
Address (of):	105 Oakland Lane, Goshen, NY.
Date (this day of):	third day of January 1997.

9. Spell check.

10. Preview your work.

11. Print one copy.

12. Save the file; name it WILL.

13. Close the document window.

PART I

AutoText Name: **Will1**

> I, *, of *, do make, publish and declare this to be my Last Will and Testament, hereby revoking all wills and codicils heretofore made by me.

AutoText Name: **Will2**

> IN TESTIMONY WHEREOF, I have to this my Last Will and Testament, subscribed my name and affixed my seal, this * day of *, 199*.
>
> _____
>   *
>
> Signed, sealed, published and declared by the above-named testator, as and for his Last Will and Testament, in our presence, and we at his request, in his presence and in the presence of each other, do hereunto sign our names and set down our addresses as attesting witnesses, all on this * day of * , 199*.
>
> _____ residing at _____
>
> _____ residing at _____
>
> _____ residing at _____

AutoText Name	AutoText Entry
PSA	*PsA* Micro**Computer** Systems, Inc.
CO	*Computer Technology Group, Inc.*
CL	Sincerely, Chad Chasin Manager cc/
RV	*Rave Sunglasses* *(set text to script 20 point.)*

PART II

Insert Will 1.

LAST WILL AND TESTAMENT
OF
JOHN RICHARD ADAMS

FIRST: I direct that all my just debts, the expenses of my last illness and funeral and the expenses of administering my estate be paid as soon as convenient.

SECOND: I give all my articles of personal, household or domestic use or adornment, including automobile and boats, to my wife, Mary Adams, or, if she does not survive me, to my children, Thomas Adams and Betsy Adams, as shall survive me, in shares substantially equal as to value.

THIRD: I give and devise all my residential real property, and all my interest in any policies of insurance thereon, to my wife, Mary Adams, if she survives me or if she does not survive me, to my surviving children, to be held by them jointly.

Insert Will 2.

KEYSTROKES

CREATE AN AUTOTEXT ENTRY

1. Select (highlight) text/graphics to store as an AutoText entry.
2. Click **Insert**..........................Alt + I
3. Click **A**utotext..................................A
4. Click **N**ew..N
5. Type name for AutoText entry....... *name*
6. Click **OK**.....................................Enter

DELETE AN AUTOTEXT ENTRY

1. Click **Insert**..........................Alt + I
2. Click **A**utoText.................................A
3. Click **A**utoTe**x**t.................................X
4. Select AutoText name to delete.
5. Click **D**elete.........................Alt + D
6. Click **OK**.....................................Enter

INSERT AN AUTOTEXT ENTRY

USING KEYBOARD SHORTCUT

1. Place insertion point where AutoText entry will be inserted.
2. Type name of AutoText entry.
3. Press **F3**...F3
   OR
   (If AutoComplete is turned on)
   Press **Enter** when Word suggests the desired AutoText entry.

USING THE INSERT MENU

1. Place insertion point where AutoText entry will be inserted.
2. Click **Insert**..........................Alt + I
3. Click **A**utoText...............................A
4. Click **A**utoTe**x**t.............................X
5. Select or type desired AutoText name.
6. Click **Insert**..........................Alt + I

USING THE AUTOTEXT TOOLBAR

1. Right-click on Standard (or any) toolbar and select **AutoText** to turn on toolbar.

2. Place insertion point where AutoText entry will be inserted.
3. Click All Entries.
4. Click template where AutoText entry is stored. (By default all AutoText entries are stored in Normal template unless you select another template where you want to store them.)
5. Select desired entry from list.

EDIT AN AUTOTEXT ENTRY

1. Insert AutoText into document.
2. Edit as desired.
3. Select (highlight) the edited text.
4. Click **Insert**..........................Alt + I
5. Click **A**utoText...............................A
6. Click **A**utoTe**x**t.............................X
7. Select or type desired AutoText name.
8. Click **A**dd..........................Alt + A
9. Click **Y**es..........................Alt + Y
   when asked if you want to redefine the AutoText entry.

Exercise 56

■ **Insert AutoText**

NOTES

Insert AutoText

■ To insert an AutoText entry into a document, type the AutoText name and press F3.

■ If AutoComplete is on, a pop-up box will suggest the entry contents after the first four or more letters of the entry name are typed. Press Enter if you want to accept Word's suggestion.

■ However, before typing the AutoText name, be sure your insertion point is at the beginning of a line or preceded by a space or punctuation mark. Otherwise, the abbreviation will not be replaced with the AutoText entry.

In this exercise, you will create a letter and, where indicated, insert AutoText entries you created in the previous exercise. You will note that this document contains a Re line, which is commonly used in legal correspondence. "Re" means "in reference to" or "subject." Press the Enter key twice before and after keying the Re line.

EXERCISE DIRECTIONS

1. Create a NEW document.

2. Use the default margins.

3. Keyboard the letter shown in the exercise.

4. Begin the document At approximately 2".

5. Insert the PSA, CO, and CL AutoText entries wherever they appear in the text.

6. Spell check.

7. Preview your work.

8. Print one copy.

9. Save the file; name it **TRANSFER**.

10. Close the document window.

Today's date

Samantha Goodwin, Esq.
Goodwin, Escada & Maldanato
803 Park Avenue
New York, NY 10023

Dear Ms. Goodwin:

Re: [PSA] vs. ABC Manufacturing Company

I am enclosing a copy of the Bill of Sale that transfers all Gordon's assets to [PSA]

In addition, you asked us to represent [CO] in their $200,000 payment to [PSA] Because of this payment, [CO] became subrogated to the claim made by [PSA], and [PSA] cannot settle this matter without the approval of [CO]

[CO] would also be entitled to recover some portion of any judgement recovered by [PSA] in the above action. In order to get a settlement in this matter, we will need to obtain a release of ABC Manufacturing Company by [CO]

Let's discuss this so that we can quickly settle this matter.

[CL]

enclosure

KEYSTROKES

INSERT AUTOTEXT

USING KEYBOARD SHORTCUT

1. Place insertion point where AutoText entry will be inserted.

2. Type name of AutoText entry.

3. Press **F3** F3
   OR
   (If AutoComplete is turned on)

   Press **Enter** when Word suggests the desired AutoText entry.

Exercise

57

■ **Record a Macro**

NOTES

Record a Macro

- A macro is a saved series of commands and keystrokes that may be played with a single keystroke or mouse click. It is different from an AutoText entry in that it may contain procedures and/or commands in addition to text.

- For example, a macro may be used to automate a particular task, like changing margins or line spacing. Rather than press many keys to access a task, you can record the process and play it with one keystroke.

- To record a macro, select <u>R</u>ecord New Macro from the <u>M</u>acro submenu of the <u>T</u>ools menu.

- In the Record Macro dialog box that follows, keyboard the name of your macro in the <u>M</u>acro name text box. Macro names may be up to 82 characters in length. Macro names may include letters and numbers, but they may not contain any spaces or special characters.

- It is important to type a <u>D</u>escription of what each macro accomplishes. This will enable others to use it. Also, because macro names are easy to forget, you can always find out what a macro does by reading the description.

Record Macro Dialog Box

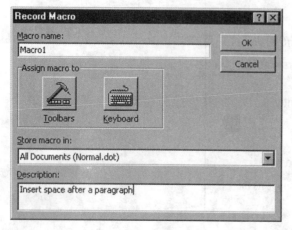

- You can assign your macro to become a toolbar button or a combination of keystrokes on the keyboard.

  ✓*Note:* *To create a toolbar button for a particular macro, you must customize the toolbar. See Office documentation to customize toolbars.*

Macro Dialog Box

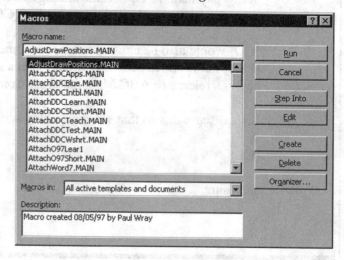

- For the exercises in this text, click <u>K</u>eyboard to assign shortcut keystroke(s) for each macro you record (*See keystrokes on page 247*).

- After you click OK, the Macro Control box appears on the screen, and any key you press will be captured into the macro.

- To stop recording, click the Stop button on the Macro control box.

- After entering the name and description of your macro, click OK.

Stop button ——→   ——— Pause

In this exercise, you will create three macros to automate tasks. In the next exercise, you will run the macros.

EXERCISE DIRECTIONS

1. Create a NEW document.

2. Close the Office Assistant (if it is displayed).

3. Create macro #1 as indicated below (spell check and print preview); name it **CLOSING** and use **Alt + C** as the shortcut keys.

4. Create macro #2 as indicated below (font size and margin change); name it **MARGINS** and use **Alt + M** as the shortcut keys.

5. Create macro #3 as indicated below (line spacing change); name it **LINESPACING** and use **Alt + L** as the shortcut keys.

6. Close the document window.

Macro #	Macro Name	Shortcut keys	Procedures to Record
1	CLOSING	Alt + C	Click Spelling button on toolbar. Respond to all prompts. Click File. Click Print Preview.
2	MARGINS	Alt + M	Click Font size button on toolbar. Select 12 point. Click File. Click Page Setup. Click Margins. Change left and right margins to 1". Click OK.
3	LINESPACING	Alt + L	Click Format. Click Paragraph. Click Line Spacing list arrow. Select 1.5 Lines. Click OK.

KEYSTROKES

RECORD A MACRO

1. Click **Tools** .... `Alt` + `T`

2. Click **Macro** .... `M`

3. Click **Record New Macro** .... `R`

4. Type a name for the macro.

5. Click **Description** .... `Alt` + `D`

6. Type a description of the macro's function.

7. Click **Keyboard** button .... `Alt` + `K`

8. Press **Alt** plus a desired shortcut key.
   ✓ *Do not use a key that is assigned to another function. Word will indicate whether each key you suggest is unassigned.*

9. Click **Assign** .... `Tab` , `Alt` + `A`

10. Click **Close**.

11. Type keystrokes to store in the macro.
    ✓ *Mouse actions in menus and dialog boxes may be used in a macro, but mouse actions that select text or position the insertion point may not be stored in a macro.*

STOP RECORDING A MACRO

Click **Stop** button .... ▪
on Macro Control box to stop recording keystrokes.

OR

1. Click **Tools** .... `Alt` + `T`

2. Click **Macro** .... `M`

3. Click **Stop Recording** .... `R`

DELETE A MACRO

ALT + F8

1. Click **Tools** .... `Alt` + `T`

2. Click **Macro** .... `M`

3. Click **Macros** .... `M`

4. Select macro name .... `↓` `↑`

5. Click **Delete** .... `Alt` + `D`

6. Click **Yes** .... `Y`

7. Click **Close** .... `Esc`

Exercise 58 ■ Run a Macro

NOTES

Run a Macro

■ Once a macro has been recorded and saved, it can be *run* (or played) into your document whenever desired.

■ To run a macro, press the keystroke(s) assigned to the macro. Or open the <u>T</u>ools menu, select Macro, then select <u>M</u>acros from the submenu. Select the name of the macro and click <u>R</u>un.

✓Note: *You can also use this dialog box to create, delete, or access the edit macro feature.*

■ If you select Word commands from the M<u>a</u>cros in drop-down list box, numerous macros that you did not create will be listed in the macro window. Word has provided you with numerous macros to automate a variety of tasks. To determine what each macro does, click the macro and note the description at the bottom of the dialog box.

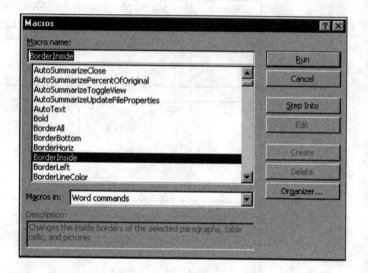

In this exercise, you will create an advertisement and insert an AutoText entry as well as run two macros you created earlier.

EXERCISE DIRECTIONS

1. Create a NEW document.

2. Begin the exercise At 1".

3. Use the default margins.

4. Center the first two lines. Set the text to a serif 18-point bold font. Set the Q and A to a different serif 22-point font. Press the Enter key twice.

5. Run the LINESPACING macro (Alt+L).

6. Set the side heading text to a sans serif 12-point font (use Britannic Bold, if available). Set the paragraph text to a serif 14-point font.

7. Key the advertisement as shown. Insert the **RV** AutoText entry wherever *Rave Sunglasses* appears in the text.

8. Justify paragraph text.

9. Center the page vertically.

10. Run the CLOSING macro (Alt+C) to spell check and print preview the document.

11. Print one copy.

12. Save the file; name it **RAVE**.

13. Close the document window.

Q: **What is the difference?**

A: **The difference is *Rave Sunglasses*.**

With *Rave Sunglasses* you can see the difference.

Rave Sunglasses has developed lens technologies that control light frequencies. The "bad" ones like UV are kept out, while the "good" ones that help vision are let in. You will notice more light gets through, so you can distinguish objects better.

You can feel the difference in the way *Rave Sunglasses* fit.

Rave Sunglasses don't pinch or feel too heavy on your face. They're easily adjustable for a perfect fit, and many styles have details like spring hinges and silicone nosepads.

Experience a difference in the way you see the world with *Rave Sunglasses*.

You'll be amazed once you wear *Rave Sunglasses* around town for a few days. You'll wonder how you ever lived without them. Buying a pair of *Rave Sunglasses* is like making an investment in your eyes!

KEYSTROKES

RUN A MACRO

ALT + F8

1. Click **Tools** .... `Alt` + `T`
2. Click **Macro** .... `M`
3. Click **Macros** .... `M`
4. Select desired macro name ..... `↓` , `↑`
5. Click **Run** .... `Alt` + `R`
   OR
   Press shortcut keys for desired macro.

Exercise 59

■ Summary

In this exercise, you will create an AutoText entry and two macros. You will then create a document and use the AutoText entry and macros you created.

EXERCISE DIRECTIONS

1. Create the following AutoText entry in italics; name it **AD**.

   Ride the Track Exerciser

2. Create a macro that will create a continuous section break and change left and right margins to 1.5". Name the macro BREAK and assign Alt+B as the shortcut keys.

3. Create another macro that will create a continuous section break and change left and right margins to 1.25". Name the macro BREAK2 and assign Alt+G as the shortcut keys.

   ✔ *You must type the desired margin measurements even if those same measurements are displayed already for the macro to be effective.*

4. Close the document window.

5. Keyboard the advertisement shown.

6. Begin At 2".

7. Play the macros and AutoText entries indicated.

8. Print one copy.

9. Save the file; name it **WORKOUT**.

10. Close the document window.

MARGINS (Alt + M)

DISCOVER AN EXCITING NEW WAY TO *Serif 12-point*
ACHIEVE WELLNESS OF BODY AND MIND *bold*

2x

LINESPACING (Alt + L)

According to medical fitness experts, regular aerobic exercise is essential for
achieving all-around wellness. Aerobic exercise helps you prevent illness, feel better *Serif*
physically and mentally, boost your energy level, and increase the years on your life. *12-point*
That's why you need **[AutoText AD]**. **[AutoText AD]** will provide you with the
following benefits:

[Return to single space]

BREAK (Alt + B)

Format list
with bullets.

- you can burn more fat than on other exercisers and burn up
  to 1,100 calories per hour!
- you can improve your cardiovascular fitness and lower your
  overall cholesterol level.
- you'll feel more mentally alert, relaxed, positive and self-confident.

BREAK2 (Alt + G)
LINESPACING (Alt + L)

With regular workouts on a **[AutoText AD]**, you'll feel wonderful because you're
doing something positive for yourself.

Seven out of ten **[AutoText AD]** owners use their machines an average of three
times per week.

Call your **[AutoText AD]** representative today at 1-800-555-4444 to receive a
FREE video and brochure.

[AutoText AD]

CLOSING (Alt + C)

Exercise 60

■ Summary

In this exercise, you will create two AutoText entries. You will then create a letter and use the AutoText entries you created.

EXERCISE DIRECTIONS

1. Create NEW document.

2. Create the following AutoText entry in a sans serif 12-point bold italics font; name it **MM**.

   Mark Mutual Funds

3. Create the following AutoText entry in a serif 12-point bold font; name it **VS**.

   Vector Special Investment Trust

4. Close the document window.

5. Create NEW document.

6. Keyboard the letter below in a serif 12-point font.

7. Begin the exercise At 2.5".

8. As you type, play the macros and AutoText entries indicated.

9. Print one copy.

10. Save the file; name it **INVEST**.

11. Close the document window.

MARGINS (Alt + M)
Today's date

Mr. Peter Streedham
One Casey Place
Cincinnati, OH 45227

Dear Investor:

Effective August 1, 1997, **[MM]** was reorganized and became a series of **[VS]**, a business trust organized under the laws of the Commonwealth of Massachusetts.

Prior to the reorganization, **[MM]** had been a series of **[VS]**, which was also a Massachusetts business trust. Except for the fact that **[MM]** is now a series of **[VS]**, shares of **[MM]** represent the same interest in the Fund's assets, are of the same class, are subject to the same terms and conditions, fees and expenses, and confer the same rights as when **[MM]** was a series of **[VS]**.

If you need further clarification on this issue, please phone me at 1-800-777-7777.

[CL]

CLOSING (Alt + C)

NEXT LESSON

Word 97

LESSON 9

Columns and Tables; Calculate and Sort

- Columns
- Format Columns
- Columns with Custom Widths
- Tabular Columns
- Set Custom Tabs
- Tabular Columns with Dot Leaders
- Create a Table
- Default Borders, Gridlines and Endmarks
- Move within a Table
- Enter Text in a Table
- Create a Parallel Column Table
- Alignment within Table Cells
- Indents and Tabs within Table Cells
- Insert and Delete Columns and Rows

- Change Column Widths
- Horizontal Positioning of a Table
- Draw a Table
- Change Direction of Text in a Table
- Change Borders and Add Shading and Patterns to a Table
- Use AutoFormat
- Merge Cells
- Split Cells
- Row Height
- Calculate in Tables
- Number Formats
- Sort within a Table

Exercise 61 ■ **Columns**

Standard Toolbar

Columns

NOTES

Columns

- The Column feature allows text to flow from one column to another. When the first column is filled with text, additional text automatically flows into the next column.

- Columns are particularly useful when you are creating newsletters, pamphlets, brochures, lists or articles.

- You can access the Column feature by selecting Columns from the Format menu.

- In the Columns dialog box that appears, you may select the number of columns you desire for a document or section of a document. (You may vary the number of columns used in different sections of a document by selecting This point forward in the Apply to drop-down list box or by creating continuous section breaks between sections).

- You can also change the distance between columns (often called the gutter space), or you may let Word set it automatically. To change the spacing between columns, enter the amount of space that you want between columns in the Spacing text boxes. You also have the option of adding a vertical line between the columns. Click Line Between to add a vertical line.

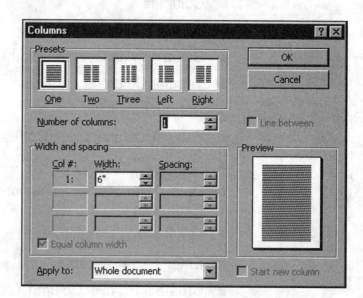

- To create columns quickly without accessing the Column dialog box, you may click the Columns button on the Standard toolbar and drag to highlight the desired number of columns.

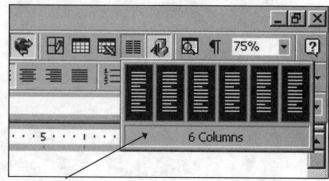

Drag to indicate number of columns.

- If you desire a centered title before the column text, you must first key the title, create a continuous section break, then turn on the column feature. If you do not create the continuous section break after the title, the title will become part of the first column text.

- You can move the insertion point quickly by clicking in the desired column.

- In order to see columns side by side as they will print, you must switch to Page Layout view or Print Preview.

In this exercise, you will create a two-column report.

EXERCISE DIRECTIONS

1. Create a NEW document.

2. Use the default margins.

3. Begin the exercise At 1.3", or open ⊟61EMAIL.

4. Center the title in a sans serif 22-point bold font as shown; press Enter twice.

5. Create a continuous section break.

6. Create the article shown using a two-column, newspaper-style format. Use the default gutter space between columns.

   ✓ *Before keyboarding this exercise, access the AutoCorrect dialog box. Be sure that Internet and network paths with hyperlinks is deselected on the AutoFormat as You Type tab.*

7. Set column text to a serif 14-point font. Italicize and bold where indicated.

8. Set a first line indent of .5" for column text.

9. Set line spacing in column text to exactly 20 points.

10. Insert a vertical line between columns.

11. Justify column text.

12. Spell check.

13. Hyphenate the document. Limit consecutive hyphens to 2.

14. Preview your document.

15. Print one copy.

16. Save the file; name it EMAIL.

17. Close the document window.

E-MAIL

E-mail, otherwise known as *electronic mail*, is the Internet's most used function. It is used to send letters, documents, or pictures, much as the post office is used to send a letter. However, e-mail does not require paper, stamps or much travel time. In order to send e-mail, the sender and the receiver must each have an Internet account and an e-mail address. An e-mail address may look something like this: **jaimeb@sas.upenn.edu**

The word or name before the "@" is the login name or *username*. The words after the "@," which are separated by periods, are known as the domain names. An e-mail address may have up to five domain names. The address above is that of a student at the University of Pennsylvania. The first domain name is the name of a specific computer connected to the Internet. In the illustration above, *sas* represents the *School of Arts and Sciences* connection at the University of Pennsylvania. The school name is abbreviated as the next domain for easy identification. The final domain, known as the "top-level domain," categorizes the e-mail address. For example, *.edu* means that this address belongs to someone at a college, university or secondary school.

Before e-mail can be sent, an e-mail header must be filled out. The header includes the name of the addressee (to whom the mail is being sent), copy or attachment notations, and the subject of the mail. The e-mail is sent to a "mailbox," where it is saved until it is either deleted or downloaded onto a disk. The sender of the e-mail can determine whether the person to whom the mail was sent retrieved the message.

Nowadays when you ask for a person's address, you need to specify whether you want their postal address, e-mail address or both!

KEYSTROKES

CREATE COLUMNS

USING MOUSE AND TOOLBAR

1. Highlight text to format for columns.
2. Click **View**.......................... `Alt` + `V`
3. Click **Page Layout**......................... `P`
   to switch to Page Layout view.
4. Click **Column** button .... `▦`
   on Standard toolbar.
5. Drag down and to the right to select desired number of columns.

USING DIALOG BOX

1. Click **Format**....................... `Alt` + `O`
2. Click **Columns** .... `C`
3. Click **Number of columns** .... `Alt` + `N`
4. Click up or down arrow to set desired number of columns.
   OR
   - Click **One**........................ `Alt` + `O`
   - Click **Two**........................ `Alt` + `W`
   - Click **Three** .... `Alt` + `T`
   OR
   Click **Left** or **Right**........ `Alt` + `L`/`R`
5. Click **Apply to** list arrow .... `Alt` + `A`
6. Select desired option:
   - **Whole document**
   - **This point forward**
   - **This section**
   - **Selected text**

   ✓ *This option is available if you have highlighted text that you want formatted as columns.*
7. To set gutter width:
   a. Click in **Spacing** box........ `Alt` + `S`
   b. Type distance .... *number* to place between columns.
   c. Repeat in spacing boxes below for additional columns.

   To add vertical line between columns:
   Select **Line between**............. `Alt` + `B`
   check box.
8. Click **OK** .... `Enter`

MOVE INSERTION POINT FROM COLUMN TO COLUMN

Click in desired column.

Exercise

62

■ **Format Columns**

Standard Toolbar

Columns

NOTES

Format Columns

■ As indicated in Exercise 61, to create different styles or different numbers of columns in different parts of the same document, you must divide the document into sections.

■ A section break may be created in three ways:

- Select Break, Continuous from the Insert menu at the point where you wish to change the column format.

- Select Columns from the Format menu and select *This point forward* in the Apply to drop-down list box.

- Highlight the text you want to appear in a different column format and then select Columns from the Format menu.

■ To force text to wrap to the next column before you reach the bottom of the current column, you may insert a column break at the point where you wish the current column to end.

■ To balance uneven columns, so they end at the same point, you may insert a continuous section break at the end of the last column.

In this exercise, you will create an advertisement using a two- and three-column newspaper format within the same document. You will gain practice using section and column breaks to format this document as shown.

EXERCISE DIRECTIONS

1. Create a NEW document.

2. Use the default margins.

3. Begin the exercise At 1".

4. Left align "Welcome To" and set it to a sans serif 18-point bold font. Right-align "The Vacation of a Lifetime" and set it to a script 36-point font.

5. Insert a continuous section break. Change text back to 12 point and left-align. Press Enter twice.

6. Create the top of the advertisement using a two-column, newspaper-style format. Use the default gutter space between columns. Set heading "Flotilla Cruises" to a narrow sans serif bold font.

7. Set column text to a serif 13-point font.

8. Justify and hyphenate column text. Do not limit consecutive hyphens.

9. Insert a column break approximately where shown. Be sure to insert the column break at the end of a line.

10. Insert a Continuous Break and press Enter three times. Create the bottom of the advertisement using a three-column, newspaper-style format. Use the default gutter space between columns.

11. Set each city and country to a sans serif narrow 10-point bold font. Set each description to a serif 10-point font. Justify and hyphenate column text. Do not limit consecutive hyphens.

12. Insert column breaks where shown.

13. Spell check.

14. Preview your document.

15. Print one copy.

16. Save the file; name it **ATSEA**.

17. Close the document window.

Welcome to...

The Vacation of a Lifetime!

Insert Continuous Section Break.

Flotilla Cruises—*the best private clubs on earth are at sea.*

Flotilla Cruises offer you an atmosphere of elegance that comes only with the most precise attention to detail. During your stay, our staff remains attentive to your every need.

Flotilla Cruises' accommodations are all outside suites, spacious and luxurious. Our fine dining is second to none. You can select from a variety of menu choices, all delicious and created by world-class chefs. Our guests find the same relaxed atmosphere on our

expansive decks as in our public areas. You can browse our fully stocked library for a favorite bestseller, or view the latest video in our private theater. Spend a few hours at our spectacular pool, or just gaze at the horizon as the ship glides to the next destination.

Call Ms. Judith Fiorella, our tour director, at **1-800-888-8888** for more information or to book this exciting vacation of a lifetime. Here is just a sampling of the places we visit on our Mediterranean 13-day cruise.

Insert Continuous Section Break.

Insert Column Break at end of this line.

ROME, Italy

Imperial Rome is yours to explore, with an endless parade of fountains, forums, ancient ruins and Renaissance treasures. See St. Peter's, the Vatican, the Coliseum and the Pantheon. Marvel at the works by da Vinci and Michaelangelo.

SORRENTO, Italy

Time has been arranged for you to fully explore this serene port, with its many flowering gardens as well as orange and lemon groves. After a day trip to nearby Pompeii, be sure to visit the glorious Amalfi Coast and the Isle of Capri.

Insert Column Break and press Enter twice.

TAORMINA, Italy

It's only natural that the seasoned traveler should make Taormina their favorite retreat. With a backdrop of snow-capped Mt. Etna, it is Sicily's most beautiful city.

OLYMPIA, Greece

The tiny port of Katakolon is your gateway to ancient Olympia, where the first Olympic torch was lit. See where Hellenic athletes trained and played in the Gymnasium and Stadium. Marvel at the larger-than-life Temple of Zeus.

Insert Column Break and press Enter twice.

CORINTH CANAL, Greece

Nero attempted to build the Corinth Canal but failed. Now you can realize his dream while voyaging through the rock-walled canal linking the Ionian and Aegean Seas. In Itea, follow the mythic call of the Pythian Oracle to ancient Delphi.

ATHENS, Greece

Ancient Athens abounds with treasures. The spectacular ruins of the Acropolis, the awe-inspiring Parthenon and the venerable Agora are but a few of the wonders you will discover on our fascinating shore excursions.

KEYSTROKES

SECTION BREAK

1. Highlight text you want to appear in a different column format.

   OR

   Position insertion point where new column format will begin.

2. Click **Insert**...........................[Alt] + [I]

3. Click **Break**.......................................[B]

4. Click **Con<u>t</u>inuous**..............................[T]

COLUMN BREAK

CTRL + SHIFT + ENTER

1. Position insertion point where column is to end.

2. Click **Insert**...........................[Alt] + [I]

3. Click **Break**.......................................[B]

4. Click **<u>C</u>olumn break**.......................[C]

Exercise

63

■ **Columns with Custom Widths**

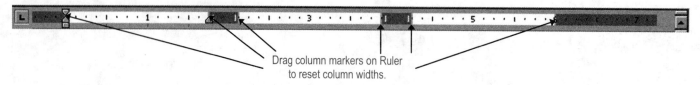

Drag column markers on Ruler
to reset column widths.

NOTES

Columns with Custom Widths

- Word lets you create **columns with custom widths**. As indicated in the Columns dialog box, the default width of a column in a two-column document using default margins is 2.75"; the gutter space is 0.5". To change the column width, click the Equal column width option to OFF. Then click in the Col #1/#2 Width and Spacing text boxes and type the desired widths.

- You can also change column widths by dragging the left and right column width markers on the Ruler bar.

- If you want to create two unequal columns, one twice as wide as the other, choose the Left or Right preset options in the Columns dialog box.

Column width and
spacing text boxes

Columns Dialog Box

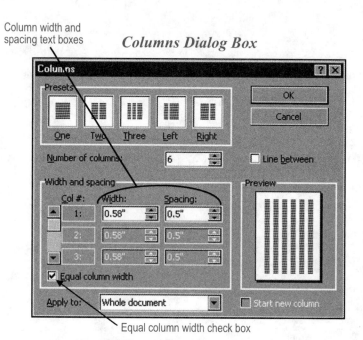

Equal column width check box

In this exercise, you will create an article using a two-column, newspaper-style format in which the second column is narrower than the first. The text does not fill up the first column and requires that you force the insertion point to the top of the second column. This is done by inserting a column break when you are ready to move to the top of the second column. You will also change your line spacing back to single space when you begin the second column.

EXERCISE DIRECTIONS

1. Create a NEW document and keyboard the exercise as shown, or open ⊟63GOODBYE.

2. Begin the exercise At approximately 2".

3. Set left and right margins to 1".

4. Set the first line to all capitals in a sans serif 24-point bold italic font; set the "V" to 56 points.

5. Insert the ampersand from the Wingdings symbols; set the size to 72 points.

6. Set GUIDEBOOKS in all capitals; right-align it and set the size to a 24-point bold sans serif font.

7. Begin the column text At 4.4".

8. Create two columns. Select This point forward from the Apply to drop-down list box.

9. Change the width of Column One to 4.5"; change the width of Column Two to 1.5". Use the default gutter space between columns (0.5").

10. Set Column One text to a sans serif 12-point font; insert a column break after the word "Enjoy." Set Column Two text to all capitals in a sans serif 10-point bold font.

11. Justify and hyphenate Column One text. Hyphenate Column Two text.

12. Set line spacing to double for the first column; set line spacing to single for the second column.

13. Spell check.

14. Preview your work.

15. Print one copy.

16. Save the file; name it GOODBYE.

17. Close the document window.

VACATION PLANNING &

GUIDEBOOKS

It can be very exciting to plan a vacation. There are a number of ways to go about it. Of course, you could have a travel agent make all the arrangements. But it is more exciting to investigate all the possibilities of travel.

First, you can check the hundreds of guidebooks which can be purchased at bookstores. Then you can send away to the government tourist offices in the country you are planning to visit. They will send you lots of free literature about the country – places to visit and a list of accommodations. The travel advertisements in your newspaper will tell you where the bargains are. After you have planned your trip by looking through the guidebooks listed to the right, ask your travel agent to do the actual booking.

Enjoy!

Insert column break here.

OFFICIAL AIRLINE GUIDE

RUSSEL'S NATIONAL MOTOR COACH GUIDE

STEAMSHIP GUIDE

HOTEL AND RESORT GUIDE

RESTAURANT, INN AND MUSEUM GUIDE

SIGHTSEEING GUIDE

FARM VACATIONS AND ADVENTURE TRAVEL GUIDE

KEYSTROKES

CREATE COLUMNS WITH CUSTOM WIDTHS

1. Click **F**o**rmat** .... `Alt` + `O`
2. Click **C**olumns .... `C`
3. Click **N**umber of columns .... `Alt` + `N`
4. Click up or down arrow to set desired number of columns.

   OR

   Click **O**ne .... `Alt` + `O`

   OR

   Click T**w**o .... `Alt` + `W`

   OR

   Click **Three** .... `Alt` + `T`
5. Click **Apply to** list arrow ...... `Alt` + `A`
6. Select **This Point Forward**.
7. Click **E**qual column width .... `Alt` + `E` to turn it off.
8. Click in **Wi**dth box .... `Alt` + `I` for Column 1 and type desired width.
9. Click in **Wi**dth box .... `Tab` , `Tab` for Column 2 and type desired width.
10. Repeat for 3rd column, if necessary.
11. Click **OK** .... `Enter`

CREATE TWO UNEQUAL COLUMNS WITH CUSTOM WIDTHS

1. Click **F**o**rmat** .... `Alt` + `O`
2. Click **C**olumns .... `C`
3. Click **Left** .... `Alt` + `L`

   OR

   Click **R**ight .... `Alt` + `R`
4. Click **OK** .... `Enter`
5. Drag column markers on Ruler as desired to adjust column width.

CHANGE COLUMN WIDTH

Column markers on Ruler

1. Place mouse pointer over a column marker on the Ruler until it assumes the shape of a two-headed arrow.
2. Click and drag the column marker to size the column as desired.

   ✓ *If the columns are equal, all columns will change as you drag the column marker for one column. However, when columns are unequal, only the column you are adjusting will change.*

Exercise 64

- Tabular Columns ■ Set Custom Tabs
- Tabular Columns with Dot Leaders

NOTES

Tabular Columns

- Tabs may be used to align columns of information. However, since Word does have a Table feature that organizes information into columns and rows without using tabs or tab settings, using tab settings to align columns is not the most efficient way to tackle this task. (*Tables will be introduced in Exercise 65.*)

- Nonetheless, it is important for you to understand the tab types available in Word (other than left-aligned) and how tabs are used for **tabular columns**.

- When you change tab settings in a document, changes take effect from that point forward. If you wish to change tab settings for existing text, you must first select the text.

- When you open a document, there are left-aligned tabs set every half-inch. This is the default setting. Whenever you press the Tab key, the insertion point jumps to the next tab stop, and the space is filled with a tab character (→). This character does not print and will display on screen *only* if you have chosen to display special characters (Show/Hide).

Set Custom Tabs

- It is possible to change the location and type of tab settings. **Custom tabs** are set in Word in two steps:

  - Click the **Tab Type** icon at the left side of the ruler to set the desired tab type.

  - Click the Ruler bar at the position where a custom tab is desired.

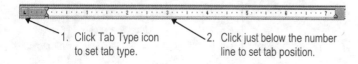

1. Click Tab Type icon to set tab type.
2. Click just below the number line to set tab position.

- When a custom tab has been set, default tabs to the left of it are deleted.

- There are four different tab types. Each tab type is represented on the Ruler bar by a different symbol.

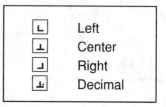

- Note the effect each tab type has on text:

Left Tab

- Text moves to the right of the tab as you type.

```
XXXXXXX
XXXX
XXXXXX
```

Centered Tab

- Text centers at the tab stop.

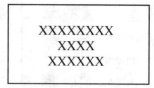

Right Tab

- Text moves to the left or backwards from the tab as you type.

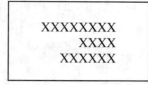

Decimal Tab

- Text before the decimal point moves to the left of the tab. Text you type after the decimal point moves to the right of the tab. The decimals stay aligned.

```
123.65
 56.77
  4.66
```

- Tab settings become part of paragraph formatting, and all paragraph formatting is stored in the **paragraph mark** (¶) at the end of the paragraph. If this mark is deleted, or if you move the insertion point to another paragraph, you may not have the tab settings you expect.

- Tabs may be set on the Ruler or in the Tabs dialog box. To set tabs in the Tabs dialog box, select Tabs from the Format menu.

Set Tabs on the Ruler

- As illustrated in Exercise 3, tab settings are displayed on the bottom of the Ruler as gray dots set 0.5" apart.

- **To set a new left-aligned tab**, click anywhere on the Ruler bar where a new tab is desired; a new tab marker is inserted. To delete a tab setting, drag the tab marker off the Ruler bar.

- To set right-aligned, centered or decimal tabs, you must first change the tab type by clicking the tab type icon at the left end of the Ruler. After you select the Tab Type, each click on the Ruler will insert the tab type you have chosen. *(See keystrokes on page 224.)*

Set Tabs in the Dialog Box

- You may also set tabs using the Tabs dialog box (Format, Tabs). This method lets you set and clear tab positions and tab types in one operation. You cannot, however, see the result of your changes on text until all settings have been made.

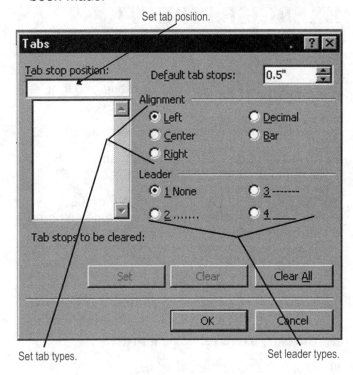

Set tab position.

Set tab types.

Set leader types.

Tabular Columns with Dot Leaders

- A **dot leader** is a series of dots that connect one column to another to keep the reader's eye focused.

- To create dot leaders, select a dot leader tab type from the Leader section of the Tabs dialog box when you set your tabs.

- After all tab settings are made, use the Tab key to advance to each column. The dot leaders will automatically appear preceding those columns that contain a dot leader tab setting.

In Part I of this exercise, you will create a four-column tabular document in which the first and second columns are left-aligned, the third is right-aligned, and the fourth is decimal-aligned. In Part II of this exercise, you will create a two-column table in which the first column is left-aligned and the second column is right-aligned with dot leaders.

EXERCISE DIRECTIONS

PART I

1. Create a NEW document.

2. Use the default margins, font style and font size.

3. Center the title lines; press Enter three times.

4. Set a left tab at 1.5". Set a left tab at 2.75". Set a right tab at 4". Set a decimal tab at 4.5".

5. Left-align and type the remainder of the exercise, using the Tab key to create columns as indicated.

6. Vertically center the exercise.

7. Preview your work.

8. Print one copy.

9. Save the exercise; name it **PHONE**.

10. Close the document window.

PART II

1. Create a NEW document.

2. Use the default margins.

3. Center the title lines in a sans serif 16-point font; set the second title line to bold italics. Press Enter twice after the first title line. Press Enter three times after the second title line.

4. Left-align and set font to 13-point sans serif.

5. Set a left-aligned tab for the first column and a right-aligned dot leader tab at the end of the second column.

6. Type the remainder of the exercise using tabs to create columns as shown.

7. Vertically center the exercise.

8. Preview your work.

9. Print one copy.

10. Save the exercise; name it **TC**.

11. Close the document window.

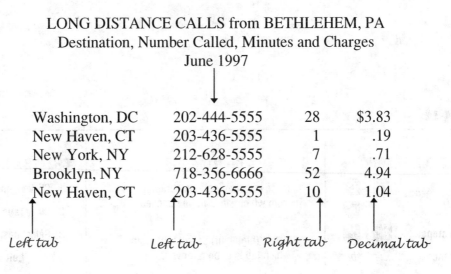

PART I

LONG DISTANCE CALLS from BETHLEHEM, PA
Destination, Number Called, Minutes and Charges
June 1997

Washington, DC	202-444-5555	28	$3.83
New Haven, CT	203-436-5555	1	.19
New York, NY	212-628-5555	7	.71
Brooklyn, NY	718-356-6666	52	4.94
New Haven, CT	203-436-5555	10	1.04

Left tab   *Left tab*   *Right tab*   *Decimal tab*

PART II

BIOLOGY TODAY

TABLE OF CONTENTS

The Nature of Life 1
The Chemistry of Living Things 23
Taxonomy and Evolution 47
Nutrition 70
Transport 97
Respiration 114
Excretion 142
The Nervous System 180
The Endocrine System 197
Photosynthesis 221
Plant Transport 247
Respiration 255

KEYSTROKES

CHANGE DEFAULT TAB SETTING

1. Click **F**ormat........................ Alt + O
2. Click **T**abs .... T
3. Click **Default tab stops**......... Alt + F
4. Type desired distance............... *number* between tabs.

   OR

   Select **Increase/Decrease**....... ↑ ↓ buttons to set desired distance.
5. Click **OK**.................................... Enter

SET A CUSTOM TAB

1. Place insertion point in paragraph in which tabs are to be set.

   OR

   Select (highlight) paragraphs for which tabs are to be set.

2. Click one of the following **Tab Type** buttons to the left of the Ruler to set desired tab type:

   - **Left-aligned** tab .... ∟
   - **Center-aligned** tab................. ⊥
   - **Right-aligned** tab.................. ⌐
   - **Decimal-aligned** tab.............. ⊥

3. Click below number line in Ruler where tab is to be set.

REMOVE A CUSTOM TAB

1. Place insertion point in paragraph from which tab is to be removed.

   OR

   Select (highlight) paragraphs from which tab is to be removed.

2. Drag desired tab symbol *down* off of the Ruler.

MOVE A TAB

1. Place insertion point in paragraph in which tabs are to be moved.

   OR

   Select (highlight) paragraphs in which tabs are to be moved.

2. Drag tab symbol on Ruler to desired location.

CLEAR CUSTOM TABS

1. Place insertion point in paragraph containing tabs to clear.

   OR

   Select (highlight) paragraphs containing tabs to clear.

2. Click **F**ormat........................ Alt + O
3. Click **T**abs .... T
   to open **Tabs** dialog box.
4. Click **Clear All** .... Alt + A
   or make desired changes.

   OR

   a. Click in **Tab Stop** .... Alt + A
      list box and select tab to clear.

   b. Click **Clear**...................... Alt + E

5. Click **OK**.. Alt

   ✓ *Default tab settings will remain after you clear all custom tabs.*

CREATE A TAB WITH A DOT LEADER

1. Click **F**ormat........................ Alt + O
2. Click **T**abs .... T
3. Select desired alignment option:

   - **Left**
   - **Center**
   - **Right**
   - **Decimal**
   - **Bar**

4. Select desired Leader option:

   - **1 None** .... Alt + 1
   - **2 (dots)**...................... Alt + 2
   - **3 (dashes)**.................. Alt + 3
   - **4 (solid line)**.............. Alt + 4

5. Click **OK**.................................... Enter

NEXT EXERCISE

Exercise 65

- ■ **Create a Table** ■ **Default Borders, Gridlines and Endmarks**
- ■ **Move within a Table** ■ **Enter Text in a Table**
- ■ **Create a Parallel Column Table**

Standard Toolbar

Borders button   Tables button

NOTES

- ■ The **Table** feature lets you organize information into columns and rows without using tabs or tab settings.

- ■ A table consists of **rows**, which run horizontally, and **columns**, which run vertically. The rows and columns intersect to form boxes called **cells**. Note the example below of a table with three rows and four columns:

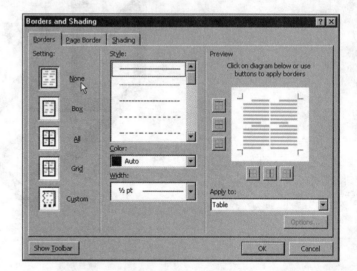

- ■ Text, graphics, numbers or formulas are entered into cells after you have defined the structure of your table—that is, how many columns and rows you require for your table.

Default Borders, Gridlines and Endmarks

- ■ By default, tables display with ½-point inside and outside border lines. In these next few exercises, you will use a table without border lines. To remove the border lines, *right* click inside the table, select Borders and Shading and click None. *(Borders and Shading will be covered more extensively in Exercise 68.)*

- ■ When you remove the default border from a table, gridlines will display onscreen, but they will not print. Gridlines make it easier to navigate in and format the table. However, if you want to hide the gridlines, you can select Hide Gridlines on the Table menu.

- ■ When the Show/Hide button ¶ is on, Endmarks display in a table. There are two types of Endmarks. End-of-cell marks indicate where the contents of a cell end; end-of-row marks indicate the end of a row.

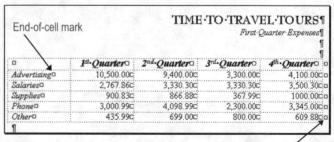

End-of-cell mark

TIME·TO·TRAVEL·TOURS¶
First·Quarter·Expenses¶

	1ˢᵗ·Quarter	2ⁿᵈ·Quarter	3ʳᵈ·Quarter	4ᵗʰ·Quarter
Advertising	10,500.00	9,400.00	3,300.00	4,100.00
Salaries	2,767.86	3,330.30	3,330.30	3,500.30
Supplies	900.83	866.88	367.99	1000.00
Phone	3,000.99	4,098.99	2,300.00	3,345.00
Other	435.99	699.00	800.00	609.88

End-of-row mark

Create a Table

- Select <u>I</u>nsert Table from the T<u>a</u>ble menu. In the Insert Table dialog box that follows, indicate the desired Number of <u>c</u>olumns and Number of <u>r</u>ows.

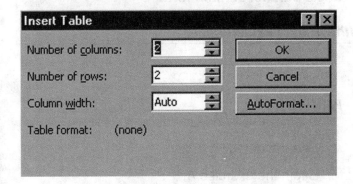

- You can also create tables quickly by clicking the Insert Table button 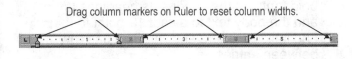 on the Standard toolbar and dragging the mouse to select the desired number of columns and rows.

- The columns adjust automatically to fit between the left and right margins.

- After the table is created, the Ruler displays table markers that indicate the left and right boundaries of the table columns.

Drag column markers on Ruler to reset column widths.

✓Note: Changing table column widths will be covered in Exercise 67.

Move within a Table

- The insertion point moves in a table the same way it moves in a document. You may use the mouse to click in the desired cell, or you may use the Tab key to move to the next column. When the insertion point is in the last cell of the right-most column of a table, pressing the Tab key creates a new row.

Enter Text in a Table

- As you enter text in a table cell, the cell expands downward to accommodate the text.

- Pressing Enter in a cell extends the cell vertically. It will not advance you to the next cell.

Create a Parallel Column Table

- **Parallel columns** are used to create a list, script, itinerary, minutes of a meeting or any other document in which text is read horizontally.

Monday	Meeting with John Smith at 9 a.m.
Tuesday	Lunch appointment with Randy Grafeo to discuss merger.

- To create parallel columns, you must create a two-column table. After entering text in the left column cell, press the Tab key and enter the necessary text in the right column cell. Remember that the cell expands downward to accommodate the desired text.

> *In Part I of this exercise, you will create minutes of a meeting using a table with 2 columns and 11 rows. Skip one row after each entry. In Part II of this exercise, you will create an itinerary using a table with 2 columns and 20 rows. Both exercises use a parallel column format.*
>
> ✓*Note: You will learn to adjust table column widths in the next exercise.*

EXERCISE DIRECTIONS

PART I

1. Create a NEW document.

2. Use the default margins.

3. Begin the exercise At approximately 1.8".

4. Center the main heading in a sans serif 18-point bold font. Use the book symbol in the Wingdings font collection before and after the heading, as shown. Center the minor headings in a sans serif 12-point font. Press Enter twice after the time.

5. Center four symbols to separate the time from the body text. Press Enter three times after the symbols. Change to left alignment.

6. Create a table using 2 columns and 15 rows.

7. Place insertion point in table, then remove the default border from the entire table (Alt + O, B, N).

8. Set the side headings (Column 1 text) to a sans serif 12-point font; italicize and bold where indicated; set the body text to a serif 12-point font. Skip one row between entries.

9. Spell check.

10. Preview your work.

11. Print one copy.

12. Save the exercise; name it **BOOKMEET**.

13. Close the document window.

PART II

1. Create a NEW document.

2. Use the default margins.

3. Begin the exercise At 1".

4. Right-align the first line of the heading in a sans serif 18-point bold italic font. Right align the three remaining heading lines in a sans serif 12-point italic font.

5. Press Enter twice after the date and return to left alignment. Change font to a serif 10-point font.

6. Create a table using 2 columns and 20 rows.

7. Remove the default border from the entire table.

8. Set the side headings (Dates) to a serif 10-point bold font; set the minor side headings (times) and the body text to a serif 10-point font. Bold and italicize where shown. Skip one row between entries.

9. Spell check.

10. Preview your work.

11. Print one copy.

12. Save the exercise; name it **ONTIME**.

13. Close the document window.

📖 📖 BLOOMSBURY BOOKS, LTD. 📖 📖

Marketing Meeting Minutes
September 12, 199-
9:30 a.m.

📖 📖 📖 📖

Present	Laurie James, Adrian Monroe, Jill Robinson, Chris Powell, Robert Johnson, Brian Murphy
Announcements	David presided over the meeting in John's absence. Next week's meeting will be held on Thursday at 9:30 a.m., at which time Jill and Brian will present the findings of the Marketing Task Force meeting.

NEW TITLES

Journey through Tomorrow	The publishing date has been pushed to December. Alice to check with production and firm up all dates.
Perfect Pasta	May publishing date to coincide with Mother's Day. In-store promotional display. Author to offer cooking demonstrations at major chains during tour.
The Book of Healing	Jacket art has been delayed until March 22. Coordinate with publicity to run print ads in corresponding cities with author's tour.
Waiting for the Light	We will run ads in the *San Francisco Chronicle, Los Angeles Times, Denver Post, Chicago Tribune, New York Times* and *Boston Globe* to correspond with author tour.
Adjournment	The meeting was adjourned at 11:00 a.m.

SELECT INVESTMENTS
Private Placement Group
Timetable
October 27-28, 199-

Tuesday, October 27

9:00 a. m.

Arrive Brussels, Belgium
Check in at the hotel begins at 10:00
a.m.
Hotel Amigo
rue de l'Amigo 1-3
1000 Bruxelles
Tel. 32-2-555-55-55
Fax 32-2-666-66-66

6:30 p.m.

Meet in lobby of hotel

7:00 p.m.

Dinner with Private Placement
Group
John Canny, Chief Financial Officer
Pierre LeFere, Director of Corporate
Finance
Les Brigittines
5 place de la Chapelle
1000 Bruxelles
Tel. 32-2-444-55-55
Fax 32-2-888-66-66

Wednesday, October 28

8:30 a.m.

Arrive at ARB's office:
ARB SA
Chaussee de La Hulpe 185
Brussels, Belgium
Tel. 32-2-999-55-55
Fax 32-2-878-00-66

9:15 a.m.

Brandon Fallon, Chief Executive
Officer
Presentation
Question and Answer Period

12:00 p.m.

Working Lunch

1:30 p.m. - 3:30 p.m.

Meeting with Laurence Volpe

6:30 p.m.

Return to Hotel

KEYSTROKES

CREATE A TABLE

1. Click **Table** button.............................. 🔲
   on the Standard toolbar.

2. Drag to the right and down to indicate
   desired number of columns and rows.

   USING THE MENU

1. Click **Ta̲ble**.......................... `Alt` + `A`

2. Click **I̲nsert Table** .... `I`

3. Click **Number of c̲olumns** .... `Alt` + `C`

4. Type number of columns. ....*number*

5. Click **Number of r̲ows** .... `Alt` + `R`

6. Type number of rows ....*number*

7. Click **Column w̲idth**............. `Alt` + `W`

8. Type desired width ....*number*

9. Click **OK** .... `Enter`

REMOVE DEFAULT BORDER(S) FROM TABLE

1. Right-click inside table.

2. Click **B̲orders and Shading** .... `B`

3. Click **B̲orders** tab.................. `Alt` + `B`

4. Click **N̲one**........................... `Alt` + `N`
   in Setting section.

5. Click **OK** .... `Enter`

SHOW/HIDE GRIDLINES

   ✓ *Gridlines will not appear if a table
     has a border or lines on it.*

1. Click inside table.

2. Click **Ta̲ble** .... `Alt` + `A`

3. Click **Hide G̲ridlines**........................ `G`
   OR
   Click **Show G̲ridlines** .... `G`

MOVE FROM COLUMN TO COLUMN IN A TABLE

Press **Tab** to move .... `Tab`
one column to the right.

OR

Press **Shift+Tab** .... `Shift` + `Tab`
to move one column to the left.

Exercise 66 ■ Alignment within Table Cells ■ Indents and Tabs within Table Cells

NOTES

Alignment within Table Cells

- Word allows you to change the alignment of data for a cell, a column or the entire table.

- You may left-, center-, right- or decimal-align data either during the table creation process or afterward.

Left Align	Decimal Align: .001 10.00 1000.00 1.000
Center Align	**Full justify** needs several lines of text to illustrate the effect that it will have on a paragraph.
Right Align	

- To align data in a table, place the insertion point in any cell or select (highlight) several cells or columns in which you wish to align data. Click the alignment button on the Formatting toolbar or set a tab type (center, right or decimal).

- It is recommended that you use the alignment buttons on the Formatting toolbar to center or right-align data and use the tab type to set decimal alignments within a table.

Indents and Tabs within Table Cells

- Indents and tabs may be created within table cells using the same techniques used to create them in text paragraphs.

- To change the indent, first-line indent or tab set within a table cell, you must first place the insertion point in the cell, or select the cells to affect, then use the same procedures you learned earlier to set the indent, first-line indent or tab.

- Once a tab is created within a table cell, you must use Ctrl + Tab to advance the insertion point to the tab stop.

- For example, to decimal-align data in a table, click the decimal tab type ⊥, then click the Ruler bar where the decimal alignment is desired. Press Ctrl + Tab to advance the insertion point to decimal-align the data.

In Part I of this exercise, you will create a table and align text within table cells.
In Part II of this exercise, you will align text in a previously created table.

EXERCISE DIRECTIONS:

PART I

1. Create a NEW document.

2. Use the default margins.

3. Center the page vertically.

4. Center the title as shown. Set the main title to a sans serif 14-point bold font; press Enter twice after the first title line. Set the second and third lines of the title to a sans serif 12-point font; set the third line to italic. Press the Enter key three times after the third title line.

5. Create the table shown on the next page using 4 columns and 5 rows.

6. Enter the table text using a serif 12-point font. Bold the column headings. Whatever font is selected when you create a table becomes the table's default font.

7. Center all headings and the text in the third and fourth columns.

8. Remove the table borders.

9. Preview your work.

10. Print one copy.

11. Save the file; name it **CRUISE**.

12. Close the document window.

PART II

1. Create a NEW document.

2. Open ⌨ **BOOKMEET**, or open 💾**66BOOKMEET**.

3. Display both windows by selecting Arrange All from the Window menu.

4. Copy the centered heading, BLOOMSBURY BOOKS, LTD. along with the book symbols to the new document.

5. Close **BOOKMEET**.

6. Center the subtitle, February Sales, below the main title in a sans serif 12-point font. Press Enter three times.

7. Return to left alignment and create the table using 4 columns and 8 rows.

8. Remove the table border.

9. Enter the table text using a sans serif 12-point font. Center and bold the column headings. Leave a blank row after the column headings.

10. Right-align the text in Columns 3 and 4.

11. Center the page vertically.

12. Preview your work.

13. Print one copy.

14. Save the file; name it **BOOKSALE**.

15. Close the document window.

PART I

FESTIVAL TRAVEL ASSOCIATES

WORLD CRUISE SEGMENTS
SPRING 199-

DESTINATION	DEPARTS	NO. OF DAYS	COST
Panama Canal	March 6	13	$2,529
Trans Pacific	March 19	11	$4,399
Israel to New York	March 19	18	$5,299
Naples to New York	March 19	11	$3,499

PART II

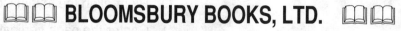

BLOOMSBURY BOOKS, LTD.
February Sales

Title	Author	Gross Units To Date	Net Units To Date
The Peacemaker	Allen	15,283	8,987
September Queen	Ewing	11,876	11,515
The Fifth Dimension	Mitchell	11,888	9,777
Where There's Smoke	Kasdam	18,732	16,231
Spider's Web	Newman	12,802	3,343
Learning to Earn	Cameron	20,777	20,690

KEYSTROKES

ALIGN TEXT WITHIN CELLS, COLUMNS, OR TABLE (CENTER, RIGHT, LEFT)

1. Place insertion point in desired cell.

   OR

   Select a cell, several cells, or columns to receive alignment change.

2. Click desired alignment button on Formatting toolbar:

   - **Left**.. ▤
   - **Right** .... ▤
   - **Center** .... ▤
   - **Justify** .... ▤

SELECT (HIGHLIGHT) A CELL, ROW, COLUMN, OR TABLE

To highlight a row:

1. Position insertion point to the left of the row to be selected until the insertion point changes to a white, upward-pointing arrow.

2. Click the left mouse button once.

   OR

1. Place insertion point anywhere in row.

2. Click **Table** .... Alt + A

3. Click **Select Row** .... R

To highlight a column:

1. Position insertion point above the column to be selected until the insertion point changes to a black, downward-pointing arrow.

2. Click the left mouse button once to select the column or drag to select multiple columns.

   OR

1. Place the insertion point anywhere in column.

2. Click **Table** .... Alt + A

3. Click Select **Column** C

To highlight the table:

1. Position insertion point above the first column until the insertion point changes to a black, downward-pointing arrow.

2. Drag the arrow right to highlight all columns in the table.

   OR

1. Place insertion point anywhere in table.

2. Click **Table** .... Alt + A

3. Click **Select Table** .... A

To select a cell:

Click in cell to left of cell contents.

OR

Triple-click anywhere in the cell.

SET TABS IN A TABLE CELL OR COLUMN (PREFERABLY FOR DECIMAL ALIGNMENT)

1. Place insertion point in desired cell.

   OR

   Select desired columns.

2. Click **Tab Type** icon .... ⊥ to set desired type of tab.

3. Click desired position in the Ruler.

4. Drag tab symbol to adjust position if necessary.

5. Press **Ctrl** + **Tab** to advance insertion point to tab alignment position.

Exercise 67

- ■ **Insert and Delete Columns and Rows**
- ■ **Change Column Widths** ■ **Horizontal Positioning of a Table**

NOTES

Insert and Delete Columns and Rows

- ■ Rows and/or columns may be inserted or deleted in a table.

- ■ To insert a row, click in the table and select Insert Rows from the Table menu. A new row will be inserted above the insertion point position.

- ■ To insert a column, highlight the column to the *right* of the column to be inserted. Then select Insert Columns from the Table menu.

- ■ To insert a column as the last column in a table, you must click the Show/Hide button to turn on the table codes. Position the insertion point at the end of the last row, outside the table but in front of the end-of-row mark, choose Select Column from the Table menu, then select Insert Columns from the Table menu. To insert additional columns to the right of the table, press F4.

- ■ The text in the inserted column or row takes on the same formatting as that in the row or column containing the insertion point.

- ■ To delete a column, highlight the column to be deleted and select Delete Columns from the Table menu.

- ■ To delete a row, position the insertion point in the row to be deleted, select Delete Cells from the Table menu, and select Delete entire row from the Delete Cells dialog box that follows. Or highlight the row to be deleted and select Delete Rows from the Table menu.

Delete a Table

- ■ You can also delete the entire table by selecting the entire table, then selecting Delete Rows from the Table menu.

- ■ When a column or row is deleted, the contents of that column or row are also deleted.

Change Column Widths and Margins

- ■ **You can change Column widths** using a specific measurement or by dragging the vertical lines between columns to the desired width.

- ■ To adjust column widths and see the immediate effect of the change on the table as it is being made, place the mouse pointer on a vertical line bordering a column to be sized. (To adjust table size, place mouse pointer on the far left or right vertical line.) The pointer's shape changes to a table sizing arrow ←‖→. Press and hold the mouse as you drag the dotted line left or right to the desired width or table size.

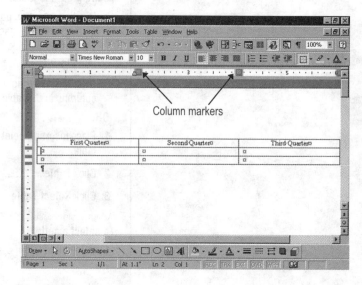

Column markers

284

- To adjust column widths and margins using a specific measurement, select Cell Height and Width from the Table menu and make desired changes in the Width of column and Space between columns boxes on the Column tab.

- You can also adjust column widths and see the immediate effect by dragging the column boundary markers on the Ruler bar. To change column margins, drag the left and right indent markers on the Ruler.

- The **AutoFit** feature lets you adjust the width of a cell or column to automatically fit the maximum width of text in that cell or column. Place the insertion point in the column to adjust and select Cell Height and Width from the Table main menu. In the Cell Height and Width dialog box illustrated below, select the Column tab, then choose AutoFit.

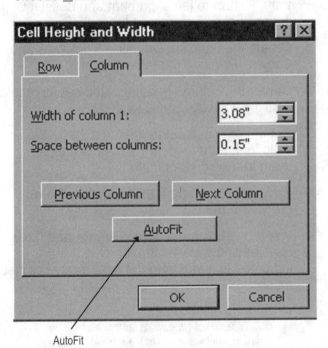

AutoFit

Horizontal Positioning of a Table

- Word sets column widths in a table to spread out evenly between the margins whether your table contains two or ten columns. When you change column width, Word keeps the same left margin. This means the table is no longer centered across the page.

- To center the table horizontally, select Cell Height and Width from the Table menu. In the Cell Height and Width dialog box that follows, select the Row tab and click Center (Alignment).

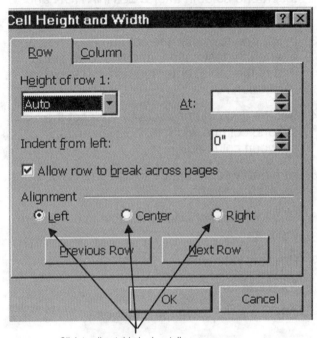

Click to align table horizontally across page.

- You may also align the table to the Left or Right of the page or a specific amount from the left edge of the page.

> *In Part I of this exercise, you will open a previously created table, insert one column and row, adjust column widths using specific amounts and AutoFit, and reposition the table horizontally. In Part II of this exercise, you will create a new table and gain more practice inserting columns and rows and adjusting column widths.*

EXERCISE DIRECTIONS

PART I

1. Open 🖮 **CRUISE**, or open 🖫 **67CRUISE**.

2. Insert one column after DESTINATION and enter the text as shown.

3. Insert one row after the column headings and after each destination, and two rows at the end of the table; enter the text as shown in Illustration A.

4. Set the first column width to 1.5"; set the second column width to 1.5"; leave 0.25" between columns.

5. Use the AutoFit feature to size the third, fourth and fifth columns.

6. Horizontally reposition the table to center on the page.

7. Preview your work.

8. Print one copy.

9. Close the file; save the changes.

PART II

1. Create a NEW document, or open 🖫**67EXPENSES**.

2. Use the default margins.

3. Begin the exercise At 1".

4. Right-align the titles as shown in Illustration B. Set the company name to a serif 16-point bold font; set the subtitle to a serif 12-point italic font. Return to left alignment and deselect italics. Press Enter three times.

5. Create the table shown using 5 columns and 6 rows. Remove the table borders.

6. Center the column headings and set them to a serif 14-point bold italic font.

7. Set the expense categories to a serif 12-point italic font; right-align the amounts and set them to a serif 12-point font.

8. Save the file; name it **EXPENSES**. **Do not close the file.**

9. Insert one column after 4th Quarter and three rows as shown in illustration C; enter the indicated text and bold the total expenses cell, as shown.

   ✔ *To insert a column as the last column, you must display table codes (click Show/Hide button) and position the insertion point at the end of the last row, outside the table, but in front of the end of row mark.*

10. Use the AutoFit feature to size columns 2, 3, 4 and 5.

11. Horizontally reposition the table to center on the page.

12. Preview your work.

13. Print one copy.

14. Close the file; save the changes.

FESTIVAL TRAVEL ASSOCIATES

Insert Column.

WORLD CRUISE SEGMENTS
SPRING 1997

Insert Rows.

DESTINATION	PORTS	DEPARTS	NO. OF DAYS	COST
Panama Canal	New York, Cartegena, Panama Canal, Acapulco	March 6	13	$2,529
Trans Pacific	Los Angeles, Ensenada, Kona, Honolulu, Fiji, Auckland	March 19	11	$4,399
Israel to New York	Haifa, Kusadasi, Istanbul, Athens, Naples, Cannes, New York	March 19	18	$5,299
Naples to New York	Naples, Cannes, Lisbon, Southampton, New York	March 19	11	$3,499
Trans-Atlantic	Fort Lauderdale, Madeira, Lisbon, Gibraltar, Genoa	April 16	15	$2,599

ILLUSTRATION B

TIME TO TRAVEL TOURS

First Year Expenses

	1st Quarter	2nd Quarter	3rd Quarter	4th Quarter
Advertising	10,500.00	9,400.00	3,300.00	4,100.00
Salaries	2,767.86	3,330.30	3,330.30	3,500.30
Supplies	900.83	866.88	367.99	1,000.00
Phone	3,000.99	4,098.99	2,300.00	3,345.00
Other	435.99	699.00	800.00	609.88

ILLUSTRATION C

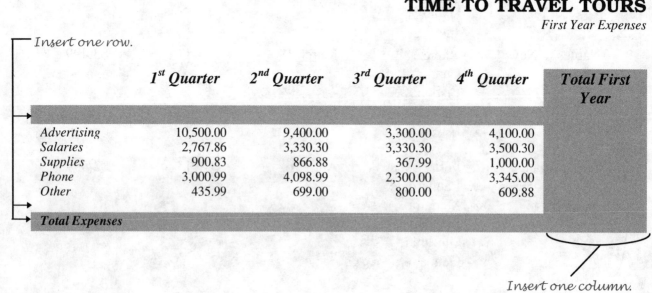

TIME TO TRAVEL TOURS

First Year Expenses

Insert one row.

	1st Quarter	2nd Quarter	3rd Quarter	4th Quarter	*Total First Year*
Advertising	10,500.00	9,400.00	3,300.00	4,100.00	
Salaries	2,767.86	3,330.30	3,330.30	3,500.30	
Supplies	900.83	866.88	367.99	1,000.00	
Phone	3,000.99	4,098.99	2,300.00	3,345.00	
Other	435.99	699.00	800.00	609.88	
Total Expenses					

Insert one column.

KEYSTROKES

INSERT ROWS/COLUMNS

ROWS

1. Place insertion point inside table, in row below which desired insertion is to occur.
2. Click **Table** .... `Alt` + `A`
3. Click **Insert Rows** .... `I`

COLUMNS

1. Highlight column to the right of desired insert.
2. Click **Table** .... `Alt` + `A`
3. Click **Insert Columns** .... `I`

AS THE LAST COLUMN

1. Click **Show/Hide** button on Standard toolbar to turn on table codes.
2. Position insertion point at the end of the last row, outside the table, butin front of the end of row mark.
3. Click **Table** .... `Alt` + `A`
4. Click **Select Column** .... `C`
5. Click **Table** .... `Alt` + `A`
6. Click **Insert Columns** .... `I`

DELETE ROWS/COLUMNS

1. Select columns or rows to delete.
2. Click **Table** .... `Alt` + `A`
3. Click **Delete Rows** .... `D`

   OR

   Click **Delete Columns** .... `D`

DELETE TABLE

1. Select entire table.
2. Click **Table** .... `Alt` + `A`
3. Click **Delete Rows** .... `D`

CHANGE COLUMN WIDTH

To see immediate changes:

1. Place mouse pointer on a vertical line separating the column until it changes to a table sizing arrow `←|→` .
2. Drag sizing arrow left or right to adjust column width.

OR

1. Place insertion point in the table.
2. Drag column boundary markers to change the table.
3. Drag left and right indent markers to change table margins.

OR

1. Place insertion point in cell containing longest text.
2. Click **Table** .... `Alt` + `A`
3. Click **Cell Height and Width** .... `W`
4. Click **Column** tab .... `Alt` + `C`
5. Click **AutoFit** .... `Alt` + `A`

To set specific settings:

1. Place insertion point in column to format.

   OR

   Select several columns to format.
2. Click **Table** .... `Alt` + `A`
3. Click **Cell Height and Width** .... `W`
4. Click **Column** tab .... `Alt` + `C`

To set column width:

1. Click **Width of Column** .... `Alt` + `W`
2. Type column width amount .... *number*

To set table margins:

1. Click **Space** .... `Alt` + `S` **between columns**.
2. Type distance to place between columns .... *number*

HORIZONTALLY POSITION A TABLE

1. Select table.
2. Click **Table** .... `Alt` + `A`
3. Click **Cell Height and Width** .... `W`
4. Click **Row** .... `Alt` + `R`
5. Click Alignment option:
   a. **Left** .... `Alt` + `L`
   b. **Center** .... `Alt` + `T`
   c. **Right** .... `Alt` + `I`
6. Click **OK** .... `Enter`

Exercise 68

■ **Draw a Table** ■ **Change Direction of Text in a Table**

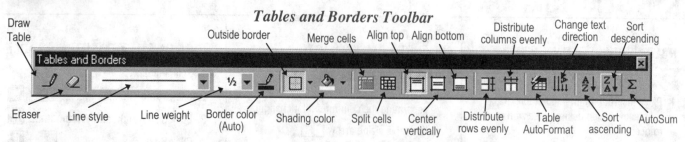

Tables and Borders Toolbar

Draw Table · Eraser · Line style · Line weight · Border color (Auto) · Shading color · Outside border · Split cells · Merge cells · Center vertically · Align top · Align bottom · Distribute rows evenly · Distribute columns evenly · Table AutoFormat · Change text direction · Sort ascending · Sort descending · AutoSum

NOTES

Draw a Table

■ To create a more complex table, for example one with cells that are irregular in height or width, you can use the Draw Table feature. After you "draw" your table, you can adjust the width and height of cells by dragging the table lines where you want them. You can use the eraser to remove any unwanted lines.

■ Click the Tables and Borders ⊞ button on the Standard toolbar, or select Draw Table on the Table menu to activate the Draw Table tool. The mouse pointer will change to a pencil ✐. When you activate this tool, the Tables and Borders toolbar will automatically appear.

■ Click where you want the upper-left corner of the table to appear, and drag to the right and down to insert a one-cell table.

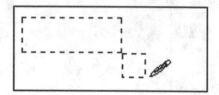

■ With the drawing tool, you can then create table cells by drawing horizontal and vertical lines to insert the cells.

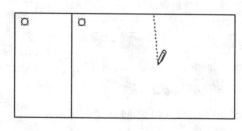

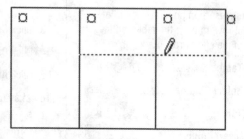

■ If you do not drag far enough in either direction, you may get a message from the Office Assistant suggesting that you draw a little farther in the direction that you want to go.

■ Press Escape to turn off the Draw Table tool.

To erase lines in a table:

- On the Borders and Table toolbar, click the Eraser 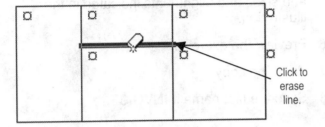 icon. Position the Eraser over the line(s) that you want to remove and start to drag. When the portion of the line that you want to remove is highlighted, release the mouse.

Click to erase line.

Change Direction of Text in a Table

- Using the **Text Direction** command, you can change the direction of text in a table cell. (You can also change the direction of text in text boxes.) Click in the cell containing the text you want to change. Select Text Direction from the Format menu. In the Text Direction dialog box that follows, select the direction you want the text to take. The Preview window displays the new direction. Click OK.

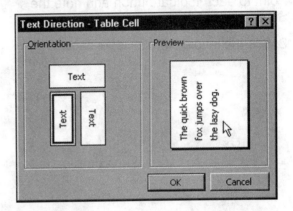

- If the Tables and Borders toolbar is displayed, you can also click the Text Direction button to change the direction of text in the table cell where the insertion point is located. Keep clicking the Text Direction button until the text assumes the direction you want.

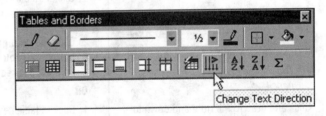

In this exercise, you will use the Draw Table feature to create an invoice.

EXERCISE DIRECTIONS

1. Access the Draw Table feature.

2. Using the pencil, draw the invoice as shown below. Size it to approximately 5" wide x 5" tall.

3. Point to each toolbar button and note the Screentip that displays.

4. Divide the invoice into cells as shown.

5. Type the text where shown with the font styles and sizes and alignments indicated in the illustration.

6. Preview the exercise.

7. Print one copy.

8. Save the file; name it **INVOICE**.

KEYSTROKES

DRAW A TABLE

1. Click **Draw Table** button ⊞ on Standard toolbar.

   OR

   a. Click **Table** .... `Alt` + `A`

   b. Click **Draw Table** .... `B`

   ✓ *The mouse pointer will look like a pencil ✎.*

2. Click and drag to the right and down to insert the table.

   ✓ *This inserts a one cell table.*

3. Draw horizontal and vertical lines to create individual cells.

4. Click **Esc** .... `Esc` to turn off Draw Table.

To erase lines:

1. Click **Eraser** ⬜ on Borders and Tables toolbar.

2. Drag Eraser over lines to delete.

3. Click **Esc** .... `Esc` to turn off Eraser.

CHANGE ORIENTATION OF TEXT IN A TABLE CELL

1. Click in table cell containing text whose orientation you want to change.

2. Click the **Change Text Direction** ..... ⬛ button on **Tables and Borders** toolbar until the desired location is selected.

   OR

1. Click in table cell containing text whose orientation you want to change.

2. Click **Format** .... `Alt` + `O`

3. Click **Text Direction** .... `X`

4. Click desired **Orientation**.

5. Click **OK** .... `Enter`

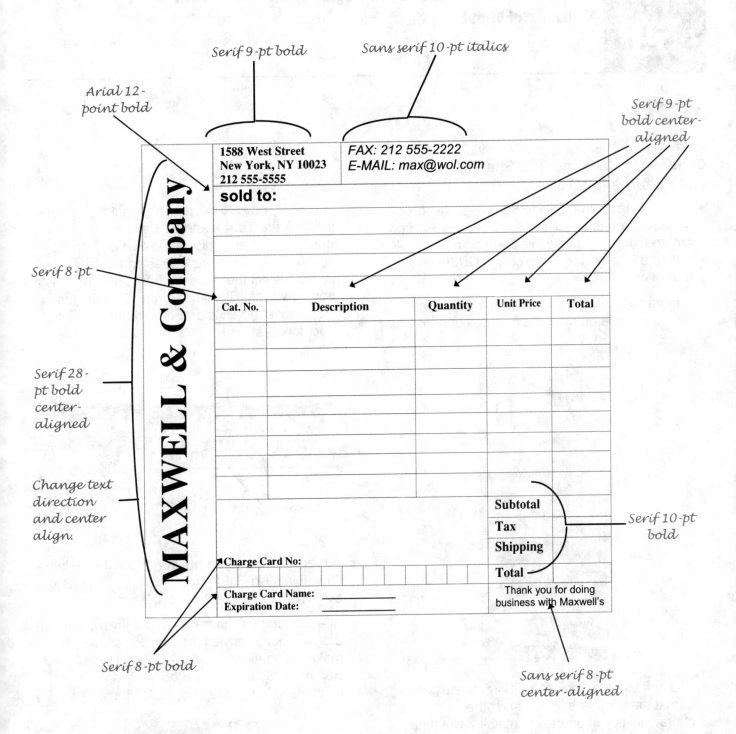

Serif 9-pt bold

Sans serif 10-pt italics

Arial 12-point bold

Serif 9-pt bold center-aligned

1588 West Street
New York, NY 10023
212 555-5555

FAX: 212 555-2222
E-MAIL: max@wol.com

sold to:

Serif 8-pt

Cat. No.	Description	Quantity	Unit Price	Total

Serif 28-pt bold center-aligned

Change text direction and center align.

MAXWELL & Company

Subtotal

Tax

Shipping

Total

Serif 10-pt bold

Charge Card No:

Charge Card Name:
Expiration Date:

Thank you for doing business with Maxwell's

Serif 8-pt bold

Sans serif 8-pt center-aligned

Exercise

69

- ■ **Change Borders and Add Shading and Patterns to a Table**
- ■ **Use AutoFormat**

NOTES

Change Borders and Add Shading and Patterns to a Table

- As you learned in Exercise 65, a ½-point border appears around all cells of a table when it is first created. If you remove this border, you can still view the boundaries of the cells if **Gridlines** is turned on.

- To turn Gridlines on/off, select Show <u>G</u>ridlines from the T<u>a</u>ble menu. Gridlines do not print.

- You can use the Tables and Borders toolbar to format the thickness, color, and other characteristics of borders in a table. Note the table below, which has a 4½-point table border, ¾-point inside table lines, a shaded cell and a patterned cell.

- ■ **To modify a table border**, highlight the table and click the Tables and Borders button on the Standard toolbar to display Tables and Border toolbar. Then from the Tables and Borders toolbar, select the line style from the Line Style drop down list. Click the Border Style list arrow and choose the Outside Border button from the drop down list.

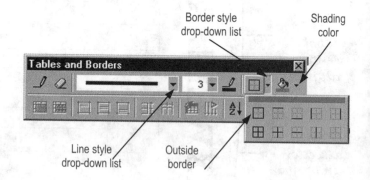

- ■ **To remove the table border**, highlight the table, then select No Border from the Line Style drop-down list.

- ■ After clicking the Border Style list arrow, you can drag the border styles drop-down list menu to make it a floating toolbar. If you drag the Borders toolbar up to the toolbar area, it will insert itself below the existing toolbars.

- **To add a shade to a cell**, column or row, select the cells you wish to shade, then select a gray shading percentage, or a different color, from the Shading Color drop-down list on the Tables and Borders toolbar. Note the illustration below.

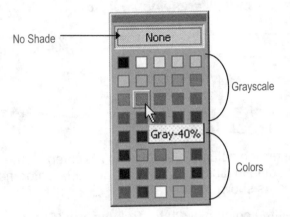

- You can also add borders around a cell or cells. Note the table below, which has a 2¼-point double-line table border, ¾-point dashed inside border lines and a ½-point double line border around one cell.

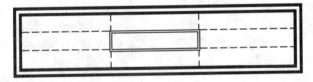

- You may also change the line style of individual lines within a table or cell. This is an effective way of emphasizing data within a cell.

- To change the line style of individual lines, select the cell(s) to receive the line change, select the line style from the drop-down list, then click the Border Style button on the Borders toolbar and select the cell border to modify. Note the table below, which has 3-point bottom and right lines in one cell and 1½-point double top lines in another cell.

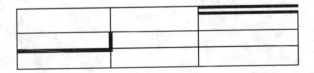

- To add patterns to a cell, column, row, or table, select the cells to which you wish to add a pattern. Then select Borders and Shading from the Format menu and click the Shading tab. Click the Style list arrow, scroll down, and select a desired pattern. Click OK.

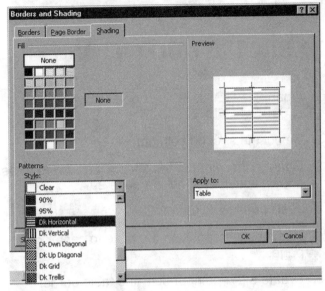

Use AutoFormat

- Word provides a quick way to enhance the appearance of tables through its **Table AutoFormat**. Word provides 34 predefined formatting styles from which you can select to apply to your table.

- You may access AutoFormat by selecting Table AutoFormat from the Table menu. In the Table AutoFormat dialog box that follows, available styles are listed on the left, and a preview window displays the selected style.

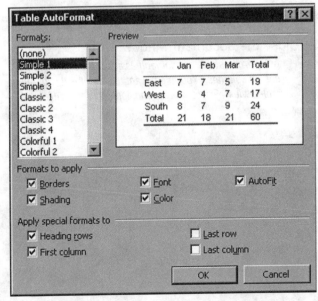

In Part I of this exercise, you will adjust column widths by dragging column boundary markers, change line and border styles and add shading to a previously created table. You will also apply an AutoFormat style to this table. In Part II of this exercise, you will gain more practice inserting and deleting columns and rows, adjusting column widths as well as applying an AutoFormat style to another previously created table.

EXERCISE DIRECTIONS

PART I

1. Open ⌨ BOOKMEET, or open 💾 69BOOKMEET.

2. Select the second column.

3. Change the width of the second column to 4" as shown in Illustration A on page 297.

4. Justify text in column 2.

5. Horizontally reposition the table to center on the page.

6. Create a 2¼-point double line table border.

7. Create ¾-point inside border lines.

8. Use 10% shading to shade Column 1.

9. Preview your work.

10. Print one copy.

11. Save the file as **BOOKMEET**. **Do not close the file.**

12. Apply the Simple 2 AutoFormat as shown in Illustration B on page 298.

13. Print one copy.

14. Save the file as **BOOKMEET1**.

15. Close the document window.

   ✓ *AutoFormat styles will sometimes affect the alignment of data in columns. You might want to experiment with other table styles. Select another and apply it to this table.*

PART II

1. Open ⌨ BOOKSALE, or open 💾 69BOOKSALE.

2. Insert the column and rows as indicated by the shading in Illustration C on page 299. Enter the text as shown.

3. Set the column width for Column 1 to 2"; set the column widths for Columns 2, 3, 4 and 5 to 1.2".

4. Horizontally reposition the table to center on the page.

5. Create a 1½-point line border around the column headings.

6. Create a 1½-point line between columns, select table and use vertical inside border button.

7. Use a 20% shading for the column headings.

8. Preview your work.

9. Print one copy.

10. Save the file as **BOOKSALE**. Do not close the document.

11. Apply the Grid 8 AutoFormat as shown in Illustration E on page 300.

12. Print one copy.

13. Save the file; name it **BOOKSALE1**.

14. Close the document window.

📖📖 BLOOMSBURY BOOKS, LTD. 📖📖
Marketing Meeting Minutes
September 12, 199-
9:30 a.m.

📖 📖 📖 📖

Present	Laurie James, Adrian Monroe, Jill Robinson, Chris Powell, Robert Johnson, Brian Murphy
Announcements	David presided over the meeting in John's absence. Next week's meeting will be held on Thursday at 9:30 a.m., at which time Jill and Brian will present the findings of the Marketing Task Force meeting.
NEW TITLES	
Journey through Tomorrow	The publishing date has been pushed to December. Alice to check with production and firm up all dates.
Perfect Pasta	May publishing date to coincide with Mother's Day. In-store promotional display. Author to offer cooking demonstrations at major chains during tour.
The Book of Healing	Jacket art has been delayed until March 22. Coordinate with publicity to run print ads in corresponding cities with author's tour.
Waiting for the Light	We will run ads in the *San Francisco Chronicle, Los Angeles Times, Denver Post, Chicago Tribune, New York Times* and *Boston Globe* to correspond with author tour.
Adjournment	The meeting was adjourned at 11:00 a.m.

ILLUSTRATION B

📖📖 BLOOMSBURY BOOKS, LTD. 📖📖

Marketing Meeting Minutes
September 12, 199-
9:30 a.m.

📖 📖 📖 📖

Present	**Laurie James, Adrian Monroe, Jill Robinson, Chris Powell, Robert Johnson, Brian Murphy**
Announcements	David presided over the meeting in John's absence. Next week's meeting will be held on Thursday at 9:30 a.m., at which time Jill and Brian will present the findings of the Marketing Task Force meeting.
NEW TITLES	
Journey through Tomorrow	The publishing date has been pushed to December. Alice to check with production and firm up all dates.
Perfect Pasta	May publishing date to coincide with Mother's Day. In-store promotional display. Author to offer cooking demonstrations at major chains during tour.
The Book of Healing	Jacket art has been delayed until March 22. Coordinate with publicity to run print ads in corresponding cities with author's tour.
Waiting for the Light	We will run ads in the San Francisco Chronicle, Los Angeles Times, Denver Post, Chicago Tribune, New York Times and Boston Globe to correspond with author tour.
Adjournment	The meeting was adjourned at 11:00 a.m.

ILLUSTRATION C

📖📖 BLOOMSBURY BOOKS, LTD. 📖📖
February Sales

Title	Author	Sales	Gross Units To Date	Net Units To Date
The Peacemaker	Allen	41,000	15,283	8,987
September Queen	Ewing	44,999	11,876	11,515
The Fifth Dimension	Mitchell	35,000	11,888	9,777
Where There's Smoke	Kasdam	50,000	18,732	16,231
Spider's Web	Newman	14,566	12,802	3,343
Learning to Earn	Cameron	69,654	20,777	20,690
No Entry	Zaccaro	18,600	4,900	4,000

ILLUSTRATION D

📖 📖 BLOOMSBURY BOOKS, LTD. 📖 📖
February Sales

Title	Author	Sales	Gross Units To Date	Net Units To Date
The Peacemaker	Allen	41,000	15,283	8,987
September Queen	Ewing	44,999	11,876	11,515
The Fifth Dimension	Mitchell	35,000	11,888	9,777
Where There's Smoke	Kasdam	50,000	18,732	16,231
Spider's Web	Newman	14,566	12,802	3,343
Learning to Earn	Cameron	69,654	20,777	20,690
No Entry	Zaccaro	18,600	4,900	4,000

ILLUSTRATION E

📖📖 BLOOMSBURY BOOKS, LTD. 📖📖
February Sales

Title	Author	Sales	Gross Units To Date	Net Units To Date
The Peacemaker	Allen	41,000	15,283	8,987
September Queen	Ewing	44,999	11,876	11,515
The Fifth Dimension	Mitchell	35,000	11,888	9,777
Where There's Smoke	Kasdam	50,000	18,732	16,231
Spider's Web	Newman	14,566	12,802	3,343
Learning to Earn	Cameron	69,654	20,777	20,690
No Entry	Zaccaro	18,600	4,900	4,000

KEYSTROKES

TABLE BORDERS AND LINES

1. Select the table or individual cells to receive lines.
2. Click the **Line Style**.. [_____▼] button on the Borders toolbar and select a line style from the drop-down list.
3. Click the **Border Style** button on the Borders toolbar and select borders to add.

ADD SHADING TO A TABLE

1. Select the table or individual cells to receive shading.
2. Click the **Shading Color** button ...... [🔲] on the Borders toolbar and select a shade from the drop-down menu.

ADD PATTERNS TO CELLS, ROWS, COLUMNS, OR TABLES

1. Select cell(s) to which to add a pattern.
2. Click **Format** menu..............[Alt] + [O]
3. Select **Borders and Shading** ....[B] from drop-down menu.
4. Click **Style** drop-down..........[Alt] + [Y] list box.
5. Scroll down and select pattern .. [↑][↓] to apply.
6. Click **OK** ....[Enter]

TABLE AUTOFORMAT

1. Place insertion point anywhere in table to format.
2. Click **Table** ....[Alt] + [A]
3. Click **Table AutoFormat** ....[F]
4. Select desired style ....[Alt] + [T] from list of **Formats**.
5. Click any or all of the following **Formats to Apply** to turn check boxes on or off as desired:
   - **Borders** ....[Alt] + [B]
   - **Shading**...........................[Alt] + [S]
   - **Font**.............................[Alt] + [F]
   - **Color** ....[Alt] + [C]
   - **AutoFit**..........................[Alt] + [I]
6. Click any or all of the following to **Apply special formats to** specified parts of the table:
   - **Heading rows**................[Alt] + [R]
   - **First column**..................[Alt] + [O]
   - **Last row** ....[Alt] + [L]
   - **Last column** ....[Alt] + [U]
7. Click **OK**..................................[Enter]

Exercise 70

■ **Merge Cells** ■ **Split Cells** ■ **Row Height**

NOTES

Merge Cells

■ Merging cells lets you create a single larger cell by removing the dividing lines between cells. This feature may be used, for example, to create a heading row within a table or to provide room for longer cell entries without adding additional lines within an individual cell.

■ Cells can be merged horizontally and/or vertically.

■ You can merge cells by highlighting the cells that you want to combine, then selecting Merge Cells from the Table menu.

OR

Merge cells by selecting the cells to merge, right-clicking in selected cells, and clicking Merge Cells on the shortcut menu.

OR

Display the Tables and Borders toolbar and use the eraser ⬛ to remove the lines between cells.

Original Table

Table with Merged Cells

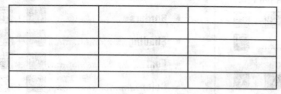

Three cells merged vertically		
	Two cells merged horizontally	
Three cells merged horizontally		

Split Cells

■ **Splitting Cells** lets you divide cells. When a cell is split into multiple cells, the space of a single cell is divided into the number of cells you specify.

Table with Split Cells

■ You can split cells by positioning your insertion point in the cell to be split, then selecting Split Cells from the Table menu. In the Split Cells dialog box that follows, you must indicate into how many columns and rows you wish to split your cell.

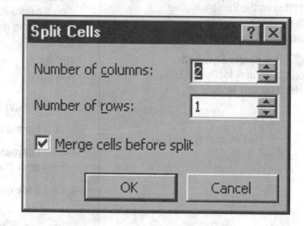

Row Height

■ Each row is defaulted to accept the default font size for text. When you change the font size, Word automatically adjusts the row height to accommodate the size of the text.

- You may, however, adjust the row height as desired to make text more readable or to add special effects by selecting Cell Height and Width from the Table menu.

- In the Cell Height and Width dialog box that follows, select the Row tab and make the necessary adjustments.

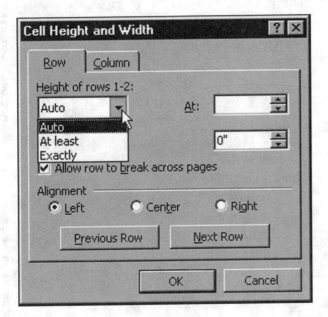

- If you select At Least from the Height of Rows drop-down list, you can specify a minimum row height in the At text box. If you select Exactly, you can specify a fixed row height in the At text box.

- You can also position the pointer on the horizontal line separating the rows and drag to adjust the height of a row.

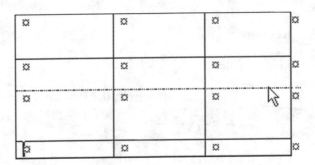

In this exercise, you will create an income statement using the table feature.

EXERCISE DIRECTIONS

1. Create a NEW document.

2. Display the Tables and Borders toolbar.

3. Set 0.5" left and right margins.

4. Create the table on the following page using 3 columns and 22 rows. Remove the default border from the entire table.

5. Change the row height to At Least 20 points.

6. Change column 1 width to 4.5".

7. Change column width of columns 2 and 3 to 1".

8. Right align text in columns 2 and 3.

9. Create a ¾-point dotted border around the table.

10. Merge cells in the first row, and center all title lines.

11. Set the first two lines to a sans serif 14-point bold font; set third line to italics.

12. Set column text to a serif 12-point bold font where indicated. Press Ctrl + Tab to insert a tab where necessary.

13. Add 20% shading to the rows as illustrated.

14. Center the table vertically.

15. Spell check.

16. Preview your work.

17. Print one copy.

18. Save the file; name it **IS**.

19. Close the document window.

JUDY'S CARD SHOPPE
INCOME STATEMENT
For the Month Ended April 30, 199-

Revenue:

Sales	25700	
Less Sales Returns and Allowances	700	
Net Sales		25000

Cost of Merchandise Sold:

Merchandise Inventory, April 1	50250	
Purchases	9250	
Merchandise Available for Sales	59500	
Less Merchandise Inventory, April 30	40000	
Cost of Merchandise Sold		19500

Gross Profit on Sales | | 9000

Operating Expenses:

Salaries	4000	
Rent	1666	
Taxes	400	
Utilities	345	
Advertising	500	
Depreciation on Equipment	210	
Insurance	65	
Total Operating Expenses		7186

Net Income: | | 1814

KEYSTROKES

MERGE CELLS VERTICALLY/HORIZONTALLY

USING THE MENU

1. Select cell or group of cells to merge.
2. Click **Table** .... **Alt** + **A**
3. Click **Merge Cells** .... **M**

USING THE TOOLBAR

1. Display the **Tables and Borders** toolbar.
2. Select cell or group of cells to merge.
3. Click **Merge** button ....

SPLIT CELLS

USING THE MENU

1. Select cells or group of cells to split.
2. Click **Table** .... **Alt** + **A**
3. Click **Split Cells** .... **P**
4. Type number .... *number*
   in **Number of columns** text box.
   AND/OR
   Type number .... *number*
   in **Number of rows** text box.
5. Click **OK** .... **Enter**

USING THE TOOLBAR

1. Display the **Tables and Borders** toolbar.
2. Select the cell(s) to split.
3. Click **Split Cells** button ....

ROW HEIGHT

1. Select row or group of rows.
2. Click **Table** .... **Alt** + **A**
3. Click **Cell Height and Width** .... **W**
4. Select **Row** tab and select desired options:

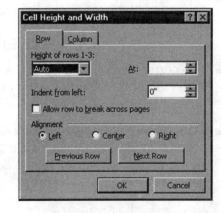

   a. Click **Height of rows** .... **E**
   b. Select Height of rows option:
      - **Auto**
      - **At Least**
      - **Exactly**
5. If you selected **At Least** or **Exactly**:
   a. Click **At** .... **Alt** + **A**
   b. Type row height .... *number*
6. Click **OK** .... **Enter**

Exercise

71

■ **Calculate in Tables** ■ **Number Formats** ■ **Sort within a Table**

NOTES

Calculate in Tables

■ Word can add consecutive numbers in table columns or rows. You can also perform subtraction, multiplication and division within a table cell. This exercise will focus on performing addition. If your data requires subtraction, multiplication, division, averaging, finding the highest or lowest value or more extensive calculations, use a spreadsheet software application, such as Excel.

■ To add numbers in a table, place the insertion point in the cell where the answer should appear. Then select Formula from the Table menu.

■ The correct formula for computing the sum of a column of numbers above the insertion point cell is:

=SUM(ABOVE)

■ The correct formula for adding a row of numbers to the left of the insertion point cell is:
=SUM(LEFT)

■ If one of the numbers in a calculation includes a dollar sign ($), the answer will include a dollar sign and will appear with two places after the decimal.

Number Formats

■ Word provides seven formats for numerical data including currency, percent and several decimal place options. Therefore, if you desire a dollar sign or another format for your numerical data, select Formula from the Table menu. In the Formula dialog box that follows, click the Number format list arrow and choose a desired format. A number format should be selected at the same time you enter your formula.

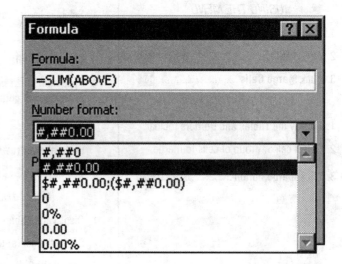

Sort within a Table

- Word's Sort feature lets you arrange text in a table alphabetically or numerically in ascending order (from A to Z or 1 to 9) or descending order (Z to A or 9 to 1).

- To begin the sort, select text to be sorted and select Sort from the Table menu. In the Sort dialog box that follows, indicate which column is to be sorted, which direction to sort in, ascending or descending, and identify the text as text, number or date.

  ✓Note: It is important to save your document before you begin a sort. If your sort produces unexpected results, you can close your file without saving it, open the file again, and repeat the sort process.

Sort Dialog Box

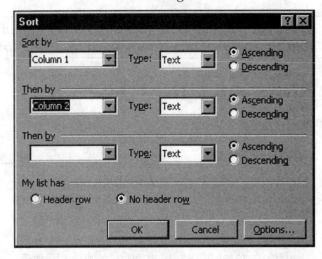

- Word allows you to sort by up to 3 columns of data.

  ✓Note: This exercise will focus on simple sorts. If you require extensive sorting and/or selective data sorts, use database software.

- It is possible to sort by one criterion and then subsort by another. Note the illustration of records sorted on one criterion and subsorted by another.

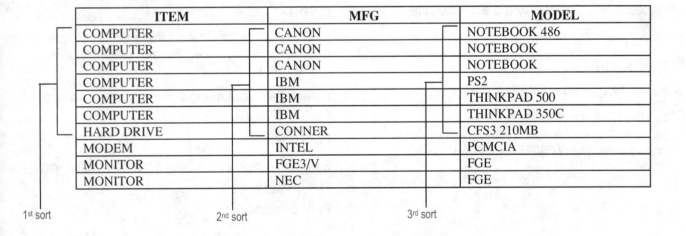

ITEM	MFG	MODEL
COMPUTER	CANON	NOTEBOOK 486
COMPUTER	CANON	NOTEBOOK
COMPUTER	CANON	NOTEBOOK
COMPUTER	IBM	PS2
COMPUTER	IBM	THINKPAD 500
COMPUTER	IBM	THINKPAD 350C
HARD DRIVE	CONNER	CFS3 210MB
MODEM	INTEL	PCMCIA
MONITOR	FGE3/V	FGE
MONITOR	NEC	FGE

1st sort   2nd sort   3rd sort

> *In Part I of this exercise, you will use the calculate feature to find totals in a previously created table. In Part II of this exercise, you will find totals and sort in a column.*

EXERCISE DIRECTIONS

PART I

1. Open ⌨ **EXPENSES**, or open 💾**71EXPENSES**.

2. Merge the cells in row 2 and then merge the cells in row 8 as shown in Illustration A on page 309.

3. Insert ¾-point double-line left, right, and top outside border lines, as shown in Illustration A.

4. Use a 20% shading for the last row.

5. Find the total expenses for 1ˢᵗ Quarter, 2ⁿᵈ Quarter, 3ʳᵈ Quarter and 4ᵗʰ Quarter. Then find the total expenses for the year.
   [Use =SUM(ABOVE) for quarter totals and =SUM(LEFT) for Total First Year totals.]
   Format the Total First Year totals for currency.

6. Sort the first column to arrange the expenses alphabetically. (Select only the expense names.)

7. Preview your document.

8. Print one copy.

9. Save the file; name it **EXPENSES**.

10. Close the document window.
    ✓ *If you made an error in any of the steps in Part I, you may close this file, open EXPENSES or 71EXPENSES, and begin again.*

PART II

1. Open ⌨ **BOOKSALE**, or open 💾**71BOOKSALE**.

2. Insert two rows at the bottom of the table as shown in Illustration B on page 310.

3. Merge cells in row 2, the next to the last row and the first two cells of the last row.

4. Insert and center the word Totals in the last row as shown. Shade Totals row with 20% gray as shown.

5. Create a 3-point border around the last row as shown. Insert ¾-point inside border lines for the entire table. Create a pattern for row 2.

6. Delete blank rows between entries except for row below "No Entry." Insert ¾-point left and right outside borders lines for rows 2-10 as shown.

7. Find the totals for Sales, Gross Units to Date and Net Units to Date. Format the total Sales for currency.

8. Select cells containing author names and sort alphabetically.

9. Print one copy.

10. Select the cells containing sales data and sort in ascending order.

11. Print one copy.

12. Select cells containing book titles and sort in alphabetical order.

13. Preview your work.

14. Print one copy.

15. Save the file; name it **BOOKSALE3**.

16. Close the document window.

TIME TO TRAVEL TOURS

First Year Expenses

	1st Quarter	2nd Quarter	3rd Quarter	4th Quarter	Total First Year
Advertising	10,500.00	9,400.00	3,300.00	4,100.00	
Salaries	2,767.86	3,330.30	3,330.30	3,500.30	
Supplies	900.83	866.88	367.99	1000.00	
Phone	3,000.99	4,098.99	2,300.00	3,345.00	
Other	435.99	699.00	800.00	609.88	
Total Expenses					

ILLUSTRATION B

BLOOMSBURY BOOKS, LTD.
February Sales

Title	Author	Sales	Gross Units To Date	Net Units To Date
The Peacemaker	Allen	41,000	15,283	8,987
September Queen	Ewing	44,999	11,876	11,515
The Fifth Dimension	Mitchell	35,000	11,888	9,777
Where There's Smoke	Kasdam	50,000	18,732	16,231
Spider's Web	Newman	14,566	12,802	3,343
Learning to Earn	Cameron	69,654	20,777	20,690
No Entry	Zaccaro	18,600	4,900	4,000
Totals				

KEYSTROKES

CALCULATE/USE FORMULAS

1. Place insertion point in cell where answer will appear.

2. Click **AutoSum** .... Σ
   on Tables and Borders toolbar.

   OR

   a. Click **Table** .... Alt + A

   b. Click **Formula** .... O

   c. Click **OK** .... Enter
      if Word proposes the
      correct formula.

   OR

   Edit expression in parentheses as
   necessary.

3. Click **OK** .... Enter

SORT

1. Place insertion point in column to be sorted.

   OR

   Highlight data to sort.

2. Click **Table** .... Alt + A

3. Click **Sort** .... S

4. Click **Sort by** .... Alt + S

5. Select column .... ↓, ↑
   by which to sort.

6. Click **Type** .... Alt + Y

7. Select data type to sort............ ↓, ↑

8. Select a sort order:

   Ascending .... Alt + A

   OR

   Descending .... Alt + D

9. Click **Then by** if desired .... Alt + T

10. Select second column............. ↓, ↑
    by which to sort.

11. Click **Type** .... Alt + P

12. Select data type to sort............ ↓, ↑

13. Select a sort order:

    Ascending .... Alt + C

    OR

    Descending .... Alt + N

14. Click **Then by** if desired .... Alt + B

15. Select third column .... ↓, ↑
    by which to sort.

16. Click **Type** .... Alt + E

17. Select data type to sort............ ↓, ↑

18. Select a sort order:

    Ascending .... Alt + I

    OR

    Descending .... Alt + G

19. Click **OK** .... Enter

Exercise 72   ■ **Summary**

In this exercise, you will create a monthly sales table and use the Calculate feature to find quarterly totals.

EXERCISE DIRECTIONS

1. Create a NEW document, as shown in Illustration A.

2. Set the left and right margins to 0.5".

3. Center the main heading in a serif 14-point bold font and set other headings in a 12-point font; set the first and second headings in all caps; set the third heading in italics. Press Enter three times.

4. Return to left alignment. Set font to a 12-point serif.

5. Create a table using 5 columns and 11 rows.

6. Enter the data as shown. Center and bold the column headings in all caps; bold and italicize TOTALS. Skip a row after the heading row and before the Totals row.

7. Right-align money amounts.

8. Save the file; name it **MICRO**.

9. Set width of columns 2-5 to 1.25". Use AutoFit to adjust Column 1 width.

10. Find the totals for JANUARY, FEBRUARY, and MARCH and QTR TOTALS.

   [Use =SUM(ABOVE) for JANUARY, FEBRUARY, and MARCH and =SUM(LEFT) for QTR TOTALS.]

11. Format the totals for currency.

12. Sort the first column to arrange the names alphabetically. (Select only the names before sorting, or totals will be sorted also.)

13. Highlight the cells that contain numerical data and left-align data. Set a decimal tab in the second column so the data centers within the column (at 2") as shown in Illustration B.

14. Horizontally and vertically center the exercise.

15. Apply any desired Table AutoFormat to the exercise.

16. Preview your document.

17. Print one copy.

18. Save the file; name it **MICRO1**.

✓ If you made an error in any of the steps above, you may close this file without saving the changes, open MICRO, and begin again.

MICRO ELECTRONICS

MONTHLY SALES BY SALESPERSON
First Quarter 199-

	JANUARY	FEBRUARY	MARCH	QTR. TOTALS
Mauro, John	$3456.99	$3456.88	$2345.99	
Singh, Chandra	8634.88	3466.88	2356.66	
Doyle, Ebony	7643.99	5558.99	4765.00	
Dunn, Brad	7777.00	7776.55	6668.00	
Ho, Bruce	7745.00	3456.99	5666.95	
Kennedy, Sharon	5987.00	6575.85	4556.88	
Yerman, Jonathan	6432.25	6554.00	5090.00	

TOTALS

ILLUSTRATION B

MICRO ELECTRONICS

MONTHLY SALES BY SALESPERSON
First Quarter 199-

	JANUARY	FEBRUARY	MARCH	QTR. TOTALS
Doyle, Ebony	$7643.99	5558.99	$4765.00	17967.98
Dunn, Brad	7777.00	7776.55	6668.00	22221.55
Ho, Bruce	7745.00	3456.99	5666.95	16868.94
Kennedy, Sharon	5987.00	6575.85	4556.88	17119.73
Mauro, John	3456.99	3456.88	2345.99	9259.86
Singh, Chandra	8634.88	3466.88	2356.66	14458.42
Yerman, Jonathan	6432.25	6554.00	5090.00	18076.25
TOTALS	$47677.11	$36846.14	$31449.48	$115972.73

Word 97

LESSON 10

Merge; Envelopes and Labels

- Mail Merge
- The Main Document
- The Data Source Document
- Merge Main and Data Source Documents
- Create and Merge Main and Data Source Documents
- Merge Selected Records
- Prepare Envelopes and Labels while Merging
- Envelopes and Labels

Exercise

73

■ **Mail Merge** ■ **The Main Document** ■ **The Data Source Document**
■ **Merge Main and Data Source Documents**

NOTES

Mail Merge

■ The **Merge** feature allows you to mass-produce letters, envelopes, mailing labels and other documents so that they appear to be personalized.

■ The exercises in this lesson illustrate the mail merge feature using typical letters. However, other document types may be merged, such as reports or catalogs.

■ The merge process combines the **main document** (sometimes referred to as the form letter) with a **data source document** (the actual names and addresses of those who will receive the letter) to produce a **merged** document.

■ The same data source file may then be used to produce envelopes and/or labels, thus making it unnecessary to type the name and address list a second time.

■ There are three steps in a mail merge process:

1. Create a **main document** containing text that will not change and codes where variable information will be inserted (see illustration to the right).

2. Create a **data source document** that contains the variable information (actual names and addresses of those receiving the letter).

3. **Merge** the main and data source documents to create individual, personalized letters.

✓*Note:* *Before you create the main and data source documents, we recommend that you create a rough copy of the letter you wish to send and determine what variables will be included in your letter. This will ensure that you create and insert the proper merge codes in your main and data source documents.*

The Main Document

■ The main document contains information that does not change. All formatting, margins, spacing, etc., as well as graphics and paper size information, should be included in the main document. The main document is often referred to as the form letter. However, the main document can also take the form of a report or a catalog. Since the Mail Merge feature is most frequently used to personalize letters, we will use a letter as the main document to illustrate the merge process.

■ Information that *does* change is called a **variable**. Each variable is indicated on the form letter as a code. Each code is named for what will eventually be inserted into that location. These code names are called **merge field names**. Note the form letter below, which contains merge field names for each variable in the letter. In a typical letter, the variable information would include the person's title (Ms., Mr., Dr.), first name, last name, address, city, state, and zip.

Today's date

«Title» «FirstName» «LastName»
«Address1»
«City», «State» «PostalCode»

Dear «Title» «LastName»:

We are sorry for the delay in processing your order. The items you ordered have been out of stock; however, we anticipate delivery within the next few days.

We will process your order as soon as the merchandise reaches our warehouse. We are sorry for any inconvenience this delay may have caused you.

Sincerely,

Ralph Jones

- Word provides a list of the most commonly used merge field names for you to insert as codes in your form letter.

- To create a main document, select Mail Merge from the Tools menu. In the Mail Merge Helper dialog box that follows, select Create, Form Letters.

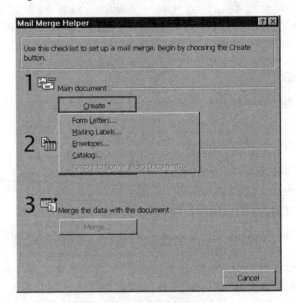

- You will be prompted to use the active window to create your form letter or to create a new main document. Select Active Window if you have a blank document screen ready for entering text. Otherwise, select New Main Document.

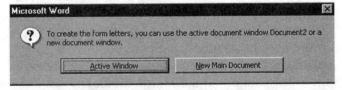

- The Mail Merge Helper dialog box will again display:

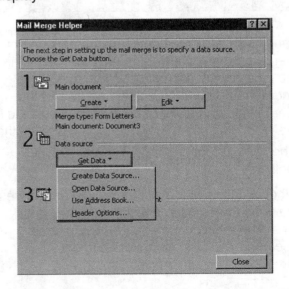

- At this point, you will want to establish the merge field codes you will use for each variable in your main document. To do this, select Get Data, Create Data Source. The Create Data Source dialog box displays, listing merge field code names that are typically used for variables in a letter.

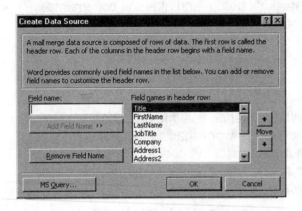

- If you see field names you probably will not use in your main document, select the names from the Field names in header row box and click the Remove Field Name button. If there is a name you wish to add, type it in the Field Name box and click the Add Field Name button.

- When you are satisfied with your list, click OK. The Save As dialog box will then appear for you to save your data source document (even though you have not entered actual names and addresses yet).

- Once you save your data source document, you will be prompted to either enter data into your data source document (Edit Data Source) or to create your main document (Edit Main Document).

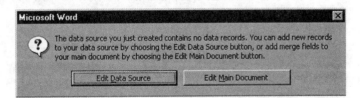

- Click Edit Main Document. The blank document screen displays, ready for you to create your main document. The Mail Merge toolbar also displays at the top of the screen.

Mail Merge Toolbar

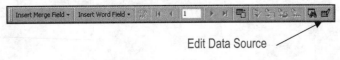

Edit Data Source

- To complete the main document, type your letter as you normally would. (Begin the date At 2.5" from the top of the page, press Enter four times, etc.) For each variable in the main document, click the Insert Merge Field button on the Merge toolbar and select an appropriate merge field name. A merge field name code will appear with brackets before and after the code name. Example:

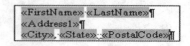

- When entering field merge codes, place space where you want spacing to appear when text is substituted for the codes. Punctuation must also be added before or after merge field codes where appropriate.

- After completing the letter, save it. You are now ready to complete the data source document.

- To create the data source document, click the Edit Data Source button on the Merge toolbar.

The Data Source Document

- The data source document contains the variable information (title, first name, last name, etc.) for those people who will be receiving the letter created as the main document.

- A data source document contains many records. A record is a collection of related information about one person or one thing. When you click the Edit Data Source button on the Mail Merge toolbar, a Data Form dialog box displays one record. The record lists the field names you entered in your main document and space for you to fill in the actual information for those fields.

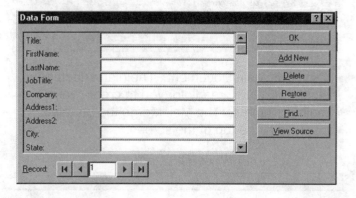

- After entering all the information for the first record, click Add New to get a new blank data form, and fill in the next record.

- When you finish entering all records, you may view your data source document by clicking the View Source button in the Data Form dialog box. The data source document will appear as a table of columns and rows with merge field names at the top of each column. Do not be concerned if the column widths do not accommodate the information.

- Click the Mail Merge Main Document button on the Database toolbar to return to the main document display.

- You are now ready to merge the two documents.

Merge Main and Data Source Documents

- The main document and data source document may be merged to a new, third document on screen. Or the two documents may be merged and sent directly to the printer without first displaying them on screen. We recommend that you merge the documents and display them on screen so that if the documents do not merge properly, you can check them and remerge them, if necessary, before you print.

- To merge the documents and create a new, third document on screen, click the Merge to New Document button on the Mail Merge toolbar. To merge the documents and print them (without displaying them on the screen), click the Merge to Printer button on the Merge toolbar.

- If the main and data source documents do not merge properly, check to make sure the text in the data source document has been entered under the proper merge field names and that merge field names have been properly placed in the main document. For help with this, click the Check for Errors button on the Merge toolbar.

- When working with Mail Merge, you may have as many as three documents open at the same time: the main document, the data source document, and the merged document. To cycle through the documents, press Ctrl + F6.

In this exercise, you will create the main and data source documents, merge the two documents to a third document and print them.

EXERCISE DIRECTIONS

1. Create a NEW document.

2. Review the main document shown on the following page and note the merge field name codes used. Create the merge field name codes list in the Create Data Source dialog box using the field name codes used in the main document.

3. Save the data source document; name it **HUGDATA**.

4. Create the main document illustrated on the following page using the merge field names indicated. Begin the date At 2.5".

5. Spell check.

6. Print one copy.

7. Save the main document; name it **HUGMAIN**.

8. Edit the data source document and enter the information in the data source document shown on page 320.

9. View the source document.

10. Switch to the main document. (Click the Mail Merge Main document button.)

11. Merge the main and data source documents using the *merge to new document* option.

12. Scroll through the new merged document; check the form letter for errors.

13. Save the merged letters under a new filename, **HUGFINAL**.

14. Print one copy of the merged letters.

15. Close all files.

MAIN DOCUMENT

Today's date

«Title» «FirstName» «LastName»
«Address1»
«City», «State» «Postal_Code»

Dear «Title» «LastName»:

The New York Chapter of the HUG Computer Users' Group cordially invites you to attend our first annual computer conference. The conference will take place at the Plaza Hotel in New York City on Thursday, June 22 at 8:30 a.m.

We are confident that this year's conference will be inspiring and informative. We have several leading representatives of the computer industry who will be conducting seminars at the conference. A conference program and registration form is enclosed.

Please let me know, **«Title» «LastName»,** if you plan to attend by returning the completed registration form no later than June 1.

Sincerely,

Thomas Mann
President
NY Chapter

tm/yo
enclosure

DATA SOURCE DOCUMENT

Title	FirstName	LastName	Address1	City	State	Postal Code
Mr.	Peter	Ringler	23 Preston Avenue	Bellemore	NY	11010
Mr.	Fred	LeBost	98-67 Kew Gardens Road	Forest Hills	NY	11432
Ms.	Mary	McClean	765 Belmill Road	Roslyn	NY	11577
Ms.	Rosa	Napolitano	34-38 202 Street	Bayside	NY	11361

KEYSTROKES

CREATE A MAIN DOCUMENT

1. Type the document you wish to use as a main document.

   OR

   Open an existing document you wish to use as a main document.

2. At locations in the document where variable information will be inserted, type the **merge field name** for that information.

   OR

   Type an asterisk (*) as a placeholder for the variable information.

   ✓ *You may make up your own merge field names, use those on the list provided by Word, or use a combination of both your own names and Word's. It is also okay to type an asterisk (*) as a placeholder instead of a merge field name.*

3. Click **Tools** .... `Alt` + `T`

4. Click **Mail Merge** .... `R`

5. Click **Create** .... `Alt` + `C`
   to define document as a main document.

6. Click **Form Letters** .... `L`

7. Click **Active Window** .... `Alt` + `A`

8. Click **Close** .... `Esc`

9. Click **File** .... `Alt` + `F`

10. Click **Save** .... `S`

CREATE A DATA SOURCE DOCUMENT

1. Open the main document.

2. Click **Tools** .... `Alt` + `T`

3. Click **Mail Merge** .... `R`

4. Click **Get Data** .... `Alt` + `G`

5. Click **Create Data Source** .... `C`

6. Click **Field names** .... `Alt` + `N`
   in header row list box.

   ✓ *Word suggests a list of commonly used field names. You may add new field names, delete suggested names, or use the suggested fields in their entirety.*

Do one of the following:

   a. Select field name to delete ..... `↑`, `↓`

   b. Click **Remove Field Name** .. `Alt` + `R`

   c. Repeat steps a-b for each field name not wanted.

AND/OR

   a. Click **Field name** .... `Alt` + `F`

   b. Type name of new merge field to add to list.

   c. Click **Add Field Name** ..... `Alt` + `A`

   d. Repeat steps a-c for each new field name you wish to add.

7. Click **OK**.

8. Key a name for the data source document in the **File name** box .... *name*

9. Click **Save** .... `Enter`

   ✓ *A message will appear indicating that there are no records in the data source file. By selecting Edit Data Source, you cause the Data Form dialog box to appear.*

10. Click **Edit Data Source** .... `Alt` + `E`
    to open **Data Form** dialog box.

11. Key information for the first field.

12. Press **Enter** .... `Enter`
    to move to next field.

13. Repeat for each field.

    ✓ *Press **Shift** + **Tab** to go back to edit a field.*

14. Click **Add New** .... `Alt` + `A`
    after entering information for last field.

    ✓ *See illustration of **Data Form** dialog box in the **Notes** section of this exercise, page 318.*

15. Repeat steps 11 -14 for each person who will receive the form letter.

16. Click **View Source** .... `Alt` + `V`
    to see data source document.

17. Save and close data source document in the usual way.

18. Save and close main document in the usual way.

SWITCH FROM DATA DOCUMENT TO MAIN DOCUMENT

Click **Main Document** button ....
on Database toolbar.

SWITCH FROM MAIN DOCUMENT TO DATA DOCUMENT

1. Click **Edit Data Source** button ....

2. Click **View Source** .... `Alt` + `V`

INSERT MERGE FIELD NAMES INTO MAIN DOCUMENT

1. Open the main document.

2. Select (highlight) the first placeholder in the **main document**.

3. Click

   Insert Merge Field ..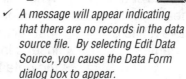
   button on Mail Merge toolbar.

4. Click the merge field name that will replace the placeholder.

5. Add spacing or punctuation before or after the merge field name, if needed.

6. Repeat steps 2-5 at each location where a merge field name is to be inserted.

7. Resave the main document.

MERGE MAIN AND DATA DOCUMENTS

1. Open the main document.

2. Click **View Merged Data** button ....
   on Mail Merge toolbar.

3. Click **Next Record** button ....

   OR

   Click **Previous Record** button ....
   to view additional records.

4. Click **Merge to Printer** button ....
   to print merged form letters.

   OR

   Click **Merge to New Document** ....
   button on Mail Merge toolbar to merge to new document to create a new file of merged documents.

5. Save and close the main document and the merge document.

CHECK MAIN DOCUMENT AND DATA DOCUMENT FOR ERRORS

1. Click **Main Document** button ....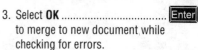
   to switch to main document, if necessary.

2. Click **Error Check** button ....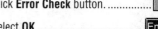

3. Select **OK** .... `Enter`
   to merge to new document while checking for errors.

Exercise 74

■ Create and Merge Main and Data Source Documents

NOTES

■ In the previous exercise, each of the records in the merged file contained the same number of variables. However, this is not always the case. Not all inside addresses are three lines. Some people receiving a form letter may have a title or an address that contains a company name.

■ When creating the main document, include a merge field code for every possible variable. When filling out the data form, you will not fill in any information in a field if it is not relevant for that record. During the merge process, Word inserts into the letter any information included in the data form.

In this exercise, you will create a main document and a data source document and merge the two files. The main document will contain more variables than the previous exercise.

EXERCISE DIRECTIONS

1. Create a NEW document.

2. Use the default margins.

3. Review the main document shown on the following page and note each place where a merge field code is to be inserted. Review the data source document shown and note the merge field codes to be used.

4. Create the merge field names list in the Create Data Source dialog box using the merge field code names shown in the data source document.

5. Save the data source document; name it **DUEDATA**.

6. Create the main document illustrated on the right using the appropriate merge field name codes. Begin the date At 2.5".

7. Spell check.

8. Print one copy.

9. Save the main document; name it **DUEMAIN**.

10. Edit the data source document and enter the data shown.

11. View the data source document.

12. Switch to the main document.

13. Merge the main and data source documents using the *merge to new document* option.

14. Scroll through the new merge document; check the form letter for errors.

15. Save the merge letters under a new filename, **DUEFINAL**.

16. Print one copy of the merged letters.

17. Close all files.

Today's date

░░░ ░░░ ░░░░░

░░░░░░░░

░░░░░░░░

░░░░░ , ░░ ░░░░░

Dear ░░░░ ░░░░░ :

Just a brief reminder, ░░░░ ░░░░░░ , that your account is now past due. As you can see from the enclosed statement, you still have an outstanding balance of $ ░░░░░ , which was due on ░░░░░ .

We need your cooperation so that we can continue to give you the service we have provided you for many years.

Please mail your remittance for $ ░░░░░ today, so we are not forced to send your account to our collection agency.

Cordially,

Brenda Nadia
Collection Manager

bn/yo
enclosure

Title	FirstName	LastName	Company	Address1	City	State	PostalCode	Amount	Date
Ms.	Vanessa	Jackson	Ace Chemical Co.	48 Endor Avenue	Brooklyn	NY	11221	256.98	March 1
Mr.	Kenneth	Hall		5 Windsor Drive	West Long Branch	NJ	07764	450.50	March 15
Mr.	Glenn	Babbin		187 Beach Street	Queens	NY	11694	128.86	February 28
Ms.	Stefanie	Eaton	XYZ Broadcasting Company	137 Brighton Avenue	Perth Amboy	NJ	08861	612.75	February 15

Exercise 75

■ Merge Selected Records

Mail Merge Toolbar

Mail Merge

NOTES

Merge Selected Records

- It is possible to merge selected records rather than all the records contained in the data file.

- To merge records 1-5, for example, open the main document and click the Mail Merge button ![icon] on the Merge toolbar.

- In the Merge dialog box that follows, click the From button and specify the record numbers to be merged in the From and To text boxes. Then click the Merge button.

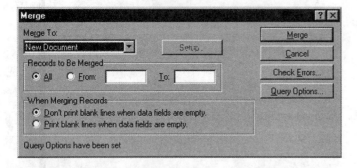

- In addition to merging specific records, you can define conditions that data records must meet to be included in the merge. For example, you might want to merge only those records with a specific zip code or job title. Or you might want to merge letters for only those individuals who owe more than $200 and live in New Jersey.

- To define conditions for a merge, open the main document, click the Mail Merge button on the Mail Merge toolbar, and click the Query Options button in the Merge dialog box.

- In the Query Options dialog box that follows, click the **Field** drop-down list to select a field you want to limit. For example, if you wanted to send letters to only those in a particular zip code, you would select Postal Code from the drop-down list. The words *Equal To* will appear in the Comparison box.

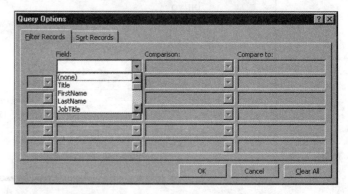

- In the Compare to text box, type the text you want selected.

- Note the Query Options dialog box below. It is set to merge letters for only those individuals who live in New Jersey and owe more than $200.

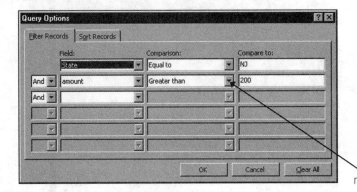

Click to select relational operators.

- Word provides numerous relational operators to set criteria in a search. "Greater than" in the illustration to the left is selected by clicking the Comparison drop-down list box.

- After you set the conditions for your merge and click OK, Word returns to the Merge dialog box. Click the Merge button to complete the process. The documents will merge to the screen.

- Before merging again with different conditions, you must clear all settings in the Query Options dialog box by clicking the Clear All button.

In this exercise, you will create a main document and a data source document and merge selected records.

EXERCISE DIRECTIONS

1. Create a NEW document.

2. Use the default margins.

3. Review the main document shown on the following page and note the merge field code names used.

4. Create the merge field code names list in the Create Data Source dialog box using the merge field codes shown in the main document.

5. Save the data source document; name it **JACOBDATA**.

6. Create the main document using the appropriate merge field name codes. Begin the date At 2.5".

7. Spell check.

8. Print one copy.

9. Save the main document; name it **JACOBMAIN**.

10. Edit the data source document and enter the data shown in the Data Source Document on page 326.

11. View the data source document.

12. Switch to the main document. (Click the Mail Merge Main document button.)

13. Merge the main and data source documents using the following conditions for the merge: those who live in the zip code 10021 and contributed more than $200.00.

14. Save the merge letters under a new filename, **JACOBFINAL**.

15. Print one copy of the merged letters.

16. Close all files.

Today's date

«Title» «FirstName» «LastName»
«JobTitle»
«Company»
«Address1»
«City», «State» «PostalCode»

Dear «Title» «LastName»:

Thank you for showing your support for the benefit reading of *Jacob's Room*, to be held at the Canby Theater on April 25.

Your tax-deductible donation of $«donation» includes admission to the reading, a banquet dinner, and two free raffle tickets.

Your support of our theater is most appreciated. We will be honored to have you at the benefit on April 25. You may pick up your tickets at the box office before the performance. The reading will begin promptly at 7:30 p.m.

Sincerely,

Karen Vasquez
Benefit Coordinator

kv/yo

Title	FirstName	LastName	JobTitle	Company	Address1	City	State	PostalCode	donation
Ms.	Elizabeth	Winters	Director of Communications	Bali, Inc.	142 First Avenue	New York	NY	10003	100
Ms.	Andrea	Mendez			111 East 85 Street	New York	NY	10021	150
Mr.	Todd	Wilkes	President	Landis Products	555 Fifth Avenue	New York	NY	10023	275
Mr.	Paul	Bergman			440 Third Avenue	New York	NY	10023	325
Mr.	Peter	Rojas	Vice President	Stern Investments	55 Wall Street	New York	NY	10003	500
Ms.	Shirley	Lee			18 Willow Place	Brooklyn	NY	11236	300
Ms.	Mara	Lexmark			888 Park Avenue	New York	NY	10021	500
Mr.	Ted	Needham	Manager	Calahan Realty, Inc.	867 Madison Avenue	New York	NY	10021	400
Mr.	William	Shabaz	President	Updike Car Parts	76 Bronx River Parkway	Bronx	NY	10433	350

KEYSTROKES

MERGE WITH CONDITIONS

1. Open the main document.

2. Click the **Mail Merge button** ....
   on the Mail Merge toolbar.

3. Click **Query Options** .... <kbd>Alt</kbd> + <kbd>Q</kbd>

4. Select **Filter Records** tab ..... <kbd>Alt</kbd> + <kbd>F</kbd>

5. Click drop-down list arrow next to
   Field text box.

6. Select a field on which to set a
   condition.

7. Click drop-down list arrow next to
   Comparison text box.

8. Select a relational operator for your
   search.

9. Type the text or data you want selected
   in the Compare to text box.

10. Click **OK** .... <kbd>Enter</kbd>

11. Click **Merge** .... <kbd>Alt</kbd> + <kbd>M</kbd>

Exercise

76

■ **Prepare Envelopes and Labels while Merging**

NOTES

Envelopes

■ Rather than typing an envelope for each form letter, you can automatically print an envelope for each merged letter using the same data source document used to prepare the merged letters. Rather than merge the data source document with the main document (which is typically your form letter), you must create an envelope main document.

■ An envelope main document contains only those merge field codes needed for the address (Title, FirstName, LastName, Address, City, State, PostalCode).

■ To create an envelope main document, you must activate the main document and click the Mail Merge Helper button ▦ on the Mail Merge toolbar.

■ In the Mail Merge Helper dialog box that follows, click Create, Envelopes.

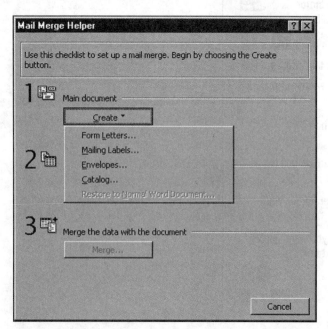

■ Another dialog box appears. Since you need to set up a new envelope main document, select New Main Document.

■ The Mail Merge Helper dialog box again displays. Click Get Data, Open Data Source. Open the data source document you prepared earlier.

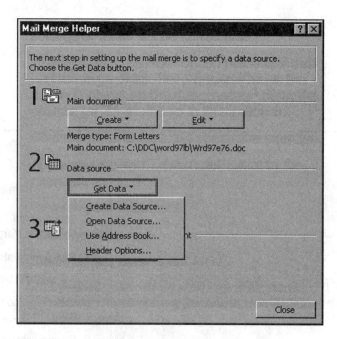

■ In the next dialog box that appears, click Set Up Main Document. In the Envelope Options dialog box that follows, make the necessary choices for envelope size and click OK.

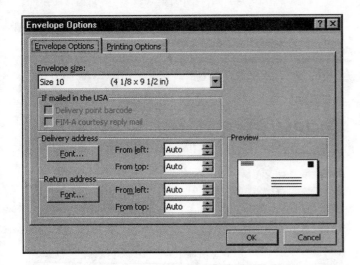

■ In the Envelope Address dialog box that follows, you must enter the appropriate field code names for an envelope address in the Sample Envelope Address window. To do so, click the Insert Merge Field button and select the relevant field name codes. Be sure to insert the appropriate spaces and punctuation as if text were in place of the codes.

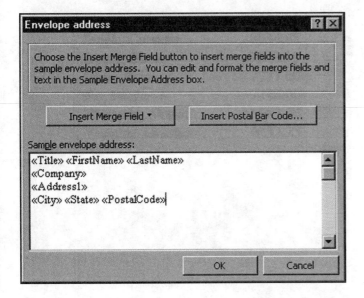

■ When you finish entering the fields, click OK. The Mail Merge Helper dialog box appears again. Click Merge. Your data source document merges with the envelope merge document to display a sample envelope on screen. Load your envelopes into the printer and print in the usual way. If you plan to use the envelope file again, save it.

Labels

■ You can prepare mailing labels for each merged letter using a method similar to the one for preparing envelopes. *(See keystrokes on page 331.)*

■ Label paper contains removable labels that are placed on envelopes. Word provides a list of product numbers for Avery brand label paper. If you are using a different brand, you can find an equivalent product number. Otherwise, you can experiment to find product equivalents.

In this exercise, you will open a previously created main document, create a label file, and merge it with the data source document to create labels.

EXERCISE DIRECTIONS

1. Open ⌨DUEMAIN, or open 💾76DUEMAIN.

2. Create and save a mailing label main document; name it **DUELABEL**.

3. Merge the mailing label main document with the data source document, **DUEDATA**.

4. Print one copy. (Use plain paper to see how labels print on a page.)

5. Close all files.

KEYSTROKES

CREATING MAILING LABELS WHILE MERGING

1. Open the main document.

2. Click the **Mail Merge Helper** .... 📇
   button on the Mail Merge toolbar.
   OR
   a. Click **Tools** .... Alt + T
   b. Click **Mail Merge** .... R

3. Click **Create** .... Alt + C

4. Click **Mailing Labels** .... M

5. Click **New Main Document** .... N
   if no document is on screen.
   OR
   Click **Change Document Type** C
   if main document is on screen.

6. Click **Get Data** .... Alt + G

7. Click **Open Data Source** .... O

8. Select document containing
   address data.

9. Click **Open** .... Enter

10. Click **Set Up Main Document** .... S
    OR
    Click **Set Up** .... Alt + S

11. Click **Laser and ink jet** .... Alt + L
    OR
    Click **Dot matrix** .... Alt + M

12. Click **OK** .... Enter

13. Click **Insert Merge Field** ...... Alt + S

14. Click desired merge fields to include in
    envelope address.

15. Enter any necessary spaces, returns or
    punctuation between fields.

16. Click **OK**.

MERGE THE DATA WITH THE DOCUMENT

1. Click **Merge** twice .... Alt + M

2. Close the label documents without
   saving.

CREATE ENVELOPES WHILE MERGING

1. Activate main document.

2. Click **Mail Merge Helper** .... 📇
   button on Merge toolbar
   OR
   a. Click **Tools** .... Alt + T
   b. Click **Mail Merge** .... R

3. Click **Create** .... Alt + C

4. Click **Envelopes** .... E

5. Click **New Main Document** .... N
   to set up a new label main document.
   OR
   Click **Change Document Type** C
   to change open Form Letter Main
   document to a label main document.

6. Click **Get Data** .... Alt + G

7. Click **Open Data Source** .... O

8. Select document containing address
   data.

9. Click **Open** .... Enter

10. Click **Set Up Main Document** .... S
    OR
    Click **Set Up** .... Alt + S

11. Click **Printing Options** tab .... P
    and select feed options.

12. Click **OK** .... Enter

13. Click **Insert Merge Field** ...... Alt + S

14. Click desired merge fields to include
    in first line of envelope address.

15. Type any necessary spaces, returns or
    punctuation between fields.

16. Click **OK**.

17. Click **Main Document, Edit** . Alt + E

18. Select envelope .... ↑, ↓
    document name.

19. Edit return address as desired.

20. Click **Merge to Printer** button .... 📄
    on the Mail Merge toolbar.

21. Close the envelope document without
    saving.

Exercise 77 ■ **Envelopes and Labels**

NOTES

■ In Exercise 76, you created labels as part of the merge process. Envelopes and labels can also be created independently of the merge process.

Envelopes

■ To create an envelope independently of merge, select Envelopes and Labels from the Tools menu. The Envelopes and Labels dialog box displays. Click the Envelopes tab.

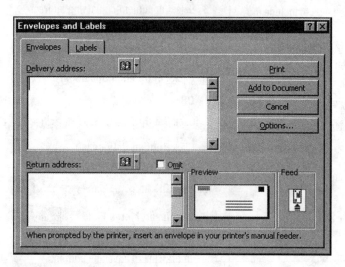

■ If a document is on screen, Word automatically retrieves its mailing address into the Delivery address window.

■ If you wish to use a name and address that you previously entered in the Address Book, click the Address Book list arrow and select the desired name from the drop-down list. Word pastes the name and address in the Delivery address window.

■ You may enter a return address in the Return Address window. To omit the return address, click the Omit check box.

■ To change the envelope specifications, click the Options button.

■ Clicking the Add to Document button inserts the envelope file at the end of your active document, so you can print it at a later time. The Print button allows you to print your envelope without appending it to the document.

Labels

■ Labels may also be created independently of the merge process.

■ To create labels, select Envelopes and Labels from the Tools menu. The Envelopes and Labels dialog box displays. Click the Labels tab.

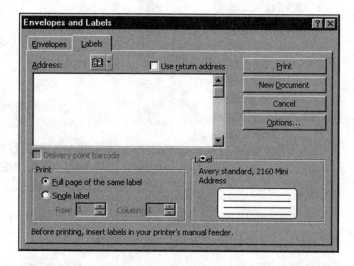

■ To change label specifications, click the Options button.

■ You can prepare labels in three different ways. You can:

• **Print a full page of the same label** by entering a name and address in the Address window, selecting the Full page of the same label button and clicking New Document. A full page of labels displays; each label contains the name and address shown in the Address window.

- **Print a single label** by entering the name and address in the Address window, selecting the Single label button and indicating the location of the label on which you want to print. For full page labels, specify the label location by row and column number.

✓Note: When printing a full page of the same label or printing a single label, you may insert a name and address from the address book by clicking the list arrow next to the address book button and selecting a listed address. Or, if a document is on screen, Word automatically retrieves its mailing address into the Address window.

- **Print a full page of different names and addresses**. Specify the label type you desire in the Label Options dialog box and then click the New Document button. A full page of blank labels displays, ready for you to enter names and addresses. Use the Tab key to advance from label to label.

■ To view the labels as they will be arranged when printed, select Print Preview from the File menu.

> *In this exercise, you will create labels for three addresses.*

EXERCISE DIRECTIONS

1. Create a NEW document.

2. Create three labels using the addresses below.

> Mr. Harold Dembo
> Holistic, Inc.
> 654 Sanborn Street
> Denver, CO 80202

> Ms. Jennifer Downing
> 766 Utica Avenue
> San Antonio, TX 78202

> Mr. Daniel Davis
> Acme Plumbing Supply
> 90 Plaza Z
> Milwaukee, WI 53212

3. Use Avery Standard 5160 Address Labels as your label type.

4. Print one copy of the page.

5. Create a new document and merge a new mailing label main document with the data source document, ⌨**JACOBDATA** or 💾**JACOBDATA**.

6. Print one copy. (Use plain paper to see how labels print on a page.)

7. Close all files.

KEYSTROKES

CREATE ENVELOPES

1. Click **Tools** .... `Alt` + `T`
2. Click **Envelopes and Labels** .... `E`
3. Click **Envelopes tab** .... `Alt` + `E`
4. Click **Delivery address** .... `Alt` + `D`
   window.
5. Type mailing address.
   OR
   Click **Address Book** button and select address.
   ✓ *If a letter was on screen, the address should automatically appear in Delivery address window.*

To change envelope specifications:

1. Click **Options** .... `Alt` + `O`
2. Click **Envelope Options** tab.. `Alt` + `E`
3. Make desired changes.
4. Click **OK** .... `Enter`

To change Printing feed specifications:

1. Click **Options** .... `Alt` + `O`
2. Click **Printing Options** tab .... `Alt` + `P`
3. Make desired changes.
4. Click **OK** .... `Enter`
5. Load envelope into printer.
6. Click **Print** .... `Enter`

CREATE MAILING LABELS

1. Click **Tools** .... `Alt` + `T`
2. Click **Envelopes and Labels** .... `E`
3. Click **Labels tab** .... `Alt` + `L`
4. Select a label type:
   a. Click **Options** .... `Alt` + `O`
   b. Make desired changes.
   c. Click **OK** .... `Enter`

To create a sheet of different names and addresses:

1. Click **New Document** .... `Alt` + `D`
2. Type names and addresses.

To create one label or full page of the same label:

1. Click **Address** window .... `Alt` + `A`
2. Type name and address.
   OR
   Click **Address Book** button and select address.
   ✓ *If letter was on screen, the address should automatically appear in Address window.*
3. Select method to print.
   • **Full page** .... `Alt` + `F`
     of the same label
   • **Single label** .... `Alt` + `N`
4. Type **Row** .... `Alt` + `W`, `Alt` + `C`
   and **Column** of Label
   if you selected single label.
5. Load label paper.
6. Click **File** .... `Alt` + `F`
7. Click **Print** .... `P`

Exercise 78

■ **Summary**

EXERCISE DIRECTIONS

1. Create a data document and a main document from the information below and on the next page.

2. Format the main document in any letter style.

3. You must italicize the "brochureon" merge code in the main document; it may be necessary to click twice.

4. Use the default margins; begin the date At 2.5".

5. Save the main document; name it **TRVLMAIN**.

6. Save the data document; name it **TRVLDATA**.

7. Preview your document.

8. Spell check.

9. Merge the main and data documents to the printer; print an envelope for each merged letter.

   Hint: *Delete the return address after envelope main document is created but before it is merged by editing the main document and then accessing merge again.*

10. Close the document window.

Title	FirstName	LastName	Company	Address1	City	State	PostalCode	cruiseto	brochureon	sailings	rep
Ms.	Beverly	Oberlin		65 Court Street	Portland	ME	04141	Spain	*Hidden Treasures*	December 15 and February 12	Sarah
Mr.	Wayne	Viscosa	ABC Incorporated	690 Eldridge Drive	Richmond	VA	23808	The Bahamas	*Caribbean Coral*	June 29 and August 1	Patricia
Ms.	Edna	Hamilton		76 Rider Avenue	Baltimore	MD	21201	Trinidad	*Breathtaking Voyages*	December 15 and February 12	Michael

Today's date

«Title» «FirstName» «LastName»
«Company»
«Address1»
«City», «State» «PostalCode»

Dear «Title» «LastName»:

Thank you for your inquiry about a cruise to «cruiseto». We are enclosing a brochure on «brochureon», which might be of interest to you if you should decide to sail to «cruiseto».

There are two sailings scheduled in the next season: «sailings». The cost varies depending upon your accommodations.

If you would like more information about the vacation of a lifetime, call «rep», who is one of the representatives in our office who will be delighted to help you.

Sincerely,

Susan Crawford
Travel Agent

sc/yo
enclosure

Exercise 79

■ Summary

EXERCISE DIRECTIONS

1. Create a data document and a main document from the information below and on the next page.

2. Use the Contemporary Letter template to create the main document. Complete the letterhead information as shown. Delete logo reference at the bottom of the letter.

   ✓ *To insert title and last name field merge codes, first highlight the existing salutation text (including paragraph mark) and insert field codes. Then place the insertion point at the beginning of the salutation line and type the word "Dear".*

3. Begin the dateline At 3.1". Use the default margins and font size.

4. Save the main document; name it **ORDERMAIN**.

5. Save the data document; name it **ORDERDATA**.

6. Preview your document.

7. Spell check.

8. Merge the main and data documents for only those individuals who ordered by American Express.

9. Print a label for each merged letter.

10. Close the document window.

Title	FirstName	LastName	Company	Address1	City	State	PostalCode	paymentmethod	catno	amount	purdate
Ms.	Gail	Reddy		98 Federal Lane	Orem	UT	84060	American Express	8845	85.00	January 19
Ms.	Patricia	Lakis		98 Spruce Street	Lawrenceville	NJ	08648	Visa	8888	102.99	January 18
Mr.	Steve	Harmon	The Harmon Group	555 Madison Avenue	New York	NY	10018	American Express	9901	124.00	January 23
Mr.	Howard	Title		23 Kelly Boulevard	Staten Island	NY	10314	Discover	5555	167.50	January 14
Ms.	Sandra	Lakani		99-99 Sand Lane	Lakewood	NJ	08701	Visa	2234	118.12	January 28
Ms.	Donna	Brown		24 Apple Way	Manalapan	NJ	07726	American Express	3333	79.00	January 28

PrecisionWear MAIL ORDER

August 11, 1997

«Title» «FirstName» «LastName»
«Company»
«Address1»
«City», «State» «PostalCode»

Dear «Title» «LastName»:

Thank you for placing an order with PrecisionWear Mail Order, Inc. on «purdate» for catalog number «catno».

Unfortunately, we no longer have the item you selected in stock. We will credit your «paymentmethod» account in the amount of $«amount».

If you would like to make another purchase, please call our order department at 1-800-777-7777. We are sorry for any inconvenience this might have caused you.

Sincerely,

Mary Kinning
Catalog Manager

mk/

NEXT LESSON

Word 97

LESSON 11

Desktop Publishing and Draw

- Work with Clip Art
- Import a Picture
- Size a Picture
- Text Boxes
- Text Box Borders and Shading
- Wrap Text
- Drop Caps
- Create a Newsletter
- WordArt
- AutoShapes
- Rotate WordArt Text
- Reverse Text
- Create Lines and Arrows
- Line Styles and Colors
- Create Shapes
- Group and Ungroup
- Copy/Move/Size a Shape
- Add Colors to Shapes
- Create Shadow and 3-D Effects
- Bring in Front of Text and Send Behind Text
- Bring to Front and Send to Back
- Watermarks

Exercise

80

■ **Work with Clip Art**   ■ **Import a Picture**   ■ **Size a Picture**

Picture Toolbar

Insert Picture

Line Style   Text Wrapping   Reset Picture

NOTES

Work with Clip Art

■ You can include objects such as clip art (bitmap images and photos), Excel charts, AutoShapes, sound clips, and even video clips in a document. Several clip art images are installed when you install Word. If you have a connection to the Internet, you can download additional images from Microsoft. The ability to combine pictures and text can help you communicate your message more effectively.

■ Word provides the Microsoft Clip Gallery, which contains numerous pictures covering a wide range of topics. Each picture has its own filename and contains the extension .WMF (Windows Metafile Format).

Import a Picture

■ To insert a clip art image into a Word document, select Picture from the Insert menu. Then select Clip Art from the Picture submenu.

■ In the Microsoft Clip Gallery that follows, a list of categories appears on the left side of the Gallery window, and images relating to the category are displayed on the right. A description of the picture and its filename display at the bottom of the window. Select the image you want to appear in your document and click Insert.

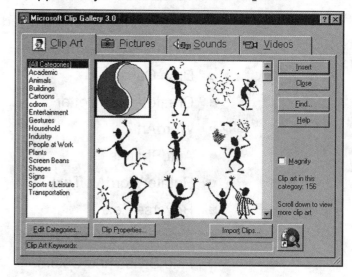

■ You can also insert a picture by clicking the Picture button on the Picture toolbar (see illustration at top of page).

Size a Picture

- When a picture is imported, its size is determined by Word. However, after a picture is imported, you may make it smaller, larger, stretch it into exaggerated shapes, move it or delete it.

- To change the size of a graphic, move it or delete it, you must first select it by clicking on the image. A selected image appears below. Note the sizing handles that appear once the graphic is selected. When the mouse pointer is placed on one of the sizing handles, it changes to a double-headed arrow. You may then change the size or shape of the image by simply dragging the sizing handle.

Selected Graphic

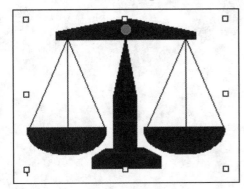

- When any of the four corner handles is dragged, the size of the entire image changes (becomes smaller or larger) and the picture retains its proportions. When any of the four middle handles is dragged, only the height or the width changes, thus changing the proportions or scale of the image and giving it a different appearance. Note the stars below.

- You can adjust the image by a specific amount by selecting the picture, then selecting Picture from the Format menu. In the Format Picture dialog box, click the Size tab and enter the desired measurements in the Width and Height text boxes.

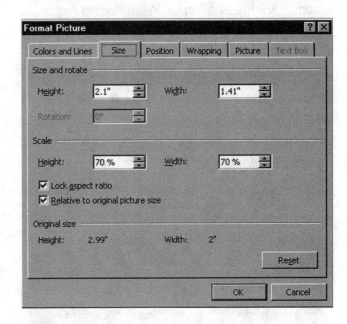

- You can return the picture to its original size by clicking the Reset button on the Size tab in the Format Picture dialog box. You can also click the Reset Picture button 🖼 on the Picture toolbar.

- To delete a picture, select it and press Delete.

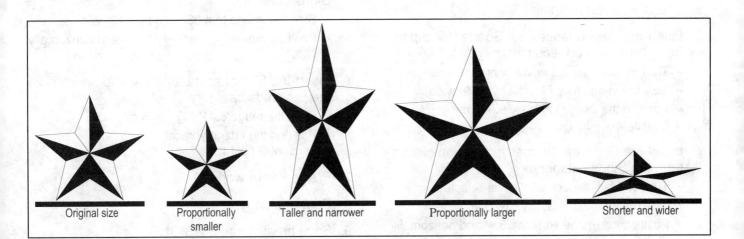

Original size	Proportionally smaller	Taller and narrower	Proportionally larger	Shorter and wider

Position a Picture

■ By default, when a picture is imported into Word, it is aligned at the left margin. However, the alignment may be changed using several techniques. You can select the picture and drag it to a position on the page. You can also select Picture from the Format menu, click the Position tab in the Format Picture dialog box and enter a horizontal or vertical position in the appropriate text box.

■ If you are in Normal view when you insert clip art, Word will automatically switch to Page Layout view. If you switch back to Normal view after you insert a picture, you will not see the picture, even though it is there.

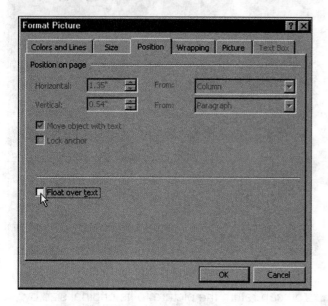

In this exercise, you will insert several pictures, align, size and position them.

EXERCISE DIRECTIONS

1. Create a NEW document.

2. Use the default margins.

3. Insert the Performance Fast Sports Car clip art from the Transportation category.
   - Turn off Lock aspect ratio, if it is selected.
   - Size the image to 1.71" high by 5.49" wide.
   - Position the image vertically 6.88" and horizontally –0.31".

4. Insert the Direction Alternative Solution clip art from the Signs category.
   - Turn off Lock aspect ratio, if it is selected.
   - Size the image to 4.3" high by 2.38" wide.
   - Position the image vertically 5.4" and horizontally -0.95".

5. Insert the Barrier Obstacle Wait clip art from the Signs category.
   - Size the image to 4.08" high by 2.22" wide.
   - Position the image vertically 5.63" and horizontally 4.86".

6. Insert the Skyscraper Large Tall clip art from the Buildings category.
   - Size the image 8.41" high by 5.47" wide.
   - Position the image vertically –0.95" and horizontally 0.14".

7. Preview your work.

8. Print one copy.

9. Save the file; name it **SIGNS**.

10. Close the document window.

KEYSTROKES

DISPLAY DRAWING TOOLBAR

Click **Drawing** button ....
on Standard toolbar.

DISPLAY PICTURE TOOLBAR

1. Right-click on menu bar or any displayed toolbar.

2. Click **Picture**.

OR

1. Click **View** .... `Alt` + `V`

2. Click **Toolbars** .... `T`

3. Click **Picture** .... `↑` `↓`

INSERT A PICTURE

1. Place insertion point where clip art is to be inserted.

2. Click **Insert** .... `Alt` + `I`

3. Click **Picture** .... `P`

4. Click **Clip Art** .... `C`

5. Click **Clip Art** tab .... `Alt` + `C`

6. Select desired category .... `↑` `↓`

7. Click desired image .... `↑` `↓`

8. Click **Insert** .... `Enter`

SELECT A PICTURE

Click anywhere in the picture.

DESELECT A PICTURE

Click anywhere outside the picture.

SIZE OR SCALE A PICTURE

USING THE MOUSE

1. Select the picture.

2. Drag any of the four middle handles to scale the height or width of the picture.

   OR

   Drag any of the four corner handles to change the size of the entire picture proportionally.

USING THE MENU

1. Select the picture.

2. Click **Format** .... `Alt` + `O`

3. Click **Picture** .... `I`

4. Click **Size** tab .... `←` `→`

5. Click **Height** .... `Alt` + `E`
   and enter measurement.

6. Click **Width** .... `Alt` + `D`
   and enter measurement.

7. Click **OK** .... `Enter`

RETURN A PICTURE TO ITS ORIGINAL SIZE

1. Display **Picture** toolbar.

2. Select the picture.

3. Click **Reset Picture** ....

OR

1. Select the picture.

2. Click **Format** .... `Alt` + `O`

3. Click **Picture** .... `I`

4. Click **Size** tab .... `←` `→`

5. Click **Reset** .... `Alt` + `S`

6. Click **OK** .... `Enter`

DELETE A PICTURE

1. Select picture.

2. Press **Delete** button .... `Delete`

   OR

   Click **Cut** button .... `✄`

NEXT EXERCISE

Exercise 81

■ **Text Boxes** ■ **Text Box Borders and Shading** ■ **Wrap Text**

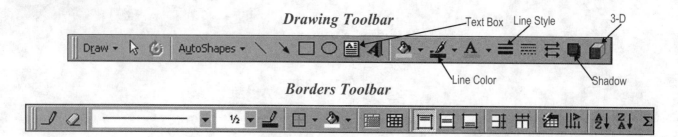

Drawing Toolbar

Borders Toolbar

NOTES

Text Boxes

■ A text box is a drawing object that allows you to place text or an inserted picture anywhere on a page.

■ Text boxes are typically used for setting off special text such as tables, charts, sidebars, and callouts. Text or pictures in a text box can be sized, moved and positioned almost anywhere in a document. The text direction within the box can also be changed.

■ Create a text box by clicking the Text Box button ▤ on the Drawing toolbar, then dragging the mouse pointer (now a crossbar) to the desired box size and typing the desired text. If the Drawing toolbar is not visible, point to the toolbars at the top of the screen, right-click, and select Drawing from the Toolbar options.

■ A text box may be resized or repositioned using the same techniques used to resize or reposition a picture. A picture inserted or text typed inside a text box becomes part of the box and moves as the box is moved.

■ You can rotate text, but not the textbox. To rotate text, click anywhere in the textbox, then select Te**x**t Direction on the F**o**rmat menu. Select the desired direction in the dialog box that displays.

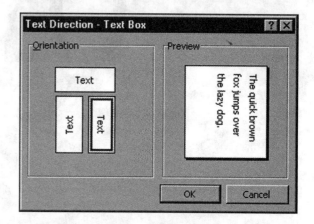

Text Box Borders and Shading

■ Word automatically places a border around a text box. You can change the line style or line color of the border, add shading to the contents of the text box or change the font color within the text box. In addition, you can create a shadow or 3D effect on the text box.

> This is an example of text within a text box. Note the ¾-point default border. You can change the border style, the font color, or the size of the text within the box.

> This is an example of a text box in which shading has been added and the border line style has been changed. Note, too, that the text has been centered within the box.

> Text Direction with 3D effect

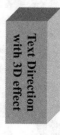

> Text Direction with Shadow Effect.

- You may set the thickness and/or color of the line around the text box by clicking the Line Style button ☰ and/or Line Color button 🖊▾ on the Drawing toolbar. Change the box color by clicking the Fill Color button. You can also set these options by selecting Text Box from the Format menu.

- A text box may be used to draw a border around an entire page. To do this, you must create a text box and size it so it fits around the page, then select a desired border and/or color fill.

- **To change the line style or line color**, select the text box (so handles appear), then click the Line Style button and/or the Line Color list arrow on the Drawing toolbar and choose a desired line style and/or line color.

- **To shade the contents of the text box**, select the text box, then click the Fill Color list arrow on the Drawing toolbar and choose a desired fill.

- **To create a shadow or 3D effect**, select the text box, then click the Shadow or 3D button on the Drawing toolbar. Select desired Shadow or 3D setting.

Wrap Text

- Word provides several options for wrapping text around a picture or text box.

- To wrap text around a picture or text box, select the picture, then select Picture or Text Box from the Format menu. In the Format Picture dialog box, illustrated below, select the Wrapping Tab and select a desired text wrap option.

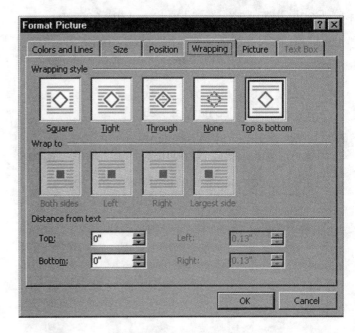

- When using text wrapping, carefully proofread the text that flows around the picture. You may need to adjust the picture position to avoid awkward word breaks.

In this exercise, you will create an advertisement using graphics and text boxes.

EXERCISE DIRECTIONS

1. Create a NEW document.

2. Set .5" top and bottom margins.

3. Begin the exercise at the top of the screen.

4. Insert the Harmony Teamwork Consensus picture, found in the Shapes category of the ClipArt Gallery.
   - Size it to 3.5" high by 3.5" wide.
   - Position it horizontally at 1.25".

5. Center and bold the headline text in any desired font using 28 points. Press Enter twice.

6. Return to left alignment and enter the text in a serif 12-point font. Set the line spacing to 1.5.

7. Create a text box below the headline and insert the text as shown in a sans serif 10-point font.
   - ✓ *You can adjust the frame size of the text box at any time to suit your needs.*
   - Bold and center the heading. Press Enter twice.
   - Use any bullet other than the round dot.
   - Use a dotted border.
   - Shade the text 20% gray.
   - Position the text box in the middle of the text as shown. Use a Both sides, Tight text wrap.

8. Set Coastal Electronics and the phone number to the same font style used in the headline text in a 10-point bold font.

9. Spell check.

10. Preview your work.

11. Print one copy.

12. Save the file; name it **COASTAL**.

13. Close the document window.

Send and Receive Computer Data and Faxes From Wherever You Happen To Be.

With Phone/Data Link, physical constraints of really lose touch. The business tool from gives you the freedom communicate anytime Link allows you to equipped computer or cellular telephone and and receive data and

Phone/Data Link Advantages

➢ Connects any modem-equipped computer or fax machine to a portable cellular telephone.
➢ Enables you to send and receive computer data or faxes via your cellular phone.
➢ Compatible with your existing software.
➢ Compact design.
➢ Features simple two-cable connection.

you can leave behind the your office, but never Phone/Data Link is a new Coastal Electronics that to compute and or anywhere. Phone/Data connect your modem-fax machine to a portable have the ability to send faxes from virtually

anywhere that cellular service is available. **Coastal Electronics. 1-800-555-5555.**

KEYSTROKES

DISPLAY DRAWING TOOLBAR

Click **Drawing** button .... 🖉
on Standard toolbar.

CREATE A TEXT BOX

1. Click **Text box** button .... 📇
   on Drawing toolbar.

   OR

   a. Click **Insert** .... `Alt` + `I`

   b. Click Te**x**t Box .... `X`

   ✓ *Mouse pointer assumes shape of*
     crossbar.

2. Position crossbar pointer where you
   want top left corner of text box to
   appear.

3. Hold down left mouse button and drag
   down and to the right until desired text
   box size is created.

4. Release the mouse.

5. Size, scale, reposition, or format text
   box as desired.

FORMATTING PICTURES AND TEXT BOXES

Formatting options for borders, fills,
position, size, and wrapping options are
similar for both text boxes and pictures.

1. Select the picture or text box.

2. Click F**o**rmat .... `Alt` + `O`

3. Click **P**icture .... `I`

   OR

   Click Text B**o**x .... `O`

Colors and Lines

1. Click **Colors and Lines** tab.

   To change Fill options:

   Click **C**olor .... `Alt` + `C`
   and select desired fill color/shade.

To change Line options:

a. Select line **C**olor............. `Alt` + `O`

b. Select **D**ashed style .... `Alt` + `D`

c. Select **S**tyle..................... `Alt` + `S`

d. Select **W**eight .... `Alt` + `W`

2. Click **OK**............................ `Enter`

Size

1. Click **Size** tab.

   To change Size options:

   a. Enter **H**eight .... `Alt` + `E`
      measurement.

   b. Enter Wi**d**th .... `Alt` + `D`
      measurement.

   To change Scale options:

   a. Enter **H**eight .... `Alt` + `H`
      percentage.

   b. Enter **W**idth .... `Alt` + `W`
      percentage.

2. Click **OK**............................ `Enter`

MOVE/POSITION A TEXT BOX OR PICTURE

1. Place mouse pointer on any side of the
   image or text box until four-arrow shape
   appears at end of mouse pointer.

2. Drag framed image to desired location.

ALIGN TEXT WITHIN A TEXT BOX

1. Place insertion point in desired
   paragraph in text box.

   OR

   Select desired text.

2. Click **Left Align** button .... 🗎

   OR

   Click **Right Align** button .... 🗎

   OR

   Click **Center** button .... 🗎

DISPLAY BORDER TOOLBAR

1. Right-click on any toolbar.

2. Click **Tables and Borders**.

   To float Borders toolbar:

   a. Click **down arrow** .... ▾
      next to **Outside Border** button 🔲▾
      on Tables and Borders toolbar.

   b. Click on the Title bar of **Borders**
      toolbar.

   c. Then drag away to float toolbar.

   d. Select desired border style.

   To close Borders toolbar:

   Click **Close** button........................... ✖
   on Title bar `Borders            ✖`

WRAP TEXT

1. Click text box or picture.

2. Click F**o**rmat .... `Alt` + `O`

3. Click **Text B**o**x**............................... `O`

   OR

   Click **P**icture .... `I`

   OR

   Click **O**bject .... `O`

4. Click **Wrapping** tab.

5. Select desired Wrap option.

   ✓ *Options not available for the current*
     situation will be dimmed.

6. Click **OK** .... `Enter`

NEXT EXERCISE

Exercise 82 ■ Drop Caps ■ Create a Newsletter

NOTES

Drop Caps

■ A drop capital is an enlarged capital letter that drops below the first line of body text. It is usually the first letter of a paragraph. It is often used to draw the reader's attention to chapter beginnings, section headings and main body text.

> **D**rop capitals are large decorative letters often used to mark the beginning of a document, section or chapter. Drop caps are set to a much larger font than the text, and often span the height of three or four lines.

■ To create a drop capital, place the insertion point in the paragraph where the drop cap will appear. Then select <u>D</u>rop Cap from the F<u>o</u>rmat menu.

■ If you want to include several letters, highlight the letters you want to include in the drop cap style, then open the Drop Cap dialog box.

■ In the Drop Cap dialog box, select the desired options for the Drop Cap. You can have the text wrap under the large letter (or letters) or let the text wrap to the right of the letter.

Create a Newsletter

■ A newsletter is a document used by an organization to communicate information about an event, news of general interest, or information regarding new products.

■ Newsletters consist of several parts:

- **Nameplate** – may include name of the newsletter, the organization publishing the newsletter, and/or the logo (a symbol or distinctive typestyle used to represent the organization).

- **Dateline** – may include the volume number, issue number, and the date.

- **Headline** – title preceding each article.

- **Body Text** – the text of the article.

■ Newsletters may also be created using the Newsletter Wizard. The Wizard steps you through the procedures for creating a newsletter. You can access the Newsletter Wizard from the Publications tab in the New dialog box.

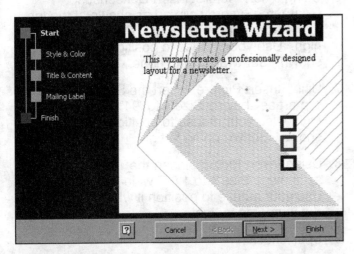

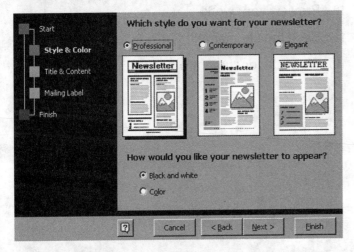

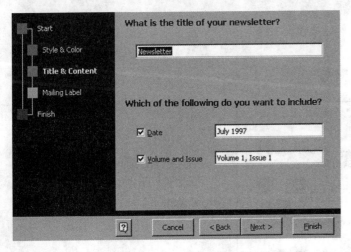

In this exercise, you will create a newsletter and include pictures, a text box and a drop cap.

EXERCISE DIRECTIONS

1. Create a NEW document.

2. Set left and right margins to 1". Set top and bottom margins to 0.5".

3. Type the nameplate as shown using a serif 30-point bold font for "Cablecom," serif 48-point font for "News Briefs," and serif 10-point font for A monthly Publications of CableCom..."

4. Press Enter five times.

5. Format the remainder of the document for 3 columns (Format, Columns).

   - Keyboard the newsletter as shown; note the following:
   - Center the headlines; set them to a sans serif 14-point bold font.
   - Create the drop cap as shown.
   - Set paragraph text to a serif 12-point font.
   - Full justify column text.
   - Set the paragraph spacing to 6 point after each paragraph.
   - Select the Please Note information and insert a border around it. Use a 1½-point double line border and shade the text 25%.
   - Use Manual hyphenation to hyphenate the document. Limit consecutive hyphens to 2. Do not hyphenate words in article headings
   - Insert column breaks where shown.
   - ✓ *Use any relevant Clip Art, if the pictures listed here are not available.*

6. Using Insert Picture, insert Consensus GuaranteeSynergy clip art as shown at the top of the newsletter. Size it to 2.7" wide by .75" high. Use your mouse to position it where shown. Set wrapping to none.

7. Using Insert Picture, insert the Soccer Game clip art as shown. Size it to .94" wide by 1.2" high. Use your mouse to position it where shown. Set wrapping to tight.

8. Using Insert Picture, insert the Trophy clip art as shown. Size it to 1.07" wide by 1.5" high. Use your mouse to position it where shown. Set wrapping to tight.

9. Spell check

10. Preview your work.

11. Save the file; name it **CABLE**.

12. Close the document window.

KEYSTROKES

CREATE A DROP CAP

1. Place insertion point in paragraph where drop cap will appear.

2. Click **F**ormat .... `Alt` + `O`

3. Click **D**rop Cap .... `D`

4. Click desired position:

   - **N**one .... `N`
   - **D**ropped .... `D`
   - In **M**argin .... `M`

5. Select **F**ont .... `F`
   (if different from rest of text.)

6. Click **L**ines to drop .... `Alt` + `L`

7. Select increase or .... `↑` `↓`
   decrease arrows to set desired number of lines.

8. Click **D**istance from te**x**t .... `Alt` + `X`

9. Select increase or .... `↑` `↓`
   decrease arrows to set desired distance from text.

10. Click **OK** .... `Enter`

CABLECOM
News Briefs

A Monthly Publication of CableCom ■ December 1998

Insert column breaks.

Senior Vice President of Human Resources Named

David Duffy has been named Senior Vice President of Human Resources for Cablecom. He is being promoted from General Manager, and will assume his new position on April 1. In his new role, David will report directly to Chief of Corporate Operations.

David has been with Cablecom for 12 years and has held a variety of positions of increasing responsibility in Human Resources.

Employee Health Club Construction Update

The men's upstairs locker room will be closed through April 19, at which time construction is expected to be completed. As soon as the men's room is finished, construction will begin in the women's locker room and is expected to last four weeks.

Fire Procedures

All employees should take notice of the new fire procedures posted on each floor. Please become familiar with the fire exits located in the same area on every floor:

- **Exit A** is located in the back freight elevator lobby.
- **Exit B** is the outside fire escape located at the end of the main hallway.
- **Exit C** is located in the front elevator lobby.

In the event that a fire alarm does sound on your floor, please wait for an announcement from the Fire Warden who will instruct you as to which exit to use.

Computer Workshops

The Information Services department is conducting the following monthly workshops. These workshops will be offered during lunch hours and will be open to all employees.

⇒ *Now Up To Date 3.0.* This calendar program lets you schedule appointments and "to do" items for one or more people. The workshop will address creating a new calendar, scheduling events, using categories and reminders, customizing and printing schedule views. *Thursday, January 9, 12-2.*

⇒ *Windows 95 Upgrade.* This workshop will present the new features of Windows 95. *Thursday, January 16, 12-2.*

Please Note: Workshops have limited seating capacity, so sign up early if you wish to attend. Call Mary Rizzo at Extension 444.

Achievement Awards Dinner

This year's annual Cablecom Achievement Awards Dinner will be held at the Marriott Hotel on Thursday, April 25. Cocktails will be served at 6:30 p.m. followed by dinner at 8:00 p.m.

■ **WordArt** ■ **AutoShapes**

Drawing Toolbar

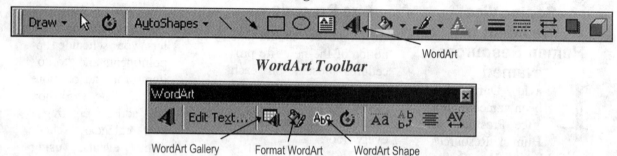

WordArt

WordArt Toolbar

WordArt Gallery   Format WordArt   WordArt Shape

NOTES

WordArt

■ WordArt lets you create special effects with text. You can create stretched, shadowed, skewed, rotated or vertical text. Several predefined shapes are also available. Essentially, WordArt lets you treat text as a picture.

■ Note some of the effects you can achieve using the WordArt program.

■ To access WordArt, click the WordArt button on the Drawing toolbar. You can also click Insert, Picture on the menu. Then select WordArt on the submenu. The WordArt Gallery, illustrated below, appears.

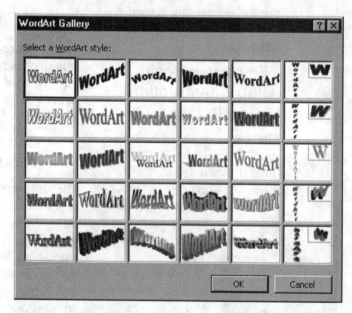

■ Select the desired shape and click OK. The following Window, illustrated on the next page, will appear. Type the text you want to appear as WordArt, then click OK. Your text will replace the words "Your Text Here."

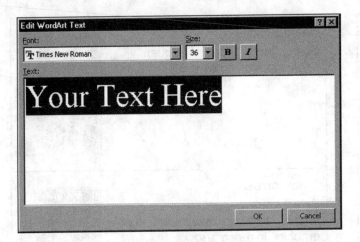

✓Note: You will be able to change many aspects of the WordArt shape once you have inserted it into a document.

- Your text will appear in the shape and formatting of the selected style, with selection handles that let you size and reshape the object without opening any other dialog box. The WordArt toolbar will automatically appear. You can use the buttons on the WordArt toolbar to format the WordArt object.

- The following is an explanation of the buttons on the WordArt toolbar:

◢	Opens the WordArt Gallery. Start here to insert a new WordArt object into a document.
Edit Text...	Opens the Edit WordArt Text dialog box. Use this to change the content, font, font size and font style of the WordArt object.
◩	Opens the WordArt Gallery. Select this button to select a new style for an existing object.

◈	Opens the Format WordArt dialog box. Use this to customize the WordArt object using the features available on the tabs in this dialog box. 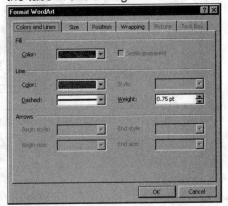
Abc	Opens the WordArt shape palette. Use this to retain some of the formatting of original, but change the shape of the object immediately.
♺	Activates Free Rotate tool. Click the WordArt object, then click this button. The Mouse pointer changes to a rotate tool. Point to the round selection handles on the WordArt image and change the direction of the object by dragging in the desired direction. (Rotating text will be covered in Exercise 84.) 
Aa	Makes all the letters in the object the same height. Lowercase letters stretch to the height of uppercase letters. 
Ab b♪	Changes text in the WordArt object to vertical position. Click again to restore horizontal position.

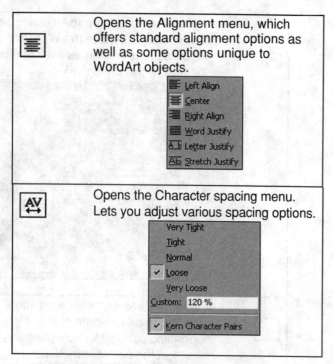

Opens the Alignment menu, which offers standard alignment options as well as some options unique to WordArt objects.

Opens the Character spacing menu. Lets you adjust various spacing options.

- WordArt graphics may be sized or positioned just like any other graphic object.

AutoShapes

- In addition to WordArt and various Drawing tools, you can enhance documents using features available on the AutoShapes menu.

- When you select AutoShapes on the Drawing toolbar, several menus containing a variety of shapes (lines, connectors, flowchart elements, callouts, etc.) display.

- Below and to the right is an illustration and explanation of each category available on the AutoShapes menu.

Lines

Create curves, freeform, and scribble lines. The straight line and arrow tools are also available on this menu. (See Exercise 85.)

Basic Shapes

Select from a group of frequently used shapes and symbols.

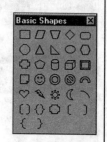

Block Arrows

Select from various directional arrows. You can easily add text or graphics to these arrows.

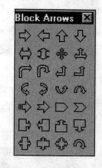

Flowchart

Select from a variety of shapes used to create a flow chart.

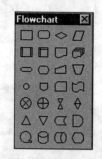

Stars and Banners

Select from shapes useful in creating graphics, bullets, even callouts.

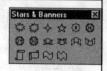

Callouts

Use to illustrate various sections of a document.

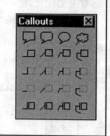

- To draw an AutoShape, select the desired shape from the appropriate palette, then click the place where you want the AutoShape to begin and drag the mouse to expand the shape to the desired size.

- You can easily change the fill color of an AutoShape. Click on the shape, then click the list arrow next to the Fill Color button on the Drawing toolbar 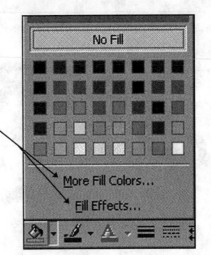 to open the color palette.

- Select the desired color. If you click More Fill Colors or Fill Effects, you can select from even more options, or create your own.

In this exercise, you will create a flyer enhanced with WordArt.

EXERCISE DIRECTIONS

1. Create a NEW document.

2. With your insertion point at the top of the screen, access WordArt.

3. Select the Arch Up design (the third one in first row).

4. Using a sans serif bold font, type CYBER CAFE on the first line. Accept the default 36-point font size.

5. Size the graphic object to 4" wide by 2" high. Drag the graphic to the center of the page.

6. Insert the Stress Frustration Anger Chaos clip art from the Cartooon category. Size it to 2" wide by 1.5" high and position it as shown.

7. Position the insertion point At 4.3". (Reposition the WordArt and the clip art if it moves down the page as you press Enter.)

8. Type and center Announces in a script 36-point font; type and center the remaining text in a script 28-point font.

9. To insert the AutoShape:
   - Click Autoshapes on the Drawing toolbar and select Stars and Banners
   - Click the Stars and Banners 4-Point Star.
   - Position the stars as shown. Size them to 0.7" high by 0.8" wide.
   - Color the AutoShapes black.

10. Access WordArt.

11. Select the Arch Up design again.

12. Using a serif bold font, type the address and Internet numbers on three lines.

13. Be sure that the WordArt object is selected and that the WordArt toolbar is displayed. Click the WordArt Shape button on the WordArt toolbar and select the Button (Curve) design ⊖ on the palette.

14. Size the graphic to 2" wide by 2" high and position it at the bottom center of the page.

15. Preview your work.

16. Make any necessary adjustments so that all elements are horizontally centered.

17. Print one copy.

18. Save the file; name it **OPENING**.

19. Close the document window.

CYBER CAFE

Announces
the opening
of its newest cafe

105 Spring Street

New York

http://www.cybercafe.com

KEYSTROKES

CREATE WORDART

1. Click Insert **WordArt** button ....
   on the Drawing toolbar.
   OR
   a. Click **Insert**...................... Alt + I
   b. Click **Picture**............................. P
   c. Click **WordArt**............................. W
2. Select **WordArt**............. ↓ ↑ → ←
   style from gallery.
3. Click **OK** .... Enter
4. Enter text to appear in WordArt object.

   To change Font:
   Select **Font** from list............ Alt + F

   To change Size:
   Select **Size** from list............ Alt + S

   To Bold text:
   Click **Bold** button .... Alt + B

   To Italicize text:
   Click **Italic** button .... Alt + I
5. Click **OK** .... Enter

DELETE WORDART OBJECT

1. Select the graphic.
2. Press **Delete** .... Del

INSERT AN AUTOSHAPE

1. Click **AutoShapes**................. Alt + U
   on the Drawing toolbar.
2. Select desired category:
   - **Lines**
   - **Basic Shapes**
   - **Block Arrows**
   - **Flowchart**
   - **Stars and Banners**
   - **Callouts**
3. Select desired shape.
4. Position crosshair (+) at point where
   shape will start.
5. Click and drag to desired end point.

   ✓ *Most drawing shapes require the
   same procedure: you click and drag
   the mouse pointer to the right and
   down. Some shapes, however,
   require additional actions to get the
   desired result. The distance and
   drag direction determine the size and
   shape of the object. Experiment to
   determine how the shape will look.
   You can always resize and reshape
   the object after it is in place.*
6. Release mouse to insert shape.

CHANGE WORDART SHAPE

1. Select WordArt object.
   *The WordArt toolbar will appear
   automatically.*
2. Click **WordArt Shape** button.......... Abc
3. Select desired shape from palette.
4. Position and size WordArt object.

CHANGE FILL COLOR OF WORDART OBJECT

1. Select WordArt object.
   *The WordArt toolbar will appear
   automatically.*
2. Click **Format WordArt** button ....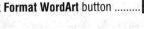
   OR
   - Right-click on object.
   - Click **Format WordArt**............... O
3. Click **Colors and Lines** tab.
4. Click **Fill Color** .... Alt + C
   AND/OR
   Click **Line Color**................... Alt + O
5. Select desired color.
6. Click **OK**................................... Enter

Exercise

84

■ **Rotate WordArt Text** ■ **Reverse Text**

WordArt Toolbar

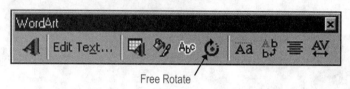

Free Rotate

NOTES

Rotate WordArt Text

■ You can rotate WordArt by clicking the Free Rotate button on the WordArt toolbar. Then position the tool over the round selection handles that appear on the WordArt object.

■ Click and drag the WordArt object in the direction you want the text to rotate. Release the mouse when you reach the desired location.

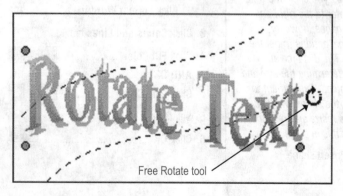

Free Rotate tool

■ You can also use the Rotate or Flip command on the Draw menu. Select the WordArt object, click Draw (on the Drawing toolbar), then select Rotate or Flip, and select desired option from the submenu.

✓ *Note the effect on WordArt objects that are flipped horizontally and vertically.*

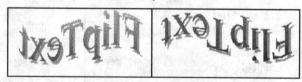

■ Since WordArt objects are graphics, not text, you can use the commands on the Drawing toolbar to format and position them.

Reverse Text

- Reverse text appears white against a dark background. Reverse text adds interest to text and can be used as an attention-getting device.

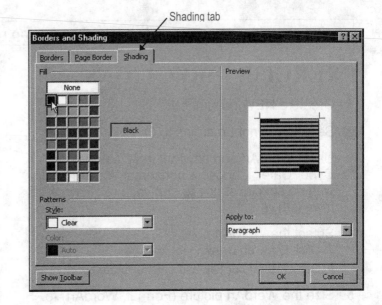

Reverse Text

- Select the text you want to reverse. Select Format, Font on the menu. In the Color box, be sure that Auto is selected. This ensures that the letters will become white when you apply shading to the text. Close the Font dialog box. With the text still selected, open the Format, Borders and Shading dialog box. Click the Shading tab, then select black in the Fill section. Click OK to return to the document. Click away from the text that you selected to view the results.

> *In this exercise, you will create a letterhead using rotated WordArt text, clip art, and reverse text.*

EXERCISE DIRECTIONS

1. Create a NEW document.

2. Set left and right margins to 0.75".

3. Using WordArt and any font in 72 point, type Cyber Café. Choose a horizontal WordArt style with no special shape to start with (3rd Row, 1st from left).

4. Select the WordArt object.
   - Click Draw on Drawing toolbar.
   - Select Rotate or Flip and select Rotate Left.

5. Size the WordArt picture (Format, WordArt) to 1" high by 4.75" wide and position it as shown.

6. Using Insert Picture, insert the StressFrustrationAngerChaos clip art from the Cartoon category; size it to 1.5" wide by 1.5" high. Position it below the rotated WordArt as shown.

7. Copy the picture. (Hold down Ctrl and drag the graphic below the other picture.)

8. Keyboard the name and address information in the same font used for WordArt using a 12-point font. Set the text to reverse.

9. Preview your work.

10. Save the file; name it **CYBERLETHEAD**.

11. Close the document window.

KEYSTROKES

ROTATE WORDART OBJECT

USING THE WORDART TOOLBAR

1. Click WordArt object to rotate.

2. Click **Free Rotate** button .... ⟳ on WordArt toolbar.

3. Position tool over one of the round selection handles that appear.

4. Click and drag tool in direction the text is going to appear.

USING THE DRAW MENU

1. Click WordArt object to rotate.

2. Click **Dr̲aw** .... Alt + R on Drawing toolbar.

3. Click **Rotate or Fli̲p** .... P

Select desired direction:

- **Free Ro̲tate** .... T

   ✓ *See directions at left to use the Free Rotate tool.*

- **Rotate L̲eft** L

- **Rotate R̲ight** .... R

- **Flip H̲orizontal** .... H

- **Flip V̲ertical** V

REVERSE TEXT

1. Select text to reverse.

2. Click **F̲ormat** .... Alt + O

3. Click **F̲ont** .... F

4. Click **Auto** .... Alt + C , A in the **C̲olor** list box.

5. Click **OK** .... Enter

6. Click **F̲ormat** .... Alt + O

7. Click **B̲orders and Shading** .... B

8. Click **S̲hading** tab .... Alt + S

9. Click desired color to apply to background.

   ✓ *Black is frequently used, although other colors can be used as well.*

10. Click **OK** .... Enter

105 Spring Street
New York, NY
(212) 666-6666
http://www.cybercafe.com

Cyber Cafe

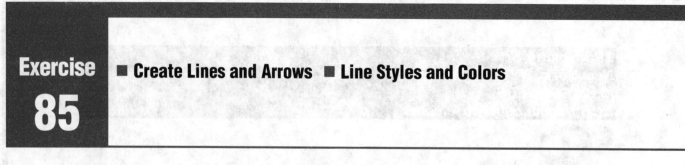

Exercise 85 ■ **Create Lines and Arrows** ■ **Line Styles and Colors**

Drawing Toolbar

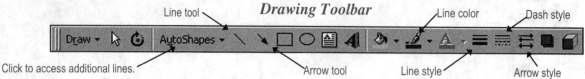

NOTES

Create Lines and Arrows

- You can create a variety of lines (straight, curved, freeform, arcs, scribbles) using a variety of tools available on the Drawing toolbar. Separate tools are available for creating various arrow styles.

- You must be in Page Layout View to see lines and arrows.

- The following is an explanation of the various Drawing toolbar buttons that you can use to create and format lines.

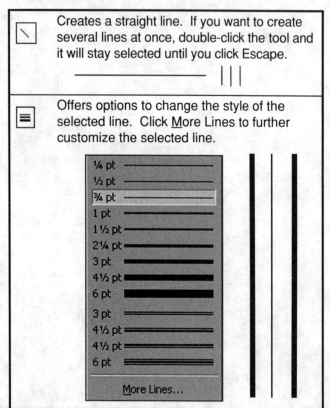

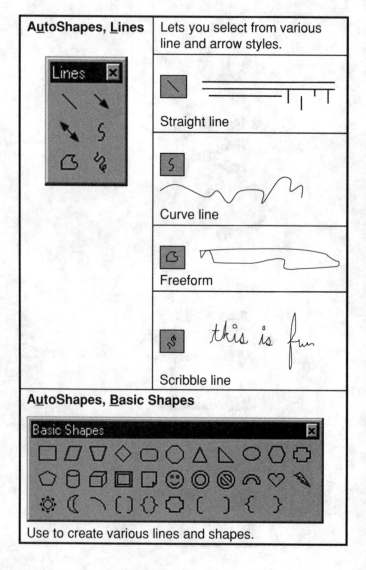

- Various arrow styles are available from the Drawing toolbar. To draw an arrow, click the arrow tool 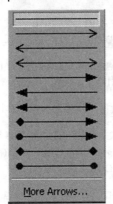. Click and drag to insert the arrow. Then select the desired arrow style from the Arrow Style palette.

- Click <u>M</u>ore Arrows to access even more arrow styles.

Line Styles and Colors

- You can change the style and color of lines and arrows.

- To change the style of a line or arrow, select that line or arrow, then click the line, dash, or arrow style button on the Drawing toolbar and select the desired style. Note some of the examples below.

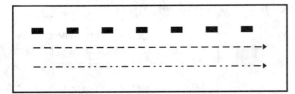

- To change the line color of a line or arrow, select the line or arrow, then click the list arrow next to the **Line Color** button on the Drawing toolbar.

Pop-up Menu

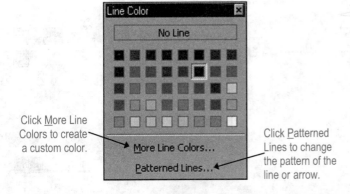

Click <u>M</u>ore Line Colors to create a custom color.

Click <u>P</u>atterned Lines to change the pattern of the line or arrow.

- In the Colors dialog box that follows, select the Standard or Custom tab, then select a custom color.

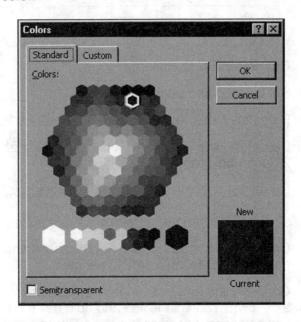

- In the Patterned Lines dialog box that appears after clicking Patterned Lines option, select a desired line pattern.

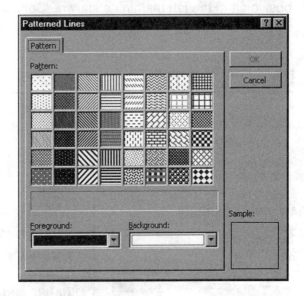

- When handles appear on a selected line, you can change the line style and color, and also the line length and position.

- To change the line length, select the line, then drag on a handle until the desired length is achieved. To change the line position, select the line, then drag the line (not the handle) to move it to the desired position. If you hold down the Alt key while dragging, you will have greater precision placing the line.

In this exercise, you will create a letterhead using various line styles.

EXERCISE DIRECTIONS

1. Create a NEW document.

2. Set 0.5" top and bottom margins.

3. Press the Enter key twice.

4. Center the line The Palm Court using a script 28-point bold font.

5. Create a horizontal line between the margins, and position it above the centered text, as shown. Use the default thickness (3/4 point).

6. Create a 1" line using 2.4-point thickness and position it at the left margin as shown.

7. Copy the line and position it at the right margin as shown. (Select the line and hold down the Ctrl key as you position the line. This will make a copy of the line.)

8. Create a 1" line using a 4.5-point thickness and position it at the left margin as shown. Color it blue.

9. Copy the line and position it at the right margin as shown. Color it blue.

10. Insert a relevant picture. Size it to 1" wide by 1" high and position it as shown.

11. Position the insertion point At 10.1".

12. Create a footer and center the address text using a serif 9-point font for the text and any desired Wingdings symbol between the text.

13. Create a 1" arrowhead using a 2-point line and position it at the left margin.

14. Copy the line and position it at the right margin. Change the arrowhead direction.

15. Preview your work

16. Print one copy.

17. Save the file; name it **PALM**.

18. Close the document window.

KEYSTROKES

The Drawing toolbar must be displayed on screen to do the following procedures. Click the Drawing button 🖉 *on the Standard toolbar to display the Drawing toolbar.*

DRAW LINE OR ARROW

1. Click **Line** button .... ◻
   OR
   Click **Arrow** button .... ◼
2. Place mouse pointer where arrow or line will begin.
3. Drag mouse pointer to where arrow or line will end.
4. Release mouse.

CHANGE LINE OR ARROW STYLE

1. Select line or arrow.
2. Click **Line Style** button .... ▤ on Drawing toolbar.
   AND/OR
   Click **Arrow Style** button .... ⇄
3. Click desired line or arrow style.

CHANGE LINE OR ARROW COLOR

1. Select line or arrow.
2. Click list arrow next to
   Line Color button .... on Drawing toolbar.
3. Click desired color.

REPOSITION LINE OR ARROW

1. Place mouse pointer on line or arrow until a four-headed arrow is added to the end of the mouse pointer.
2. Drag object to desired position.

RESIZE A LINE OR ARROW

1. Select line or arrow.
2. Drag handles.
   OR
1. Select line or arrow.
2. Click **Format** .... Alt + O
3. Click **AutoShape** .... O
4. Click **Size** tab.
   AND/OR
   Click **Position** tab.
5. Select desired options.
6. Click **OK** .... Enter

The Palm Court

87 Collins Avenue ✠ Miami Beach ✠ Florida 33140 ✠ 305-555-5555

Exercise 86

- ■ **Create Shapes** ■ **Group and Ungroup** ■ **Add Colors to Objects**
- ■ **Create Shadows and 3-D Effects**

Drawing Toolbar

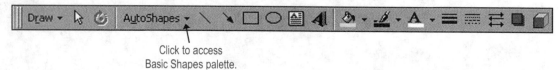

Click to access
Basic Shapes palette.

NOTES

Create Shapes

- You can draw a variety of shapes using various tools available on the Drawing toolbar. In addition to the rectangle and oval tools on the Drawing toolbar, you can select from several shapes on the AutoShapes menu.

- To draw an **oval** or **circle**, select the Oval tool 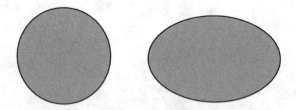 on the Drawing toolbar. The mouse pointer changes to a crosshair. Place the crosshair pointer where you wish the shape to begin and drag in the desired direction. To draw a perfect circle, hold down the Shift key as you drag. When you release the mouse button, a circle or oval appears.

- Similarly, if you wish to draw a **rectangle**, click on the Rectangle tool  and drag diagonally. To draw a perfect square, hold down the Shift key as you drag.

- You can select from a variety of shapes (parallelogram, trapezoid, triangle, cube, etc.) on the **Basic Shapes** palette on the AutoShapes menu.

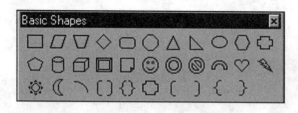

- You can use the selection handles to adjust the object once it is in place. Note the selection handles on the object below. Many shapes also have a diamond-shaped adjustment handle that will not change the size of the entire shape, but will allow you to adjust or size some aspect of the shape. In the illustration below, the adjustment handle was dragged up to change the smile to a frown.

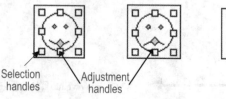

Selection
handles

Adjustment
handles

- To draw irregular shapes, select the freeform tool 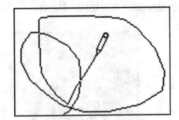 from the Lines submenu of the AutoShapes menu, then click where your line will begin. Hold down the mouse button and drag. The mouse pointer will change to a pencil shape.

- Draw the shape; double-click when finished. The mouse pointer will return to the default shape.

Group and Ungroup

- **Grouping** creates one object out of individual parts. Note the individual parts in the exercise illustration. Grouped objects behave like a single graphic object. Grouping is achieved by holding the Shift key as you select several objects, then clicking Group on the Draw menu, or by clicking the Select tool and drawing a box around the objects to group (click the mouse at top left of objects and drag diagonally to create the box).

- Grouped objects may be sized as if they were a single drawing object.

- If, after you group an object, you wish to edit part of it, you must **ungroup** it by selecting it and clicking Ungroup on the Draw menu.

Copy/Move/Size a Shape

- You can quickly copy a shape by selecting the shape, then holding the Ctrl key down while you drag.

- To move an object, select the object and drag it into place. Position your pointer on the object, not on a handle, when dragging.

- To size a shape, select the shape and position the pointer on a handle until it becomes a two-headed arrow. Then drag a handle. Drag a corner handle to change the object's height and width proportionally; drag a top or bottom middle handle to change the height; drag a middle side handle to change the width.

- To size an object by a specific amount, select the object, then select AutoShape from the Format menu. You can also right-click on the object and select Format AutoShape on the shortcut menu. In the Format AutoShape dialog box that follows, click the Size tab and enter the size of the object in the Height and Width text boxes.

Add Colors to Shapes

- Closed objects (circle, square, rectangle, triangle) can be filled with various colors by selecting the object, then clicking the arrow next to the Fill Color button and selecting from a palette of colors. You need a color printer, however, to obtain color output.

Create Shadows and 3-D Effects

- You can change the shape of the beginning and end of a line by selecting the line, then selecting AutoShape from the Format menu. In the arrow section of the Colors and Lines tab in the Format AutoShapes dialog box, select from the Begin and End styles available. These options are also available when you create an arrow.

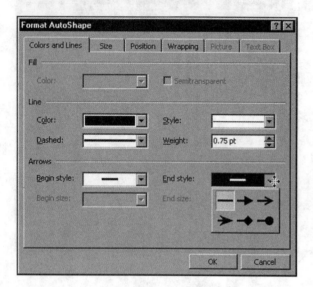

- You can also add shadows or 3-D effects to drawing objects.

To add shadows to an object:

- Select the object.
- Click the Shadow button 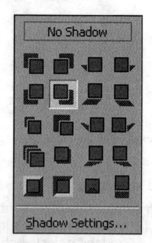 on the Drawing toolbar.
- Select desired shadow effect.

To add 3-D effects to an object:

- Select the object.
- Click the 3-D button 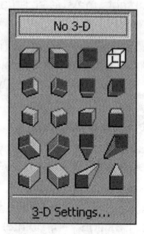 on the Drawing toolbar.
- Select desired 3-D effect.

In this exercise, you will create shapes and objects.

EXERCISE DIRECTIONS

PART I

1. Create a NEW document.

2. Set 0.5" top and bottom margins.

3. Access the circle tool.

4. Create a circle in the center of your page, approximately 1.5" wide by 1.5" tall for the body of the bug. Fill it any desired shade of blue. Use a 6-point black line around the circle.

5. Divide the circle in half using a 6-point black line.

6. Create the bug using circles and lines as shown. Use the copy procedure to duplicate the same elements (the two circles and the legs). Use an 8-point line for the legs. Color the legs blue.

7. Using the Select Drawing Objects tool, select the entire bug. Click the Group button to group the objects.

8. Select the bug by clicking on the edge of the graphic; size it to 1.5" wide by 1.5" tall and move it to the middle of the page.

PART II

9. Create a text box and insert and center the text shown in a 16-point font. Use a script or decorative font for the title; use a serif font for the address and phone information. Change the text box border line to 2 point. Center the text box.

10. Make a copy of the bug. Move one copy to the left of the framed text box; move one copy to the right of the framed text box.

11. Preview your work.

12. Print one copy.

13. Save the file; name it **BUG**.

14. Close the document window.

PART I

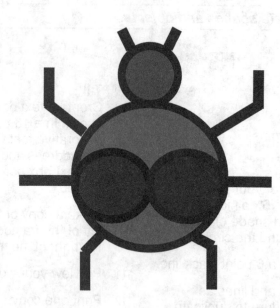

PART II

Ace Exterminators

90 Quest Lane
Mission, KS 66201
1-800-BUG-5555

KEYSTROKES

✓ *The Drawing toolbar must be displayed on screen to do the following procedures. Click the Drawing button on the Standard toolbar* 🔀 *to display the Drawing toolbar.*

DRAW AN OVAL OR RECTANGLE

1. Click **Oval** button .... ⬭

   OR

   Click **Rectangle** button .... ▢

2. Place crosshair-shaped mouse pointer above and to the left of where ellipse or rectangle will begin.

3. Drag down and to the right to point where object will end.

4. Set line style as desired.

   To draw a perfect circle or square:

   Hold down **Shift** .... Shift
   while dragging down and to the right.

REPOSITION AN OBJECT

Drag entire object.

RESIZE AN OBJECT

Drag side handles or corner handles.

DRAW BASIC SHAPES

1. Click **AutoShapes** .... Alt + U
   on Drawing toolbar.

2. Click **Basic Shapes** .... B

3. Click desired shape.

4. Place crosshair-shaped mouse pointer above and to the left of where shape will begin.

5. Drag down and to the right to point where shape will end.

COPY OBJECT

1. Click object to be copied.

2. Press and hold **Ctrl** .... Ctrl

3. Drag shape to desired location.

GROUP OBJECTS

1. Click **Select Objects** tool .... ⬉

2. Place crosshair-shaped mouse pointer above and to the left of the objects to be selected.

3. Drag down and to the right to enclose all desired objects.

4. Click **Draw** .... Alt + R
   on Drawing toolbar.

5. Click **Group** .... G

   To ungroup objects:

   a. Select grouped objects.

   b. Click **Draw** .... Alt + R
      on Drawing toolbar.

   c. Click **Ungroup** .... U

RESIZE AN OBJECT

1. Select the object.

2. Drag the side handles to change only the height or width of the object.

   OR

   Drag a corner handle to change the height and width proportionally.

   If object has adjustment handle:

   Click and drag to adjust object.

SET FILL COLOR FOR OBJECTS

1. Select desired object.

2. Click arrow next to **Fill Color** ....
   button on Drawing toolbar.

3. Select desired fill color.

APPLY SHADOW OR 3-D EFFECT

1. Select object.

2. Click **Shadow** button .... ▣
   on Drawing toolbar.

   OR

   Click **3-D** button .... ▱
   on Drawing toolbar.

3. Select desired effect.

NEXT EXERCISE

Exercise
87

- ■ **Bring in Front of Text and Send Behind Text**
- ■ **Bring to Front and Send to Back** ■ **Page Border**

Click to access Order commands.   *Drawing Toolbar*

Order Floating Toolbar

NOTES

Bring in Front of Text and Send Behind Text

- When you use a text box to create an object (shape, picture, chart) and a text box, you have the option of stacking one on top of the other. It is like using a new transparency page for each object and text box you draw and overlaying it on the previous object.

- You can change the layering of the objects/text boxes that overlap by selecting the object or text box, then using the Bring in Front of Text 🔲 or Send Behind Text 🔲 features. To access these commands, select Order from the Draw menu on the Drawing toolbar.

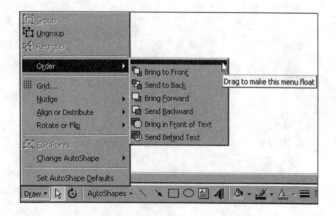

- If you are working with several objects, you may want to float the Order toolbar.

  Hint: *If you can't find an object in a stack, press Tab to cycle forward (or Shift+Tab to cycle backward) through the objects until you find it.*

Bring to Front and Send to Back

- The **Send to Back** button 🔲 and **Bring to Front** button 🔲 on the Order toolbar move objects (shapes, pictures or bitmaps, *not text boxes*) to the front or back of all items in the stack.

- When you have several objects layered and you use the Send to Back or Bring to Front command, the selected object will go to the bottom or top of the stack. If you use the **Bring Forward** 🔲 or **Send Backward** 🔲 command, the selected object will move through the stack one object at a time. This gives you more control over the order of objects.

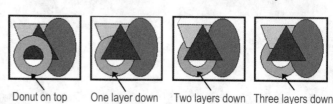

Donut on top   One layer down   Two layers down   Three layers down

Add Page Border

- **To add a border to a page**, select <u>B</u>orders and Shading on the F<u>o</u>rmat menu and click the <u>P</u>age Border tab. In the Page Border dialog box, illustrated below, select the desired border style.

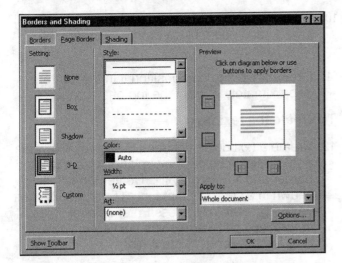

- You can specify where the border will appear on a page (top, bottom, left/right side) by using the C<u>u</u>stom settings. Click where you want the border to appear in the Preview section of the Page Border dialog box.

- You can also specify what part of a document (page, section, entire document) to apply the page border to by selecting an option in the App<u>l</u>y to drop-down list.

- To specify the position of the border on a page, select the options you want in the <u>O</u>ptions dialog box, illustrated below.

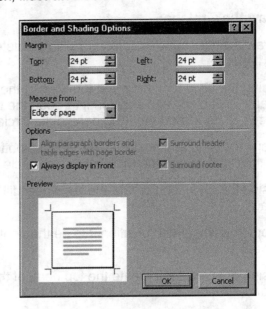

In this exercise, you will create a flyer using text boxes and other drawing tools.

EXERCISE DIRECTIONS

1. Create a NEW document.

2. Set 1" left and right margins.

To draw the airplane:

3. Draw a circle, approximately 0.75" in diameter; fill it black.

4. Using the Oval tool, draw the top wing of the plane, fill it black and position it through the top of the circle. (Send the wing behind the circle.)

5. Copy the wing and position it through the bottom of the circle. (Send the wing behind the circle.)

6. Using the Oval tool, create the left wheel; fill it black.

7. Copy the wheel and position it to be the right wheel.

8. Using the Oval tool, create the top head of the plane; fill it black.

9. Create a smaller circle within the black circle; fill it white.

10. Create a smaller circle within the white circle; fill it white and use a black border to create the "ring" effect.

11. Group the plane and position it in the center, approximately 2" from the top of the page.

To create the text box:

12. Create a text box measuring 5" high by 1.5" wide and position it below the airplane. Use a dashed border and a 20% gray fill. Center the text as shown in a serif 24-point font. (To center the text vertically in the box, press Enter several times before typing the text.) Use a different font in bold for the words "Glide Airlines."

13. Using the Format, Borders and Shading option, create a dashed page border.

14. Preview your work.

15. Print one copy.

16. Save the file; name it **AIRPLANE**.

17. Close the document window.

All of us

at

Glide

Airlines

wish
you a
pleasant
journey.

KEYSTROKES

The Drawing toolbar must be displayed on screen to do the following procedures.

Click the Drawing button 🖊 *on the Standard toolbar to display the Drawing toolbar. You can also float the Order toolbar by dragging it away from the Order submenu on the Draw menu.*

BRING A DRAWING OBJECT IN FRONT OF TEXT

1. Select the object you want to move.

2. Click **Bring in Front of Text** button .... 🔲
   on Order floating toolbar.

   OR

   a. Click **D**r**aw** .... `Alt` + `R`
      on Drawing toolbar.

   b. Click **O**r**der** .... `R`

   c. Click **Bring in F**r**ont of Text** .... `R`

SEND A DRAWING OBJECT BEHIND TEXT

1. Select the object you want to move.

2. Click **Send Behind Text** button .... 🔲
   on Order floating toolbar.

   OR

   a. Click **D**r**aw** .... `Alt` + `R`
      on Drawing toolbar.

   b. Click **O**r**der** .... `R`

   c. Click **Send Be**h**ind Text** .... `H`

BRING A DRAWING OBJECT TO THE FRONT

1. Select the object you want to move.

2. Click **Bring to Front** button .... 🔲
   on Order floating toolbar.

   OR

   a. Click **D**r**aw** .... `Alt` + `R`
      on Drawing toolbar.

   b. Click **O**r**der** .... `R`

   c. Click **Bring to Fron**t .... `T`

SEND A DRAWING OBJECT TO THE BACK

1. Select the object you want to move.

2. Click **Send to Back** button .... 🔲
   on Order floating toolbar.

   OR

   a. Click **D**r**aw** .... `Alt` + `R`
      on Drawing toolbar.

   b. Click **O**r**der** .... `R`

   c. Click **Send to Bac**k .... `K`

BRING AN OBJECT TO THE FRONT ONE OBJECT AT A TIME

1. Select the object you want to move.

2. Click **Bring Forward** button .... 🔲
   on Order floating toolbar.

   OR

   a. Click **D**r**aw** .... `Alt` + `R`
      on Drawing toolbar.

   b. Click **O**r**der** .... `R`

   c. Click **Bring F**o**rward** .... `F`

SEND AN OBJECT TO THE BACK ONE OBJECT AT A TIME

1. Select the object you want to move.

2. Click **Send Backward** button .... 🔲
   on Order floating toolbar.

   OR

   a. Click **D**r**aw** .... `Alt` + `R`
      on Drawing toolbar.

   b. Click **O**r**der** .... `R`

   c. Click **Send B**a**ckward** .... `B`

ADD A PAGE BORDER

1. Click **F**o**rmat** .... `Alt` + `O`

2. Click **B**o**rders and Shading** .... `B`

3. Click **P**a**ge Border** .... `Alt` + `P`

4. Select desired options.

5. Click **OK** .... `Enter`

NEXT EXERCISE

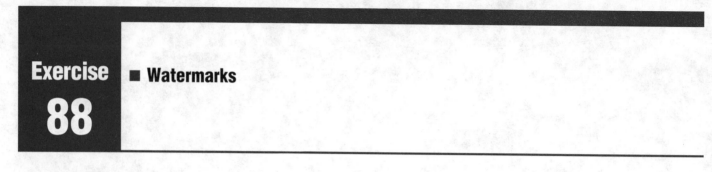

Exercise 88

■ **Watermarks**

NOTES

Watermarks

■ A **watermark** is any text or picture that appears behind regular text in a document. Below is an example of a watermark.

The California Bar Association

Invites You

To its

Annual Awards Luncheon

May 15, 1998

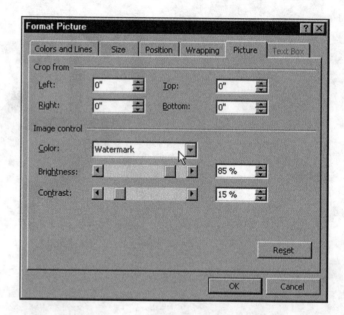

■ You can insert pictures and other objects to use as a watermarks and then format them to achieve the look that you want. You can create a watermark before or after you enter text.

■ To insert a picture into the document, click Picture on the Insert menu. Select the clip art or picture that you want to use as a watermark and click OK.

■ To lighten the image so that it does not interfere with the content of your document, select Picture from the Format menu. In the Format dialog box that follows, click the list arrow next to Color and select Watermark. Note that the Brightness and contrast level indicators change. You can also adjust these controls manually.

■ You have to change the Wrapping style of the picture so that the document text appears on top of the watermark and not to one side or the other. To change the wrapping style, click the Wrapping tab in the Format Picture dialog box. Click None in the Wrap Style section.

■ To send the object behind the text so that the object does not cover the text, click Draw on the Drawing toolbar. Select Order and Send Behind Text.

In this exercise, you will create a flyer using watermarks.

EXERCISE DIRECTIONS

1. Create a NEW document.

2. Set 0.5" left, right, top and bottom margins.

3. Begin the text At 0.9". Center the text and set it to a sans serif 24-point bold font. Use spacing as desired to balance the page. Format the text as illustrated.

4. Insert the String Beans Accomplishment clip art.

5. Select the image. Right-click on it, select Format Picture, and do the following:
   - Click the Picture tab. Select Watermark in the Image Control Color box.
   - Click the Wrapping Tab and select None.
   - Click OK to return to the document.

6. Position it in the center of the page as shown.

7. Select the picture and Send it Behind the Text.

8. Size the picture to fit the page (7.2" high by 7.09" wide).

9. Preview your work.

10. Print one copy.

11. Save the file; name it **CONDUCT**.

KEYSTROKES

CREATE A WATERMARK

1. Enter text that will appear on the page.

2. Click **Insert** .... `Alt` + `I`

3. Click **Picture** .... `P`

4. Select desired picture.

5. Click **Insert** .... `Enter`

6. Right-click on picture to display shortcut menu.

7. Click **Format Picture** .... `I`

8. Click **Wrapping** tab.

9. Select **None** .... `Alt` + `N`
   in Wrapping Style section.

10. Click **Picture** tab.

11. Select **Watermark** .... `Alt` + `C`
    in **Color** box.

12. Click **OK** .... `Enter`
    to return to document.

13. Drag selected object to desired location.

14. Resize selected object by dragging a sizing handle.

15. Select picture.

16. Click **Draw** .... `Alt` + `R`
    on Drawing toolbar.

17. Click **Order** .... `R`

18. Click **Send Behind Text** .... `H`

Reserve Your Seats
NOW
for great performers at
Victoria Music Hall
1997-1998

24-point Arial Black

H = 7.2"
W = 7.09"

24-point

Great Performers —— great rewards
The best subscriber benefits in town!

Call 212-555-5555 to order your tickets and for details about subscriber benefits, including ticket exchange.

16-point Arial Black

NEXT EXERCISE

Exercise

89

■ **Summary**

In this exercise, you will create an invitation using AutoShapes and a watermark.

EXERCISE DIRECTIONS

1. Create the invitation shown.

2. Set 0.5" left, right, top and bottom margins.

3. Enter the invitation text as shown.
   - Start At approximately 3.1" down from the top of the page.
   - Center the text.
   - Set the name to a 22-point serif bold font.
   - Set CONGRATULATIONS to a serif 16-point bold font.
   - Set all remaining text to a 26-point script font.

4. Insert the down ribbon Autoshape from the Stars and Banners palette
   - Size it to 9" high by 7.43" wide.
   - Fill it light turquoise. Select the Semitransparent option.
   - Set the Wrapping to None.
   - Send the image behind the text.
   - Move the shape so that it is centered on the page.

5. Line space the text as desired to fill the center of the banner.

6. Insert the sailboat image from the Transportation category of the Clip Gallery.
   - Size it to 7" high by 3" wide. Set Wrapping to None. Deselect lock aspect ratio, if it is selected.
   - Position the image in the middle of the banner as shown.
   - Set to a watermark.
   - Send the image behind the text.

7. Insert ½-point art page border as shown.

8. Preview your work.

9. Make any necessary adjustments to the text or graphics to align the elements as shown.

10. Print one copy.

11. Save the file, name it **RETIRE.**

12. Close the document window.

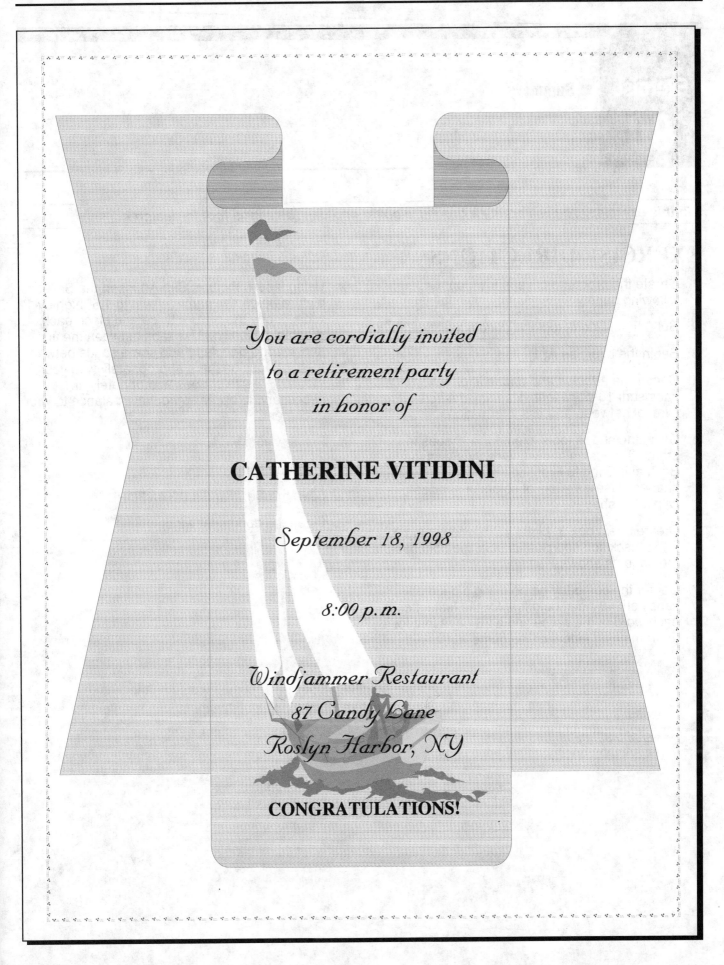

You are cordially invited
to a retirement party
in honor of

CATHERINE VITIDINI

September 18, 1998

8:00 p.m.

Windjammer Restaurant
87 Candy Lane
Roslyn Harbor, NY

CONGRATULATIONS!

Exercise

90

■ **Summary**

In this exercise, you will create a brochure cover and use the shape tool to design it.

EXERCISE DIRECTIONS

1. Create the brochure cover shown on the following page.

2. Set 0.5" left, right, top and bottom margins.

3. Begin the exercise At 1".

4. Center the address and phone information in a sans serif 10-point font. Use any desired symbol between address information.

5. Using the shape tools, create the shapes to create the design shown. Use the Send to Back and Bring to Front commands to layer the shapes. Use a variety of colors or shades within the shapes.

6. Create a text box 3" high by 7.5" wide using a 0.25" black line and position it at the bottom of the page as shown.

7. Center the company name using a decorative sans serif 48-point bold font for the first letter in each word of the name and a 28-point font for the remaining letters of the name.

8. Using Insert, Picture, Clip Art insert the Sailboat picture below the name; size it to 1.5" high by 1" wide. Copy the picture twice and place each graphic as shown. Use tabs between the first and second picture to add some space between them or position them appropriately with your mouse. Resize shapes appropriately, if necessary, to apply appropriate balance to your document.

9. Preview your work.

10. Print one copy.

11. Save the file; name it **BRANFORD**.

12. Close the document window.

12 Palm Tree Lane ● Union, NJ ● 07311 ● Phone: 908-777-0777 ● Fax: 908-777-9999

Branford **T**ours **&** **T**ravel

Word 97

LESSON 12

Word and the Internet

- Introduction
- Internet Basics
- Using Word 97 to Access the Internet
- Search the Internet
- Getting Help from the Microsoft Web Site
- Print Web Site Information
- Save Current Web Page
- Copy Text from a Web Site into a Word Document
- Uniform Resource Locators (URL)
- Access a Web Site Using a URL Address
- Favorites Folders
- Add Sites to the Favorites Folder
- Add New Folders to Favorites Folder
- Delete Web Sites from Folders
- Inserting Hyperlinks in a Word Document to Access a World Wide Web Site
- Access a World Wide Web Site from a Hyperlink in Word
- Insert Hyperlinks from a Word Document to Another Word Document
- Move Back and Forth between Hyperlinks
- Select, Copy, and Delete Hyperlinks

Exercise

91

■ **Introduction** ■ **Internet Basics** ■ **Using Word 97 to Access the Internet**
■ **Search the Internet**

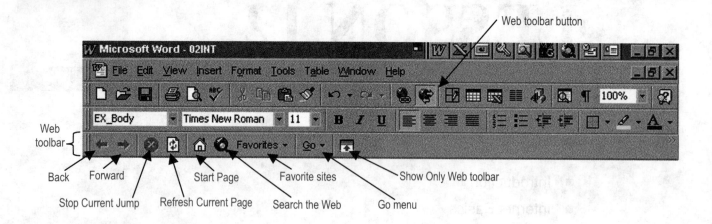

Web toolbar button

Web toolbar

Back   Forward   Start Page   Favorite sites   Show Only Web toolbar

Stop Current Jump   Refresh Current Page   Search the Web   Go menu

NOTES

Introduction

■ This lesson will introduce you to accessing the Internet directly from Word 97. You will also learn how to use information gathered from various Web sites in your Word document. If you are not connected to the Internet, you can use the DDC Internet Simulation CD-ROM, included with this book, to simulate Internet searches. (For more information on the DDC Internet Simulation see page 394 and the Introduction to this book.)

Internet Basics

■ The **Internet** is a worldwide network of computers. These computers may be located in businesses, schools, research foundations and/or individuals' homes. Those who are connected to this network can share information with each other, communicate via e-mail and search for information.

■ The **World Wide Web** (WWW) is a service of the Internet in which pages, created by companies, individuals, schools and government agencies around the world, are linked to each other.

■ In order to access the Internet, you (or your company, or school) must sign up with an Internet service provider (ISP). Some popular service providers include America Online, Microsoft Network (MSN), and CompuServe.

■ A **Web browser** is a program on your computer that displays the information you retrieve from the Internet in a readable format. The most popular Web browsers are Microsoft Internet Explorer and Netscape Navigator. Some service providers give you a Web browser when you subscribe. If your service provider does not give you a Web browser, you will need to purchase and install one.

Using Word 97 to Access the Internet

- Microsoft Word 97, like all the applications in Microsoft Office 97, provides easy access to the Internet through menus and toolbar buttons.

  When you click the **Web toolbar** button 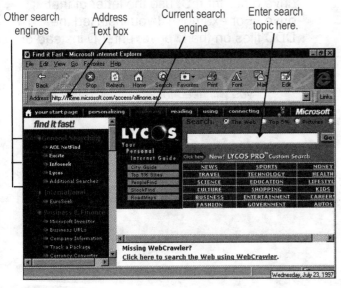 on the Standard toolbar, the Web toolbar, illustrated on the previous page, displays.

Search the Internet

> ✓Note: If you are using Microsoft Office 97, Internet Explorer is probably already set up on your computer. The exercises in this lesson assume your are accessing the Internet using Internet Explorer.

- To begin searching the Internet from Word 97, click the Web toolbar button on the Standard toolbar to display the Web toolbar. Then, click the Search the Web button [Q]. This will bring you to the General Search page of Internet Explorer. The Internet Explorer window will replace the Word window. Note the General Search page illustrated below.

Other search engines — Address Text box — Current search engine — Enter search topic here.

- A search text box and a list of search engine names (Yahoo, InfoSeek, Magellan, Lycos, Excite, etc.) display on the page. A **search engine** searches databases around the world for results of your search topic. Some search engines return more results than others. To start a search, first select the search engine you want to use. Then enter the search topic in the search text box and click the appropriate button (e.g., Submit, Search, Go Get It) to start the search.

- You will go to the search site, and the results of your search will display. When a site is contacted, the Web address (for example, http://www.excite.com) displays in the address text box. (A Web address is also referred to as a URL – Uniform Resource Locator. Opening a Web Site using URL address will be covered in Exercise 93.)

- For example, if you were searching for information about the Peace Corps, you would enter the words "Peace Corps" in the search text box. After you clicked the appropriate search button, the results would display. Below is an example of the kind of result you might get.

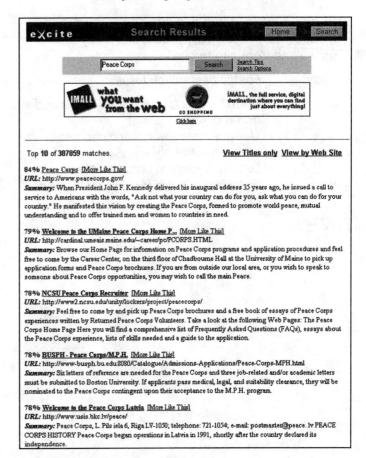

- Once you have contacted a site, some words appear in a different color, underlined, or both. Clicking on one of these **hypertext links** takes you to a new page with related information.

- To move among the links that you have accessed during the current session, click the Back and Forward buttons ⬅️➡️ on the Internet Explorer toolbar

- You can scroll through the results of your search by clicking on a hypertext link, or you can return to the Search Page and enter a new search topic and launch a new search.

- If the page seems to take too long to load, click the Refresh button 🔄 on the Internet Explorer toolbar. If you decide to take a different action, click the Stop button ❌ on the Internet Explorer toolbar.

- Search Sites are updated constantly, so the results you get can vary greatly from day to day as well as from site to site.

  Hints: *For the best search results:*
  - *Always check for misspelled words and typing errors.*
  - *Use descriptive words and phrases to narrow the search.*
  - *Use synonyms and variations of words.*

- If you don't find what you are looking for, connect to a different search site and try the search again.

- You will gather information from the Internet for the rest of the exercises in this lesson.

  - If you are connected to the Internet, use the suggested sites or select other appropriate Web sites.

  - If you are not connected to the Internet, use the CD-ROM that accompanies this book. All the Internet actions described in the exercises are simulated on this CD. You can use the information on the CD-ROM to complete the exercises in this book.

- If you want to use the CD-ROM for these exercises, follow the installation directions on pages vii-viii.

To launch the simulation from a hard drive:

  - On the Web toolbar, Click **Go**, then select **Open**.

  - Type **C:\DDCPUB\WOR97INT.IMR** on the address line. If you installed the files to a drive other than C, use the letter of that drive. For example, if you installed the DDC files on the D drive, enter D instead of C.

  ✓ *Note:*   *If you did a "Typical" install of the files, you will need to leave the CD in your CD-ROM drive for all the graphics to display.*

  - Click **OK** to open the simulation.

  - Double-click on an exercise name to select it.

In this exercise you will launch the Web from inside Word 97 and search the Web for information.

IMPORTANT: If you plan to use the DDC Internet simulation, be sure that the files have been installed on your hard drive (see pages vii-viii for installation directions).

EXERCISE DIRECTIONS

✓ If you have a live Internet connection, follow Directions A. Since you will be working with an active web site and web sites are constantly changing, the following steps may have to be modified to reflect changes. If you plan to use the **DDC Simulation**, follow Directions B.

DIRECTIONS A

1. Start Microsoft Word 97.

2. Open a new document.

3. Display the Web toolbar.

4. Move the mouse pointer over each button on the Web toolbar and note the ScreenTip that displays for each one.

5. Click the Search the Web button on the Web toolbar.

6. Select the Excite Search Engine on the main search page in Internet Explorer.

7. Type *fossil energy international* in the textbox and click the Search button.

   ✓ Search words are not case sensitive.

   ✓ The results of your search will appear.

8. Scroll down and locate a link that reads **U.S. Dept. of Energy–Fossil Energy International Activities**. It should have the following URL: **http://www.fe.doe.gov/int/international.html.** Click this link.

9. Scroll down to view the world map. Click on the link below the map for **Western Hemisphere**.

10. Scroll down to view the country flags. Click on the flag for **Brazil**.

11. Scroll down and locate a link that reads **Trade Point USA**. Click this link.

12. Find information relating to Export Opportunities for Brazil.

13. Close Internet Explorer.

14. Close Microsoft Word.

DIRECTIONS B

✓ If you make a mistake as you go through the simulation, click menu and start the exercise over.

1. Launch the DDC Internet Simulation:

   • Click **Go**, **Open** on the Web toolbar.

   • Type **C:\DDCPUB\WOR97INT.IMR.** (Be sure that the simulation has been installed on your hard drive and that the CD is in the CD-ROM drive. If files are on a drive other than C, replace C with the correct letter.)

   • Click **OK**.

2. Double-click on **Exercise 91: Brazil Economy**.

3. Click [Search] button on the Internet Explorer toolbar.

4. Type *Brazil economy* in the Search textbox and click the Search button.

   ✓ The search words are not case sensitive.

   ✓ The results of your search will appear .

5. Scroll down and locate a link that reads **Brazil**. It should display the following URL: **http://www.fe.doe.gov/int/brazil.html**. Click this link.

6. Scroll down and locate a link that reads **Trade Point USA**. Click this link.

7. Find information relating to Export Opportunities for Brazil.

8. Close the DDC simulation.

DESIRED RESULTS FOR LIVE CONNECTION (DIRECTIONS A)

✓ *Since you are using an active Web site, your results may vary.*

89% Energy and the Environment: Resources for a Networked World [More Like This]
URL: http://zebu.uoregon.edu/energy.html
Summary: Comprehensive collection of environment and earth science publications. Sustainable Development Dimensions, including sections on Environmental information, Environmental policy, planning and management and Energy for development.

Click Here.

86% U.S. Dept. of Energy - Fossil Energy International Activities [More Like This]
URL: http://www.fe.doe.gov/int/international.html
Summary: Select a Region Africa Russia/Newly Independent States Eastern Europe Western Europe South Asia/Near East Pacific Rim Western Hemisphere Fossil Energy Home Page Options.
Africa | Eastern Europe | Western Europe | Pacific Rim | Western Hemisphere.

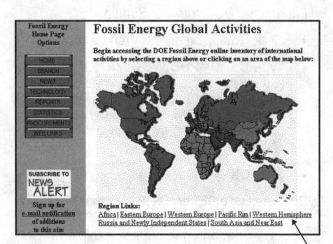

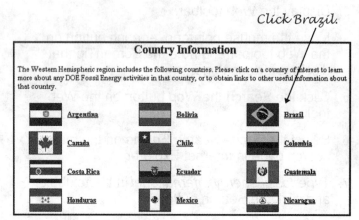

Click Brazil.

Click Western Hemisphere.

Trade Point USA - U.S. Global Trade Outlook for Brazil, including a summary overview of the Brazilian economy with sections on trade climate & trends and export opportunities for U.S. companies. Elsewhere at this site is a 10-year summary of Brazil's National Economic Indicators and International Trade.

Locate and click this link.

Return to International Initiatives page   **Return to Western Hemisphere page**

Export Opportunities-Brazil

Find this information.

Computer Software. U.S. exports are expected to reach $250 million in 1995. The United States now has a 97 percent share of Brazilian imports. U.S. software manufacturers are responsible for 70 percent of Brazil's software sales; local competitors, principally word processing software producers, account for the rest. Best sales prospects for U.S. exporters include software for personal computers, LANs (local area networks), and graphics.

Computers and Peripherals. U.S. exports were an estimated $892 million in 1994. The United States now has a 60 percent share of total imports, and 15 percent of the market. The Brazilian market reserve policy, restricting foreign participation in the computer industry, ended in October 1992, but the government still offers incentives to the domestic computer industry. The most promising products for U.S. companies include notebooks, subnotebooks, handheld and palmtop computers, high-end microcomputers, disk drives, monitors, and printers.

Plastic Materials and Resins. U.S. exports will be a projected $178 million in 1995. The United States now has a 40 percent share of total imports, but only 4 percent of the overall market. The liberalization of imports since 1990 has had a positive impact on production costs in the Brazilian plastics industry. Imports of plastic materials and resins jumped 74 percent between 1992 and 1993. The packaging industry, the leading national consumer of raw materials, absorbs about 60 percent of the domestic resin supply. Local manufacturers account for more than 90 percent of the production of plastic materials and resins in Brazil.

KEYSTROKES

DISPLAY WEB TOOLBAR

Click **Web toolbar** button ....
on Standard toolbar.

OR

1. Click **View** .... [Alt] + [V]

2. Click **Toolbars** .... [T]

3. Click **Web** .... [↓] [Enter]

  ✓ Web toolbar displays.

ACCESS INTERNET EXPLORER'S GENERAL SEARCH PAGE FROM WORD

Click **Search the Web** button ....
on Web toolbar in Word.

  ✓ If you are not connected to your Internet Service Provider, a dialog box that lets you sign on to your provider appears. Follow whatever steps are necessary to connect to your ISP.

PERFORM A SIMPLE SEARCH

FROM INTERNET EXPLORER GENERAL SEARCH SITE

  ✓ *The featured Search Site (Lycos, Excite, Yahoo, InfoSeek, etc.) will appear.*

1. Enter Search topic in Search textbox.

2. Click **Search** button.

  ✓ *In some Search Engines, this button might contain different text. Lycos, for example, might say, "Go Get It."*

  ✓ *The results of the Search display.*

USE A HYPERLINK TO GO TO ANOTHER WEB SITE

1. Point to a link to a site you want to jump to.

2. Click the underlined or graphic link to access the new site.

Exercise

92

- **Get Help from the Microsoft Web Site** ■ **Print Web Site Information**
- **Save Current Web Page**
- **Copy Text from a Web Site into a Word Document**
- **Copy Images from the Internet**

Internet Explorer Toolbar

NOTES

Get Help from the Microsoft Web Site

- In addition to the Help features that you have learned about earlier in this book, you can also get help from Microsoft Web sites. To do this, select Microsoft on the Web from the Help menu. A submenu displays several links to Microsoft support and information.

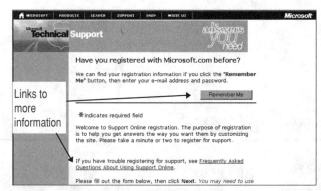

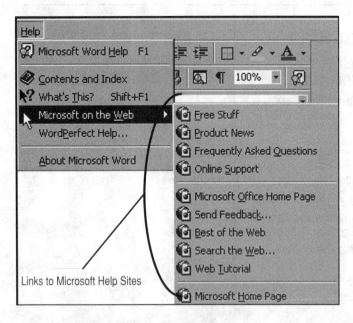

- For example, if you click Frequently Asked Questions, you will go to a page on the Microsoft Web site that displays questions and answers about issues related to Microsoft Word (see illusration on right).

- You can access any other area of the Microsoft site for additional help from this or any page you open. You do not have to return to Word to click another link.

Print Web Site Information

- You can print Web pages or specified text that you find on the Web.

- To print a Web page, click the Print button on the browser's toolbar or select Print from the File menu.

  ✓ *Web pages are constantly changing. You may print a page one day and the page may be different the next day.*

Save Current Web Page

- To save a Web page, open the page, then select Save as File from the File menu. Type the name of the file in the File name box and click Save.

  ✓*Note:* *Text will be saved in the file; graphics will not be saved.*

Copy Text from a Web Site into a Word Document

- It is possible to copy text that you find on the Web into a Word document. To copy Web text, highlight the text you want copied, and select Copy from the File menu. You may also highlight the desired text on the Web site, right-click and select Copy. Text is then copied to the clipboard. Open or switch to your Word document and select Paste from the Edit menu or click the Paste button ▣ on the Formatting toolbar to insert the text into your document.

Copy Images from the Internet

- In addition to Clip Art images available free from Microsoft, many Web sites offer images such as cartoons, icons, art and photographs that you may copy and paste into your document. Locate the object you want to copy, right-click on it and select Copy from the Shortcut menu that appears. Then switch to the Word document and paste the object. Microsoft Office applications accept images in .pcx or .bmp format.

In this exercise, you will access a Microsoft Help site. You will also use a template to create a memo, copy information from a Web site and paste it into the memo.

EXERCISE DIRECTIONS

✓   *If you have a live Internet connection, follow Directions A. If you plan to use the DDC Simulation, follow Directions B.*

DIRECTIONS A

1. Create the memo shown in Illustration A or open 🖫**92GETHELP** from the data file.
   - Use the Contemporary Memo Template.
   - Type the paragraphs shown. Insert a footnote after the word Microsoft, as illustrated.
   - Change the word Confidential at the bottom of the memo to read, SOS—Support on Site. Set it to 18-point Arial Black.

2. Select Microsoft on the Web from the Help menu.

3. Click the link to Frequently Asked Questions.

4. Register with Microsoft Technical Support by entering the information requested. Use the drop-down lists where available to enter your choices. Click Next.

5. Enter your name as requested. Choose the bullet for Basic Site Options. Click Finish.

6. In the My search is about drop-down list, select Word for Windows. Enter the word "signature" in the Search text box.

7. Click Find.

8. Scroll down through the search results and click the link to **WD: How to Add Automatic Signatures to WordMail Messages**.

9. Print a copy of this article.

10. Select the portion of the article indicated in Illustration B, and copy it to the clipboard.

11. Switch to the Word document.

12. Paste information from the clipboard into the memo where shown.

13. Format the memo as follows:
    - Use the Format Painter to apply the Heading 1 style to the heading for the numbered steps.
    - If necessary, delete extra returns from the numbered steps.
    - Delete the numbers from the steps.
    - Highlight the five steps and apply automatic numbering.

14. Italicize the notes in steps one and four.

15. Preview the document.

16. Print one copy.

17. Save the file; name it **EMAILSIGNATURE**.

18. Close the document window.

19. Disconnect from your Internet Service Provider and close your browser.

DIRECTIONS B

1. Create the memo shown in Illustration A or open 🖫92GETHELP from the data file.
   - Use the Contemporary Memo Template.
   - Insert a footnote after the word Microsoft, as illustrated.
   - Change the word Confidential at the bottom of the memo to read, SOS—Support on Site. Set it to 18-point Arial Black.

2. Launch the DDC Internet Simulation:
   - Click **Go**, **Open** on the Web toolbar.
   - Type **C:\DDCPUB\WOR97INT.IMR**. (Be sure that the simulation has been installed on your hard drive and that the CD is in the CD-ROM drive. If files are on a drive other than C, replace C with the correct letter.)
   - Click **OK**.

3. Double-click on **Exercise 92: GETHELP**.

4. Select Microsoft on the Web from the Help menu.

5. Click the link to Frequently Asked Questions.

6. Click the link to Microsoft Word 97 for Windows.

7. Enter the word "signature" in the Search text box in the Word 97 for Windows Frequently Asked Questions window.

8. Click Find.

9. Scroll down through the search results and click the link to **WD: How to Add Automatic Signatures to WordMail Messages**.

9. Select the portion of the article indicated in Illustration B, and copy it to the clipboard.

10. Switch to the Word document.

11. Paste information from the clipboard into the memo where shown.

12. Format the memo as follows:
    - Use the Format Painter to apply the Heading 1 style to the heading for the numbered steps.
    - If necessary, delete extra returns from the numbered steps.
    - Delete the numbers from the steps.
    - Highlight the four steps and apply automatic numbering.

13. Italicize the notes in steps one and four.

14. Preview the document.

15. Print one copy.

16. Save the file; name it **EMAILSIGNATURE.DOC**.

17. Close the document window.

18. Close the document window.

ILLUSTRATION A

Memorandum

To: Janet Landis, Eastern Division Tech Support Coordinator

CC: Western Division Tech Support Personnel

From: Maggie Martinez

Date: Today's date

Re: Attachments to E-mail Messages

Insert footnote here.

Insert information from Web site here.

Add signatures to e-mail messages
In response to several inquiries about adding signatures to e-mail messages, the following information from the Microsoft[1] Help center should clear up any confusion.

If you have any additional questions, please send me e-mail at Landis@wwa.com

---

[1] Information courtesy of Microsoft on the Web Help Site.

SOS–SUPPORT ON SITE ← *18-point Arial black*

ILLUSTRATION B
DESIRED RESULTS (WEB PAGE SENT DIRECTLY TO THE PRINTER)

Select and copy to the clipboard.

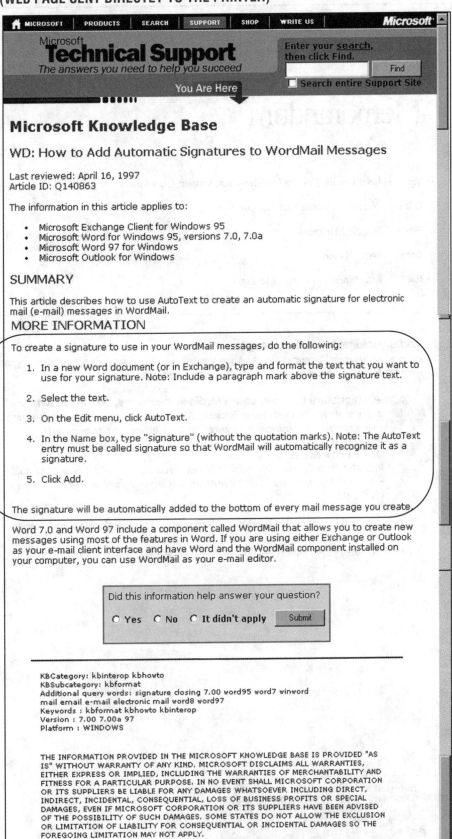

ILLUSTRATION B
DESIRED RESULTS

Memorandum

To: Janet Landis, Eastern Division Tech Support Coordinator

CC: Western Division Tech Support Personnel

From: Maggie Martinez

Date: Today's date

Re: Attachments to E-mail Messages

Add Signatures to email messages

In response to several inquiries about adding signatures to email messages, the following information from the Microsoft[1] Help center should clear up any confusion.

To create a signature to use in your WordMail messages, do the following:

1. In a new Word document (or in Exchange), type and format the text that you want to use for your signature. *Note: Include a paragraph mark above the signature text.*
2. Select the text.
3. On the Edit menu, click AutoText.
4. In the Name box, type "signature" (without the quotation marks). *Note: The AutoText entry must be called signature so that WordMail will automatically recognize it as a signature.*
5. Click Add.

The signature will be automatically added to the bottom of every mail message you create.

If you have any additional questions, please send me email at Landis@wwa.com

---

[1] Information courtesy of Microsoft on the Web Help Site.

SOS–SUPPORT ON SITE

1

KEYSTROKES

GET HELP ON THE WEB

1. Click **Help** .... `Alt`+`H`
2. Click **Microsoft on the Web** .... `W`
3. Click link to desired location:
   - **Free Stuff** .... `F`
   - **Product News** .... `P`
   - **Frequently Asked Questions** .... `Q`
   - **Online Support** .... `S`
   - **Microsoft Office Home Page** .... `O`
   - **Send Feedback** .... `K`
   - **Best of the Web** .... `B`
   - **Search the Web** .... `W`
   - **Web Tutorial** .... `T`
   - **Microsoft Home Page** .... `H`

PRINT INFORMATION FROM THE WEB DIRECTLY TO THE PRINTER

1. Go to a Web site that you want to print.
2. Click **Print** button 🖶 on Internet Explorer toolbar.

   OR
   a. Click **File** .... `Alt`+`F`
   b. Click **Print** .... `P`
   c. Click **OK** .... `Enter`

COPY TEXT FROM A WEB SITE TO A WORD DOCUMENT

1. Go to a Web site containing text that you want to copy.
2. Highlight text that you want to copy.

   OR
   Select the entire page............. `Ctrl`+`A`
3. Copy the text......................... `Ctrl`+`C`
   to the clipboard.
4. Switch to the Word document where text will be inserted.

   OR
   Open a new Word document where text will be inserted.
5. Copy text into document .... `Ctrl`+`V`
   - ✓ *Placeholders will mark the location of graphics.*

COPY IMAGES FROM A WEB SITE TO A WORD DOCUMENT

1. Go to a Web site containing an image that you want to copy.
2. Right-click on the image that you want to copy.
3. Select **Copy** .... `Ctrl`+`C`
   from the Shortcut menu that appears.
4. Switch to the Word document where the image will be inserted.

   OR
   Open a new Word document where the image will be inserted.
5. Paste the image .... `Ctrl`+`V`
   into the document.

Exercise

93

- ■ **Uniform Resource Locators (URL)**
- ■ **Access a Web Site Using a URL Address**

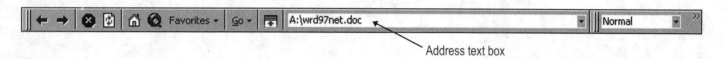

Address text box

NOTES

Uniform Resource Locators (URL)

- As indicated in Exercise 91, a Uniform Resource Locator, frequently referred to as a URL, is a World Wide Web address. These addresses can provide a direct link to a particular Web site. Instead of clicking hypertext links to get to a particular page, you can enter the URL to go directly to a location on the Web.

- A typical URL address looks like: http://www.vicinity.com. The http stands for HyperText Transfer Protocol, which simply refers to the communication protocol that allows Web pages to connect to one another.

Access a Web Page Using a URL Address

- In Exercise 91, you learned that you could enter a search topic into a search text box, select a search engine and perform a search. The search would lead you to a Web page with results of your search. When a site is contacted, the Web address is indicated in the Address text box.

- You can also access a Web page directly by entering a Web address into the Address text box.

- To access a Web page, using a URL Address, click Go on the Web toolbar and select Open. The Open Internet Address dialog box, illustrated below, displays.

- Enter the address of the Web site and then click OK.

    ✓*Note:*   *You can also open files and other documents from this dialog box.*

In this exercise, you will use a URL address to open a WWW site, then record and copy information from the site into a table within a letter.

EXERCISE DIRECTIONS

✓ If you have a live Internet connection, follow Directions A. If you plan to use the DDC Simulation, follow Directions B.

DIRECTIONS A

1. Create a new document as shown in Illustration A on page 413 or open 🖫93CURRENCY.

2. Begin the letterhead at the top of page.

3. Set up the letter as follows:
   - Set the left margin to 2". Use the default margins for the top, bottom, and right margins.
   - Set letterhead text to 14-point bold serif font.
   - Use a 12-point serif font for the rest of the letter.

4. Insert and position the clip art from the Sign group in the Clip Gallery. Use another graphic if this clip art is not available.
   - Size it to 2.5" high by 1.38" wide.
   - Select the Tight Wrapping option.
   - Select Wrap to Largest Side.

5. Save the file; name it **CURRENCY**.

6. Create and format a table as shown in Illustration B on page 414.
   - Create a table using 5 rows and 3 columns.
   - Enter the labels as shown.
   - Use the List 7 Table AutoFormat to format the table.
   - Insert a decimal tab at 3" in rows 2-5 of the third column.
   - Select the entire table and center align it.

7. Resave the file.

8. Display the Web toolbar.

9. Select Open from the Go menu.

10. Enter one of the following URL addresses:
    ✓ If you cannot access any of these sites, use a Search Engine to search for currency convert.
    - http://www.xe.net/currency/
    - http://www.travlang.com/money/
    - http://www.oanda.com/cgi-bin/ncc

11. Copy the conversion rate for Austria and paste it into the appropriate location in the table. Repeat this procedure for the conversion rates for France, Italy, and Switzerland.

12. Preview your work.

13. Resave the file.

14. Print one copy.

15. Exit from your browser.

16. Close all files.

DIRECTIONS B

1. Create a new document as shown in Illustration A on page 413 or open 🖫93CURRENCY.

2. Begin the letterhead at the top of page.

3. Set up the letter as follows:
   - Set the left margin to 2". Use the default margins for the top, bottom, and right margins.
   - Set letterhead text to 14-point bold serif font.
   - Use a 12-point serif font for the rest of the letter.

4. Insert and position the clip art from the Sign group in the Clip Gallery. Use another graphic if this clip art is not available.
   - Select the Tight Wrapping option.
   - Size it to 2.5" high by 1.38" wide.
   - Select Wrap to Largest Side.

5. Save the file; name it CURRENCY.

6. Create and format a table as shown in Illustration B on page 414.
   - Create a table using 5 rows and 3 columns.
   - Enter the labels as shown.
   - Use the List 7 Table AutoFormat to format the table.

7. Resave the file.

8. Display the Web toolbar.

9. Launch the DDC Internet Simulation:
   - Click **Go**, **Open** on the Web toolbar.
   - Type **C:\DDCPUB\WOR97INT.IMR.** (Be sure that the simulation has been installed on your hard drive and that the CD is in the CD-ROM drive. If files are on a drive other than C, replace C with the correct letter.)
   - Click **OK**.

10. Double-click on **Exercise 93: Currency** and follow the directions at the bottom of the screen to search for currency convert.

11. Write down the conversion rates for Austria, France, Italy, and Switzerland. Exit from the DDC Simulation. Enter the exchange rates into the table.

12. Use the List 7 Table AutoFormat to format the table.

13. Preview your work.

14. Resave the file.

15. Print one copy.

16. Close and save the file.

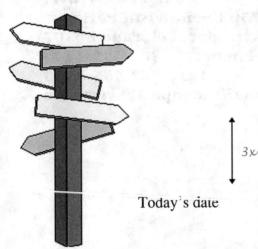

SignPost Travel
3750 Buena Vista Parkway
Breckenridge, Colorado 80307
Phone: 303 555-4444
Fax: 303 555-3333
Email: signpost@wwa.com

14 pt serif

3x

Today's date

Ms. Wendy Ascend, President
Upson Downs Ski Club
234 Summit Ridge
Keystone, CO 80305

Dear Ms. Ascend:

Thank you for your inquiry about group rates for European ski vacations.

We will be glad to present a seminar to your group on the premier European ski resorts and the unique features of each.

Traveling to Europe can be very expensive. After hearing our presentation, you will be able to decide which vacation best suits your travel needs.

Our Leisure Travel Department is available for consultation from 9 a.m. to 7 p.m., 7 days a week. We look forward to working closely with your group.

Sincerely,

Avi Lanch, Vice President
Leisure Travel Department

av/yo

ILLUSTRATION B

SignPost Travel
3750 Buena Vista Parkway
Breckenridge, Colorado 80307
Phone: 303 555-4444
Fax: 303 555-3333
Email: signpost@wwa.com

Today's date

Ms. Wendy Ascend, President
Upson Downs Ski Club
234 Summit Ridge
Keystone, CO 80305

Dear Ms. Ascend:

Thank you for your inquiry about group rates for European ski vacations.

We will be glad to present a seminar to your group on the premier European ski resorts and the unique features of each.

Traveling to Europe can be very expensive. After hearing our presentation, you will be able to decide which vacation best suits your travel needs.

Country	Currency	1.00 US Dollar =
Austria	Schilling	
France	French Franc	
Italy	Lira	
Switzerland	Swiss Franc	

Insert current rates from Web site here.

Our Leisure Travel Department is available for consultation from 9 a.m. to 7 p.m., 7 days a week. We look forward to working closely with your group.

Sincerely,

Avi Lanch, Vice President
Leisure Travel Department

av/yo

KEYSTROKES

USE A URL TO GO TO A WEB SITE FROM WORD

1. Display the Web toolbar ... `Alt`+`V`, `T` if necessary.

2. Click **Go** on the Web toolbar..... `Alt`+`G`

3. Click **Open**.................................. `O`

4. Enter the address of the Web site you want to open.

5. Click **OK** .... `Enter`

   ✓ *You will be prompted to connect to your Internet Service Provider, if you are not already connected.*

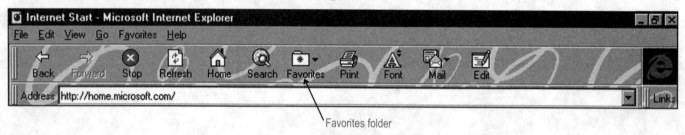

Exercise 94

- **Favorites Folders** ■ **Add Sites to the Favorites Folder**
- **Add New Folders to Favorites Folder**
- **Move Web Sites from Folder to Folder** ■ **Delete Web Sites from Folders**
- **Open a Web Site from the Favorites Folder in Word**

Internet Explorer Toolbar

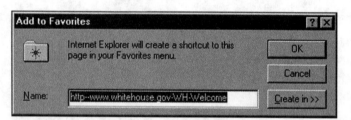

Favorites folder

NOTES

Favorites Folders

- Sometimes it takes you a good deal of time to find a site that you like. You might want to visit this site frequently. You can save addresses of favorite sites in a **Favorites Folder** by adding them to the Favorites folder in Internet Explorer. You can also access the Favorites folder by clicking the Favorites button `Favorites ▾`, on the Web toolbar in Word.

Add Sites to the Favorites Folder

> ✓*Note:*   *Because it is more complicated to add favorites from within Word, this exercise will only cover adding and accessing the Favorites folder from within Internet Explorer.*

- To add sites to the Favorites Folder, go to the Web site that you want to add to your Favorites folder. Click the Favorites button `📷 Favorites` on the Internet Explorer toolbar and select Add to Favorites. *(If the Internet Explorer toolbar is not displayed, click the View menu and select Toolbars, Web.)*

- The address of the Web site that you are currently visiting appears in the Name box. Click OK to add the web address to the Favorites folder.

Add New Folders to Favorites Folder

- To keep your files organized on your computer, you created folders for your word processing, spreadsheet and other files. You can also do this in the Favorites folder for your Web site addresses.

- To create new folders, access Internet Explorer and click the Favorites button. Select Organize Favorites. The contents of your Favorites folder displays.

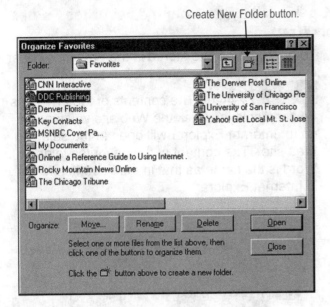

Create New Folder button.

- Click the Create New Folder button 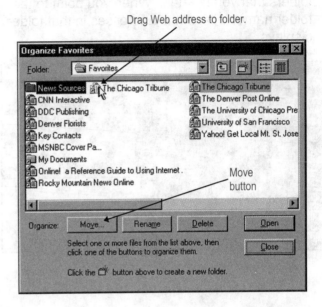.

- Type the name of the new folder and press Enter.

- You can create as many folders and subfolders as you would like.

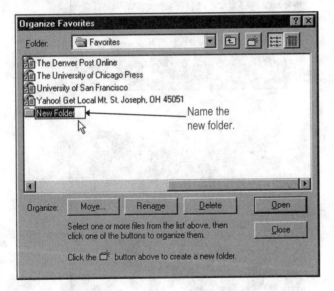

Name the new folder.

To move addresses into a new location:

- Open the Organize Favorites dialog box.

- Click once on the Web site to highlight it.

- Hold down the left mouse button and drag the highlighted Web site to the desired folder.

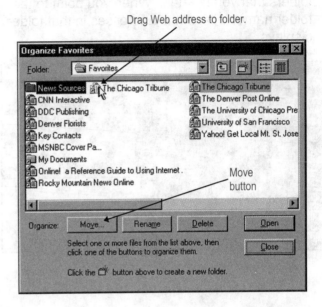

Drag Web address to folder.

Move button

- You can also select the address that you want to move, click Move and select the folder where you want to move the address.

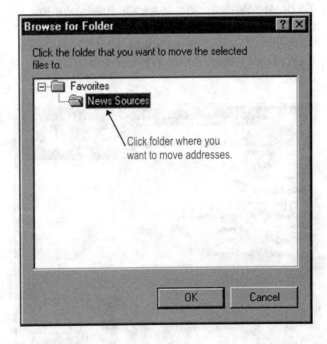

Click folder where you want to move addresses.

- If you want to drag several related addresses at the same time, hold the Ctrl key, click on the addresses you want to move, then drag the entire group to the new folder.

- When you open the Favorites folder in Internet Explorer or in Word 97, you will see the new folders that you created. When you point to the folder name, a list of the addresses in that folder displays.

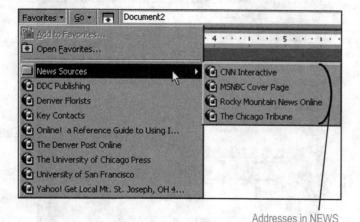

Addresses in NEWS sources folder

Delete Web Sites from Folders

- You can delete web addresses from folders.

- To delete Web addresses, click the Favorites button in Internet Explorer and select <u>O</u>rganize Favorites. Select the site you want to delete, then click <u>D</u>elete. Click <u>Y</u>es to confirm the deletion.

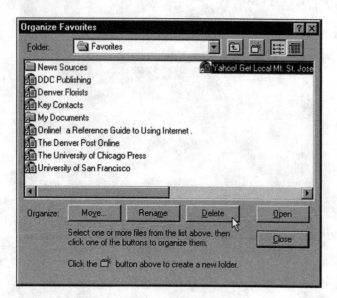

Open a Web Site from the Favorites Folder in Word

- To go to a Web site stored in the Favorites folder in Word, display the Web toolbar and click Favorites ▾ button. The contents of the Favorites Folder displays. Click the Web site you want to go to; Internet Explorer will open at the selected Web site. The content of the Favorites folder in Word is the same as that in the Favorites folder in Internet Explorer.

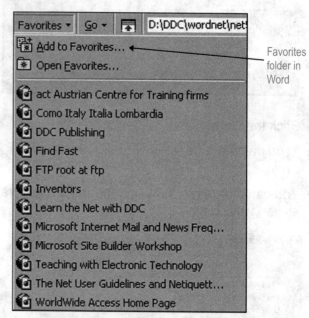

Favorites folder in Word

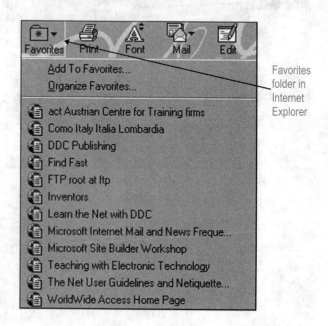

Favorites folder in Internet Explorer

In this exercise, you will create a new folder in your Favorites folder, move and add Web site addresses to it. You will not save any files in this exercise.

EXERCISE DIRECTIONS

✓ *If you have a live Internet connection, follow Directions A. If you plan to use the DDC Simulation, follow Directions B.*

DIRECTIONS A

1. Start Word.

2. Open a blank document.

3. Click the Search the Web button on the Web toolbar.

   ✔ *Since you are not going to save a document, you can go directly to Internet Explorer to complete this exercise. The results will be available to you when you open the Favorites Folder in Word. If you do go directly into Internet Explorer, click the Search button on the Internet Explorer toolbar and complete the exercise as directed.*

4. Enter the topic *universal currency converter* in the search textbox. Use any Search Engine.

5. Click on a site that contains current currency conversion rates.

6. Add this site to your Favorites folder.

7. Visit two other sites that convert currency, and add them to your Favorites folder.

8. To create another folder in your Favorites folder, do the following:
   - Open the Favorites folder and select Organize Favorites.
   - In the Organize Favorites dialog box, click the New Folder button 📁.

     ✓ *If you accidentally click the Up One Level button 📤, click Close and start the procedure again.*
   - Name the new folder, **Currency**.
   - Click the Close button
   - Reopen the Favorites folder. *Note the Currency folder that you have just created is listed on the menu.*

9. To move web addresses to this new folder, do the following:
   - Open Organize Favorites.
   - Select the three addresses that you just added to your Favorites folder. Hold down the Ctrl key while you click on the name of each web address.

   - Release the Ctrl key, point to one of the highlighted addresses, click and drag the group of Web address to the **Currency** folder. Release the mouse when the **Currency** folder is highlighted.
   - Double-click on the **Currency** folder and note the addresses that you have moved to this new folder.
   - Close the Organize Favorites folder.

10. Go to one the sites that you have added to your **Currency** folder. Open the Favorites menu, point to the **Currency** folder and select one of the currency sites. *The currency converter site will display.* Return to your Start page.

11. To delete web address from Favorites folders:
    - Open the Organize Favorites dialog box.
    - Open the Currency folder.
    - Highlight two sites that you no longer want in this folder.
    - Click Delete button. Click Yes in Confirm File Deletion box.
    - Close the Organize favorites dialog box.

12. Create another new folder in your Favorites folder for Web sites in your folder that are related. For example, you could have a folder for News Sources and within that folder you could have additional folders that further group those Web sites (TV, radio, newspapers, magazines, etc.).

13. Search for and add sites to this new folder.

14. Close Internet Explorer and disconnect from your Service Provider.

15. Close but do not save any changes to the Word document.

DIRECTIONS B

1. Start Word.

2. Open a blank document.

3. Launch the DDC Internet Simulation:
   - Click **Go**, **Open** on the Web toolbar.
   - Type **C:\DDCPUB\WOR97INT.IMR.**
     (Be sure that the simulation has been installed on your hard drive and that the CD is in the CD-ROM drive. If files are on a drive other than C, replace C with the correct letter.)
   - Click **OK**.

4. Double-click on **Exercise 94: Currency**.
   - ✓ *Prompts on the bottom of the screen will help guide you through the steps.*

5. Click the Search button on the Internet toolbar or the Search tab on the Microsoft Home page.

6. Click in the Search textbox and enter the topic *universal currency converter*, then click the Search button.

7. Select link to Universal Currency Converter.

8. Click Favorites on the menu, then select Organize Favorites.

9. Click Create New folder button .

10. Follow the onscreen prompts to create a folder, then add a site to the folder.

11. Close the simulation.

12. Minimize or exit Word.

Click hyperlink to go to Web site.

Xenon Labs: The Universal Currency Converter(tm)
THE UNIVERSAL CURRENCY CONVERTER[TM] NOTE: Use your BACK button (or right mouse button) to return to previous pages. I WANT TO CONVERT... CAD Canadian...
http://www.sofa-inc.com/currentc.htm - size 6K - 5 Nov 96

Xenon Labs: The Universal Currency Converter(tm)
This is a direct FORM link to the XENON. UNIVERSAL CURRENCY CONVERTER™ I WANT TO CONVERT... CAD Canadian Dollars. USD American Dollars. GBP British Pounds.
http://www-itp.unibe.ch/~kunszt/currency.html - size 4K - 27 Dec 96

Create New
Folder button.

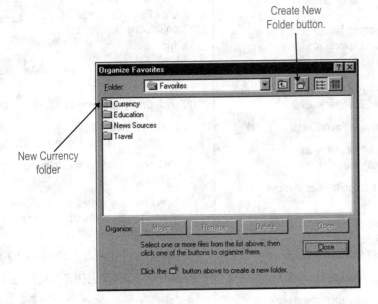

New Currency
folder

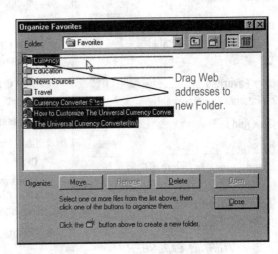

Drag Web
addresses to
new Folder.

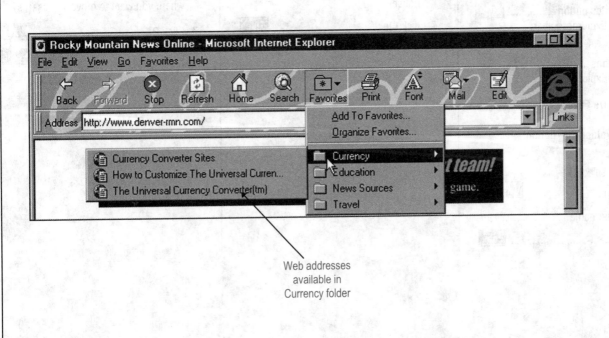

Web addresses
available in
Currency folder

KEYSTROKES

ADD WEB ADDRESSES TO FAVORITES FOLDER

IN INTERNET EXPLORER

1. Open Internet site you want to add to Favorites folder.

2. Click **Favorites** button ....
   on Internet Explorer toolbar.
   OR
   Click F**a**vorites .... Alt + A
   on Internet Explorer menu.

3. Click **Add to Favorites** .... A

4. Click **OK** .... Enter
   to add address to Favorites Folder.

ADD NEW SUBFOLDERS TO FAVORITES FOLDER

IN INTERNET EXPLORER

1. Click **Favorites** button ....
   on Internet Explorer toolbar.
   OR
   Click F**a**vorites .... Alt + A
   on Internet Explorer menu.

2. Click **Organize Favorites** .... O

3. Click **New Folder** ☐ button.
   OR
   Right-click, select
   New, **F**older .... W + F

4. Type in folder name .... *name*

5. Click **OK** .... Enter

MOVE WEB ADDRESS(ES) FROM MAIN FAVORITES FOLDER TO SUBFOLDER

1. Click **Favorites** button ....
   on Internet Explorer toolbar.
   OR
   Click F**a**vorites .... Alt + A
   on Internet Explorer menu.

2. Click **Organize Favorites** .... O

3. Open subfolder containing address(es) you want to move.

4. Click once on addresses to move.
   OR
   Select multiple addresses by holding down Ctrl key as you click once on addresses that you want to move.

5. Point to selected addresses.

6. Drag to new location and release the mouse.

7. Click **Close** .... Enter

MOVE WEB ADDRESS(ES) FROM SUBFOLDERS

1. Click **Favorites** button ....
   on Internet Explorer toolbar.
   OR
   Click F**a**vorites .... Alt + A
   on Internet Explorer menu.

2. Click **Organize Favorites** .... O

3. Open subfolder containing address(es) you want to move.

4. Click once on addresses) to move.
   OR
   Select multiple addresses by holding down Ctrl key as you click once on address that you want to move.

5. Click **Mo**v**e** button .... Alt + V

IN BROWSE FOR FOLDER DIALOG BOX

6. Select desired folder .... ↓, ↑
   where you want to move address(es).

7. Click **OK** .... Enter

8. Click **Close** .... Enter

NEXT EXERCISE

Exercise 95

- Inserting Hyperlinks in a Word Document to Access a World Wide Web Site
- Access a World Wide Web Site from a Hyperlink in Word
- Insert Hyperlinks from a Word Document to Another Word Document
- Create a Link to a Specific Location in a Document
- Move Back and Forth between Hyperlinks
- Select, Copy, and Delete Hyperlinks

Standard Toolbar

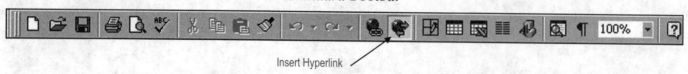

Insert Hyperlink

NOTES

Inserting Hyperlinks in a Word Document to Access a World Wide Web Site

- By now you have become accustomed to clicking on underlined words in different colors that take you to another location on the Web. These **hyperlinks** are one of the elements that make it easy to navigate the Web. You can insert hyperlinks to World Wide Web addresses into your Word 97 documents. Then, when you click on the link, you will go to that site.

  For example: if you insert hypertext links in a document, you can click on those links and go to the Web site, if you are connected to the Web and if the address still exists.

To insert a hyperlink to a World Wide Web site in a Word Document:

- Open the Web site that you want to link to a Word document.

- Click once in the Address line to highlight the URL address.

- Press Ctrl + C to copy the address to the Clipboard, then switch back to the Word document where you want to insert the hyperlink.

- Click the Insert Hyperlink button 🌐 on the Standard toolbar. In the Insert Hyperlink dialog box click in the Link to file or URL text box and press Ctrl + V to paste the URL address from the Clipboard. Click OK.

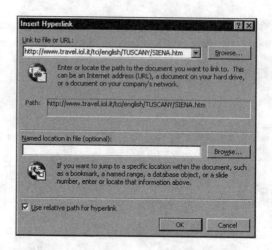

- The hyperlink will appear in a different color and underlined in the document.

  EXAMPLES:
  http://www.travel.iol.it/tci/english/ TUSCANY/SIENA.htm
  http://www.denverpost.com/index.htm

- If you know the entire Web address, you can type the URL in the <u>L</u>ink to file or URL text box. If you want to insert a link to an address stored in your Favorites folder, you can use the <u>B</u>rowse feature to locate the Favorites folder, then select the URL address.

Access a World Wide Web Site from a Hyperlink in Word

- Be sure that you are connected to your Internet Service Provider, then click the URL address embedded in the Word document to go to the Internet address.

  - If you click Back 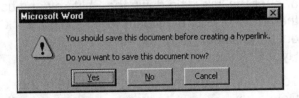 on the Internet Explorer toolbar you will return to your Word document.

Insert Hyperlinks from a Word Document to Another Word Document

- In addition to inserting hyperlinks to World Wide Web addresses, you can insert hyperlinks to other Word documents and all other Microsoft Office applications. When you click a hyperlink to a Word document, the document will open. If you have hyperlinks to other Office applications, the appropriate application will open when you click the link.

  To insert a hyperlink from a Word document to another Word document:

  - Open the Word document where you want to insert a hyperlink.

  - If you do not save your changes, you will be asked if you want to when you click the Insert Hyperlink button on the Standard toolbar. It's a good idea to save your changes if you want to create a relative link *(see below).*

- Click the Insert Hyperlink button on the Standard toolbar. In the Insert Hyperlink dialog box, click in the <u>L</u>ink to file or URL textbox. Enter the path to the file you want to create a link to, or click <u>B</u>rowse, locate the file and click OK. The name of the file will appear on the line. A truncated path appears in the Path section of the dialog box.

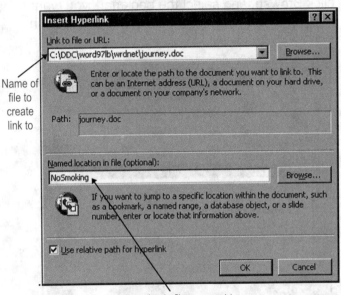

Name of file to create link to

Location in file you want to jump to when the file is opened

- If <u>U</u>se relative path for hyperlink is selected, the link between the files will remain intact as long as *all* files are moved together.

Create a Link to a Specific Location in a Document

- If you want go to a specific location in the Word document, mark the location with a Bookmark in the Word document. When you click in the <u>N</u>amed location in file box in the Insert Hyperlink dialog box, type the name of the Bookmark you want to jump to in the other Word document, or, click Bro<u>w</u>se, and select the bookmark you want to jump to from the list of bookmarks available in the document. Click OK.

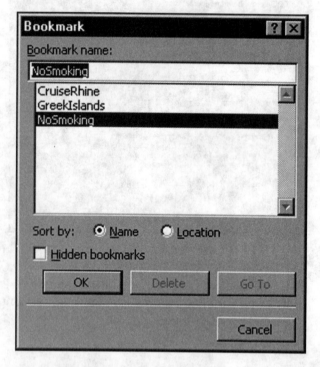

- The path to the file and the location you will jump to, will display in the Insert Hyperlink dialog box. Click OK to return to the document. The hyperlink will be inserted into the Word document.
  EXAMPLES: <u>Journey.doc - NoSmoking</u>

The entire path to the hyperlink will display if you point to it.

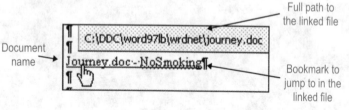

Document name → ... Journey.doc.--NoSmoking¶

Full path to the linked file → C:\DDC\word97lb\wrdnet\journey.doc

Bookmark to jump to in the linked file

Move Back and Forth between Hyperlinks

- When you click a link to another Word document, you can click on the Forward and Back buttons ← → on the Web toolbar to move back and forth between the linked documents. The arrows remain grayed until you click on a link.

Select, Copy, and Delete Hyperlinks

- If you click on a hyperlink to highlight it, you will go the link instead of selecting it. To highlight, or select, a hyperlink, move the mouse pointer over the path name in a hyperlink. When the pointer changes to a hand, right-click to open the shortcut menu. Select <u>H</u>yperlink, then select <u>C</u>opy Hyperlink on the submenu.

  ✓*Note:*   *If you point to the specific location part of a hyperlink and right-click, you might not see Hyperlink on the Shortcut menu. Be sure to position the mouse over the filename portion of the Hyperlink.*

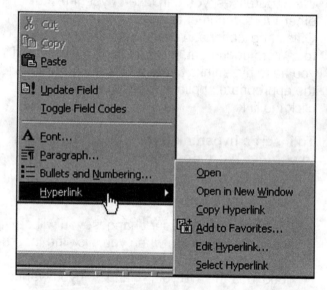

- You can also position the mouse pointer before or after the link, hold down the Shift key and use the arrow keys to highlight the link. Right-click on it and select <u>C</u>opy Hyperlink from the <u>H</u>yperlink submenu.

- To delete a hyperlink, select it and press the Delete key.

In this exercise, you will insert a hyperlink in a Word document that links to a WWW address and to bookmarks in a Word document. You will then access the Web site and the links to bookmarks in the Word document.

EXERCISE DIRECTIONS

✓ *If you have a live Internet connection, follow Directions A. If you plan to use the DDC Simulation, follow Directions B.*

DIRECTIONS A

1. Create a new document or open 95TICKLE.DOC

2. Format the document as shown in Illustration A.
   - Use 1" margins for top, bottom, left, and right margins.
   - Use square bullets for the list.

3. Open 95TOYDATA.DOC
   - Insert the following three bookmarks in the locations indicated in Illustration B.
   - Bookmark1   Plant_locations
   - Bookmark2   East_Div_Production_volume
   - Bookmark3   Virginia_production

4. Close and save the 95TOYDATA.DOC

5. In the Word document, go to each hyperlink location, delete the bracketed information, and insert a hyperlink to the 95TOYDATA bookmarks as follows:

   - Click Insert Hyperlink button on Standard toolbar.
   - Enter 95TOYDATA in the **Link to File or URL box** or Browse to locate the file.
   - Enter the appropriate bookmarks in the **Named location in file** box or browse to locate the bookmarks.

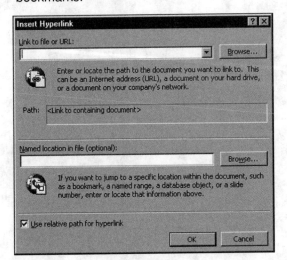

   - Repeat this procedure for each hyperlink to bookmarks in the TOYDATA.

6. In the last hyperlink location, delete the bracketed information and enter the Internet address http://www.toy-tma.com to point to a World Wide Web site created by the Toy Manufacturers of America.

7. Click on each link to the information in the TOYDATA file.
   The file will open, and you will jump directly to the bookmark inserted in the hyperlink.

8. If you have an Internet connection, select the Internet hyperlink to the Toy-tma.com World Wide Web site.

9. Exit from you browser and disconnect from your service provider.

10. Close and save the file; name it **TICKLE**.

DIRECTIONS B

1. Create a new document or open 95TICKLE.DOC.

2. Format the document as shown in Illustration I.
   - Use 1" margins for top, bottom, left, and right margins.
   - Use square bullets for the list.

3. Open 95TOYDATA.DOC.
   - Insert the following three bookmarks in the locations indicated in Illustration II.
   - Bookmark1   Plant_locations
   - Bookmark2   East_Div_Production_volume
   - Bookmark3   Virginia_production

4. Close and save the 95TOYDATA.DOC file.

5. In the Word document, go to the first hyperlink location and delete the bracketed information, and Insert a hyperlink to the 95TOYDATA bookmarks as follows:

   - Click Insert Hyperlink button on Standard toolbar.
   - Enter 95TOYDATA.DOC in the **Link to File or URL box** or Browse to locate the file.
   - Enter the appropriate bookmarks in the **Named location in file** box or browse to locate the bookmarks.

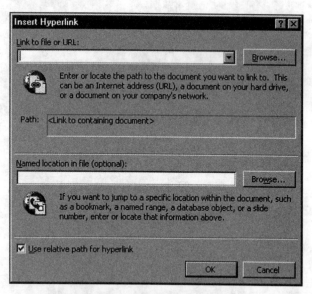

   - Repeat this procedure for each hyperlink to bookmarks in the TOYDATA.DOC.

6. Click on each link to the information in the TOYDATA file.

   The file will open and you will jump directly to the bookmark inserted in the hyperlink.

7. In the last hyperlink location, delete the bracketed information and enter the Internet address http:\\www.toy-tma.com to point to a World Wide Web site created by the Toy Manufacturers of America.

8. Close and save the file; name it **TICKLE**.

9. Launch the DDC Internet Simulation:
   - Click **Go**, **Open** on the Web toolbar.
   - Type **C:\DDCPUB\WOR97INT.IMR.** (Be sure that the simulation has been installed on your hard drive and that the CD is in the CD-ROM drive. If files are on a drive other than C, replace C with the correct letter.)
   - Click **OK**.

10. Double-click on **Exercise 95: Toys**.

11. Follow the onscreen prompts.

12. Close the simulation.

TICKLE TOY COMPANY
PRODUCTION ANALYSIS-EASTERN DIVISION
First Quarter – 199-

We will be looking at our production capacities in the Eastern Division with an eye to improving efficiencies and increasing capacities.

Our Eastern Division consists of plants in Delaware, Georgia, and Virginia. The plant in Reston, Virginia is our largest in this division and its production data reflects that fact. Our Newark, Delaware plant is our next largest plant and the data is unsatisfactory in comparison to that from Marietta, Georgia, our smallest plant. Click on **<Enter hyperlink to 95TOYDATA.DOC, bookmark Plant_locations>**.

The product lines manufactured at Eastern Division plants are Toys, Games and Stuffed Toys. This year our marketing department has succeeded in promoting our Toy line, especially the Tickle Tot Dolls. We have geared up our production capacity in our other divisions to meet the demand. The primary product of all Eastern Division plants has been Toys. Click on **<Enter hyperlink to 95TOYDATA.DOC, bookmark Virginia_production>**.

In order to improve the efficiency and output of the Newark, Delaware plant, we have had the plant under study by the Meister Efficiency Company. We have hired Mr. Tony Playsome to implement their recommendations as follows:

- Bring production equipment into good repair.
- Set manufacturing goals and develop production team involvement
- Institute Quality Control circles within the production area.
- Upgrade employee facilities.
- Establish standards for the workplace and apply them evenly.

We are looking forward to improvement in the second quarter this year.

The overall production of the Eastern Division was satisfactory, and we expect that our Newark, Delaware plant will begin to show improvement. Click on **<Enter hyperlink to 95TOYDATA.DOC, bookmark East_Div_Production_Volume>**.

You can view the Web site prepared by the Toy Manufacturers of America, of which we are members, by clicking on **<Enter hyperlink to http://www.toy-tma.com>**.

ILLUSTRATION B

Tickle Toy Eastern Division Locations

Bookmark1   Plant_locations

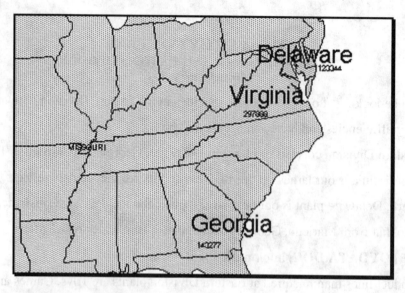

Eastern Division production volume

Bookmark2   East_Div_Production_Volume

TICKLE TOY COMPANY			
PRODUCTION SUMMARY EASTERN DIVISION			
	Toys	Games	Stuffed Toys
Delaware	123344	89654	54888
Georgia	143277	95654	64733
Virginia	297888	135333	53456

Reston Virginia production

Bookmark3   Virginia production

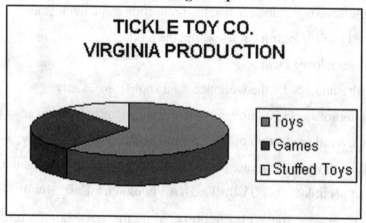

KEYSTROKES

INSERT A HYPERLINK IN A WORD DOCUMENT

1. Open Word document where you want to insert a hyperlink to a World Wide Web site.

2. Open a Web site that you want to link to a Work document.

3. Click once in the **Address** ... `Ctrl` + `Tab` **line** to highlight the URL address.

4. Press **Ctrl + C** .... `Ctrl` + `C` to copy address to clipboard.

5. Switch to Word document .. `Alt` + `Esc` where you want to insert hyperlink.

6. Click **Insert Hyperlink** .... `Ctrl` + `K` button on Standard toolbar.

IN INSERT HYPERLINK DIALOG BOX

7. Click in **Link to file or** .... `Alt` + `L` **URL** box.

8. Click **Ctrl + V** .... `Ctrl` + `V` to paste address from Clipboard.

9. Click **OK** .... `Enter`

The hyperlink will appear underlined and in a different color in the Word document.

LINK A WORD DOCUMENT WITH ANOTHER WORD DOCUMENT

1. Open Word document where you want to insert a hyperlink to another Word document.

2. Save the document .... `Ctrl` + `S`

3. Click **Insert Hyperlink** .... `Ctrl` + `K` button on Standard toolbar.

IN INSERT HYPERLINK DIALOG BOX

4. Click in **Link to file** or URL box .... `Alt` + `L`

5. Enter the path and filename...... *filename* to file you want to create a link to.

   OR

   a. Click **Browse** button .... `Alt` + `B`

   b. Click on file to create link to.

   c. Click **OK** .... `Enter`

To create a link to a specific location in the document:

   ✓ *The location in the Word document where you want to jump to must be marked with a bookmark to complete the following steps.*

   a. Click in **Named location in** .... `Alt` + `N` file box.

   b. Enter the path and filename .. *filename* to file you want to create a link to.

   OR

   a. Click **Browse** button .... `Alt` + `W`

   b. Click on file to create link to.

   c. Click **OK** .... `Enter`

6. Click **OK** .... `Enter`

   ✓ *The link to the document will appear underlined and in a different color in the document.*

SELECT A HYPERLINK

   ✓ *If you want to select, not access, a hyperlink (to a Web site, or a Word document), follow these steps.*

1. Position the mouse over the pathname in a hyperlink.

2. When the pointer changes to a hand right-click to open shortcut menu.

3. Click **Hyperlink** .... `H`

4. Click **Select Hyperlink** .... `S`

To delete a hyperlink:

Select it, then press **Delete** .... `Delete`

Exercise 96 ■ Summary

You are the President of Blooming Investments. You are meeting with prospective investors from Spain who are coming to New York City next month for a three-day meeting. You will send them a letter informing them of where they will be staying, their meeting itinerary and tourist attractions that are near their hotel. You will need to research the Internet for some of this information.

EXERCISE DIRECTIONS

✔ *If you have a live Internet connection, follow Directions A. If you do not have a live connection, use the DDC Simulation and follow Directions B.*

DIRECTIONS A

1. Create a new word document.

2. Start the exercise at the top of the page.
   - Use the default margins.

3. Create the company name and address as shown in the Illustration.
   - Use any decorative font for the company name and address.
     - ◆ Size the first letter of the word Blooming in the company name to 12 point. Increase the size of each subsequent letter 2 points.
     - ◆ Change to 12 point and press Enter five times after the word Investments.
       - ✔ *Hint: Highlight character and press Ctrl + Shift + > to increase font size.*
     - ◆ Use expanded character spacing for the word Investments so that it becomes the same width as Blooming.
   - Create a centered footer in 10 point for the address.
   - Copy the flower from the Web.
     - ◆ Search for *Clipart Collection* on the Web.
     - ◆ Scroll down and surf the web until you find a relevant graphic.
     - ◆ Copy a flower image from a desired web site and insert it into the letterhead where shown.
     - ◆ Adjust the size, wrap option and position.

4. Type the remainder of the letter. Begin the dateline At 3.1".

5. Insert five tourist attractions that are located near the client's hotel. Search the Internet as follows to find this information and insert it where indicated in the letter.
   - Enter the URL, http://www.mapblast.com.
   - Click on "Come on in!"
   - Enter 275 Madison Avenue (the hotel location) in the Address or Intersection box.
   - Enter New York, NY 10016 in the City & State box.
   - Click Mapblast!
   - Print one copy of the map.
   - Copy the five tourist attractions into the letter where indicated.
   - Add this site to your Favorites folder.

6. Insert the following sentence to the last paragraph of the first page. Include an enclosure notation below the typist's initials.
   > Enclosed is a map of your hotel location and surrounding tourist attractions.

7. Spell check.

8. Print one copy.

9. Save the file; name it **MEET**

10. Close the Word document window.

11. Exit the Web.

DIRECTIONS B

1. Create a new word document.

2. Start the exercise at the top of the page.
   - Use the default margins.

3. Create the letterhead shown in Illustration.
   - Use any decorative font for the company name.
   - Size the first letter of the word Blooming in the company name to 10 point. Increase the size of each subsequent letter 2 points.
   - Change to 12 point and press Enter five times.
   - ✔Hint: *Highlight character and press Ctrl + Shft + > to increase font size.*
   - Use expanded character spacing for the word Investments so that it becomes the same width as Blooming.
   - Create a centered footer in 10 point for the address.

4. Use the DDC Simulation to copy a flower graphic.
   - Click **Go**, **Open** on the Web toolbar.
   - Type **C:\DDCPUB\WOR97INT.IMR.**
     (Be sure that the simulation has been installed on your hard drive and that the CD is in the CD-ROM drive. If files are on a drive other than C, replace C with the correct letter.)
   - Click **OK**.
   - Click on **Exercise 96: Clipart Search**.
   - Follow on-screen prompts to copy the flower.
   - Insert the flower between the words Blooming and Investments as shown.
   - Adjust the size, wrap option and position.

5. Type the remainder of the letter. Begin the dateline At 3.1"

6. Insert five tourist attractions in New York City that are located near the client's hotel. Use the DDC Simulation to find this information.

7. Double-click on **Exercise 96: City Maps**.

8. Spell check.

9. Print one copy.

10. Save the file; name it **MEET**.

11. Close the Word document window.

12. Exit the DDC simulation.

bLOOMING

INVESTMENTS

Today's Date

Mr. Antonio Herreros, CFO
Banco de Madrid
Lopes de Hoyos 143
28002 Madrid

Dear Mr. Herreros:

We have scheduled several meetings to review investment possibilities that we have been discussing these last few weeks. All meetings will take place at our main office. The schedule is as follows:

Date	Time	BI Participants	Location
Monday, May 5	9:30 a.m.	John Rogers, Managing Director Paula Jenkins, Associate	Conference Room A
Tuesday May 6	11:00 a.m.	Michael Strauss, DEO Rosa Cruz, Managing Director	Conference Room A
Wednesday May 7	9:00 a.m.	John Rogers, Managing Director Karen Akers, Vice President Jamal Mitchell, Vice President	Conference Room B

We have reservations for you at the Moran Hotel, located at 275 Madison Avenue. We chose this hotel because it is located near our office as well as several New York City attractions. Enclosed is a map of your hotel location and surrounding tourist attractions.

200 Park Avenue ✳ New York, NY 10016 ✳ Phone: 212-555-5555 ✳ Fax: 212-555-6666

Mr. Antonio Herreros
Page 2
Today's date

Listed below are tourist sites near your hotel that you might want to visit.

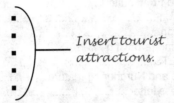

Insert tourist attractions.

Feel free to contact me if you have any questions or concerns regarding the arrangements that we have made for you. We look forward to seeing you on May 5.

Sincerely,

Jamal Mitchell, Vice President
Structured Finance Department

jm/yo
enc.

Index

Note: Entries in all capital letters indicate keystroke procedures.

DDC VISUAL REFERENCE BASICS

The Fastest Technique Ever Developed For Teaching 100 Basic Software Functions

THE POWER OF SIMPLICITY

Introducing a whole new way to learn software skills *fast*. DDC Publishing's Visual Reference Basics books teach program essentials with clarity and speed.

We tell *and* show, making learning simple, immediate. Color pictures and callouts explain your screen's elements—icons and dialog boxes—while step-by-step instructions lead you through the program's 100 most common functions. Spiral binding keeps the book open so you can type as you read.

Finally, concise and intuitive software guides.
Find the answers quickly and get back to the keyboard fast.

DDC Publishing's **Visual Reference Basics Series**— Simply Essential.

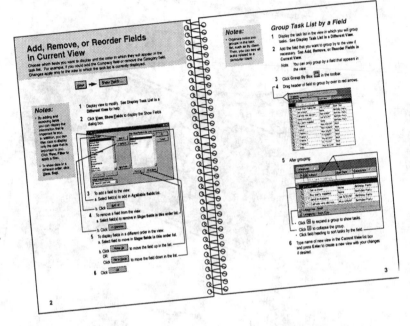

Order by Phone: (800) 528-3897　　Fax: (800) 528-3862　　URL: http://www.ddcpub.com

275 Madison Avenue,
New York, NY 10016

Name _____

School/Firm _____

Address _____

City, State, Zip _____

Phone _____

ACCEPT MY ORDER FOR:

Qty.	Cat. No.	Name	Price
_____	G-19	Visual Reference MS Office 97	$15
_____	G-20	Visual Reference MS Word 97	$15
_____	G-21	Visual Reference MS Excel 97	$15
_____	G-22	Visual Reference MS PowerPoint 97	$15
_____	G-23	Visual Reference Outlook 97	$15

❏ Check enclosed.　❏ Please bill me.　❏ Visa　❏ Mastercard

Add $2.50 for postage & handling.
NY State residents add local sales tax.

Orders for less than $25 must be prepaid.

Card No. _____

Exp. Date _____

Learning the Internet

Now includes our Internet Simulation on CD-ROM

- No Modems
- No Connection Fees
- No Extra Phone Lines
- No Waiting for Downloads

What we teach:

- **Basic Internet concepts**

- **Web Browsers**
  - MS Internet Explorer
  - Netscape Navigator

- **Search Engines, including**
  - Yahoo
  - Excite

- **FTP**
  - Communicate with other computers
  - Download software
  - Download graphics

- **E-mail**
  - Send and receive e-mail
  - Download attached files
  - Download e-mail software

Cat. No. Z-15   ISBN 1-56243-345-8

Learning the Internet......$27

Network Site License on CD-ROM

- Simulates actual WWW sites and hyperlinks used in DDC's *Learning the Internet* book.

- Install on all your network workstations.

Cat. No. Z-15CD..........$150

275 Madison Avenue, NY, NY 10016

More Fast-teach Learning Books

Did we make one for you?

Title	Cat. No.
Corel WordPerfect 7 for Win 95	Z12
DOS 5–6.2 (Book & Disk)	D9
DOS + Windows	Z7
Excel 5 for Windows	E9
Excel 7 for Windows 95	XL7
INTERNET	Z15
Lotus 1-2-3 Rel. 2.2–4.0 for DOS	L9
Lotus 1-2-3 Rel. 4 & 5 for Windows	B9
Microsoft Office	M9
Microsoft Office for Windows 95	Z6
Windows 3.1 – A Quick Study	WQS-1
Windows 95	Z3
Word 2 for Windows	K9
Word 6 for Windows	1-WDW6
Word 7 for Windows 95	Z10
WordPerfect 5.0 & 5.1 for DOS	W9
WordPerfect 6 for DOS	P9
WordPerfect 6 for Windows	Z9
WordPerfect 6.1 for Windows	H9
Works 3 for Windows	1-WKW3
Works 4 for Windows 95	Z8

DESKTOP PUBLISHING LEARNING BOOKS

Word 6 for Windows	Z2
WordPerfect 5.1 for DOS	WDB
WordPerfect 6 for Windows	F9
WordPerfect 6.1 for Windows	Z5

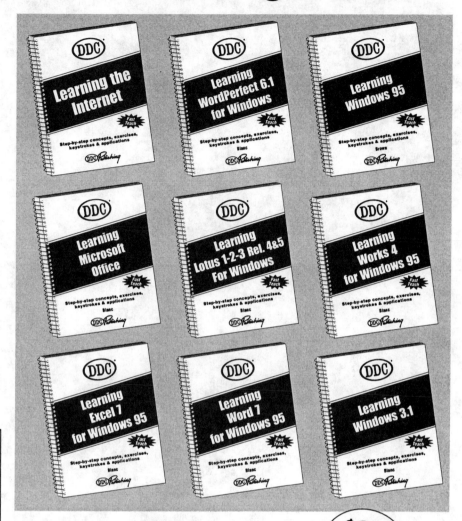

ETURN FREE CATALOG
FOR: AND
UPDATED LISTING

275 Madison Avenue,
New York, NY 10016

☐ Please send me your catalog and put me on your mailing list.

Name _____

Firm (if any) _____

Address _____

City, State, Zip _____

**SEE OUR COMPLETE CATALOG ON THE
INTERNET** @: http://www.ddcpub.com

ORDER FORM

$27 EACH

275 Madison Avenue,
New York, NY 10016

$29 hardcover edition

QTY.	CAT. NO.	DESCRIPTION

☐ Check enclosed. Add $2.50 for postage & handling & $1 postage for each additional guide. NY State residents add local sales tax.

☐ Visa   ☐ Mastercard   **100% Refund Guarantee**

No._____ Exp._____

Name_____

Firm _____

Address_____

City, State, Zip _____

Phone (800) 528-3897   Fax (800) 528-3862

New One-Day Courses

Title	Cat. No.	Title	Cat. No.
Access 7 for Win 95	**DC-1**	**Netscape Navigator**	**DC-10**
Access 97	**DC-2**	**& Simulation**	
Excel 7 for Win 95	**DC-3**	**Outlook 97**	**DC-11**
Excel 97	**DC-4**	**PageMaker 5**	**DC-12**
Internet E-Mail & FTP	**DC-5**	**PowerPoint 7 for Win**	**DC-13**
Simulation		**PowerPoint 97**	**DC-14**
Intro to Computers	**DC-6**	**Windows NT 3.5**	**DC-15**
Macintosh Sys. 7.5	**DC-7**	**Word 7 for Win 95**	**DC-17**
MS Explorer	**DC-8**	**Word 97**	**DC-18**
& Simulation		**WordPerfect 6.1**	**DC-19**
MS Project 4	**DC-9**	**Visual Basics 3.0**	**DC-20**

DDC can't promise you will master your software with these books, but you will be using it the very next day. These books are great for instructor-led one-day workshops or seminars. They are also ideal for the home computer owner or student who wants to get up and running with software . . . fast.

ORDER FORM

DDC Publishing   275 Madison Ave. NY, NY 10016   **$22 ea.**

QTY.	CAT. NO.	TITLE

☐ Check enclosed. Add $2.50 for post. & handling & $1.50 for ea. additional. guide. NY State res. add local sales tax.

☐ VISA   ☐ Mastercard   ***100% Refund Guarantee***

No._____ Exp._____

Name_____

Firm _____

Address_____

City, State, Zip _____

Phone (800)528-3897   Fax (800)528-3862

SEE OUR COMPLETE CATALOG ON THE INTERNET

FREE CATALOG
AND
UPDATED LISTING

We don't just have books that find your answers faster; we also have books that teach you how to use your computer without the fairy tales and the gobbledygook.

We also have books to improve your typing, spelling and punctuation.

Return this card for a free catalog and mailing list update.

275 Madison Avenue,
New York, NY 10016

☐ Please send me your catalog and put me on your mailing list.

Name

Firm (if any)

Address

City, State, Zip

Phone (800) 528-3897   Fax (800) 528-3862

SEE OUR COMPLETE CATALOG ON THE INTERNET @: http://www.ddcpub.com

---

FREE CATALOG
AND
UPDATED LISTING

We don't just have books that find your answers faster; we also have books that teach you how to use your computer without the fairy tales and the gobbledygook.

We also have books to improve your typing, spelling and punctuation.

Return this card for a free catalog and mailing list update.

275 Madison Avenue,
New York, NY 10016

☐ Please send me your catalog and put me on your mailing list.

Name

Firm (if any)

Address

City, State, Zip

Phone (800) 528-3897   Fax (800) 528-3862

SEE OUR COMPLETE CATALOG ON THE INTERNET @: http://www.ddcpub.com

---

FREE CATALOG
AND
UPDATED LISTING

We don't just have books that find your answers faster; we also have books that teach you how to use your computer without the fairy tales and the gobbledygook.

We also have books to improve your typing, spelling and punctuation.

Return this card for a free catalog and mailing list update.

DDC *Publishing*

275 Madison Avenue,
New York, NY 10016

☐ Please send me your catalog and put me on your mailing list.

Name

Firm (if any)

Address

City, State, Zip

Phone (800) 528-3897   Fax (800) 528-3862

SEE OUR COMPLETE CATALOG ON THE INTERNET @: http://www.ddcpub.com

NO POSTAGE
NECESSARY
IF MAILED
IN THE
UNITED STATES

BUSINESS REPLY MAIL
FIRST CLASS MAIL PERMIT NO. 7321 NEW YORK, N.Y.

POSTAGE WILL BE PAID BY ADDRESSEE

275 Madison Avenue
New York, NY 10157-0410

NO POSTAGE
NECESSARY
IF MAILED
IN THE
UNITED STATES

BUSINESS REPLY MAIL
FIRST CLASS MAIL PERMIT NO. 7321 NEW YORK, N.Y.

POSTAGE WILL BE PAID BY ADDRESSEE

275 Madison Avenue
New York, NY 10157-0410

NO POSTAGE
NECESSARY
IF MAILED
IN THE
UNITED STATES

BUSINESS REPLY MAIL
FIRST CLASS MAIL PERMIT NO. 7321 NEW YORK, N.Y.

POSTAGE WILL BE PAID BY ADDRESSEE

275 Madison Avenue
New York, NY 10157-0410